PENGUIN BOOKS

IMPERIAL SPAIN
1469–1716

John H. Elliott is Regius Professor of Modern History in the University of Oxford. Born in 1930, he won a scholarship to Eton College, and then to Trinity College, Cambridge. After researching in Spanish archives on the origins of the Catalan revolt of 1640 he was elected to a Fellowship at Trinity College in 1954. He was an Assistant Lecturer and Lecturer at Cambridge University from 1957 to 1967. In 1968 he became Professor of History and head of the History Department at King's College in the University of London, and from 1973 to 1990 was Professor in the School of Historical Studies at the Institute for Advanced Study, Princeton. His books include: *The Revolt of the Catalans* (1963), *Europe Divided, 1559–1598* (1968), *The Old World and the New, 1492–1650* (1970) and, with Jonathan Brown, *A Palace for a King* (1980). He is also the author of *Richelieu and Olivares* (1984) and *The Count-Duke of Olivares* (1986). In 1989 a selection of his essays was published under the title of *Spain and its World 1500–1700*. His interests extend beyond the Hispanic world to include Early Modern Europe and the Americas. He believes that historians should be willing to range widely, and to communicate their own interest and enthusiasm to a non-professional public.

J. H. ELLIOTT

IMPERIAL SPAIN

1469-1716

PENGUIN BOOKS

PENGUIN BOOKS

Published by the Penguin Group
Penguin Books Ltd, 27 Wrights Lane, London W8 5TZ, England
Penguin Books USA Inc., 375 Hudson Street, New York, New York 10014, USA
Penguin Books Australia Ltd, Ringwood, Victoria, Australia
Penguin Books Canada Ltd, 10 Alcorn Avenue, Toronto, Ontario, Canada M4V 3B2
Penguin Books (NZ) Ltd, 182–190 Wairau Road, Auckland 10, New Zealand

Penguin Books Ltd, Registered Offices: Harmondsworth, Middlesex, England

First published by Edward Arnold 1963
Published in Pelican Books 1970
Reprinted in Penguin Books 1990
7 9 10 8 6

Printed in England by Clays Ltd, St Ives plc
Set in Monotype Bembo

Acknowledgements

THIS book was read in typescript by Professor H. G. Koenigsberger of Nottingham University, and Professor A. A. Parker of the University of London. Their numerous comments were of the very greatest value in preparing the book for the press, and I have consistently taken their cogent criticisms into account when revising the text. While they bear no responsibility for the final product, it has gained immeasurably from their suggestions, and I am deeply grateful to them. In giving his comments from the standpoint of a specialist of literature, Professor Parker has rendered an additional service, at a time when contacts between historians and literary specialists are often distressingly rare. I am especially indebted to him for showing me how fruitful these contacts can be, and how historians neglect them at their peril. As a result of his labours, I hope that this book will be less misleading to those whose prime interest is in literature, than it would otherwise have been.

My wife has compiled the index, and has helped in the preparation both of the tables and of the maps, which were drawn by Miss Joan Emerson; and Dr R. Robson of Trinity College has again generously devoted his time to reading a colleague's proofs.

TRINITY COLLEGE,   J.H.E.
CAMBRIDGE.
27 *March* 1963

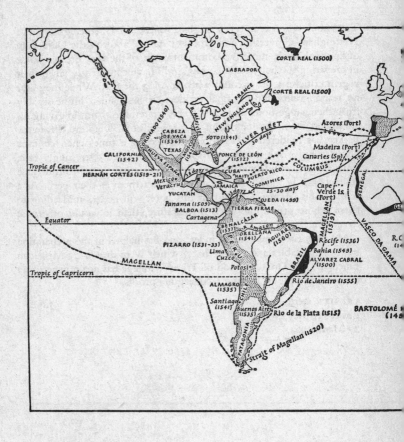

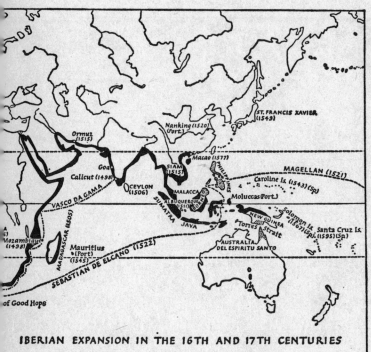

Ormuz (1515)
Nanking (1520) (Port.)
ST. FRANCIS XAVIER (1549)
Goa
Calicut (1498)
Macao (1577)
SIAM (1515)
MAGELLAN (1521)
CEYLON (1506)
MALACCA
ALBUQUERQUE (1511)
Caroline Is. (1543) (Sp.)
VASCO DA GAMA
Moluccas (Port.)
SUMATRA
JAVA
Solomon Is. (1567) Santa Cruz Is.
(Sp.) (1595) (Sp.)
NEW GUINEA
MADAGASCAR (1505)
Torres Strait
Mozambique (1498)
AUSTRALIA DEL ESPIRITU SANTO
Mauritius (Port.) (1545)
SEBASTIAN DE ELCANO (1522)
of Good Hope

IBERIAN EXPANSION IN THE 16TH AND 17TH CENTURIES

Spanish possessions and explorations

Portuguese possessions and explorations ■

Contents

Acknowledgements   5

Foreword   11

Prologue   13

1 *The Union of the Crowns*   15
   (1) Origins of the union. (2) The two Crowns. (3)
   The decline of the Crown of Aragon. (4) Unequal
   partners.

2 *Reconquest and Conquest*   45
   (1) The Reconquista completed. (2) The advance into
   Africa. (3) Medieval antecedents. (4) Conquest.
   (5) Settlement.

3 *The Ordering of Spain*   77
   (1) The 'new monarchy'. (2) The assertion of royal
   authority in Castile. (3) The Church and the Faith.
   (4) The economic and social foundations of the New
   Spain. (5) The open society.

4 *The Imperial Destiny*   130
   (1) The foreign policy of Ferdinand. (2) The
   Habsburg succession. (3) Nationalism and revolt.
   (4) The imperial destiny.

5 *The Government and the Economy in the Reign of*
   Charles V   164
   (1) The theory and practice of empire. (2) The
   organization of empire. (3) The Castilian economy.
   (4) The problems of imperial finance. (5) The
   liquidation of Charles's imperialism.

6 *Race and Religion*   212
   (1) The advance of heresy. (2) The imposition of
   orthodoxy. (3) The Spain of the Counter-
   Reformation. (4) The crisis of the 1560s. (5) The

second rebellion of the Alpujarras (1568–70). (6) The Faith militant and the Faith triumphant.

7 'One Monarch, One Empire, and One Sword' 249
(1) King and Court. (2) The faction struggles. (3) The annexation of Portugal. (4) The revolt of Aragon (1591–2).

8 Splendour and Misery 285
(1) The crisis of the 1590s. (2) The failure of leadership. (3) The pattern of society.

9 Revival and Disaster 321
(1) The reform programme. (2) The strain of war. (3) 1640. (4) Defeat and survival

10 Epitaph on an Empire 361
(1) The centre and the periphery. (2) The change of dynasty. (3) The failure. (4) The achievement.

Notes on Further Reading 387

Index 399

Maps

Iberian Expansion in the 16th and 17th Centuries 6
1. The Iberian Peninsula. Physical Features 12
2. Habsburg Spain 16
3. The Conquest of Granada 47
4. The Four Inheritances of Charles V 148
5. The Collapse of Spanish Power 358

Tables

1. The Union of the Crowns of Castile and Aragon 20
2. The Spanish Habsburgs 136
3. The Conciliar System 172
4. Imports of Treasure 184
5. The Portuguese Succession 272

Foreword to Pelican Edition

SINCE this book first appeared in 1963, one or two valuable monographs have been published on various aspects of Spanish history in
the period under review, and some important new research has been
undertaken. I had at first intended to use the opportunity afforded by
the publication of this book in a paperback edition, to incorporate
the results of recent researches into my text. But on further reflection
it seemed that they could not be convincingly integrated into the
present text, and that it would be premature at this stage – with so
much new research still to be published – to undertake the substantial
re-writing which the book will eventually require. In particular, I am
well aware that much more needs to be said about the seventeenth
century, but the pioneer work here still remains to be done. I have
therefore contented myself with correcting a number of mistakes of
fact, and with adding to the bibliographical note such titles as seem
especially deserving of notice.

KING'S COLLEGE,
LONDON.
1970

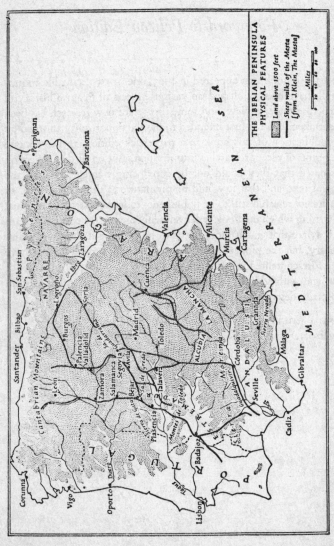

THE IBERIAN PENINSULA
PHYSICAL FEATURES

Land above 1500 feet

Sheep walks of the Mesta
[from J. Klein, The Mesta]

Miles
0 20 40 60 80 100

Map I

Prologue

A DRY, barren, impoverished land: 10 per cent of its soil bare rock; 35 per cent poor and unproductive; 45 per cent moderately fertile; 10 per cent rich. A peninsula separated from the continent of Europe by the mountain barrier of the Pyrenees – isolated and remote. A country divided within itself, broken by a high central table-land that stretches from the Pyrenees to the southern coast. No natural centre, no easy routes. Fragmented, disparate, a complex of different races, languages, and civilizations – this was, and is, Spain.

The lack of natural advantages appears crippling. Yet, in the last years of the fifteenth century and the opening years of the sixteenth, it seemed suddenly, and even miraculously, to have been overcome. Spain, for so long a mere geographical expression, was somehow transformed into an historical fact. Contemporary observers were well aware of the change. 'We have in our days,' wrote Machiavelli, 'Ferdinand, King of Aragon, the present King of Spain, who may, not improperly, be called a new prince, since he has been trans-formed from a small and weak king into the greatest monarch in Christendom.' Ferdinand's diplomats were respected, his armies feared. And in the New World the *conquistadores* were carving out for themselves an empire that could not but profoundly alter the balance of power in the Old. For a few fabulous decades Spain was to be the greatest power on earth. During those decades it would be all but the master of Europe; it would colonize vast new overseas territories; it would devise a governmental system to administer the largest, and most widely dispersed, empire the world had yet seen; and it would produce a highly distinctive civilization, which was to make a unique contribution to the cultural tradition of Europe.

How all this can have happened, and in so short a space of time, has been a problem that has exercised generations of historians, for it poses in a vivid form one of the most complex and difficult of all historical questions: what makes a society suddenly dynamic, releases its energies, and galvanizes it into life? This in turn suggests a corollary, no less relevant to Spain: how does this same society lose its impetus and its creative dynamism, perhaps in as short a period of time as it took to acquire them? Has something vital really been lost, or was the original achievement itself no more than an *engaño* – an illusion – as seventeenth-century Spaniards began to believe?

There are paradoxes here which baffled contemporaries, as they have continued to baffle ever since. No history of sixteenth and seventeenth-century Spain – least of all one so brief as this – can hope to resolve them. Nor is this a very favourable moment for such an enterprise. Outside one or two relatively specialized fields, the study of Spanish history lags several decades behind that of such countries as France and England, and the detailed monographs which would place the history of Habsburg Spain on a really solid foundation remain unwritten. This means that any historian of the period is faced with the alternative either of writing a narrative account which would lean heavily towards traditional political and diplomatic history, or of producing a more interpretative synthesis, which would attempt to incorporate the results of recent researches on social and economic developments, but which is bound in large part to remain speculative and perhaps superficial. I have chosen the second of these courses, partly because competent narratives already exist, and partly because the state of the subject would seem to demand a general survey which is prepared to raise some of the problems that seem relevant in the light of modern historical interests. Consequently, I have devoted little space to Spanish foreign policy, preferring to reserve it for less well-known aspects of the history of the age. I have also said very little about intellectual and cultural developments, not because I consider them unimportant, but because they require, for satisfactory treatment, far more space than I can give them, and have on the whole received considerable attention elsewhere. All that this book attempts to do, therefore, is to write the history of Habsburg Spain in such a way as to focus attention on certain problems that seem to me to be interesting and relevant, while indicating how much remains to be done before we can confidently claim to have found the answers.

I

The Union of the Crowns

1. ORIGINS OF THE UNION

ON the morning of 19 October 1469 Ferdinand, King of Sicily and heir to the throne of Aragon, and Isabella, the heiress of Castile, were married at a private residence in Valladolid. The events leading up to the wedding were, to say the least, unusual. The eighteen-year-old Princess, threatened with arrest by her brother, Henry IV of Castile, had been rescued from her home at Madrigal by the Archbishop of Toledo and a body of horse, and conveyed to a city where she would be safe among friends. Her bridegroom, a year younger than herself, had reached Valladolid only a few days before the ceremony after an even more eventful journey. With a handful of attendants disguised as merchants, he had travelled from Zaragoza by night through the hostile country, and had narrowly escaped death from a stone hurled by a sentinel from the battlements of Burgo de Osma. After reaching Valladolid he met his bride for the first time on 15 October, four days before the ceremony. The couple were so poor that they were compelled to borrow to meet the wedding expenses; and since they were marrying within the prohibited degrees, they required, and duly received, a papal bull of dispensation, later discovered to be a spurious document concocted by the King of Aragon, the Archbishop of Toledo, and Ferdinand himself.

There was some excuse for both the secrecy and the deceit. Many people were anxious to prevent the ceremony from taking place. Among them was Louis XI of France, who saw a grave threat to his own country in a union of the reigning houses of Castile and Aragon. But there were also enemies nearer home. Many of the powerful Castilian grandees were bitterly opposed to a matrimonial alliance which promised to strengthen the Crown's authority in Castile. Hoping to dispossess Isabella, they were now rallying to the cause of Henry IV's alleged daughter, Juana *la Beltraneja*, whose claims to

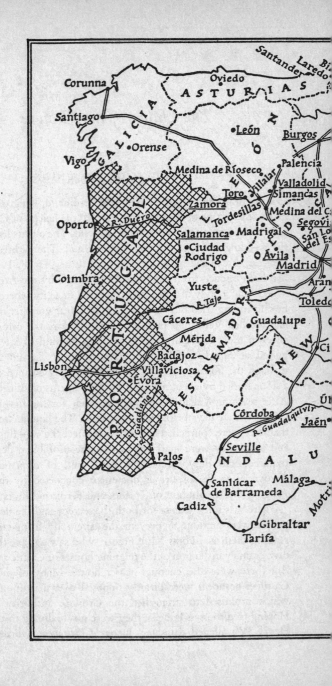

FRANCE

Fuenterrabía
Leucata
Salses
Perpiñán
Vitoria
Pamplona
NAVARRE
Logroño
Rosas
PROV
stian
ROSELLON
CERDAÑA
Seo de
Urgel
Gérona
Monzón
RIBAGORZA
CATALONIA
Soria
Zaragoza
Lérida
Cervera
Manresa
el Burgo de
sma
Calatayud
Barcelona
ARAGON
Ebro
Tarragona
Tortosa
dalajara
de Y
res
Cuenca
VALENCIA
Valencia
Albacete
MURCIA
Alicante
eal
A
Murcia
Cartagena
da
Almería

HABSBURG SPAIN

*[towns represented in
Castilian Cortes underlined]*

Key to Basque Provinces
    1 Vizcaya
    2 Guipúzcoa
    3 Álava

=== major routes in the 16th century

Miles
0 20 40 60 80 100

Map 2

the throne had recently been set aside in favour of those of his sister, Isabella. While Henry himself had been induced by the Isabelline faction in September 1468, as the price of peace, to recognize Isabella as his heiress in place of the daughter whose paternity was universally doubted, he was a vacillating and unreliable character, fully capable of going back on his word; and the pressures upon him were great. The Prince and Princess were therefore wise to seize the earliest possible opportunity of formalizing a union which would do much to strengthen Isabella's position in Castile.

Neither Ferdinand nor Isabella, however, was by nature precipitate, and their marriage was the outcome of arduously reached decisions, partly made for them, but which they ultimately made for themselves. Inevitably there was about the marriage a dynastic logic which reached back to a period long before they were born. Fifteenth-century Spain was divided among three Christian Crowns, Castile, Portugal, and Aragon. The great medieval line of the kings of Aragon had come to an abrupt end in 1410 with the death of Martin I; and in 1412 the problem of the Aragonese succession had been settled by the Compromise of Caspe, which placed on the Aragonese throne a junior branch of the Castilian house of Trastámara. From the time of the accession of Ferdinand I d'Antequera in 1412, therefore, the neighbouring Crowns of Castile and Aragon were ruled by two branches of the same, Castilian, dynasty. Might not a judicious marriage one day unite these two branches, and so bring together beneath a single monarch two of the three Christian blocs within the Iberian peninsula?

While a Castilian–Aragonese union had for some decades been an obvious possibility, it was far from being an inevitable development. There was no irrefutable economic or historical argument to bring the two Crowns together. On the contrary, the strong mutual antipathy of Aragonese and Castilians made any prospect of union unattractive to both, and the Castilian royal favourite, Don Álvaro de Luna, who was virtual master of the country from 1420 to 1453, could command the support of a Castilian nationalism which had been exacerbated by the intervention of the Infantes of Aragon in Castile's domestic affairs.

In spite of this antipathy there were, none the less, certain forces at work which might under favourable conditions prove conducive to a closer association of the two Crowns. The very presence of a Castilian dynasty on the Aragonese throne had itself multiplied contacts between them, especially since the Aragonese branch of the Trastámara owned large Castilian estates. There were also certain intellectual aspirations towards a closer unity. The word *Hispania* was in current use throughout the Middle Ages to describe the Iberian peninsula as a geographical unit. The native of medieval Aragon or Valencia thought of himself, from a geographical standpoint, as an inhabitant of Spain, and fifteenth-century sailors, although coming from different parts of the peninsula, would talk about 'returning to Spain'.[1] Even if loyalties were overwhelmingly reserved for the province of origin, growing contacts with the outer world did something to give natives of the peninsula a feeling of being Spaniards, as opposed to Englishmen or Frenchmen. Alongside this geographical concept of Spain there also existed in certain limited circles an historical concept deriving from the old Roman *Hispania*; a vision of the time when Spain was not many provinces but two, *Hispania Citerior* and *Ulterior*, united beneath the rule of Rome. This concept of the old *Hispania* was particularly dear to the little humanist group gathered round the imposing person of Cardinal Margarit, Chancellor of Ferdinand's father, John II of Aragon, in his later years.[2] Some of those closest to the Aragonese Court thus cherished the idea of re-creating Hispanic unity – of bringing together *Hispania Citerior* and *Ulterior* beneath a common sceptre.

Although a marriage alliance was, in fact, sought more eagerly by the Aragonese than by the Castilian branch of the Trastámaras, the reason for this is ultimately to be found in the grave political difficulties of the Aragonese kings, rather than in the inclinations of a little group of Catalan humanists bent on the restoration of Hispanic unity. John II of Aragon (1458–79) was faced not only by revolution in Catalonia but also by the expansionist ambitions of Louis XI of France. With inadequate resources to meet the threat on his own, his best hope seemed to lie in the assistance of Castile, and this could best be secured by a matrimonial alliance. It was, therefore, primarily the international situation – the ending of the Hundred Years' War and

1. Quoted by Richard Konetzke, *El Imperio Español* (Madrid, 1946), p. 81.
2. See Robert B. Tate, *Joan Margarit i Pau, Cardinal-Bishop of Gerona* (Manchester, 1955).

Table I THE UNION OF THE CROWNS OF CASTILE AND ARAGON

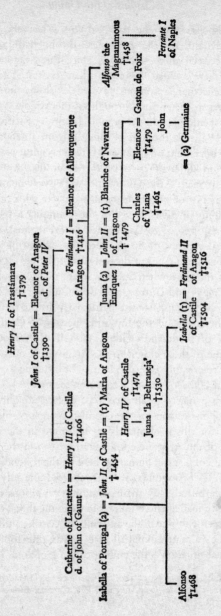

the consequent renewal of French pressure along the Pyrenees – which made a Castilian alliance both desirable and necessary to the King of Aragon. The securing of this alliance became the principal object of John II's diplomacy.

The crucial months, which were to determine the whole future of the Spanish peninsula, came between the autumn of 1468, when Henry IV recognized his half-sister Isabella as heiress, and the spring of 1469. The recognition of Isabella made her marriage a question of international concern. There were three leading candidates for her hand. She might marry Charles of Valois, the son of Charles VII of France, and so reinvigorate the old Franco–Castilian alliance. She might, as her brother intended, marry Alfonso V of Portugal, and so link the fortunes of Castile to those of her western neighbour. Finally, she might marry Ferdinand, son and heir of John II of Aragon, and thus formalize a Castilian–Aragonese alliance for which John II had been so vigorously manoeuvring. By January 1469 she had made her choice: she would marry Ferdinand.

Isabella's decision was of such transcendent importance that it is unfortunate that so little is known about the way in which it was finally reached. Strong pressure was certainly brought to bear on the Princess to choose the Aragonese match. There was a formidable Aragonese party at the Castilian court, headed by the Archbishop of Toledo; the King of Aragon's agents were very active, bribing Castilian nobles to support their master's cause; and the papal legate had been induced to use his good offices on Ferdinand's behalf. It also appears that prominent Jewish families in both Castile and Aragon were hoping to buttress the shaky position of Castilian Jewry by working for Isabella's marriage to a prince who himself, through his mother, had inherited Jewish blood. But Isabella, although highly strung by temperament, was a woman of great character and determination. She knew her own mind, and she made a choice which, both personally and politically, must have seemed the most desirable in the circumstances. Alfonso of Portugal was a widower, much older than herself, and quite without the many personal attractions generally ascribed to Ferdinand. Added to this was the fact that, since John II and Ferdinand were in no position to bargain, she could expect to dictate a settlement virtually on her own terms. The very form of the marriage contract, signed at

Cervera on 5 March 1469, showed the overwhelming strength of her position. Ferdinand was to live in Castile and fight for the Princess's cause, and it was made clear that he was to take second place in the government of the country. The terms were humiliating, but the prize before Ferdinand seemed so great and the necessity so urgent that refusal was out of the question.

The wisdom of Isabella's choice very soon became apparent. Ferdinand, wily, resolute and energetic, was to prove adept at forwarding the interests of his wife, and the couple could count on the great political experience and sagacity of Ferdinand's father, John II. Isabella needed all the help she could get if she was ever to succeed to her dubious inheritance. Her marriage had precipitated a struggle for succession to the Castilian throne which was to last for a full ten years, culminating in open civil war between 1475 and 1479. Isabella's brother, Henry IV, had been upset by the news of his sister's marriage, and Louis XI now induced him, in defiance of his agreement with Isabella, to acknowledge the rights of Juana *la Beltraneja*, who was to be given a French husband. In this delicate situation, all Ferdinand's skill was required, and the first five years of the marriage were spent in fostering Isabelline sentiment among the gentry and the towns, while at the same time attempting to secure a reconciliation with the King.

When Henry IV died on 11 December 1474, Isabella at once proclaimed herself Queen of Castile. But the anti-Aragonese faction at the Castilian court had been concerting plans with Alfonso V of Portugal, who saw in *la Beltraneja* a bride for himself, now that death had removed the French prince as a rival for her hand. At the end of May 1475 Juana, encouraged by her adherents, duly claimed the throne. Portuguese troops crossed the frontier into Castile, and risings broke out against Ferdinand and Isabella all through the country. The war of succession which followed was a genuine civil war, in which Juana enjoyed the support of several of the towns of Old Castile and of most of Andalusia and New Castile, and could also call upon the Portuguese for help. Since Isabella was eventually victorious, the history of this period was written by Isabelline chroniclers who followed the official line in declaring that Juana was not, in fact, the daughter of Henry IV the Impotent, and con-temptuously called her by her popular nickname of *la Beltraneja*, after her reputed father Beltrán de la Cueva. There is, however, some possibility that she was indeed legitimate. If so, it was the unlawful party that finally won.

But the war was much more than a dispute over the debatable legal claims of two rival princesses to the crown of Castile. Its outcome was likely to determine the whole future political orientation of Spain. If Juana were to triumph, the fortunes of Castile would be linked to those of Portugal, and its interests would correspondingly be diverted towards the Atlantic seaboard. In the event of victory for Ferdinand and Isabella, *Spain* would mean Castile and Aragon, and Castile would find itself inextricably entangled in the Mediterranean concerns of the Aragonese.

During the opening stages of the war, when everything still hung in the balance, Ferdinand's participation was of crucial importance. It was he who assumed command of the Isabelline party, and planned the campaign to restore order and unity to Castile. Ferdinand's military experts, imported from Aragon, instructed Isabella's troops in new military techniques. Ferdinand himself was a skilful negotiator, bargaining with magnates and towns for support of Isabella's cause. He could count already on the aid of the three most powerful families of north Castile – those of Enríquez, Mendoza, and Álvarez de Toledo (the ducal house of Alba), to all of which he was related; and his own energy and resourcefulness seemed to hold out promise of order and reformation to all those Castilians grown weary of civil war. All this helped gradually to give Isabella the advantage, as she herself gratefully acknowledged. She benefited also from the incompetence of Alfonso of Portugal, whose prestige was badly damaged by defeat at the battle of Toro in 1476. But progress was slow, and it was not until 1479 that all Castile was at last brought under Isabella's control. Her triumph was accompanied by the relegation of her rival to a convent.[3] Early the same year John II of Aragon died. With Castile pacified, and with Ferdinand now succeeding to his father's kingdoms, Ferdinand and Isabella had at last become joint sovereigns of Aragon and Castile. *Spain* – a

3. From which, however, she not infrequently emerged. She survived another fifty years, dying in Lisbon in 1530. She continued to sign herself throughout her life 'I, the Queen', and there were occasional threats by the kings of Portugal to revive her claims to the throne of Castile.

Spain that was Castile-Aragon, not Castile-Portugal – was now an established fact.

2. THE TWO CROWNS

The dynastic ambitions and diplomatic intrigues of many years had finally reached their consummation in the union of two of the five principal divisions of later medieval Spain – Castile, Aragon, Portugal, Navarre, and Granada. The union itself was purely dynastic: a union not of two peoples but of two royal houses. Other than the fact that henceforth Castile and Aragon would share the same monarchs, there would, in theory, be no change either in their status or in the form of their government. It was true that, in the person of Ferdinand, their foreign policies were likely to be fused, but in other respects they would continue to lead the lives they had led before the Union. The only difference was that now they would be partners, not rivals; as the town councillors of Barcelona commented in a letter to those of Seville, 'Now . . . we are all brothers.'[4]

The Union of the Crowns was therefore regarded as a union of equals, each preserving its own institutions and its own way of life. But behind the simple formula of a loose confederation lay social, political, and economic realities of the kind that can upset formulae and deflect the histories of nations into very different channels from those intended by their rulers. Castile and the States of the Crown of Aragon were, in fact, lands with different histories and characters, living at very different stages of historical development. The Union was therefore a union of essentially dissimilar partners, and – still more important – of partners markedly divergent in size and strength.

After the incorporation of Granada in 1492, the Crown of Castile covered about two-thirds of the total area of the Iberian peninsula. Its area was about three times that of the Crown of Aragon, and its population was also considerably larger. Population is difficult to measure since the figures for the end of the fifteenth century, particularly for Castile, are far from trustworthy. It is possible that Castile at that time had between five and six million inhabitants, while Portugal and the Crown of Aragon each had no more than one million. Some indication of relative size and density of popula-

4. J. Vicens Vives, *Els Trastàmares* (Barcelona, 1956), p. 240.

tion, although calculated for the end rather than for the beginning of the sixteenth century, is provided by the following table:[5]

	Sq. kilometres	Percentage of total area of peninsula	Inhabitants	Percentage of total population	Inhabitants per sq. kilometre
Crown of Castile	378,000	65·2	8,304,000	73·2	22·0
Crown of Aragon	100,000	17·2	1,358,000	12·0	13·6
Kingdom of Portugal	90,000	15·5	1,500,000	13·2	16·7
Kingdom of Navarre	12,000	2·1	185,000	1·6	15·4
	580,000	100	11,347,000	100	19·6

Perhaps the most striking fact to emerge from these figures is the superior density of the population of Castile to that of the Crown of Aragon. The awesome emptiness of the countryside in present-day Castile makes it hard to envisage a time when the population was more densely settled there than in any other part of Spain. Since the eighteenth century the peripheral areas of the peninsula have, in fact, been the most densely populated regions, but this was not true of the fifteenth and sixteenth centuries. At that time it was the centre, not the periphery, which was relatively the more populous; and this very demographic superiority of the arid central regions may itself represent one of the essential clues to the dynamic expansionist tendencies of Castile at the end of the Middle Ages.

It would, however, be wrong to assume that demographic superiority of itself necessarily ensures political and military pre-eminence in a period when governments still lacked the administrative resources and techniques to mobilize their populations for war. The medieval Crown of Aragon, although smaller in size and

5. Javier Ruiz Almansa, 'La población española en el siglo XVI', *Revista Internacional de Sociología* III (1943), pp. 115–36. Ruiz Almansa's total figures for population, which are higher than most historians would be willing to accept, are based on the exceptionally high multiplier of 6.

population, had displayed a vitality unequalled by Castile, and had triumphantly pursued a course of its own which was profoundly to influence the future political evolution of Spain.

The origins of Aragon's independent history, and of the fundamental characteristics which differentiated it so sharply from Castile, are to be found in the long struggle of medieval Spain against Islam. The Arabs had invaded the Iberian peninsula in 711, and conquered it within seven years. What was lost in seven years it took seven hundred to regain. The history of medieval Spain was dominated by the long, arduous, and frequently interrupted march of the *Reconquista* – the struggle of the Christian kingdoms of the north to wrest the peninsula from the hands of the Infidel. The speed and character of the *Reconquista* varied greatly from one part of Spain to another, and it was in those variations that the regional diversity of Spain was enhanced and reinforced.

The thirteenth century was the greatest century of the Reconquest, but it was also the century in which the divisions of Christian Spain were decisively confirmed. While Castile and Leon, under Ferdinand III, were pressing forward into Andalusia, Portugal was engaged in the conquest of its southern provinces, and Catalonia and Aragon – united in 1137 – were occupying Valencia and the Balearics. The pattern of reconquest was by no means uniform. In Andalusia, Ferdinand III handed over vast areas of the newly recovered territory to the Castilian nobles who had assisted him in his crusade. The enormous extent of the territory and the difficulties inherent in cultivating great expanses of arid land forced him to divide it into large blocs and to distribute it among the Military Orders, the Church, and the nobles. This large-scale distribution of land had profound social and economic effects. Andalusia was confirmed as a land of vast *latifundios* under aristocratic control, and the Castilian nobility, enriched by its great new sources of wealth, became sufficiently powerful to exert an almost unlimited influence in a nation where the *bourgeoisie* was still weak, and dispersed through the scattered towns of the north. In Valencia, on the other hand, the Crown was able to exercise a much closer supervision over the process of colonization and repopulation. The country was divided into much smaller parcels, and the Catalan and Aragonese settlers formed little Christian communities dotted over a Moorish landscape

– for the Moorish inhabitants of Valencia, unlike the majority in Andalusia, had stayed behind.

From about 1270 the momentum of the *Reconquista* slackened. Portugal, its path to the east blocked, turned westwards towards the Atlantic. Castile, overtaken by dynastic crises and by aristocratic revolts, became preoccupied with domestic affairs. The Levantine states, on the other hand, their work of reconquest done, and their kings succeeding to one another in unbroken succession, were now free to turn their attention eastwards, towards the Mediterranean.

These Levantine states – Catalonia, Aragon, and Valencia – together constituted the entity known as the Crown of Aragon. In fact, the name was misleading, because the kingdom of Aragon, the dry hinterland, was the least important part of the federation. The dynasty was Catalan, and it was Catalonia, with its busy seaboard and its energetic population, which played the preponderant part in the great overseas expansion of the Crown of Aragon. The Catalan achievement was prodigious. Between the late thirteenth and the late fourteenth centuries this nation of less than half a million inhabitants conquered and organized an overseas empire, and established both at home and in its Mediterranean possessions a political system in which the conflicting necessities of liberty and order were uniquely harmonized.

The Catalan-Aragonese empire of the later Middle Ages was primarily a commercial empire whose prosperity was founded on the export of textiles. Barcelona, the birthplace of the *Llibre del Consolat*, the famous maritime code which regulated the trade of the Mediterranean world, was the heart of a commercial system which reached as far as the Levant. During the fourteenth century the Catalans won, and lost, an outpost in Greece known as the Duchy of Athens; they became the masters of Sardinia and of Sicily, which was finally to be incorporated into the Crown of Aragon in 1409; Barcelona maintained consuls in the principal Mediterranean ports, and Catalan merchants were to be seen in the Levant and North Africa, in Alexandria and Bruges. They competed with the merchants of Venice and Genoa for the spice trade with the East, and found markets for Catalan iron, and, above all, for Catalan textiles, in Sicily, Africa, and the Iberian peninsula itself.

The success of the Catalan-Aragonese commercial system brought prosperity to the towns of the Crown of Aragon, and helped to consolidate powerful urban patriciates. These in practice were the real masters of the land, for, apart from a handful of great magnates, the nobility of the Crown of Aragon was a small-scale nobility, unable to compare in territorial wealth with its counterpart in Castile. Dominating the country's economic life, the *bourgeoisie* was able to hammer out, both in co-operation and in conflict with the Crown, a distinctive constitutional system which faithfully mirrored its aspirations and ideals. At the heart of this constitutional system was the idea of contract. Between ruler and ruled there should exist a mutual trust and confidence, based on a recognition by each of the contracting parties of the extent of its obligations and the limits to its powers. In this way alone could government effectively function, while at the same time the liberties of the subject were duly preserved.

This philosophy, which lay at the heart of medieval Catalan political thought and was enunciated into a doctrine by great Catalan jurists like Francesc Eixemeniç, found practical expression in the political institutions devised or elaborated in the Catalan-Aragonese federation during the later Middle Ages. Of the traditional institutions whose power had increased with the centuries, the most important were the Cortes. Catalonia, Aragon, and Valencia each had its own Cortes meeting separately, although on occasions they might be summoned to the same town and hold joint sessions as *Cortes Generales* under the presidency of the King. There were some variations in the character of the individual Cortes. Those of Aragon consisted of four chambers, the aristocratic estate being divided into two – the *ricos-hombres* and the *caballeros*. The *Corts* of Catalonia and Valencia, on the other hand, possessed the traditional three estates of nobles, clergy and towns, the latter having secured representation during the thirteenth century. The Aragonese Cortes were also unique in that, at least theoretically, unanimity was required in each estate. Meetings were held regularly (every three years in Catalonia), and the estates would deliberate separately on matters of concern to King and kingdom, considering grievances, proposing remedies, and voting subsidies to the King. More important, they had also acquired legislative power: for example in Catalonia, where this right had been won in 1283, laws could only be made and repealed by mutua consent of King and *Corts*. The Cortes were therefore by the end o the Middle Ages powerful and highly developed institutions which played an indispensable part in the governing of the land.

The rights and liberties of the subject were still further protected in the Crown of Aragon by certain institutions of a unique character. The kingdom of Aragon possessed an official known as the Justicia, for whom no exact equivalent is to be found in any country of western Europe. An Aragonese noble appointed by the Crown, the Justicia was appointed to see that the laws of the land were not infringed by royal or baronial officials, and that the subject was protected against any exercise of arbitrary power. The office of Justicia by no means worked perfectly, and by the late fifteenth century it was coming to be regarded as virtually hereditary in the family of Lanuza, which had close ties with the Crown; but none the less, the Justicia was, by the very accretion of time, an immensely influential figure in Aragonese life, and to some extent a symbol of the country's continuing independence.

There was no Justicia in either Catalonia or Valencia, but these two states possessed in the later Middle Ages, as did Aragon, another institution entrusted with certain similar functions, and known in Catalan as the *Generalitat* or *Diputació*. This had developed in the Principality of Catalonia out of the committees appointed by the *Corts* to organize the collection of the subsidies granted the King, and had acquired its permanent form and structure in the second half of the fourteenth century. It became a standing committee of the *Corts*, and consisted of three *Diputats* and three *Oidors*, or auditors of accounts. There was one *Diputat* and one *Oidor* to represent each of the three estates of Catalan society, and the six men held office for a period of three years. The original task of the *Diputació* was financial. Its officials controlled the Principality's entire system of taxation, and were responsible for paying the Crown the subsidies voted by the *Corts*. These subsidies were paid from the funds of the *Generalitat*, which were drawn principally from import and export dues, and from a tax on textiles known as the *bolla*. But alongside these financial duties it acquired others of even wider significance. The *Diputats* became the watchdogs of Catalonia's liberties. Like the Justicia in Aragon they watched out for any infringement of the Principality's laws by over-zealous royal officials, and were responsible for organizing all proper measures to ensure that the offending actions were repudiated and due redress given. They were the supreme representatives of the Catalan nation, acting as spokesmen for it in any conflict with the Crown, and seeing that the laws or 'constitutions' of the Principality were observed to the letter; and at times they were, in all but name, the Principality's government.

The Catalan *Diputació* was therefore an immensely powerful institution, backed by large financial resources; and its obvious attractions as a bulwark of national liberty had stimulated Aragonese and Valencians to establish similar institutions in their own countries by the early fifteenth century. As a result, all three states were exceptionally well protected at the end of the Middle Ages from encroachments by the Crown. In the *Diputació* was symbolized that mutual relationship between the King and a strong, free people so movingly expressed in the words of Martin of Aragon to the Catalan *Corts* of 1406: 'What people is there in the world enjoying as many freedoms and exemptions as you; and what people so generous?' The same concept was more astringently summarized in the famous Aragonese oath of allegiance to the king: 'We who are as good as you swear to you who are no better than we, to accept you as our king and sovereign lord, provided you observe all our liberties and laws; but if not, not.'[6] Both phrases, one emotionally, one legalistically, implied that sense of mutual compact which was the foundation of the Catalan-Aragonese constitutional system.

It was typical of the medieval Catalans that their pride in their constitutional achievements should naturally prompt them to export their institutional forms to any territories they acquired. Both Sardinia (its conquest begun in 1323) and Sicily (which had offered the Crown to Peter III of Aragon in 1282) possessed their own parliaments, which borrowed extensively from the Catalan-Aragonese model. Consequently, the medieval empire of the Crown of Aragon was far from being an authoritarian empire, ruled with

6. This is the form of the oath given by Antonio Pérez in his *Relaciones* of 1598, and the Venetian ambassador Soranzo provides a comparable version in his report of 1565. There are, however, reasons for believing that the oath was a sixteenth-century invention, but it expresses well enough the spirit of the contractual relationship between the Aragonese and their rulers. See Ralph A. Giesey, *If Not, Not* (Princeton, 1968).

an iron hand from Barcelona. On the contrary, it was a loose federation of territories, each with its own laws and institutions, and each voting independently the subsidies requested by its king. In this confederation of semi-autonomous provinces, monarchical authority was represented by a figure who was to play a vital part in the life of the future Spanish Empire. This figure was the viceroy, who had made his first appearance in the Catalan Duchy of Athens in the fourteenth century, when the duke appointed as his representative a *vicarius generalis* or *viceregens*. The viceroyalty – an office which was often, but not invariably, limited to tenures of three years – proved to be a brilliant solution to one of the most difficult problems created by the Catalan-Aragonese constitutional system: the problem of royal absenteeism. Since each part of the federation survived as an independent unit, and the King could only be present in one of these units at a given time, he would appoint in Majorca or Sardinia or Sicily a personal substitute or *alter ego*, who as viceroy would at once carry out his orders and preside over the country's government. In this way the territories of the federation were loosely held together, and their contacts with the ruling house of Aragon preserved.

The medieval Crown of Aragon, therefore, with its rich and energetic urban patriciate, was deeply influenced by its overseas commercial interests. It was imbued with a contractual concept of the relationship between king and subjects, which had been effectively realized in institutional form, and it was well experienced in the administration of empire. In all these respects it contrasted strikingly with medieval Castile. Where, in the early fourteenth century, the Crown of Aragon was cosmopolitan in outlook and predominantly mercantile in its inclinations, contemporary Castile tended to look inwards rather than outwards, and was oriented less towards trade than war. Fundamentally, Castile was a pastoral and nomadic society, whose habits and attitudes had been shaped by constant warfare – by the protracted process of the *Reconquista*, still awaiting completion long after it was finished in the Crown of Aragon.

The *Reconquista* was not one but many things. It was at once a crusade against the infidel, a succession of military expeditions in search of plunder, and a popular migration. All these three aspects of the *Reconquista* stamped themselves forcefully on the forms of Castilian life. In a holy war against Islam, the priests naturally enjoyed a privileged position. It was their task to arouse and sustain the fervour of the populace – to impress upon them their divinely appointed mission to free the country of the Moors. As a result, the Church possessed an especially powerful hold over the medieval Castile; and the particular brand of militant Christianity which it propagated was enshrined in the three Military Orders of Calatrava, Alcántara, and Santiago – three great creations of the twelfth century, combining at once military and religious ideals. But while the crusading ideal gave Castilian warriors their sense of participating in a holy mission as soldiers of the Faith, it could not eliminate the more mundane instincts which had inspired the earliest expeditions against the Arabs, and which were prompted by the thirst for booty. In those first campaigns, the Castilian noble confirmed to his own entire satisfaction that true wealth consisted essentially of booty and land. Moreover, his highest admiration came to be reserved for the military virtues of courage and honour. In this way was established the concept of the perfect *hidalgo*, as a man who lived for war, who could do the impossible through sheer physical courage and a constant effort of the will, who conducted his relations with others according to a strictly regulated code of honour, and who reserved his respect for the man who had won riches by force of arms rather than by the sweat of manual labour. This ideal of *hidalguía* was essentially aristocratic, but circumstances conspired to diffuse it throughout Castilian society, for the very character of the *Reconquista* as a southwards migration in the wake of the conquering armies encouraged a popular contempt for sedentary life and fixed wealth, and thus imbued the populace with ideals similar to those of the aristocracy.

The *Reconquista* therefore gave Castilian society a distinctive character in which militantly religious and aristocratic strains predominated. But it was equally important in determining the pattern of Castile's economic life. Vast estates were consolidated in the south of Spain, and there grew up a small number of great urban centres like Córdoba and Seville, living off the wealth of the surrounding countryside. Above all, the *Reconquista* helped to ensure in Castile the triumph of a pastoral economy. In a country whose soil was hard and barren and where there was frequent danger of marauding raids, sheep-farming was a safer and more rewarding occupation than agriculture; and the reconquest of Estremadura and Andalusia opened up new possibilities for the migratory sheep industry of North Castile.

But the event which transformed the prospects of the Castilian sheep industry was the introduction into Andalusia from North Africa, around 1300, of the merino sheep – an event which either coincided with, or created, a vastly increased demand for Spanish wool. The Castilian economy during the fourteenth and fifteenth centuries steadily adapted itself to meet this demand. In 1273 the Castilian Crown, in its search for new revenues, had united in a single organization the various associations of sheepowners, and conferred upon it important privileges in return for financial contributions. This organization, which later became known as the *Mesta*, was entrusted with the supervision and control of the elaborate system whereby the great migratory flocks were moved across Spain from their summer pastures in the north to their winter pastures in the south, and then back again in the spring to the north.

The extraordinary development of the wool industry under the *Mesta*'s control had momentous consequences for the social, political, and economic life of Castile. It brought the Castilians into closer contact with the outer world, and particularly with Flanders, the most important market for their wools. This northern trade in turn stimulated commercial activity all along the Cantabrian coast, transforming the towns of north Castile, like Burgos, into important commercial centres, and promoting a notable expansion of the Cantabrian fleet. But during the fourteenth century and much of the fifteenth the full extent of the transformation which was being wrought in Castilian life by the European demand for wool was partially hidden by the more obviously dramatic transformations effected by the ravages of plague and war.

The Black Death of the fourteenth century, although less catastrophic in Castile than in the Crown of Aragon, provoked at least a temporary crisis of manpower, which may have helped to give the economy a further twist in the direction of sheep-farming. Momentary economic confusion was accompanied by continuing social strife. The aristocracy was steadily gaining the upper hand in its struggles with the Crown. Enriched by the royal favours they had extorted, and by the profits from the sale of their wool, the magnates were strengthening their economic and social position during the course of the century. This was the period of the foundation of the great aristocratic dynasties of Castile – the Guzmán, the Enríquez, the Mendoza.

By the middle of the fifteenth century, some of these aristocratic houses enjoyed fabulous prestige and wealth. The famous heiress Leonor de Alburquerque, known as the *rica hembra* (the rich woman), could travel all the breadth of Castile, from Aragon to Portugal, without once setting foot outside her own estates. With such vast economic resources at their disposal, the magnates were well placed to seize the maximum political advantage at a time when the power of the Crown was fatally weakened by minorities and by disputed successions. There was, indeed, nothing to restrain them, for as yet the towns of north Castile were insufficiently developed to provide a *bourgeoisie* strong enough – as it was in the Crown of Aragon – to serve as an effective counterbalance to aristocratic ambition.

The political chaos in fourteenth-century Castile thus contrasted markedly with the public order that prevailed in the Crown of Aragon, guaranteed as it was by elaborate governmental organs. Admittedly the Castilians, like the Aragonese, had their parliamentary institutions, the Cortes of Castile, which reached the summit of their power in the fourteenth and fifteenth centuries. But there were important differences between the Cortes of Castile and those of the Crown of Aragon, which prevented them from exercising the effective political control enjoyed by their Aragonese counterparts, and which in the end were fatally to undermine their authority. There was no obligation on the kings of Castile, unlike those of Aragon, to summon their Cortes at specified regular intervals, and no one in Castile, even among the nobles and clergy, possessed a right to attend. Although it was already a recognized custom from the middle of the thirteenth century that the King of Castile must appeal to the Cortes whenever he wanted an additional subsidy or *servicio*, the strength that might have accrued to the Cortes through this practice was diminished by the Crown's ability to find alternative means of supply. It was diminished also by the fiscal exemption of nobles and clergy, whose consequent lack of interest in financial proceedings compelled the representatives of the towns to fight their battles with the Crown single-handed. Even more important, the Castilian Cortes, unlike those of the Crown of Aragon, failed to obtain a share in the legislating power. Theoretically, the Cortes's consent had to be obtained for the revocation of laws, but the power to make new laws lay with the Crown. The Cortes were allowed to draw up petitions, but they never succeeded in turning this into a right of legislation, partly because of their own lack of unity, and partly because of their failure to establish the principle that redress of grievances must precede supply.

Everything, then, conspired to make the prospects seem gloomy for Castile, and the opening years of the fifteenth century did nothing to dispel the gloom. The Castilian kings, their title dubious, had become pawns in the hands of the magnates; the Cortes were disunited and ineffectual; government had broken down, public order had collapsed, and the country was in turmoil. In the Crown of Aragon, on the other hand, the problem of succession had been solved between 1410 and 1412 without recourse to civil war, and the second king of the new dynasty, Alfonso the Magnanimous (1416–58), presided over a great new phase of imperial expansion which gave the Catalans and Aragonese a firm foothold in the Italian peninsula. The future seemed as bright for the Catalan-Aragonese federation as it appeared dark for Castile. But appearances were deceptive. Behind the grim façade of civil war, Castilian society was being transformed and invigorated by the economic changes which the growth of the wool trade was bringing in its train. If the country could once be pacified and the aristocracy be curbed, there was a real chance that Castile's great reserves of energy could be turned to new and valuable ends. In the Crown of Aragon, on the other hand, appearances were more hopeful than the reality warranted. The new overseas expansion of the fifteenth century was of itself no indication of prosperity or stability at home. On the contrary, the Catalan-Aragonese federation was now entering a period of crisis from which it took long to recover: a crisis which ensured that, in the joint monarchy of Ferdinand and Isabella, the lead, from the very first, was taken by Castile.

3. THE DECLINE OF THE CROWN OF ARAGON

The unexpected eclipse of the Crown of Aragon during the fifteenth century was largely the result of the eclipse of Catalonia. For Valencia the fifteenth century was something of a golden age, but for Catalonia it was characterized by a succession of disasters. Since it was the Catalans who had been primarily responsible for the great achievements of the confederation in the High Middle Ages, these disasters could only serve to weaken the Crown of Aragon as a whole, and leave it ill-equipped to face the many challenges which would inevitably accompany the Union of the Crowns.

The Catalan crisis of the fifteenth century has traditionally been regarded as, above all, a *political* crisis, caused by the accession to the throne of an alien, Castilian dynasty in 1412. It has been argued that the new line of Castilian kings neither understood nor sympathized with the political ideals and institutions of the Catalans. As a result, the fifteenth century marked the end of that close co-operation between dynasty and people which had been the distinguishing characteristic of Catalonia at the time of its greatness. The very fact that Alfonso the Magnanimous chose to live in the kingdom of Naples, which had fallen to him in 1443, itself symbolized the divorce between the Catalans and a dynasty from which they found themselves increasingly estranged.

This traditional interpretation has much to commend it, for in essentially monarchical societies royal absenteeism created grave problems of adjustment. It is also undeniable that the glittering imperialism of Alfonso V, dynastic in inspiration and militaristic in character, differed sharply from the commercial imperialism of an earlier age, and, by encouraging lawlessness in the western Mediterranean, directly conflicted with the mercantile interests of the Barcelona oligarchy. The policies of dynasty and merchants no longer coincided, and this itself represented a tragic deviation from the traditions of the past.

But an essential prerequisite for the coincidence of royal and mercantile policies had been the economic vitality and expansion of the thirteenth and early fourteenth centuries. By the fifteenth, these were things of the past. This ending of the expansionist phase of the

Catalan economy inevitably produced repercussions in the political system. The political crisis of fifteenth-century Catalonia therefore needs to be set – as modern historians are setting it – in the wider context of the economic recession and social upheaval of the later medieval world.

The background to the Catalan crisis was plague, recurrent and remorseless: 1333, a year of famine, came to be known as the 'first bad year', but it was between 1347 and 1351 that the Principality was first ravaged by plague. The Black Death of these years took a heavy toll of a population already stretched to its limits by the imperial adventures of the recent past. Where the visitation in Castile was harsh but swift, it proved in Catalonia to be only the first of a long and terrible succession. Although the first losses were made up with surprising speed, further waves of epidemics – 1362–3, 1371, 1396–7, and then periodically throughout the fifteenth century – steadily sapped the country's vitality. The 430,000 inhabitants of 1365 were reduced to 350,000 by 1378 and 278,000 by 1497, and the population did not return to something approaching its pre-Black Death figures until the second half of the sixteenth century. It is hardly surprising that this terrible drop in population, sharper than that experienced by Aragon or Valencia, dislocated the Principality's economic life and drastically affected its ability to adjust itself to the changed economic conditions of a plague-stricken world.

The first and most obvious consequence of the pestilence was the crisis in the countryside. Manpower was scarce, farmsteads were abandoned, and, from about 1380, the peasantry began to clash violently with landlords who, like landlords elsewhere in late fourteenth-century Europe, were determined to exploit to the full their rights over their vassals at a time when feudal dues were diminishing in value and the cost of labour was rising fast. During the fifteenth century agrarian unrest became endemic. Armed risings, murder, and arson were all employed by a class determined to emancipate itself from a legal servitude which seemed all the more bitter now that the shortage of men held out new hopes of economic gain to those who had survived. This class, technically known as the *remença* peasants – peasants tied to the land – constituted almost a third of the Principality's population. It was by no means a united social class. Some *remença* peasants were relatively wealthy, others desperately poor, and the interests of the two groups ultimately proved incompatible. But all were united at the start in their determination to win their freedom from the 'six evil customs' to which they were subjected,[7] and to obtain for themselves the abandoned farmsteads which they saw all around them. Banding together, they effectively challenged the hold of the ruling class over the countryside, and helped push the Principality towards the abyss of civil war.

In spite of the plague and the agrarian unrest, there were still impressive signs of commercial activity and of urban wealth in the late fourteenth and early fifteenth centuries. Many of the most imposing public buildings in Barcelona date from this period. But the foundations of Barcelona's economic activity were less solid than they had formerly been, and were being subjected to increasing strain. Between 1381 and 1383 there were spectacular failures of Barcelona's leading private banks. The financial crisis gravely weakened the city's standing as a market for capital, and eased the way for Italian financiers to assume the role of principal bankers to the kings of Aragon. Genoa in particular made skilful use of the opportunities created by the failure of Catalan finance, and succeeded in converting itself into the financial capital of the western Mediterranean. But it was not only in the market for capital that the Catalans saw themselves progressively outmanoeuvred by the Genoese. The late fourteenth and the fifteenth centuries were a time of bitter conflict between Catalonia and Genoa for the control of the spice, cloth, and corn trades – a conflict in which the mastery of the entire trading system of southern Europe was at stake. While the war in the Mediterranean was waged indecisively throughout the fifteenth century, the Genoese won an early and lasting victory in another vital region. This was central and southern Spain, where the expansion of the Castilian market offered the successful contender an

---

7. The first and most important of the 'six evil customs' was *remença personal*, by which the serf was obliged to purchase from his lord personal redemption from his status before he could leave his land. The other five customs allowed the lord to take a portion of the serf's goods in certain specified circumstances – as, for instance, when the serf died intestate. The six customs are described in detail in R. B. Merriman, *The Rise of the Spanish Empire*, vol. I (New York, 1918), p. 478.

exceptionally rich prize. The growth of Castile's wool trade had created new commercial opportunities, which the Catalans, embattled on so many fronts, were in no position to seize. It was, instead, the Genoese who settled in Córdoba, Cadiz, and Seville, built up a solid alliance with Castile, and secured control of the wool exports from Spain's southern ports. Once they had obtained this foothold, the Genoese were well placed to entrench themselves at one strategic point after another in the Castilian economy, and so prepare the way for their future participation in the lucrative trade between Seville and Castile's colonial empire. This Genoese predominance decisively influenced the course of sixteenth-century Spanish development. If the Catalans rather than the Genoese had won the struggle for entry into the Castilian commercial system, the history of a united Spain would have taken a profoundly different turn.

In the circumstances of the later Middle Ages it was not surprising that the Catalans missed their opportunity in Castile. Everywhere they found themselves under mounting pressure, and battling for survival. They were hard pressed by competitors in their traditional Mediterranean markets; their normal trading relations were being disrupted by the growth of piracy, some of it Catalan in origin; and their textile industry, hampered by the limited size of the home market in the Crown of Aragon, was stagnant or declining. Increasingly afflicted by the insecurity of the times, the mercantile oligarchy began to lose its enterprise and its sense of direction. From about 1350 there are signs of a rapidly increasing investment in annuities and land at the expense of trade. The Catalan upper classes were pulling out of their great commercial undertakings, and turning themselves into a society of *rentiers*.

The Principality's trade, sustaining itself with increasing difficulty, began to founder in the years round 1450. These same years of economic recession and collapse saw also a recrudescence of the agrarian conflicts, and a rapid sharpening of the divergence between the upper classes of Catalonia and a King who, from his luxurious côurt in Naples, demanded more and more money for his imperial ambitions. Alfonso the Magnanimous, master of the Mediterranean, was becoming less and less the real master of Catalonia. While he attempted to rule the Principality from Naples by means of viceroys, effective power in the country was falling into the hands of the

Generalitat. But this itself was the instrument of a closed oligarchy; and even while this oligarchy was insisting with growing vehemence on the contractual character of the Catalan constitution, against a monarchy at once increasingly authoritarian and increasingly weak, it found that its own authority was being challenged from below.

At a time when the peasantry was organizing itself into 'syndicates' and renewing its challenge to the privileged classes in the countryside, others were beginning to challenge the domination of those classes in the towns. In Barcelona in particular there was a fierce struggle for power between two parties, the *Biga* and the *Busca*. The composition of these two groups is still far from clear. The *Biga* was the party of the existing urban oligarchy of *rentiers* and large-scale merchants; the *Busca* seems to have been composed of clothiers, smaller export merchants and artisans in the guilds, although, at least in the 1450s, it assumed many of the characteristics of a genuine popular movement. These men of the *Busca*, who regarded themselves as destined to bring justice to Barcelona, gained power in the city in 1453 and systematically set about hounding their opponents out of municipal office. At the same time they tried to meet the challenge of the economic crisis by adopting certain policies, such as protectionism and devaluation of the coinage, which threatened the most deep-seated interests of the traditional oligarchy.

Nobles and urban patriciates rallied to the defence of their interests against the mounting threat of subversion in town and country. The contest, however, was to be not two-sided but triangular, for the monarchy also was inextricably involved. The viceroy, Don Galceran de Requesens, had alienated the oligarchy by his support for the *Busca*; and the King, to whom the peasants had appealed for help, suspended the 'six evil customs' in 1455 and declared the *remences* free. The Corts, in session between 1454 and 1458, reacted so violently that the King was forced to suspend his decree the following year, but the royal retreat merely encouraged the oligarchy to pursue an intransigent policy. The King in turn confirmed his decree in 1457. He died in the following year and was succeeded by his brother, John II, who was already to some extent identified with the *remença* cause. As the oligarchy prepared to break with the new King, it found itself presented with an ideal pretext in the arrest by John II on 2 December 1460 of the ambitious son of his first marriage,

Charles Prince of Viana, with whom his relations had long been strained. The arrest of the Prince of Viana, followed in 1461 by his death, which left his half-brother Ferdinand heir to the throne, was sufficient to spark off the Catalan revolution. The *Generalitat*, having espoused the cause of the Prince of Viana, renounced its allegiance to the King and prepared for war.

The civil war of 1462–72 was, therefore, in the first instance a struggle between the monarchy and a ruling class wedded to a contractual system of government which, however admirable in its original conception, seemed increasingly inadequate as a solution to the grave social and economic problems of the age. But it was much more than a simple constitutional struggle between king and oligarchy. Through it ran the cross-currents of *Busca* against *Biga*, of peasants against their lords, of rival families attempting to settle old scores. It was a struggle for the social as well as for the political domination of the Principality; a struggle, too, over the policies that should be adopted to meet the economic crisis. Finally, it was, or soon became, an international conflict, as the *Generalitat* offered the crown in turn to Henry IV of Castile, to the Constable of Portugal and to René of Anjou; while Louis XI neatly turned the situation to his own account by annexing the Catalan counties of Cerdanya and Rosselló (Cerdagne and Roussillon) in 1463.

After a long and confused struggle, John II gained the victory in 1472. He used it with moderation, granting an amnesty to his enemies and swearing to preserve Catalonia's laws and liberties intact. But in spite of his refusal to take revenge on his opponents, he failed to pacify the country, and a definitive political and social settlement continued to elude him. When he died, old and exhausted, in 1479 he left to his son Ferdinand a war-torn country, shorn of two of its richest provinces, and its problems all unsolved. Catalonia's contractual constitution had survived the upheaval, but it was left to Ferdinand to get it working once again.

4. UNEQUAL PARTNERS

While Catalonia had preserved its traditional constitutional structure, its economy had collapsed. The revolution and civil war had completed the ruin begun by the financial and commercial crisis of the preceding decades. Crops had been burnt, properties confiscated, workers and capital had fled the country. The Principality would need a long period of peace to restore its substance and recover its sense of purpose, and, in the meantime, its commercial competitors had already so established themselves in Catalonia's existing or potential markets that it would be extremely difficult to dislodge them.

The crippling of Catalonia inevitably had profound and lasting consequences for the entire Crown of Aragon. Although Valencia had replaced Barcelona as the financial capital of the federation, the Valencians failed to display the dynamism which might have preserved the momentum of the eastern kingdoms and carried them over the difficult period of the Catalan collapse. Failing this, the Crown of Aragon stagnated in the later fifteenth century, content to be left in quiet possession of a contractual constitutional system, time-honoured and sacrosanct, which Ferdinand, like his predecessors, had promised to preserve.

The weakness of the Crown of Aragon at the moment of union left the field clear for Castile. In spite of its civil wars and internal conflicts, fifteenth-century Castile was a dynamic, and expanding, society. If civil war had momentarily put a brake on expansion, there was no evidence that it had seriously impaired the workings of the economy, as it had in Catalonia. On the contrary, there were many signs of vitality, which promised well for the future. The wool industry continued to grow. The increasing importance of the port of Seville, and the continuing expansion of the Cantabrian fleet, strengthened the country's maritime tradition and tied Castile more closely to the nations of the north. Castile's new importance in international trade was reflected in the rise to prominence of the fairs of Medina del Campo, which already by the mid-fifteenth century were acting as a magnet to the leading merchants of Europe. Everywhere – even in the sporadic military expeditions against the Granada Moors – there was evidence of an upsurge of national energy, which contrasted sharply with the debilitating lassitude of the states of the Crown of Aragon.

If Isabella had chosen to marry the King of Portugal rather than Ferdinand, this crude, vigorous Castilian society might have found itself better matched. The dynamism of fifteenth-century Castile was equalled only by that of Portugal. A revolution in 1383 had brought to the Portuguese throne the House of Avis, which succeeded in forging a close alliance between the dynasty and the dynamic elements in the country's ruling class, such as had characterized medieval Catalonia in the days of its greatness. In 1385 the Castilians were defeated at the Battle of Aljubarrota, and Portugal's independence was assured. During the following decades Crown, nobles, and merchants joined forces in the great task of overseas discovery and conquest. Ceuta was occupied in 1415, an expedition was sent to the Canaries in 1425, and the Azores were settled in 1445. The union of a vigorous, expansionist Portugal to an equally vigorous and expansionist Castile would have been a well-balanced union of two nations at very comparable stages of historical development. As it was, Castile and Portugal went their separate ways, to be united only when it was already too late for the union to be durable.

Harnessed instead to Aragon – to a society in retreat – Castile was free to seize the initiative in the work of building up the Spanish Monarchy of the sixteenth century. It is true that its freedom of action was to some extent restricted by the very nature of the union. The Crown of Aragon was well protected by its traditional laws and liberties from the strong exercise of royal power, and in consequence the union represented an uneasy yoking of two very different constitutional systems, of which the Aragonese would seriously restrict the King of Spain's authority. But if, in some respects, the Crown of Aragon seemed to constitute a drag upon its partner, it also provided Castile with certain precious assets which helped it to make the most of its new opportunities. The history of Spain in the late fifteenth and early sixteenth centuries was to consist of a continuing, and fruitful, dialogue between periphery and centre, between Aragon and Castile. The Crown of Aragon may have been weak and exhausted, but if it could contribute little in the way of men and resources to the conquest of empire, it could still draw upon a vast repository of experience which proved invaluable for the organization and administration of Spain and its newly-won territories. In the Union of the Crowns, youth and experience walked hand in hand. The dynamism which created an empire was supplied almost exclusively by Castile – a Castile whose vigour and self-confidence gave it a natural predominance in the new Spanish

Monarchy. But behind Castile stood the Crown of Aragon, rich in administrative experience, and skilled in the techniques of diplomacy and government. In this sense at least the Union of the Crowns was a union of complementary partners, to which the Crown of Aragon contributed far more than might have been expected from its unhappy condition in the later fifteenth century. The marriage of Ferdinand and Isabella, so furtively arranged and incongruously celebrated, proved, in fact, to be the prelude to a vital process: the process by which medieval Castile assumed the leadership of the new Spain, and went on to acquire an empire.

2

Reconquest and Conquest

DURING the reign of Ferdinand and Isabella, the Crown of Castile, freed at last from the plague of civil war, was to launch out on a career of conquest both in Spain itself and overseas. If any one year can be taken as marking the beginning of Castilian imperialism, that year was 1492. On 6 January 1492 Ferdinand and Isabella made their victorious entry into the city of Granada, wrested after nearly eight centuries from the grasp of the Moors. On 17 April, three months after the completion of the *Reconquista*, agreement was reached at the Christian camp town of Santa Fe, six miles from Granada, on the terms for the projected voyage of exploration of the Genoese Christopher Columbus. His fleet of three caravels set sail from Palos on 3 August, and departed from the Canaries on 6 September on its voyage into the unknown. On 12 October land was sighted, and the ships anchored off an island of the Bahamas. Columbus had discovered the 'Indies'.

The conquest of Granada and the discovery of America represented at once an end and a beginning. While the fall of Granada brought to an end the *Reconquista* of Spanish territory, it also opened a new phase in Castile's long crusade against the Moor – a phase in which the Christian banners were borne across the straits and planted on the inhospitable shores of Africa. The discovery of the New World also marked the opening of a new phase – the great epoch of overseas colonization – but at the same time it was a natural culmination of a dynamic and expansionist period in Castilian history which had begun long before. Both reconquest and discovery, which seemed miraculous events to contemporary Spaniards, were in reality a logical outcome of the traditions and aspirations of an earlier age, on which the seal of success was now firmly placed. This success helped to perpetuate at home, and project overseas, the ideals, the values and the institutions of medieval Castile.

I. THE RECONQUISTA COMPLETED

During the domestic troubles of the fifteenth century Castile's *Reconquista* had nearly come to a halt. But the fall of Constantinople in 1453 revived the crusading enthusiasm of Christendom, and Henry IV of Castile dutifully responded to papal appeals for a new crusade by resuming the *Reconquista* in 1455. Six large-scale military incursions were made into the kingdom of Granada between 1455 and 1457, but they achieved nothing of importance, and no serious battles were fought. The King looked upon the crusade primarily as a useful pretext for extracting money from his subjects under papal auspices, and the real crusading zeal was found not at Court but among the ordinary Castilians, who had to be restrained in 1464 from leaving the country in large numbers to join in a crusade against the Turk.

The idea of the crusade, with its popular religious and emotional overtones, was therefore ready at hand for Ferdinand and Isabella. A vigorous renewal of the war against Granada would do more than anything else to rally the country behind its new rulers, and associate Crown and people in a heroic enterprise which would make the name of Spain ring through Christendom.

The attack began in 1482 with the Castilian capture of Alhama, and was conducted thereafter in a series of methodical campaigns designed to detach one segment after another of the Moorish kingdom until only the city of Granada remained. The character of the war – which provided valuable experience for the later campaigns in Italy of Gonzalo de Córdoba – was determined by the mountainous character of the terrain, which did not lend itself to cavalry operations. This was essentially a war of sieges, in which the role of artillery and infantry was pre-eminent. The infantry was drawn partly from mercenaries and volunteers who had come from all over Europe, and partly from a kind of national militia levied in the towns of Castile and Andalusia. The Castilian soldier already showed that capacity for endurance in extremes of heat and cold that was to make him such a redoubtable figure on the battlefields of Europe and the New World; and the Granada war, with its surprise attacks and constant skirmishes, did much to train him in the individualistic type of warfare in which he was soon to excel.

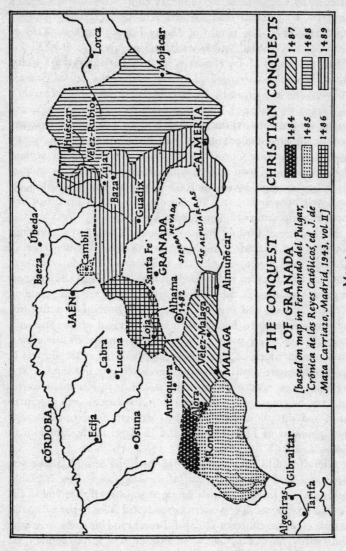

CHRISTIAN CONQUESTS

1484 · 1485 · 1486 · 1487 · 1488 · 1489

THE CONQUEST
OF GRANADA

[based on map in Fernando del Pulgar,
Crónica de los Reyes Católicos, ed. J. de
Mata Carriazo, Madrid, 1943, vol. II]

Map 3

The Granada war, however, was won almost as much by diplomacy as by Castile's sustained military effort. The Nasrid kingdom was rent by internal feuds, which Ferdinand exploited with his customary skill. The family of Mulay Hassan, the aged King of Granada, was divided within itself, and in July 1482 Boabdil and Yusuf, the sons of Mulay Hassan by his first marriage, fled to Guadix, where Boabdil was recognized as king. When the city of Granada followed the lead given by Guadix, Mulay Hassan and his brother, El Zagal ('the valiant') were compelled to retire to Málaga, and war broke out between the two halves of the kingdom of Granada. In spite of these domestic troubles El Zagal scored a great victory against an attacking Christian expedition in 1483, and his nephew Boabdil, from his own half-kingdom, rashly attempted to emulate his uncle's example by invading Christian territory. Boabdil, however, was no warrior, and his expedition ended in his defeat and capture at the battle of Lucena on 21 April.

The capture of Boabdil by the Count of Cabra proved a turning-point in the Granada campaign. Its immediate consequence in Granada itself was to reunite the kingdom under Mulay Hassan, who was later deposed and replaced as king by El Zagal. But its most important result was the establishment of a secret understanding between Boabdil and Ferdinand, by which Boabdil, in return for his freedom, pledged himself to become a vassal of the Spaniard, accepted a two-year truce, and promised to engage in war against his father, in which he would receive Spanish help. Boabdil was in practice to prove a vacillating and unreliable ally, but since he was periodically in need of Ferdinand's assistance against his powerful relatives, he continued to maintain communications with the Spaniards, and this allowed Ferdinand to strengthen his contacts with the opponents of Mulay Hassan and El Zagal in the kingdom of Granada.

After Boabdil's return to his own land, the Spanish attack was directed against the western half of the kingdom, where Boabdil's father and uncle enjoyed their strongest support. By the end of the 1485 campaign, much of western Granada had fallen to the Spaniards, in spite of all the efforts of El Zagal. Boabdil and his uncle were now temporarily reconciled, but when Boabdil was again captured, on the occasion of the fall of Loja in 1486, he was once more quick to place himself under the protection of Ferdinand and Isabella, whose help he needed in order to keep his throne. While civil war was raging between the two Granada factions, the Spaniards completed in 1487 their conquest of the western half of the kingdom with the capture of Málaga. The fall of Málaga meant that Granada itself would sooner or later become untenable, and Boabdil now declared himself willing to surrender it, and to exchange his royal title for that of a Castilian magnate, in return for jurisdiction over Guadix, Baza and one or two other towns still loyal to El Zagal.

The Spanish campaign of 1488 was therefore directed towards securing the towns to be given to Boabdil in exchange for Granada. When Baza at last fell in December 1489, El Zagal submitted to Ferdinand and Isabella, choosing rather to be subject to Christians than to his hated nephew. It was at this moment that Boabdil, never very happy in his timing, tore up his agreement with the Catholic Kings, and proclaimed his determination to fight for the remnant of his kingdom, now reduced to little more than the city of Granada. This final act of treachery by the King of Granada served only as a spur to Ferdinand and Isabella to finish for once and all with the Nasrid kingdom. During the spring of 1490 their army encamped beneath Granada, and during the following months, while elaborate preparations were being made for the siege and assault, a city was built on the site of the camp, designed on the pattern of the gridiron and bearing the name of Santa Fe. As the preparations went steadily forward, discouragement spread in the Moorish camp, and with it a feeling that honourable surrender was preferable to military conquest. Negotiations were therefore opened in October 1491. By the end of November the terms were agreed, and on 2 January 1492 Granada surrendered. Boabdil in person presented to Ferdinand the keys of the Alhambra, and the crucifix and the royal standard were raised above its highest tower.

The terms of surrender were extremely liberal. The Moors were left in possession of their arms and property, and were guaranteed in the use of their law and religion, their customs and their dress. They were to continue to be governed by their own local magistrates, and they were to pay no more in taxes than they had paid to their native kings. These terms closely resembled those which Ferdinand's ancestors had made in an earlier age with the Moors of Valencia, and there is no reason to believe that he had any intention of breaking them. The position of the conquerors was still precarious, and it would have been absurd to alienate a population which may even have welcomed a change of masters as putting an end to the anarchy that had prevailed in the Nasrid kingdom during the preceding decades. It is not therefore surprising that the first years of the new régime were distinguished by a show of moderation on the part of a Crown still preoccupied with the overriding consideration of military security.

In practice, the Crown benefited surprisingly little from the spoils of victory. By the terms of surrender, the *habices*, the revenues of certain properties traditionally set aside for religious and charitable purposes, continued to be administered by the Moorish religious authorities, while the taxes traditionally appointed for the expenses of the royal household were ceded to Boabdil, who was given an estate in the Alpujarras. This left the Crown with only the patrimonial lands of the sultanate. But some of these lands had been devastated by the advancing Christian armies, and many others had been alienated by the Nasrid kings in the fifteenth century, so that the benefit to the royal exchequer was negligible. A commission of inquiry was set up to examine the titles by which the alienated property was held, but Moorish and Christian nobles alike conspired to frustrate its work. A royal decree that no individual should acquire more than 200,000 *maravedís* worth of property in the conquered kingdom was systematically evaded with the connivance of the Crown's own officials, and a handful of nobles – among them Gonzalo de Córdoba and the Count of Tendilla – managed to acquire enormous estates, while only a small amount of land was recovered for the royal patrimony.

When the King and Queen left Granada in the spring of 1492 they handed over its administration to a triumvirate consisting of Hernando de Zafra (the royal secretary), the Count of Tendilla, a member of the powerful Mendoza family, whose ancestors had been Captain-Generals of the Granada frontier since the start of the fifteenth century, and Hernando de Talavera, the first Archbishop of Granada, whose tolerant outlook and interest in Arabic studies did much to reconcile the Moors to a Christian government. The triumvirate's immediate task was to ensure the preservation of public order and to consolidate the Crown's hold over the conquered kingdom. This was a particularly difficult task in the mountainous, bandit-infested region of the Alpujarras, to which a royal official known as the *Alcalde Mayor de las Alpujarras* was appointed in the autumn of 1492.

Fears of a revolt, especially in the Alpujarras, were ever-present among the Christian conquerors, and were made all the more real by the proximity of the Moors of North Africa. Moorish Spain and Moorish North Africa, for so long a unified civilization, had now found themselves suddenly and artificially divided. Fearing collusion between African and Spanish Moors unwilling to accept the new frontier, Ferdinand and Isabella did their best to protect it, by the building of watch-towers along the Andalusian coast, and the establishment of coastguard garrisons. They also did everything possible to induce the more influential Granadine Moors to leave the kingdom. Assistance was given to those who wished to emigrate, and in the autumn of 1493 the unhappy Boabdil and some six thousand Moors left the country for Africa, where Boabdil some years later lost his life in battle. After the emigration, very few aristocratic families were left in the conquered kingdom, and those Moorish nobles who still remained were carefully given posts in the royal administration in order to keep them contented.

It seems probable that Granada would have remained peaceful, and reasonably satisfied with its new rulers, had it not been for the question of religion. Hernando de Talavera was always scrupulous in observing the agreements of 1491, which guaranteed to the Moors the free exercise of their faith. Impressed by the Moorish cultural achievement, and by the emphasis placed by the Moors on practical works of charity, he entertained no belief in, or sympathy for, a policy of forcible conversion. His ideal was gentle assimilation, from which Spaniards, as well as Moors, would find that they had something to gain: 'We must adopt their works of charity, and they our Faith.'[1] Conversion, then, must be brought about by preaching and instruction, which itself required that the Christian clergy learn Arabic and attempt to understand the customs of the society entrusted to their charge.

1. Quoted by K. Garrad, *The Causes of the Second Rebellion of the Alpujarras* (unpublished Cambridge Ph.D dissertation, 1955), vol. I, p. 84.

While Talavera's policy achieved some remarkable successes, it unfortunately aroused strong opposition among several of his Christian colleagues, for whom the rate of conversion was insufficiently rapid. The principal advocate of a more forceful policy was Archbishop Cisneros of Toledo,[2] who came to Granada with Ferdinand and Isabella in 1499. With the blinding unawareness of the zealot, he quickly pushed aside the mild Talavera, and launched out on a policy of forcible conversion and mass baptism. His activities soon yielded predictable results: the Moors became nominal Christians in their thousands, and, in November 1499, an ill-concerted rising broke out in the Alpujarras, the densely populated slopes of the Sierra Nevada. Ferdinand advanced into the Alpujarras in March 1500; the revolt was crushed, and the Moors, on surrendering, were allowed to choose between emigration and conversion. Since the mass of the population had little alternative but to stay, this meant that, from the publication in February 1502 of a pragmatic ordering the expulsion of all unconverted adult Moors, the Moorish population of Granada became automatically 'Christian'.

The aftermath of the edict was to be unsatisfactory for the Christians and barely tolerable for the Moors. Convinced that the agreements of 1491-2 had been perfidiously broken, they clung with all the fervour of resentment to their traditional rites and customs, practising surreptitiously what was formally forbidden. The Spaniards insisted that the conversions had not been achieved by force, since the Moors had been allowed the option of emigration, but even the most zealous among them had to admit that the conversions left a good deal to be desired. But the deficiencies could only be made good by assiduous instruction, and the Andalusian clergy proved to be sadly wanting in both the skill and the desire to attend to the needs of their Moorish flocks. Since the Andalusian Church lacked the determination to convert, and the Morisco population lacked the will to be converted, deadlock was reached. During the first half of the sixteenth century an uneasy compromise prevailed in Andalusia, whereby the Moors, while nominally Christians, remained Moorish in practice, and the government refrained from

2. Known to Englishmen as Ximenes, and to Spaniards as Cisneros, his full name was Francisco Jiménez de Cisneros.

enforcing the pragmatics issued in 1508 for the prohibition of their traditional dress and customs.

2. THE ADVANCE INTO AFRICA

The dangers of rebellion among the sullen inhabitants of Granada, aided and abetted by their North African kinsmen, inevitably gave fresh impetus to a long-cherished project for the continuation of the Castilian crusade across the straits into Africa. This would be a natural sequel to the conquest of Granada, and one for which the times seemed especially propitious. The North African state system was in an advanced state of dissolution by the later fifteenth century. There were divisions between Algiers, Morocco, and Tunis, between the mountain-dwellers and the plain-dwellers, and between the traditional inhabitants and the recent émigrés from Andalusia. It was true that North Africa was difficult campaigning country, but the inhabitants were unacquainted with the new military techniques of the Castilians, and their internal feuds offered as tempting possibilities for the Spaniards as the faction struggles in the Nasrid kingdom of Granada.

Alexander VI gave his papal blessing to an African crusade in 1494, and, more important, authorized the continuation of the tax known as the *cruzada* to pay for it. But the crusade across the straits was postponed for a fateful decade. Spanish troops were heavily engaged in Italy during much of this time, and Ferdinand was in no mind to turn his attention elsewhere. Apart from the capture of the port of Melilla by the Duke of Medina-Sidonia in 1497, the new front with Islam was neglected, and it was only with the first revolt of the Alpujarras in 1499 that the Castilians really awoke to the dangers from North Africa. The revolt led to a great resurgence of popular religious enthusiasm and to new demands for a crusade against Islam, ardently supported by Cisneros and the Queen. When Isabella died in 1504, however, nothing had yet been done, and it remained for Cisneros to champion her dying request that her husband should devote himself 'unremittingly to the conquest of Africa and to the war for the Faith against the Moors'.

Cisneros's militant fervour was once again to carry all before it. An expedition was fitted out at Málaga, and set sail for North

Africa in the autumn of 1505. It succeeded in taking Mers-el-Kebir, an essential base for an attack on Oran, but Cisneros's attention was at this moment diverted to affairs nearer home, and it was not until 1509 that a new and stronger army was dispatched to Africa and that Oran was captured. But the beginning of the occupation of the North African coast in 1509–10 only served to sharpen the differences between Ferdinand and Cisneros, and to reveal the existence of two irreconcilable African policies. Cisneros, imbued with the spirit of the crusader, seems to have envisaged penetrating to the edges of the Sahara and establishing in North Africa a Spanish-Mauretanian empire. Ferdinand, on the other hand, considered North Africa a much less important theatre of operations than the traditional Aragonese preserve of Italy, and favoured a policy of limited occupation of the African coastline, sufficient to guarantee Spain against a Moorish attack.

Cisneros broke with his sovereign in 1509 and retired to the university of Alcalá. For the rest of the reign it was Ferdinand's African policy that prevailed: the Spaniards were content to seize and garrison a number of key points, while leaving the hinterland to the Moors. Spain was to pay a heavy price for this policy of limited occupation in later years. The relative inactivity of the Spaniards and their uncertain command of no more than a thin coastal strip allowed the Barbary corsairs to establish bases along the coast. In 1529 the Barbarossas, two pirate brothers who had originally come from the Levant, recaptured the Peñón d'Argel, the key to Algiers. From this moment the foundations were laid for an Algerian state under Turkish protection, which provided the ideal base for corsair attacks against Spain's vital Mediterranean routes.

The threat became extremely grave in 1534 when Barbarossa seized Tunis from Spain's Moorish vassals, and so secured for himself the control of the narrow seas between Sicily and Africa. It was obviously now a matter of extreme urgency for Spain to smoke out the hornets' nest before irreparable harm was done. In the following year Charles V undertook a great expedition against Tunis and succeeded in recapturing it, but he was unable to follow up his success with an immediate assault on Algiers, and the opportunity for destroying the Barbary pirates was missed. When the Emperor finally led an expedition against Algiers in 1541 it ended in disaster.

From now on Charles was fully occupied in Europe, and the Spaniards could do no more than hold their own in Africa. Their policy of limited occupation meant that they failed to secure real influence over the Maghreb, and their two protectorates of Tunisia and Tlemcen came under increasing Moorish pressure. By the time of Philip II's accession, Spanish North Africa was in a highly precarious state, from which the new King's efforts were unable to rescue it. Control of the Tunisian coast would have been an invaluable asset to Spain in its great naval war of 1559 to 1577 against the Turk, but although Don John of Austria was able to recover Tunis in 1573, both Tunis and its fortress of La Goletta were lost to the Moors in the following year. The fall of La Goletta was fatal to Spain's African hopes. Spanish control was gradually reduced to the garrison posts of Melilla, Oran, and Mers-el-Kebir, to which were later added the African remnants of the Portuguese Empire. Sadly, but not surprisingly, Cisneros's heroic vision of a Spanish North Africa had run to waste in the sands.

The most obvious reason for Spain's failure to establish itself effectively in North Africa lay in the extent of its commitments elsewhere. Ferdinand, Charles V, and Philip II were all too preoccupied with other pressing problems to devote more than fitful attention to the African front. The cost of failure was very high in terms of the growth of piracy in the western Mediterranean, but it is arguable that the nature of the land and the insufficiency of Spanish troops in any event made effective occupation impossible. It is conceivable, however, that the formidable natural difficulties would not have been insuperable if the Castilians had adopted a different approach to the war in North Africa. In practice they tended to treat the war as a simple continuation of the campaign against Granada. This meant that, as in the *Reconquista*, they thought principally in terms of marauding expeditions, of the capture of booty and the establishment of *presidios* or frontier garrisons. There was no plan for total conquest, no project for colonization. The word *conquista* to the Castilian implied essentially the establishing of the Spanish 'presence' – the securing of strongpoints, the staking out of claims, the acquisition of dominion over a defeated population. This style of warfare, tried and proven in medieval Spain, was naturally adopted in North Africa, in spite of local conditions which threatened to limit its effectiveness from the start. Since the country was hard and the booty disappointing, Africa, unlike Andalusia, offered few attractions to the individual warrior, more concerned to obtain material rewards for his hardships than the spiritual recompense promised by Cisneros. Consequently, enthusiasm for service in Africa quickly flagged, with entirely predictable military consequences. North Africa remained throughout the sixteenth century the Cinderella of Spain's overseas possessions – a land unsuited to the particular characteristics of the *conquistador*. The inadequacies of the crusading style of warfare of medieval Castile were here exposed; but failure in North Africa was almost immediately eclipsed by the startling success of the traditional style of warfare in an incomparably more spectacular enterprise – the conquest of an empire in America.

3. MEDIEVAL ANTECEDENTS

Medieval Castile had built up a military, crusading tradition which was to win for it in the sixteenth century an overseas empire. But it had also developed another tradition too easily overlooked – a tradition of maritime experience which was the essential prelude to its acquisition of overseas territories. The discovery and conquest of the New World was, in reality, very far from being a lucky accident for Spain. In many respects the Iberian peninsula was the region of Europe best equipped for overseas expansion at the end of the fifteenth century. Although the opening up and settlement of the New World was to be a predominantly Castilian undertaking, the enterprise had a common Iberian foundation. Different parts of the peninsula each contributed their own skills to a common store on which the Castilians drew with such spectacular results. The medieval Catalans and Aragonese had acquired a long experience of commercial and colonial adventure in North Africa and the Levant. The Majorcans had established an important school of cartography, which had devised techniques of map-making invaluable for the charting of hitherto unknown lands. The Basques, with the experience of Atlantic deep-sea fishing behind them, were skilled pilots and ship-builders. The Portuguese had played a predominant part in the perfecting of the caravel, the stout, square-rigged vessel which was to be the essential instrument of European overseas expansion in the late fifteenth and sixteenth centuries.

But the Castilians also had acquired their own commercial and maritime experience, especially during the past two centuries. The growth of the *Mesta* and the expansion of the wool trade with northern Europe stimulated the development of the ports of north Spain – San Sebastian, Laredo, Santander, Corunna – which as early as 1296 banded together in a brotherhood, the so-called *Hermandad de las Marismas*, aimed at protecting their domestic and foreign com-merical interests in the manner of the Hanseatic League. Similarly, the advance of the *Reconquista* in the late thirteenth century to Tarifa, on the straits of Gibraltar, had given Castile a second Atlantic seaboard, with its capital at Seville – itself recaptured by Ferdinand III in 1248. A vigorous commercial community established itself in Seville, including within its ranks influential members of the Andalusian aristocracy who were attracted by the new prospects of mercantile wealth. By the fifteenth century the city had become an intensely active commercial centre with thriving dockyards – a place where merchants from Spain and the Mediterranean lands would congregate to discuss new projects, form new associations and organize new ventures. It was Europe's observation post from which to survey North Africa and the broad expanses of the Atlantic Ocean.

These developments occurred at a time when western Europe as a whole was displaying a growing interest in the world overseas. Portugal in particular was active in voyages of discovery and exploration. With its long seaboard and its influential mercantile community it was well placed to embark on a quest for the gold, slaves, sugar, and spices, for all of which there was an expanding demand. Short of bread, it was also anxious for new cereal-growing lands, which it found in the Azores (rediscovered in 1427) and in Madeira. Like Castile it was inspired, too, by the crusading tradition, and the occupation of Ceuta in 1415 was itself conceived as part of a crusade which might one day encircle the earth and take Islam in the rear.

The traditional hostility of Castile and Portugal, exacerbated by Portuguese intervention in the question of the Castilian succession, provided an added incentive to Castile to acquire its own possessions overseas. One of the major battlefields in the Castilian-Portuguese conflict of the fifteenth century was to be the Canary Islands, which seem to have been discovered by the Genoese in the early fourteenth century. During the course of the Castilian War of Succession Ferdinand and Isabella attempted to substantiate their rights to the Canaries by dispatching an expedition from Seville in 1478 to occupy the Grand Canary. The resistance of the islanders and dissensions among the Castilians frustrated the intentions of Ferdinand and Isabella, and it was only in 1482 that a new expedition under Alfonso Fernández de Lugo laid the foundations for eventual success, beginning with the subjugation of Grand Canary in the following year. Even now, Palma was not taken till 1492 and Tenerife till 1493. But, in the meantime, the treaty of 1479 ending the war between Castile and Portugal had settled the dispute over the Canaries to Castile's advantage. Portugal renounced its claim to the Canaries in return for a recognition of her exclusive right to Guinea, the kingdom of Fez, Madeira, and the Azores, and so Castile acquired its first overseas possessions.

Castile's occupation of the Canaries was an event of major importance in the history of its overseas expansion. Their geographical position was to make them of exceptional value as an indispensable staging-post on the route to America: all Columbus's four expeditions put in at the Canary archipelago. But they were also to provide the perfect laboratory for Castile's colonial experiments, serving as the natural link between the *Reconquista* in Spain and the conquest of America.

In the conquest and colonization of the Canaries can be seen at once the continuation and extension of techniques already well tried in the later Middle Ages, and the forging of new methods which would come into their own in the conquest of the New World. There were marked similarities between the methods of the *Reconquista* and those adopted for the conquest of the Canaries, which itself was regarded by Ferdinand and Isabella as part of Castile's holy war against the infidel. The occupation of the Canaries, like the *Reconquista*, was a blend of private and public enterprise. Much of the *Reconquista*, especially in its later stages, had been conducted under the control of the Crown. The State also participated in the Canary expeditions, which were partly financed by the Crown and public institutions. But private enterprise operated alongside the

State. Fernández de Lugo made a private contract with a company of Sevillian merchants – one of the first contracts of the type later used to finance the expeditions of discovery in America. Even an expedition entirely organized and financed under private auspices, however, was still dependent on the Crown for its legal authority. Here again the *Reconquista* provided a useful precedent. It had been the practice for the Crown to make contracts with leaders of military expeditions against the Moors. It seems probable that these contracts inspired the document known as the *capitulación*, which later became the customary form of agreement between the Spanish Crown and the *conquistadores* of America.

The purpose of *capitulaciones* was to reserve certain rights to the Crown in newly conquered territories, while also guaranteeing to the leader of the expedition due *mercedes* or rewards for his services. These rewards might consist of an official position such as the post of *adelantado* of Las Palmas conferred upon Fernández de Lugo – *adelantado* being a hereditary title granted by medieval Castilian kings and conferring upon its holder special military powers and the rights of government over a frontier province. The leader of an expedition would also expect to enjoy the spoils of conquest, in the shape of movable property and captives, and to receive grants of land and a title of nobility, like his predecessors during the *Reconquista*.

In making *capitulaciones* of this type, the Crown was clearly bargaining away many of its rights, but generally it had no alternative. When it provided financial assistance, as it did for Columbus and Magellan, it could hope to make rather more favourable conditions, but the work of conquest and colonization had to be left largely to private enterprise. In these circumstances, the extent to which the Spanish Crown still managed to retain control over newly won territories is remarkable. It was clearly acknowledged from the start that the *capitulación* was the fundamental legal charter of any new settlement, and Ferdinand and Isabella made use of the *capitulación* to insist in writing, both on the religious purposes inherent in the conquest, and on the essential presence of the State, from which the expedition acquired its sole legal authority. Columbus and his successors would thus always take possession in the name of the Crown. Similarly, the greatest care would be taken on the conquest of new territory, to prevent the alienation of the

Crown's sovereign rights to feudal lords. The earlier history of
the Canary Islands had made Ferdinand and Isabella fully aware of the
dangers of unrestricted settlement, and they took various steps to
prevent a repetition. Governors of the islands were kept strictly
subordinate to their own control; the Crown insisted on its right to
organize *repartimientos* or distributions of land among the settlers, in
accordance with a practice already well established during the *Reconquista*; and all new towns were made dependent on a royal charter for
their rights and privileges. In this way the municipal organization of
medieval Castile was faithfully transplanted to the overseas colonies.

The cautious attitude of Ferdinand and Isabella, and their ceaseless
care for the preservation and extension of their royal rights, are
admirably illustrated by their dealings with Columbus. Here the
difficulties were both financial and political. When the Genoese
adventurer made his first appearance at Court in 1486 there were
good reasons for rejecting his proposals. The Crown was poor; it
was heavily engaged in the Granada war; and Columbus's plans
prompted a not unreasonable scepticism. The reasons why Ferdinand
and Isabella changed their minds in 1491 are still not entirely clear.
Columbus had friends in high places. These included Ferdinand's
secretary, Luis de Santángel, who helped to arrange the financing of
the expedition, and the Franciscan Juan Pérez, a former confessor of
the Queen, whose monastery at La Rábida gave shelter to the
explorer when he first sought favour at Court. But it is also probable
that the approach of victory in Granada helped to incline the
monarchs to a more benign view of some of the alleged advantages
to be derived from the project. A successful voyage by Columbus
would steal a march on the Portuguese, and might conceivably bring
riches to an empty treasury. Above all – at least as far as Isabella was
concerned – the project could be of crucial importance in the crusade
against Islam. A successful voyage would bring Spain into contact
with the nations of the East, whose help was needed in the struggle
with the Turk. It might also, with luck, bring back Columbus by
way of Jerusalem, opening up a route for attacking the Ottoman
Empire in the rear. Isabella was naturally attracted, too, by the
possibility of laying the foundations of a great Christian mission in
the East. In the climate of intense religious excitement which characterized the last months of the Granada campaign even the wildest

projects suddenly seemed possible of accomplishment. The close coincidence between the fall of Granada and the authorization of Columbus's expedition would suggest that the latter was at once a thank-offering and an act of renewed dedication by Castile to the still unfinished task of war against the infidel.

The authorization was only granted, however, after some extremely hard bargaining. Columbus's conditions seemed preposterously high. He requested for himself and his descendants in perpetuity the post of governor-general and viceroy of any lands he discovered. At a time when Ferdinand and Isabella were struggling in Spain with a considerable degree of success to assert the rights of the Crown against feudal pretensions, it was clearly impossible for them to countenance a demand which would have turned Spain's overseas territories into the feudal domain of a Genoese explorer. They also refused to let the Duke of Medinaceli help finance Columbus's voyage, fearing that participation by the magnates in colonial enterprises might similarly lead to the creation of independent domains overseas. In the end, Columbus had to be content with what were, in fact, already very large concessions – the hereditary title of Grand Admiral, and a right to the tenth of the merchandise and produce of the new territories.

When Columbus set sail in August 1492 with his three ships and his crew of eighty-eight, he was therefore the legatee of several different, and sometimes conflicting, traditions. Like a commander in the *Reconquista* he had made a private contract with the Crown for very considerable rights over the new lands that he was to win for it. But Columbus himself did not belong to the tradition of the *Reconquista*. As a Genoese, settled in Portugal and then in southern Spain, he was a representative of the Mediterranean commercial tradition, which had begun to attract Castilians during the later Middle Ages. His purpose was to discover and exploit the riches of the East in association with a State which had conferred its protection upon him. For this enterprise he could draw upon the experience acquired by Castile in its commercial ventures and its colonization of the Canaries. But unfortunately for Columbus, Castile's mercantile tradition was not yet sufficiently well established to challenge its military tradition with any hope of success. While he saw his task essentially in terms of the establishment of trading bases and commercial outposts, most Castilians were accustomed to ideas of a continuing military advance, the sharing-out of new lands, the distribution of booty and the conversion of infidels. Inevitably the two opposing traditions – that of the merchant and that of the warrior – came into violent conflict, and in that conflict Columbus himself was defeated and broken. It proved impossible for him to compete with the deeply engrained habits of a crusading society; nor could he stand alone against the growing power of a State which was quick to see both the possibilities and the dangers of overseas expansion, and was determined to keep the process of colonization firmly under its own control.

4. CONQUEST

When Columbus died in 1506, two years after Isabella, he was already a figure who belonged to the past. His attempts to colonize Hispaniola (Haiti) and to establish a commercial monopoly had failed by the end of 1498. As fresh discoveries were made, and the prospects of finding gold grew brighter with each new traveller's tale, the settlers were anxious to be up and away. Between 1499 and 1508 expeditions from Spain, sent out to explore the northern coast of South America, were establishing the existence of an American land-mass, while Columbus himself on his final voyage of 1502–4 touched Honduras and the Nicaraguan isthmus. From 1508 the pattern of discovery began to change. By that year Hispaniola was fully under Spanish control, and would replace Spain as the base for future expeditions for the discovery and conquest of Cuba and the Antilles.

By 1519 the first tentative probings were done. Núñez de Balboa had sighted the Pacific six years before, and the founding of Panama in 1519 gave Spain control of the isthmus and its first Pacific base. The years 1519 to 1540 represented the final, heroic phase of the *conquista* – the years in which Spain won its great American empire. This empire was built on the ruins of the two native empires of the Aztecs and the Incas. The conquest of the Aztec empire of Mexico was undertaken from Cuba in 1519 by Hernán Cortés with a brilliance and a daring which was to fire the imagination both of contemporaries and of future generations; Pizarro's destruction of the empire of the Incas, in fact, proved almost a carbon copy – sadly blotted in its later stages – of the triumph of Cortés a decade before

Francisco Pizarro set off from Panama in 1531 with an even smaller band of men than that of Cortés; and successfully surmounting the challenge of enormous distances and almost impassable mountain barriers, his little company overthrew the great Inca empire in the space of a mere two years. From the heart of this fallen empire the conquerors fanned out over South America in the pursuit of El Dorado. By 1540 the greatest age of the *conquista* was over. Vast areas remained as yet unexplored and unconquered; the advance into Chile was successfully checked by the fierce resistance of the Araucan Indians; but in all South America with the exception of Brazil (which fell in the area allotted to the Portuguese by the Treaty of Tordesillas of 1494), the Spanish 'presence' had been triumphantly and almost miraculously established.

The overthrow of the empires of the Aztecs and the Incas was achieved by no more than a handful of men. Cortés destroyed the empire of Montezuma with six hundred soldiers and sixteen horses; Pizarro, with thirty-seven horses, had only one hundred and eighty men. Little is known about the background and personalities of these *conquistadores*, less than a thousand all told, who captured a continent against almost inconceivable odds. There is no doubt, however, that they were drawn overwhelmingly from the Crown of Castile. America was legally a Castilian possession, in which the inhabitants of Navarre or the Crown of Aragon were regarded as foreigners. Within the Crown of Castile, it seems that natives of Andalusia and Estremadura predominated: both Cortés and Pizarro were Estremadurans by birth. The first arrivals in the New World were, naturally enough, young unmarried men, most of them with previous military experience. Socially, they were drawn from the gentry class and below, for the upper aristocracy played no part in the conquest and tended to look askance at projects for emigration which would take labourers from its estates. The strength of the *mayorazgo* system – the system of entail – in Castile did, however, provide a strong incentive for emigration by younger sons of aristocratic and gentry houses, who hoped to find in the New World the fortune denied them at home. *Hidalgos* in particular were well represented in the *conquista* – men such as Cortés himself, who came from noble but impoverished families, and were prepared to try their luck in an unknown world.

The character of these men, and especially the predominance of the *hidalgo* class in the leadership of the expeditions, inevitably set a special stamp on the whole pattern of conquest. They brought with them from Castile the ambitions, the prejudices, the habits and the values that they had acquired at home. First and foremost they were professional soldiers, schooled to hardship and war. They were also intensely legalistically minded, always drawing up documents, even in the most improbable places and situations, to determine the exact rights and duties of each member of an expedition. They had, too, the capacity for infinite wonder at the strange world unfolding before their eyes, interpreting its mysteries as much from their store of imagination as from their past experience. But their imagination was itself inspired by what they had learnt at home. The coming of printing to Spain around 1473 had given an extraordinary vogue to romances of chivalry, and *Amadis of Gaul* (1508), the most famous of them all, was known in affectionate detail by a vast body of Spaniards who, if they could not read themselves, had heard them told or read aloud. A society soaked in these works, and touchingly credulous about the veracity of their contents, naturally tended to some extent to model its view of the world and its code of behaviour on the extravagant concepts popularized by the books of chivalry. Here was an abundance of strange happenings and heroic actions. What more natural than that the mysterious world of America should provide the scene for their enactment? Uneducated and illiterate as Pizarro, Almagro and their companions may have been, all had heard of and hoped to find the kingdom of the Amazons; and it is recorded that their first sight of Mexico City reminded Cortés's men of 'the enchanted things related in the book of Amadis'.[3]

Their heads filled with fantastic notions, their courage spurred by noble examples of the great heroes of chivalry, the *conquistadores* were prepared to undergo every kind of hardship and sacrifice as they penetrated through swamps and jungles into the heart of the new continent. The spirit that animated them was later to be graphically described by Cortés: 'he highly praised the captains and companions who had been with him in the conquest of Mexico,

3. Quoted by Irving A. Leonard, *Books of the Brave* (Harvard University Press, 1949), p. 43, a remarkable study of literary fashions in the age of the conquest.

saying that they were able to suffer hunger and hardship, that wherever he summoned them he could do heroic deeds with them, and that, even when they were wounded and in rags they never failed to fight and to capture every city and fortress, however great the risk to their lives'.[4] These men were dedicated fighters – tough, determined, contemptuous of danger, arrogant and touchy, extravagant and impossible; examples, perhaps a little larger than life size, of the kind of man produced by the nomadic, warrior society which inhabited the dry tableland of medieval Castile.

The dedication, however, required a cause, and the sacrifice a recompense. Both were described with disarming frankness by Cortés's devoted companion, the historian Bernal Díaz del Castillo: 'We came here to serve God and the king, and also to get rich.'[5] The *conquistadores* came to the New World in pursuit of riches, honour, and glory. It was greed, cupidity, the thirst for power and fame that drove forward a Pizarro or a Cortés. But their ambition deserves to be set into the context of their background. They came from poor families and a poor land, members of a society acclimatized to the winning of wealth by the waging of war. Rank and social distinction were achieved in this society by the possession of land and of riches, both of them the fruits of valour in battle. Cortés, like any *caballero* of medieval Castile, aspired to obtain a fief and vassals, to secure a title, and to make a name for himself in the world – and all of these ambitions he attained through his conquest of Mexico. He ended his life as Marqués del Valle de Oaxaca, his son and daughters married into the ranks of the great aristocracy of Castile; and 'in everything – in his manner, in his conversation, in his mode of eating and dressing – he showed himself to have all the outward signs of the *gran señor*'.[6]

Any attempt to explain the extraordinary success of an enterprise undertaken by so tiny a group of men against such overwhelming superiority of numbers must necessarily take into account both the aspirations of the individual *conquistador* and the readiness

4. Bernal Díaz del Castillo, *Historia Verdadera de la Conquista de la Nueva España*, c. cciv.
5. Quoted by Lewis Hanke, *Bartolomé de las Casas* (The Hague, 1951), p. 9.
6. Bernal Díaz del Castillo, op.cit.

of the society from which he came to accept their validity and esteem their achievement. The *conquistador* knew that he faced sudden death. But he also knew that, if he survived, he would go back rich to a world in which riches conferred rank and power. On the other hand, if he should die, he had the consolation of dying in the Faith, with hope of salvation. The religion of the *conquistadores* gave them an unshakeable faith in the rightness of their cause and in the certainty of its triumph. Cortés always carried with him an image of the Virgin, and attended mass daily; and his banner, which bore a cross, was inscribed with the words: 'Amici, sequamur crucem, et si nos fidem habemus vere in hoc signo vincemus.' However often debased and traduced in practice, this conquering missionary fervour was sufficient to make the Castilians more than a match for Indians who fought bravely enough, but who lacked their zest for life.

While the *conquistadores* possessed an important advantage in the superiority of their weapons, it is in their personal characteristics that the secret of their triumph finally lies. A few small cannon and thirteen muskets can hardly have been the decisive factor in overthrowing an empire more than ten million strong. There must here have been a superiority that was more than merely technical, and perhaps it ultimately lay in the greater self-confidence of the civilization which produced the *conquistadores*. In the Inca empire they confronted a civilization that seems to have passed its peak and to have started already on its descent; in the Aztec empire, on the other hand, they successfully challenged a civilization still young and in the process of rapid evolution. Each of these empires was thus caught at a moment when it was least capable of offering effective resistance, and each lacked confidence in itself, and in its capacity for survival in a universe ruled by implacable deities, and for ever poised on the brink of destruction. The *conquistador*, hungry for fame and riches, and supremely confident of his capacity to obtain them, stood on the threshold of a fatalist world resigned to self-surrender; and in the sign of the cross he conquered it.

5. SETTLEMENT

The overthrowing of the Aztec and Inca empires represented no more than a first stage in the conquest of America. Having conquered the land, the *conquistadores* still had to take possession of it. The taking of possession, the settling of the land, the building of cities, the forcing of the native population into patterns determined for it by the Spaniards, and the gradual establishment of governmental institutions, represented the second, and perhaps the greater, conquest of America. This was to be a task extending over many generations – a task in the course of which the conquerors of the New World themselves fell victims to the bureaucrats of the Old.

This second conquest of America involved the transplanting of the institutions and the ways of life of the Castilians to the very different conditions of the new continent. In the process they were inevitably modified, and sometimes changed beyond recognition, but even the most distorted forms can shed unexpected light on the originals that inspire them.

The first task of the leader of a military expedition was to reward his followers. Before the expedition started, formal agreements were usually made about the distribution of the booty: a portion would be set aside for the Crown and the rest would be divided into fixed proportions according to the rank and status of the members of the expedition. As in the *Reconquista* the first *repartimiento* or distribution of the land after its conquest was effected on a temporary basis, the permanent division being left until it was properly occupied and surveyed. From the legal point of view it was early established that the Indians were the proprietors of all lands which they possessed and cultivated at the time of the Spaniards' arrival, while the rest of the land and all the sub-soil became the property of the State. The Crown would be expected to share out this land to the *conquistadores* as a reward for their services, following precedents already established in medieval Castile.

The land was divided among corporations and private individuals. The principal agencies for the settlement of lands recaptured from the Moors during the *Reconquista* had been the towns, and the conquest of America provided a faithful repetition of this pattern. In order to place their gains on a more permanent basis, the commanders in the New World would, as soon as possible, establish a town, secure its legal incorporation by the Crown, and put their own followers into the key municipal offices. Institutionally these towns were replicas of those of medieval Castile, displaying in their early years the same vitality as had been displayed by the Castilian towns in the heyday of municipal government during the twelfth and thirteenth centuries; but physically they were conceived on a different pattern. The principal buildings were the same – the church, the town hall, the prison fronting on to the *plaza mayor* – but the layout was more rational and spacious. The towns were built, like the camp town of Santa Fe outside Granada, on the gridiron pattern, and were probably inspired by Renaissance works on town planning, which themselves were derived from classical models. Like the Roman *civitas* and the Castilian commune, their jurisdiction extended far into the surrounding country, and the *cabildos* or town councils were immensely powerful bodies, whose independence gave the municipalities some of the character of city states.

The towns were the centres of a colonist population, which expected to live in style according to the domestic and gastronomic standards of the upper classes in Castile; and the colonists were dependent for their subsistence on a countryside that was being turned over to the cultivation of European crops, and was worked with the labour of the conquered Indian population. The legal possession of the land was thus from the start bound up with the problem of jurisdiction over the people who were to work it. In medieval Castile there had been essentially two types of lordship. In *señorios libres* (or *behetrías*), the inhabitants freely placed themselves under the protection of a lay or ecclesiastical lord, but in process of time their status tended to deteriorate until it was often indistinguishable from that of the vassals in the other type of *señorio* – the *señorio de solariego*. The character of the *señorio de solariego*, which was still a fundamental form of tenure in sixteenth- and seventeenth-century Castile, varied according to how much or how little land belonged to the lord. Its principal feature, however, was that the vassals obtained inheritance rights from their lords in exchange for dues or services. While the system of tenure in America was to develop special characteristics of its own, these Castilian models were always present in the background.

The problem of jurisdiction in America was both moral and material. The Spaniards could only survive in the New World by exploiting native labour, in the fields and the mines, but on what grounds could this exploitation be justified? This question raised the whole problem of the basis and extent of Spain's rights in the New World – itself an old problem posed in a new form.

During the Middle Ages there had been considerable discussion about the rights of Christians over pagans, and when Alexander VI issued his famous papal bulls of 1493 drawing a line of demarcation between Spain's and Portugal's spheres of influence, and confirming the status of the new territories as a papal fief held by the Spanish Crown, he was only acting in accordance with existing views about the supersession of pagan rights. The actual interpretation of the bulls, however, caused considerable difficulty in later years. It was far from clear whether the bulls unconditionally conferred full political and territorial rights on the Spanish Crown, or whether those rights were strictly subordinated to a religious end, and retained their validity only so long as Spain fulfilled its spiritual mission of converting its heathen subjects. The Spanish Crown always claimed that the bulls were no more than a reinforcement of the rights it had already acquired by conquest, but it was none the less careful to accept and insist on its own obligation to Christianize the Indians.

The Crown's obligations towards its new pagan subjects rapidly came into conflict with the economic demands of the settlers. These had their own ideas about the correct treatment of a conquered pagan population – ideas derived from the traditions of the *Reconquista*. The experiences of the *Reconquista* had led to the formulation of an elaborate code of rules about the 'just war', and the rights of the victors over the vanquished population, including the right to enslave it. These rules were extended as a matter of course to the Canary Islands. The conquerors of the Canaries used, for instance, the strange technique of the *requerimiento*, which was later employed in America, whereby the bewildered natives were presented before the opening of hostilities with a formal document giving them the option of accepting Christianity and Spanish rule. It could, however, be argued that there was a difference in kind between the Canary Islanders and the Moors of south Spain, since the islanders were totally ignorant of Christianity until the arrival of the Spaniards, whereas the Moors had heard of Christianity but rejected it. Slavery would surely seem an excessively harsh punishment for mere ignorance, and Ferdinand and Isabella did their best to prevent its growth in the Canaries.

The same problem inevitably arose again with the discovery of the Indies. Columbus sent home shiploads of Indians to be sold as slaves, but the theologians protested, the Queen's conscience rebelled, and enslavement of the Indians was formally prohibited in 1500. Exceptions were made, however, for Indians who attacked Spaniards, or practised atrocious habits such as cannibalism, and Cortés had no difficulty in finding pretexts for the enslavement of numerous men, women, and children.

With the imposition by the Government of restrictions on slavery it became essential to find some solution to the problem of providing a non-slave labour force, while at the same time giving the Indians the consolation of instruction in the rudiments of the Christian religion. The answer to this problem was provided by the institution known as the *encomienda*, which appeared to harmonize satisfactorily the Castilian ideals of lordship and the demands of pastoral care. The *encomiendas* belonging to the great Military Orders in medieval Castile consisted of temporary grants made by the Crown to private individuals, of jurisdiction over territory recaptured from the Moors. The American version of the *encomienda*, which represented a limited form of *señorío* or lordship, originated in Hispaniola, where Columbus assigned to the settlers a number of Indians who were expected to perform labour services for them. This *repartimiento* or distribution of Indians formed the basis of the *encomienda* system regularized and institutionalized by Columbus's successor Nicolás de Ovando, the Governor of Hispaniola from 1502. Under the system, the *encomendero* was given, on a strictly temporary, non-hereditary basis (at least in theory) a grant of lordship over a certain number of Indians. The *encomienda* in the New World was not, therefore, a landed estate, and indeed had nothing to do with ownership of land, the property rights of the Indians being formally respected. The *encomendero* simply accepted the obligation to protect a specified group of Indians and to instruct them in the ways of civilization and Christianity, and in return he received from the Indians labour services or tributes.

Inevitably the *encomienda* system came to assume characteristics which at times made it barely distinguishable from outright slavery. As the Spanish population grew, and a vast programme of secular and ecclesiastical building was instituted, the demand for native labour increased, and taxes in the *encomiendas* were commuted into labour services. By the middle of the sixteenth century, therefore, the economic exploitation of the New World had come to depend on the twin institutions of slavery and of labour service provided by the *encomiendas*. On these foundations arose a town-dwelling colonial society of Spaniards and *mestizos*, gradually evolving its own social élite of the families of *conquistadores* and *encomenderos*.

This duel process of the enslavement of the native population and the development of a new transatlantic feudal aristocracy was, however, halted by the combined opposition of Church and State. The friars in particular played a prominent part. Inspired by mission-ary fervour, the Mendicant Orders sent out their representatives in the wake of the *Conquista* to undertake the vast work of evangelizing the New World. The Franciscans appeared in Mexico in 1523, the Dominicans in 1526, and the Augustinians seven years later. By 1559 there were 800 Mendicants in Mexico, as against only 500 secular clergy. The first forty years after the conquest, before the secular clergy became strong enough to launch their counter-offensive against the friars, were the golden age of Mendicant evangelical enterprise. The missionaries were drawn from among the élite of the Religious Orders, and the majority of them were steeped in the humanist ideas which made so deep an impression on the intellectual leaders of early sixteenth-century Europe. The first Bishop of Mexico, for instance, the Franciscan Fray Juan de Zumárraga, was a prominent Erasmian whose policies were inspired by Erasmus's 'philosophy of Christ' and by Sir Thomas More's *Utopia*. Zumárraga and his colleagues saw in the primitive agrarian society of the American Indians the ideal material for the realization of the perfect Christian community, and they set themselves with heroic dedication to the enormous task of grouping the Indians into villages, building missions and churches, and imposing a new pattern of civilization on their bewildered charges. The results were remarkable. Within half a century the Mexican Indians had assimilated the superior techniques of their conquerors, and displayed a receptivity to European culture which had no parallel in other parts of Spain's colonial empire.

For all their own great gifts and aptitudes, the Mendicants could never have achieved so rapid a success if the Indians had not been ready to accept something of what they had to offer. The destruction of their own native civilization, controlled by a complicated calendar and based on the most intricate ceremonial, had inevitably left a vacuum in the lives of the Indians. The friars, by offering them a new set of rituals, and by occupying their time in ambitious building projects, helped to fill this vacuum. This was at once the strength and the weakness of the Mendicant achievement. After the old civilization of the Indians had been irrevocably shattered, the friars built for them a new civilization based on their acceptance of Christian ceremonial; but they were much less successful in eradicating old pagan beliefs, and in promoting among their charges a real understanding of the meaning of their faith. They entirely failed, for instance, to create a native priesthood. As the first, heroic, generation of missionaries passed away, this failure came increasingly to affect the Mendicants' general attitude to the Indian. Having at the beginning overestimated the Indian's spiritual aptitude, the friars became disillusioned by his lack of progress and began to change their views. In the end the majority probably disdained the natives, or at least came to regard them as wayward, if lovable, children to be kept in permanent tutelage; but there were some, like the great Franciscan, Fray Bernardino de Sahagún, who acquired a deep interest in native customs and language, and set out to record for posterity the characteristics of a disappearing civilization before it was finally swept away. The approach of Sahagún to the Indians resembled that of Talavera to the Granada Moors. Each was inspired by genuine curiosity, by a respect for certain aspects of an alien civilization, and by a determination to meet the natives on their own terms and to give them a thorough grounding in the principles of the Christian faith.

The missionaries naturally tended to develop an instinctive sympathy, however patronizing at times, for an Indian population as yet uncorrupted by the many vices of European civilization. Many of them, convinced of the natural dignity and rights of man, found it impossible to square the treatment that was being meted out to the natives with their own fundamental convictions about the status of mankind. 'Are these Indians not men? Do they not have rational souls? Are you not obliged to love them as you love yourselves?' These were the disturbing questions asked by the Dominican

Antonio de Montesinos in his famous sermon preached in Hispaniola before a congregation of outraged colonists in 1511.[7] They were the prelude to a great storm of moral indignation which has become associated for ever with the name of Bartolomé de las Casas. Converted to the views of Montesinos in 1514, Las Casas was to devote his life to the work of securing fair treatment for the Indians. In the New World and the Old he would insistently repeat the same refrain: that the Indians, being subjects of the Spanish Crown, should enjoy equal rights with the Spaniards; that they were intellectually capable of receiving the Faith and should be gently instructed in the ways of Christianity under the government of benevolent officials; and that the colonists should support themselves by their own efforts and had no right to enforced Indian labour.

The views of Las Casas aroused the most intense opposition, not only among those with vested interests in the supply of native labour, but also among theologians as convinced as himself of the righteousness of their cause. Chief among these was the great Aristotelian scholar Juan Ginés de Sepúlveda, for whom the Aristotelian doctrine of natural slavery was entirely applicable to the Indians on the grounds of their inferiority. For Sepúlveda, war and conquest formed an essential prelude to all attempts at evangelization, since it was just and right to take up arms against those condemned by their natural condition to obey. The great debate staged between Las Casas and Sepúlveda at Valladolid in 1550 was, in fact, to turn on precisely this theme of whether it was lawful to wage war on the Indians before preaching the Faith to them, so that afterwards they might be the more easily instructed.

The debate proved inconclusive and failed to give Las Casas the resounding victory for which he had hoped, but, in spite of this, the trend of governmental legislation continued to move, as it had for some time been moving, in the direction he desired. In 1530 a royal decree prohibited all future enslavement of Indians under any pretext, and although it was revoked under pressure four years later, it was renewed in the famous *Leyes Nuevas* of 1542, which also stipulated that the slave-owner must prove his claim to any slaves in his possession. The abolition of Indian slavery was not achieved in a

7. Quoted by Lewis Hanke, *Aristotle and the American Indians* (London, 1959), p. 15.

day, and it was tragically to be accompanied by an increasing importation of negro slaves, whose fate disturbed the Spanish conscience much less than that of the Indians; but it seems to have become effective in most areas by the end of the 1560s. Meanwhile, the *encomienda* system was badly hit by the royal decree of 1549, which forbade *encomenderos* to substitute forced labour in the mines for the payment of tribute. In some regions, like Paraguay and Chile, the old system continued in spite of the decree, but in most parts of Mexico and Peru the resistance of the colonists was overborne, and forced labour in its traditional undisguised form disappeared. Since native labour was indispensable, new methods of persuading the Indians to work more had now to be found, and this led to a system of State labour, by which the Indians received wages for work exercised under official supervision. This new system, which admittedly bore obvious similarities to the old, did much to undermine the *encomiendas*. Once Indians began to work for the State outside their *encomienda*, the *encomendero* lost control of his Indian labour force, and the role of the *encomienda* in the American economy began to decline.

The downfall of slavery and of some of the worst features of the *encomienda* system was a triumph for liberal and humanitarian sentiments and reflected a remarkable stirring of the public conscience inside Spain. It was a tribute also to the freedom and vigour of intellectual debate in the Spain of Charles V – a debate that raged in the universities, and in Court and government circles, and was publicized by controversial pamphlets and erudite tomes. But while the conscience of the Emperor and of influential officials was stirred by the incessant efforts of Las Casas, it is highly improbable that so much would have been achieved if the Spanish Crown had not already been predisposed in favour of Las Casas's ideals for less altruistic motives of its own.

For a Crown anxious to assert and preserve its own control over its newly acquired territories, the growth of slavery and of the *encomienda* system constituted a serious threat. From the outset Ferdinand and Isabella had shown themselves determined to prevent the growth in the New World of those feudal tendencies which had for so long sapped the power of the Crown in Castile. They reserved for the Crown all land not occupied by natives, in order to avoid a repetition of the first period of the *Reconquista*, when abandoned lands were occupied on private initiative without a legal title. When distributing land they took care to limit the amount given to any one individual, so as to prevent the accumulation in the New World of vast estates on the Andalusian model. Similarly, they refused to grant any *señoríos* with rights of jurisdiction, and they were very sparing in the distribution of titles. Some of the *conquistadores*, like Cortés, received grants of *hidalguía* and nobility, but the Crown had clearly set itself against anything likely to promote the growth of a powerful territorial aristocracy in America comparable to that of Castile.

The growth of the *encomienda* system, however, was perfectly capable of frustrating the Crown's intentions. There were natural affinities between the *encomienda* and the fief, and a real danger that the *encomenderos* would grow into a powerful hereditary caste. During the first years of the conquest the Court was flooded with petitions for the establishment of *señoríos indianos*, and for the perpetuation of the *encomiendas* in the families of the original *encomenderos*. With considerable skill the Government managed to sidestep these demands, and to defer decisions that the colonists were anxiously awaiting. As a result, *encomiendas* never formally became hereditary, and their value was all the time being reduced by the imposition of charges upon them whenever a vacancy occurred. Moreover, the number of *encomenderos* decreased as many *encomiendas* reverted to the Crown, and the *encomenderos* as a class gradually lost importance as the century advanced.

If, then, the abolition of slavery and the weakening of the *encomienda* represented a triumph for Las Casas and his colleagues, they also bore witness to the remarkable success of the Spanish Crown in imposing its authority on remote territories under conditions that were often extremely unfavourable. A great hereditary feudal aristocracy did not develop in the New World. Its inhabitants were not allowed to develop Cortes or representative institutions which might one day challenge the royal power. Instead, the officials of the Spanish Crown slowly asserted their authority over every aspect of American life, forcing *encomenderos* and *tabildos* to yield before them. The achievement was all the more remarkable when it is viewed against the sombre backcloth of fifteenth-century Castile. In the middle decades of the fifteenth century the kings of Castile could not even rule their own country; a hundred years later they were the effective rulers of a vast empire thousands of miles away. The change is only explicable in terms of the greatest royal achievement of the intervening years: the building of a State by Ferdinand and Isabella.

3
The Ordering of Spain

I. THE 'NEW MONARCHY'

THE late fifteenth and early sixteenth centuries are commonly described as the age of 'the new monarchies': an age in which such forceful monarchs as Henry VII of England and Louis XI of France consolidated the power of the Crown and devoted their efforts to the creation of a unified and centralized State under royal control. If, as is generally assumed, Ferdinand and Isabella conformed to the contemporary pattern, then it would be natural to expect the imposition of unity and the centralization of government to be the theme of their life work. Yet in practice the Spain created by Ferdinand and Isabella diverged in so many respects from the theoretical model of the 'new monarchy', as to make it appear either that it must be entirely excluded from the European model, or alternatively that the model itself is at fault.

The work of the Catholic Kings (a title conferred on Ferdinand and Isabella by Pope Alexander VI in 1494) deserves to be judged in the context of their own ideals and intentions, rather than in terms of the theoretical characteristics of the Renaissance State. There was little or nothing new about these ideals. Ferdinand and Isabella believed in royal justice, in good kingship, which would protect the weak and humble the proud. If they had a high sense of their own rights, they also had a high sense of their own obligations, and these included the obligation to respect the rights of others. Their divinely appointed task was to restore order and good governance, re-establishing by the exercise of their monarchical power a society in which each could freely enjoy the rights that belonged to him by virtue of his station.

The whole outlook of Ferdinand and Isabella was informed by this concept of a natural coincidence between the Crown's exercise of a God-given authority and the subject's enjoyment of his traditional rights. These rights, and the laws which guaranteed them, naturally varied considerably in Castile and Aragon, but the fact that the two Crowns were now united did not in any way imply that their legal and constitutional systems should be brought into line. Isabella, for instance, showed herself consistently unwilling to allow the smallest deviation from the succession laws of Castile. By the marriage contract of 1469, Ferdinand's personal authority in Castile was sharply restricted, and Isabella was declared, on her accession in 1474, to be the *reina propietaria* – the Queen Proprietress – of Castile, in spite of her husband's efforts to claim the throne for himself on the grounds that a female succession was invalid. In 1475 it was determined that royal documents should be headed 'Don Fernando and Doña Isabel, by the grace of God sovereigns of Castile, León, Aragon, Sicily . . .', but this was not intended to imply any fusion of the various territories, any more than the decision to place the arms of Castile before those of Aragon was intended to imply the subordination of Aragon to Castile. Each state remained in its own compartment, governed by its traditional laws; and this fact was emphasized by Isabella's will of 1504. By the terms of the will, Ferdinand, after thirty years as King of Castile, was to be stripped of his title on his wife's death, and the Crown of Castile was to pass to their daughter, Juana, who was declared to be Isabella's successor as *señora natural propietaria*.

The future development of the Spanish Monarchy was to be profoundly influenced by the essentially patrimonial concept of the State to which both Ferdinand and Isabella clung. The strength of this patrimonial concept is vividly illustrated by their handling of two outstanding problems: jurisdiction over America, and the political reorganization of the Principality of Catalonia. Both of these questions might have been regarded as matters of general Spanish concern, and handled from this standpoint. But in practice they were treated respectively as Castilian and Aragonese questions, just as they would have been treated if the Union of the Crowns had not occurred.

Although the subjects of the Crown of Aragon played some part in the discovery and colonization of the New World, the Indies were formally annexed not to Spain but to the Crown of Castile. The exact circumstances in which this occurred are by no means clear, but it seems that Alexander VI in his bull of 1493 conceded the Indies personally to Ferdinand and Isabella for their lifetime, with the intention that America should become a Castilian possession after their death. Contemporary chroniclers report that it was Isabella's wish that only Castilians should be allowed to go to America, and her will affirmed that as the Canaries and America had been discovered 'at the cost of these my kingdoms and by natives of them, it is right that trade and commerce with them should belong to these my kingdoms of Castile and León'. While there were apparently no legal restrictions on the passage of natives of the Crown of Aragon to the Indies, it was made plain that

> A Castilla y a León
> Mundo nuevo dió Colón

and that the presence of Aragonese and Catalans was not welcome (although momentarily after Isabella's death, licences for Aragonese emigrants were more freely given than hitherto). Castile was determined not to let the fabulous riches of the New World slip through its hands, and the granting in 1503 of a monopoly of American trade to the port of Seville ensured that, even if the Aragonese and Catalans enjoyed a nominal right to take part in the colonization of America, the exploitation of American wealth would in practice remain the exclusive prerogative of Castile.

It may well be that conditions in the Crown of Aragon in the late fifteenth century were such as to stifle interest in the New World, and that Castile alone was ready to seize the great opportunity afforded by the discoveries. All the same, it was very unfortunate that the colonization and subsequent exploitation of the New World should not have been undertaken jointly by Castilians and Aragonese. A close association in the common task of colonization might have done much to bring the two peoples closer together, and to break down the barriers which continued to divide a theoretically united Spain.

One way of furthering Spanish unity was to allow the natives of the peninsula equal participation in the benefits of empire. This way was rejected. But there was also another way: the imposition of a uniform administrative and legal system in every part of Spain. It has often been believed that this was indeed the intention of Ferdinand

and Isabella in their government of the Crown of Aragon. The traditional contractual constitutions of Aragon, Catalonia, and Valencia, their powerful Cortes and their strongly entrenched liberties, naturally seemed irksome to a ruler accustomed to exercising a wide degree of personal power in Castile. In 1498, for instance, Isabella was so angered by the recalcitrance of the Aragonese Cortes that she declared that 'it would be better to reduce the Aragonese by arms than to tolerate the arrogance of their Cortes'.[1] This angry outburst, however, is not necessarily to be taken as an expression of royal policy; and in any event, Isabella's personal role in the government of the Crown of Aragon was small.

Catalan historians have traditionally tended to assume that Ferdinand, no less than his wife, was anxious to destroy the liberties of the Crown of Aragon, and to bring the legal and political structure of the Levantine states into conformity with that of Castile. It has been argued that a typically Castilian outlook informed the policies of Ferdinand towards the Crown of Aragon, and in particular that his reorganization of the Principality of Catalonia after the anarchy of the civil wars was skilfully devised to smooth the way for its reduction to conformity with Castile. It is, however, far from clear that Ferdinand had any such intention. Although he came from a Castilian line, he was by upbringing more Catalan than Castilian in his outlook. His early political experience had been acquired in Catalonia and Valencia; his library was full of chronicles and judicial works which expounded the Catalan-Aragonese theory of the contractual constitution; and it would be surprising if he had not imbibed in the intellectual climate of fifteenth-century Catalonia something of the political ideals of the Principality's governing class. However regal Ferdinand's concept of his own position, this was not necessarily incompatible with a genuine willingness to accept and perpetuate the Aragonese constitutionalism which he, like his predecessors, had sworn to preserve.

Even if Ferdinand had intended to destroy the traditional liberties of the Catalans, he was scarcely in a position to do so. On the death of his father in 1479 he was faced with the gigantic task of ending the long period of civil discord in Catalonia, and this could only be

1. Quoted in J. Vicens Vives, *Política del Rey Católico en Catalonia* (Barcelona, 1940), pp. 26–7.

achieved with the help of a moderate party among the Catalans, who were bound to insist, as the price of their support, on a guarantee by Ferdinand of their customary laws and liberties. This, apart from anything else, was likely to ensure that Ferdinand's reorganization of Catalonia would be carried out on essentially moderate and conservative lines.

The most novel part of Ferdinand's reorganization of Catalonia was his agrarian settlement. By the famous *Sentencia de Guadalupe* of 1486 he provided a typically moderate solution for the hitherto intransigent problem of the relations between peasants and their lords, which had disturbed the Catalan countryside for over a hundred years. The *remença* peasants, who had been tied to the land, were freed; the 'six evil customs' exacted by the lords were abolished in return for monetary compensation; and while the lord remained legally the ultimate owner of the land, the peasant remained in effective possession of it, and could leave it or dispose of it without obtaining the lord's consent. This *Sentencia* was to become the rural charter of Catalonia, and was to remain so for many centuries. It provided a firm foundation for the Principality's agrarian life, and led to the establishment of a class of peasants who were proprietors in all but name, and whose existence gave a new and much-needed element of social stability to a war-torn land.

Ferdinand's work of reconstruction was carried over also into the Principality's institutional life. After much trial and error, a lottery system for public office was introduced into both the *Generalitat* and the municipal government of Barcelona, in order to rescue these institutions from domination by a small self-perpetuating clique. These reforms in themselves help to suggest the way in which Ferdinand's mind was working. His plan was not to abolish old institutions and replace them with new ones, but simply to bring the old institutions back into proper working order. Either by conviction or by force of circumstance he had come to the conclusion that the only feasible solution to Catalonia's troubles was to get the Principality's medieval constitutional system properly functioning once again. Accordingly, in the Catalan *Corts* of 1480–81, he accepted the Principality's traditional political system in its entirety, and capped it with the famous constitution of *Observança*, whereby the constitutional limitations on royal power were specifically recognized, and a procedure was laid down for action by the *Generalitat* in the event of any infringement of the country's liberties by the King or his officials.

The fact that Ferdinand restored peace to Catalonia by reinvigorating its traditional institutions, rather than by creating new ones, was of enormous significance for the future. So far from using the occasion to bring the Principality into closer conformity with Castile, Ferdinand chose instead to perpetuate a constitutional system which contrasted sharply with Castile's increasingly authoritarian governmental structure. Where the foundations were being laid in Castile for absolute royal power, in Catalonia the old medieval contractual State was scrupulously restored. Whether this was really the form of government best suited to the needs of a new age was apparently not considered. The history of Catalonia in the sixteenth and seventeenth centuries was indeed to make it painfully clear that a revival of traditional forms of government did not automatically ensure a revival of the spirit that had originally infused them. But in the general air of lassitude that pervaded the Principality in the late fifteenth century this was not yet apparent. It was a source of profound satisfaction that peace had at last been restored to Catalonia. For the time being this was enough and the future could look to itself.

In reviving Catalonia's archaic constitutional system Ferdinand had implicitly rejected the possibilities of furthering the unity of Spain by the introduction of administrative and legal uniformity. No effort was made to bring Castile and the Crown of Aragon into closer harmony. Instead, the dualism of the two Crowns was intensified and perpetuated. Where the kings of sixteenth-century Spain would be able to behave in many respects like absolute monarchs in Castile, they would continue to be constitutional monarchs in the states of the Crown of Aragon. They would have to summon Cortes and attend them in person whenever they required a subsidy; they would be unable to alter laws or introduce administrative changes without the Cortes's consent; they would find it almost impossible to raise troops in the Crown of Aragon without coming into conflict with regional laws and privileges; and their officials would all the time be jealously watched by the guardians of the constitutions.

If, then, the introduction of administrative uniformity and the centralizing of power in the monarch's hands were essential features of the Renaissance State, the Spain of Ferdinand and Isabella would scarcely seem to qualify. Under the government of Ferdinand no institutional change occurred in the Crown of Aragon which would formally extend the constricted area in which the Crown was compelled to operate. Monarchy remained in the Crown of Aragon what it had always been: strictly limited monarchy. Similarly, there was not the slightest attempt at administrative fusion of the two Crowns, even at the very highest level, although inevitably certain administrative adjustments were made to meet the new conditions. Since Castilian problems absorbed so much of Ferdinand's attention, royal absenteeism from the Crown of Aragon was likely to become permanent. Indeed, of the thirty-seven years of his reign, Ferdinand spent under four in the Principality of Catalonia. In order to minimize the consequences of this absenteeism, the traditional institution of viceroyalties, by means of which the Catalans and Aragonese had governed their medieval empire, now became a permanent feature of the government of the Crown of Aragon itself. Henceforth, Catalonia, Aragon and Valencia were each ruled by viceroys. At the same time, the King contrived to keep in personal touch with the affairs of his Aragonese realms by refurbishing another institution of the medieval Crown of Aragon – the Curia Regis. This council of the medieval kings of Aragon was transformed in 1494 into the Council of Aragon, presided over by a *Vice-Canciller*. It consisted of a *Tesorero-General,* who need not be a native of the Crown by origin, and five Regents representing the different states of the Crown of Aragon. It took its place at once beside the *Consejo Real,* the equivalent council for the government of Castile, as a council attendant on the person of the king, and so from the beginning spent most of its time on Castilian soil. Both its character and its composition made it the natural link between the King and the Crown of Aragon, advising the King on the policies to be pursued, and transmitting his orders to the viceroys.

This solution to the problem of Aragonese government – a solution specifically designed to preserve intact the political and administrative identity of the Crown of Aragon – played a large part in determining the future structure of an expanding Spanish Monarchy. By nature it was capable of indefinite extension, for the joint establishment of a viceroyalty and of a special council attendant on the King would make it possible for the kings of Spain to acquire new dominions without depriving them of their separate identities. But while this administrative solution allowed the kings of Spain to acquire new dominions at a minimum cost to national traditions and susceptibilities, it naturally reduced the chances of the Spanish Monarchy evolving into a unitary state. Instead, it was more likely to evolve along the same lines as the medieval Aragonese empire – as a plurality of states loosely united beneath a common sovereign. In this crucial respect at least, Ferdinand's Aragon scored a significant victory over Isabella's Castile.

The new Spain was therefore a plural, not a unitary, state, and consisted of a series of separate patrimonies governed in accordance with their own distinctive laws. The Spain of the Catholic Kings continued to be Castile and Aragon, Catalonia and Valencia. Moreover, the existing legal and political structure of these various states remained largely unaltered. Like that of other contemporary west European states, their political organization consisted of an inter-locking structure composed of different tiers. At the top was royal power, the extent of which varied from one state to another according to the respective laws of each. At the bottom was seigneurial power – the rights of jurisdiction exercised by lords over their vassals, who comprised the mass of the rural population. In between these two lay a tier of autonomous rights which came within the preserve of the Prince but were exercised by privileged bodies, such as town councils, whose authority derived from charters and privileges conceded by the Crown. Nowhere did Ferdinand and Isabella introduce any fundamental change in this three-tiered structure. They were content to respect the existing ordering of the State, insisting on the full exercise of the royal authority, but always recognizing that there were limits beyond which it could not go. They would seem, indeed, to have subscribed fully to the opinion of the contemporary jurist Palacios Rubios, that 'to the King is confided solely the administration of the kingdom, and not dominion over things, for the property and rights of the State are public, and cannot be the private patrimony of anyone'.[2]

Yet the practice of Ferdinand and Isabella was to show that, even

2. Quoted by José Cepeda Adán, *En Torno al Concepto del Estado en los Reyes Católicos* (Madrid, 1956), p. 119.

within the legal limitations on royal rights, there remained considerable scope for manoeuvre. If, for instance, Ferdinand could not be given regal powers over Castile in perpetuity, he could still be allowed to exercise them by the personal concession of his wife during her own lifetime. Ferdinand was not the man to remain in a subordinate position, and Isabella, for her part, came to feel an affection and respect for her husband which made it natural for her to entrust him with far wider powers in Castile than had originally been envisaged. The device of the sovereigns, *tanto monta, monta tanto*, which was generally thought to express their absolute equality, is now known to have been a humanistic device made for Ferdinand and intended to represent that it was a matter of indifference – *tanto monta* – as to how he should deal with the Gordian knot; but the traditional interpretation admirably conveys the spirit of their relationship. They evolved between them a working partnership unique in the annals of monarchy. Both monarchs signed royal decrees; both could administer justice in Castile, jointly when together, separately when apart; and the effigies of both appeared on Castilian coins. In some respects, it was true, Ferdinand exercised more power than Isabella, for he was an active ruler in Castile, whereas she remained simply a queen consort in Aragon; and questions of foreign policy became his special preserve. But attempts to differentiate between their powers and to elevate one at the expense of the other tend to be an unprofitable exercise. They worked in double harness, each complementing the other; united in their determination to bring greatness to their kingdoms by a full deployment of their royal power.

Inevitably their exalted sense of their own office – of their obligation as rulers to restore order and impose justice – tended to cut through many of the legal limitations by which they were surrounded. The unity of their persons transcended the disunity of their dominions, and gave reality to a Spain that was something more than merely Castile and Aragon. Their sense of regality not only strengthened the upper tier of their own royal power, but also tightened the whole governmental structure, subtly transforming it in the process, so that, in Castile at least, they left behind them a state far more subordinate at every level to royal authority than the one they had found. Like their contemporary, Henry VII of England, they laid the foundations of a new state, not by introducing new institutions but by revivifying old ones, and by bending them to serve their own ends and to assert their own authority over the entire body politic. The 'new monarchy' in Spain, as elsewhere in Europe, was in the first instance the old monarchy restored – but restored with a sense of royal authority and national purpose capable of launching it on a radically different course.

2. THE ASSERTION OF ROYAL AUTHORITY IN CASTILE

In spite of the importance of restoring peace to Catalonia, it was inevitable that the Catholic Kings should concentrate the weight of their attention on their greatest and most populous realm – Castile. Once the War of Succession had been won with the defeat of the invading Portuguese army at the battle of Toro in March 1476, the most pressing problem was clearly to curb the power of the Castilian aristocracy and bring to an end the dreary round of anarchy. This, as Ferdinand and Isabella were fully aware, was the overwhelming desire of the mass of the nation. Diego de Valera, a contemporary chronicler, asserted that Ferdinand and Isabella had come to 'restore these kingdoms and rescue them from the tyrannical government to which they have for so long been subjected'.[3] They could count on the support of all those elements which were weary of the continuing disorder and resented the long-standing abuse of power by the aristocracy. The Cortes of Castile provided a natural forum for obtaining this support, and it was in the Cortes held at Madrigal in April 1476 that the foundations were laid for that alliance between the Crown and the municipalities which gave such a powerful impulse to the reassertion of royal authority.

The most effective measure taken at the Cortes of Madrigal for the restoration of order in Castile was the creation of the *Santa Hermandad*, a perfect example of a medieval institution revived to meet new needs. The towns of medieval Castile had possessed popular bands, known as *hermandades*, or brotherhoods, to watch over their interests and help preserve the peace. At the Cortes of Madrigal, these were reorganized and placed under a unified central

3. Quoted in José Antonio Maravall, 'The Origins of the Modern State', *Cuadernos de Historia Mundial* VI (1961), p. 798.

control in the form of a council or Junta of the *Hermandad*, presided over by the Bishop of Cartagena, acting as the direct representative of the Crown. Where the medieval *hermandades* had tended to fall under the influence of local magnates, and frequently added to the very disorders they were supposed to hold in check, the reorganized *hermandades* were dependent on the Crown for their instructions. They were specifically municipal institutions placed at the disposal of the Crown, and magnates were carefully excluded from all judicial posts.

The *Hermandad* combined in itself the functions of a police force and of a judicial tribunal. As a police force, its task was to suppress brigandage and to patrol the roads and countryside. Every town and village was expected to provide its quota of troops, at the rate of one horseman to every hundred householders. There was a standing body of two thousand soldiers under the command of Ferdinand's brother, Alonso de Aragón, and each town had its company of archers who would turn out as soon as the hue and cry was raised, and pursue the malefactors to the limits of the town's jurisdiction, where the pursuit was taken up by a fresh company from the next town or village. The cost of maintaining a police force on this scale was very heavy, and it was met by fines and by a system of taxation which the Crown attempted, although without success, to extend even to the aristocracy.

If the malefactor was caught by the *Hermandad* he was also likely to be tried by it, for the tribunals of the *Hermandad* enjoyed complete jurisdiction over certain carefully specified classes of crimes – robbery, murder and arson committed in the open countryside, or in towns and villages when the criminal took to the country; together with rape, housebreaking, and acts of rebellion against the central government. These tribunals consisted of locally chosen and unpaid *alcaldes* of the *Hermandad*, of whom there was one in every village of under thirty families, and two (one a *caballero* and one of inferior rank) in all the larger centres of population. Either acting alone, or assisted by *alcaldes* from the principal judicial seat in the district, the *alcaldes* reviewed the case, pronounced judgement, and meted out the most savage penalties, which generally consisted of mutilation or a most barbarous death.

The savage punishments had the desired effect. By degrees, order was restored throughout Castile, and the country was cleared of bandits. After two or three years the very success of the *Hermandad*, combined with the cost of maintaining it, prompted the towns to ask for its dissolution; but the continuing existence of the *Hermandad* offered the Crown obvious military advantages at the time of the Granada campaign, and Ferdinand and Isabella refused to disband a body which could provide them with companies of archers to fight against the Moors. It was only in 1498 that they finally agreed to suppress the Council of the *Hermandad* and to abolish its salaried officers. While the local *hermandades* continued to survive after 1498, they inevitably lost much of their original character and effectiveness once the Supreme Council was gone. The severity of the punishments was modified; appeals were allowed to the ordinary courts; and the *Hermandad* became a modest rural police force, without either power or prestige.

The organization of the *Hermandad* was therefore essentially a temporary expedient devised to deal with an acute national emergency. The year of its creation, 1476, saw another move by the Crown to reassert its authority over the magnates – and one which this time involved a permanent change in the social and political organization of Castile. This move was directed towards securing for the Crown the mastership of the powerful Order of Santiago. The Order of Santiago was the greatest of the three military-religious Orders – Santiago, Calatrava, and Alcántara – of medieval Castile. Between them, the Orders possessed vast estates and revenues, and are thought to have exercised jurisdiction over at least a million vassals. As long as their wealth and resources remained the preserve of a handful of magnates, they inevitably constituted a State within the State. This made it essential for the Crown to secure control over them, and an opportunity arose with the death of the Grand Master of Santiago in 1476. As soon as the news reached her at Valladolid, Isabella, with characteristic intrepidity, took horse and set off for the convent of Uclés, where the dignitaries of the Order were preparing to elect a successor. Three days of hard riding brought her to the convent just in time to insist that the proceedings should be suspended and the office be conferred upon her husband. In the event, Ferdinand graciously waived his claim for the time being, but the correct precedent had been satisfactorily established. When the Grand Masterships of Calatrava and Alcántara fell vacant in 1487 and 1494 respectively, they duly went to Ferdinand; and a papal bull of 1523 definitively incorporated all three Orders into the Crown.

There is still no study of the resources of the Military Orders and of their role in the history of sixteenth- and seventeenth-century Spain, but it would be hard to overestimate the importance of their contribution to the reassertion of royal power. Their financial value to the Crown is obvious enough. The contemporary humanist, Marineo Sículo, placed the annual rental of the lands of the Order of Santiago at 60,000 ducats, of Alcántara at 45,000 and of Calatrava at 40,000,[4] and these figures rose sharply as the century advanced. Their acquisition did something to compensate for the loss of Crown lands alienated by the kings of medieval Castile, and they were to provide a useful security for royal loans from bankers. But they constituted also an invaluable source of patronage, for the Orders possessed a number of *encomiendas* (commanderies), some of them enjoying considerable incomes:[5]

Santiago	94 *encomiendas*
Calatrava	51
Alcántara	38
	‒‒‒
	183

In addition to the 183 *comendadores* there were also the so-called *caballeros de la Orden*, who possessed no *encomienda*, but were entitled to wear the *hábitos* – the ceremonial robes – belonging to one of the three Orders. This meant that, between *comendadores* and *caballeros*, nearly 1,500 dignities were now placed at the disposal of the Crown. With these it could silence the importunate and reward the deserving, and so strengthen its control over the upper ranks of Castilian society.

The steps taken by the Crown in 1476 to establish royal control over the Order of Santiago were followed by further measures designed to reduce the political power of the magnates. In particular there was the famous Act of Resumption of the Cortes of Toledo of 1480, by which the nobles were deprived of half the revenues they

4. Lucio Marineo Sículo, *Obra de las Cosas Memorables de España* (Alcalá de Henares, 1533), fs. 23v–24.

5. British Museum, Harleian MS. 3569 *Curia Española* (1615), fs. 185–204v. List of *encomiendas*.

had alienated or usurped since 1464. These Cortes, however, also saw the launching of important administrative reforms – reforms which give the Cortes of Toledo a place in Castilian history comparable to that enjoyed by the Barcelona Cortes of 1480 in the history of Catalonia.

Of all the reforms begun in the Cortes of Toledo of 1480, the most important was the refashioning of the old royal council of the kings of Castile. The *Consejo Real* – or Council of Castile, as it was often called in later years – was intended by Ferdinand and Isabella to be the central governing body of Castile, and the linch-pin of their governmental system. It advised them on appointments and the conferring of favours; it acted as the supreme court of justice in Castile; and it supervised the working of Castilian local government. It was essential that a Council with such wide powers should be composed of officials on whom the sovereigns could place total reliance, and that it should not be allowed to fall, like the old royal Council, into the hands of the magnates. To prevent this, it was arranged that the Council should consist of a prelate, three *caballeros* and eight or nine jurists (*letrados*); and although the traditional dignitaries of the realm might attend meetings if they wished, they were allowed no vote, and so enjoyed no influence. This exclusion of the great magnates from voting on matters of state meant that the traditional offices of some of the proudest families of Castile were transformed into empty dignities. The Velascos continued to be Constables of Castile, the Enríquez Admirals of Castile, but their high-sounding titles ceased to give them a prescriptive right to the exercise of political power. Instead, military commands and diplomatic and administrative offices were conferred upon 'new men': members of the lesser nobility and gentry, townsmen, and *conversos* (converted Jews).

It was symptomatic of the needs of the new age that legal training was increasingly required for governmental office. Paper work was increasing, a routine was being established, and the *letrados*, who had studied law at one of the Castilian universities, proved to be the kind of men best equipped to master bureaucratic procedures. For Castile, unlike Aragon, these procedures were relatively new. Administration in the Crown of Aragon had been vested since the fourteenth century in a highly bureaucratized chancery, which was effectively presided over by the vice-chancellor, and consisted of a *protonotario* (entrusted with the general charge of the office), three secretaries, and a series of scribes and clerks. Although the subject remains to be studied, it would be surprising if Aragonese experience were not called upon in the reconstruction of administration in Castile. But the Castilian bureaucracy, even when reformed, was much more loosely organized than the Aragonese bureaucracy and differed from it in its close dependence on the royal Council. Three members of the Council of Castile were required to sign all official documents, and the Council as a whole intervened in the most detailed decisions of day-to-day government. But alongside the members of the Council were certain other figures who were to play an increasingly important part in the administration. These were the royal secretaries, who were supposed to act as the link between the Council of Castile and the sovereign; but since they were in daily contact with him, and also prepared the agenda for the Council, they naturally acquired great influence in the making of political and administrative decisions, and on occasion entirely by-passed the Council of Castile. A man like Hernando de Zafra, secretary to the Queen and the head of the Castilian secretariat, thus became a political figure in his own right.

It was essential to choose capable officials if the momentum of the first years of the reign were to be maintained and the reforms of the 1470s and 1480s take root. Both Ferdinand and Isabella were acutely conscious of this, and took the greatest trouble over appointments, carrying with them on their travels a book in which they noted down hopeful names. Both were monarchs who knew how to be served, and they seem to have possessed an instinctive capacity for picking the right men to serve them. 'They took care,' wrote a contemporary, 'to appoint discreet and capable officials, even though they were only of middling rank, rather than important figures from the principal houses.'[6]

But if the Catholic Kings showed a preference for those of more humble rank when appointing to offices, this by no means implied any intention to exalt one social class, as a class, at the expense of another. The aristocracy may have been stripped of much of their political power, but this had been done for the benefit of the Crown

6. Galíndez Carvajal, quoted in Maravall, 'Origins of the Modern State', *op. cit.*, p. 807.

and the community at large, and not for gentry or burgesses or any other individual section of society. This soon became apparent in the Crown's treatment of the Cortes and of the municipalities. The Cortes of Castile had been of the greatest use in the early years of the reign, when it was necessary to associate the community of the realm with the Crown in its struggle against the magnates. But Ferdinand and Isabella were well aware of the danger of allowing the Cortes to acquire too great an influence. This danger was likely to last as long as the Crown remained excessively dependent on the financial grants of the Cortes, and this provided a further reason for making every effort to increase the royal revenues.

The Crown's revenues did, in fact, rise remarkably during the reign of Ferdinand and Isabella: the total revenue from taxation, which is said to have stood at under 900,000 *reales* in 1474, had risen to 26,000,000 *reales* by 1504. The increase was achieved not by the imposition of new taxes, but by the more efficient handling of old ones at a time when national wealth was growing. The traditional financial departments of the government of Castile were the *contadurías mayores*, one for account-keeping (*de cuentas*) and the other for the collection and administration of taxes (*de hacienda*). These were overhauled after the Cortes of Madrigal of 1476 and their large staff of officials was reduced. Tax-collecting became more effective once the collectors could count on support from the central and local agents of the Crown; the alienated revenues recovered by the Act of Resumption of 1480 helped to swell the royal income; and the value of the Crown's most important single source of income, the *alcabala* or sales tax, which had first become a general royal tax in 1342, rose dramatically after reforms in the early 1490s.

These sources of income were entirely independent of Cortes control, and their rising yield enabled the Crown to dispense entirely with the Cortes for a long period during the middle of the reign. Between the death of Henry IV in 1474 and that of Ferdinand in 1516 the Cortes of Castile were summoned sixteen times, and of these sessions four occurred before 1483 and the other twelve after 1497. The new recourse to the Cortes from the late 1490s is to be explained primarily by the heavy new financial demands made by the war of Granada and the Italian campaigns. The Crown's rising revenues had proved to be adequate in peacetime, but the war of Granada forced the Catholic Kings to raise loans and to sell *juros* or annuities, and financial necessity compelled them to resort to the Cortes in 1501 for a *servicio*.

Although it proved impossible to dispense entirely with the Cortes of Castile, Ferdinand and Isabella had no great difficulty in bending them to their will. Their task was eased by the constitutional deficiencies of the Cortes themselves. There was no obligation on the sovereigns to summon nobles and clergy, and after 1480 attendances by members of either of these estates were rare. This meant that the full brunt was borne by the *procuradores* of the towns. Since 1429 the towns had been limited to two *procuradores* each, and it became established under Ferdinand and Isabella that eighteen cities should be represented, so that the Crown was confronted by a body of only thirty-six burgesses. It was unlikely that these thirty-six could successfully conduct a prolonged resistance to royal demands, especially at a time when the monarchy, having moved with striking effect against the aristocracy, had begun to tighten its grasp over the towns.

Closer supervision of the municipalities was an essential prerequisite both for control of the Cortes and for a more effective assertion of royal supremacy over Castile as a whole; for the walled cities and towns which dotted the Castilian landscape had many of the characteristics of city states and enjoyed a high degree of independence of the Crown. Established one after another during the southward march of the *Reconquista*, they had been given their own *fueros* or charters of liberties by generous kings, and had been liberally endowed with vast areas of communal land, which extended their jurisdiction far into the surrounding countryside and served to meet the bulk of their expenses. Their charters gave them the right to form a general assembly or *concejo*, which was ordinarily composed of the heads of families (*vecinos*), and which chose each year the various municipal officials. The judicial officials, enjoying civil and criminal jurisdiction, were known as *alcaldes*, while the principal administrative officials were the *regidores*, who numbered anything from eight to thirty-six, and formed the effective municipal government. Beneath the *regidores* were many officials concerned with the day-to-day administration in the town – the *alguacil*, or principal police officer, the *escribano*, who kept the municipal registers, and the minor functionaries known as *fieles*, entrusted with such duties as inspecting weights and measures and superintending the municipal lands.

During the fourteenth century the vigorous democratic tradition which had characterized Castilian municipal life during the preceding two hundred years began to disappear. As the task of municipal government became more complex, and the monarchy became increasingly jealous of the powers of the municipalities, the *concejo* was undermined from within, while simultaneously coming under attack from without. During the reign of Alfonso XI (1312–50), the *concejo* everywhere lost much of its power to the *regidores*, who were appointed by the Crown instead of being elected by the house-holders. At Burgos, for instance, which provided the model for many of the towns of Castile, there were six *alcaldes* with judicial duties, and sixteen *regidores*, who administered the city as a closed oligarchy. Alongside these magistrates there also appeared in some towns during the fourteenth century a new official known as the *corregidor*, who was chosen by the King and came from outside the municipality to assist the *regidores* in its government.

The collapse of the Crown in fifteenth-century Castile inevitably checked these endeavours to bring the municipalities under effective royal control. In order to help fill its empty treasury, the monarchy under John II began to create and sell municipal offices, in direct contravention of the town charters, which carefully stipulated how many officials there should be. The growth of venality, and the decline of royal control, left the field open for local magnates and competing factions to extend their influence over the organs of municipal government, so that towns were either bitterly divided by civil feuds, or fell into the hands of small, self-perpetuating oligarchies.

In these circumstances, it was natural that Isabella should resume the policies of her fourteenth-century predecessors. Since the towns of Castile were by now more concerned with the restoration of order than with the preservation of liberty, the moment was particularly favourable. The Cortes of Toledo of 1480 accepted various measures designed to strengthen royal control over municipal administration as well as to raise the standard of urban government. All cities which did not already possess a *casa de ayuntamiento*, or town hall, were to build one within two years; written records were to be kept of all special laws and privileges; hereditary grants of offices were revoked. Most important of all, *corregidores* were in this year appointed to all the principal towns of Castile.

The generalization of the office of *corregidor* was incomparably the most effective measure taken by Ferdinand and Isabella to extend the Crown's power over the Castilian municipalities. Like the English Justice of the Peace, whom he resembled in many of his functions, he formed the essential link between the central government and the localities, but he differed from the J.P. in being a specifically royal official, unconnected with the locality to which he was appointed. His duties were both administrative and judicial. The famous decree of 1500 in which these duties were codified, shows that he was expected to watch over all the affairs of the commune, to organize its provisioning, to be responsible for the maintenance of public order, and to prevent any attempts by nobles and clergy to usurp jurisdiction.[7] In theory, a *corregidor* remained in his post for only two years, although in practice his period of office was much longer; and at the end of his term of office he was subjected to a *residencia*, or inquiry into the way in which he had conducted his duties.

By the reign of Philip II there were sixty-six *corregimientos* in Castile. These *corregimientos* supplemented rather than replaced municipal administration, although at the same time bringing much of the municipal business into the sphere of royal control. The council of *regidores*, consisting of *hidalgos* and of substantial citizens who acquired their office by royal appointment (or, as time went on, by inheritance or purchase) remained extremely influential, even though its meetings were now presided over by the *corregidor*. Municipal government therefore consisted of a delicate balance of perpetual *regidores* and a temporary *corregidor*, while a vestige of the old municipal democracy lingered in the continuing right of the *vecinos* to elect to certain of the town's other administrative offices.

While the *corregidores* had heavy administrative duties, they also became the most important judicial officers in the localities, usurping in the process many of the outstanding judicial functions previously

7. His salary was paid by the local community, and seems to have averaged between 400 and 600 ducats a year in the later sixteenth century.

exercised by municipal *alcaldes*. Well before the accession of Ferdinand and Isabella, towns had been losing to the Crown their right to choose their own *alcaldes* and *alguaciles*, and the process of royal nomination was carried still further with the coming of the new régime. The loss of this right elicited constant protests from towns and villages, and in some places a compromise was reached, whereby the commune continued to choose its own *alcaldes*, now known as *alcaldes ordinarios*, who worked alongside the *corregidor* and the *alcaldes* chosen by the King. But, outside a few privileged towns, the *alcaldes* lost much of their power to the *corregidor*, and were left with only minor civil and criminal jurisdiction, although there was a saving grace in the provision that *corregidores* could not arrogate to themselves suits that had been begun before *alcaldes*.

Towns and villages under noble or ecclesiastical jurisdiction – the so-called *villas de señorío* – nominally remained outside this system of royal justice and administration. The Crown was in no position in the late fifteenth century to launch a direct assault on private jurisdictions, and had to content itself with measures which might in process of time come to undermine seigneurial power. In particular, it pursued exactly the opposite policy to that which it had adopted towards towns holding their charters and privileges of the Crown, and insisted, as a counterweight to the power of the lord, on the right of citizens to elect their own officials. In *villas de señorío*, therefore, the *concejo*, presided over by the *alcalde*, continued to elect the *alcalde* and *regidores*, and the lord was simply expected to confirm the town's nominees. Justice was exercised in the first instance by the *alcalde*, and appeals from his decisions came before the judge or *corregidor* appointed by the lord, and then, if necessary, were carried to the lord's own council, which operated as a kind of miniature private version of the Council of Castile. While Ferdinand and Isabella made no attempt to interfere with the machinery of this private judicial system which ran parallel to the judicial system of the Crown, they did, however, insist that lords should maintain high standards of justice and were always prepared to intervene when miscarriage of justice was alleged. Over the years, the insistence of the Crown on its own judicial primacy, together with the greater competence of royal justice in many fields of litigation, sapped the foundations of the Castilian aristocracy's independent judicial power.

As a result, the influence of the *corregidor* extended by the end of the sixteenth century to every corner of Castile.

As a member of the gentry class (*de capa y espada*), the *corregidor* often lacked sufficient legal training to fulfil his judicial duties adequately, and he was therefore generally given the assistance of two trained lawyers known as *alcaldes mayores*, of whom one was a specialist in civil and the other in criminal suits. But the jurisdiction remained nominally that of the *corregidor* himself. He, or his deputies acting in his name, could pronounce sentence in civil suits involving sums of up to 10,000 *maravedís*, although appeal was allowed to a tribunal which consisted of himself and two members of the town council. In criminal cases he also enjoyed sole right of ordinary jurisdiction, but the accused possessed under Castilian law one right which he was rarely reluctant to employ. This was the right to reject (*recusar*) his judge, on a pretext either genuine or contrived. If he chose to exercise this privilege, his case had to be retried before his original judge, who was now joined by two assessors chosen by the town council from among their colleagues; and the sentence only became definitive if at least one of them agreed with the *corregidor* or his deputy. If the assessors proved obdurate, the case had to go up before one of the *chancillerías* – the highest legal tribunals in Castile. In addition, it was always possible for the accused to bring an appeal before the *chancillería* when he lost his case in the *corregidor*'s court. These two rights of *recusación* and appeal, which could be used to spin out interminably the ordinary processes of the law, therefore did something to mitigate the rigours of a system in which almost everything depended in the first instance on the decision of a single judge.

At the beginning of Isabella's reign there was no more than one *chancillería* in Castile – that of Valladolid. This was reorganized several times during the Queen's reign and that of Charles V, and came to consist of sixteen *oidores* or judges, sitting in four chambers and responsible for civil suits, and three *alcaldes de crimen*, who handled criminal cases. A subsidiary *audiencia* was established in Galicia, and in 1494 a second *chancillería* was set up at Ciudad Real. This *chancillería* was transferred to Granada in 1505, its sphere of jurisdiction being divided from that of Valladolid by the boundary line of the River Tagus. As a last recourse, appeal could be made from sentences pronounced in the *chancillería* to the Council of Castile itself, which thus acted as the highest court as well as the highest administrative organ in the country. The combined judicial and administrative functions of the Council of Castile therefore paralleled at the highest level the combined functions of the *corregidores* at the lowest.

Their reorganization of the Castilian judicial system was typical of the work of the Catholic Kings. The Crown was for them the fountainhead of justice; they constantly insisted on their so-called *preeminencia real* – the royal pre-eminence which gave them the right to intervene even in matters of seigneurial jurisdiction, in order to secure primacy for the royal power; and their interest in the impartial administration of justice made them set aside every Friday for public audiences in which they personally dispensed justice to all comers. They were the last rulers of Castile to act as personal judges in this way, for their own reforming activity was itself making such measures unnecessary. Justice was acquiring its own machinery, and in 1480 a jurist called Díaz de Montalvo was commissioned to compile the royal ordinances of Castile – the first step towards the codification of Castilian laws which was finally achieved in the reign of Philip II.

The reassertion of royal authority in the spheres of administration and justice necessarily involved some loss of liberty for the subjects of the Crown. But, after long years of civil strife, this was a price that the majority of them were willing enough to pay. According to the great chronicler Hernando del Pulgar, their wish was to 'escape from lordship into the royal liberty [*libertad real*]', and they saw no incompatibility between freedom and a greater degree of subservience to royal power. The prime reason for this is to be found in what was perhaps the greatest of all the achievements of the Catholic Kings – their uncanny skill in identifying the interests of the community of the realm with those of the Crown. Their personal attributes, their capacity to realize in institutional form the aspirations that were often but inarticulately voiced by their subjects, enabled them to shape and mould the consciousness of the community to their own design. They were, in the most real sense, national monarchs, capable of giving even their most humble subjects the feeling that they were all participating in the great task of national regeneration. This by no means implied, however, that Castile was a mere puppet to be manipulated in accordance with the royal will. If Ferdinand and Isabella were all the time giving shape and form to national aspirations, they themselves were in turn being consistently influenced by the hopes, desires, and prejudices of their subjects. The relationship between Crown and people was thus in the fullest sense a two-way relationship; and this was nowhere more apparent than in matters concerning the Faith.

3. THE CHURCH AND THE FAITH

By curbing the aristocracy, by planting their own officers in the towns, and by overhauling the judicial system, Ferdinand and Isabella had gone a long way towards ensuring the primacy of the Crown in Castile. But control of secular institutions was not enough. They could never be absolute masters in their own land until they had brought under royal control the immensely powerful Spanish Church. The power of the Church in Spain was reinforced by its vast wealth and by the extent of its privileges. There were seven archbishoprics and forty bishoprics. The joint annual income of Castile's bishoprics and its four archbishoprics (Toledo, Granada, Santiago, and Seville) in the reign of Charles V was nearly 400,000 ducats, while the Archbishop of Toledo, Primate of Spain, who ranked second only to the King in power and wealth, enjoyed a personal income of 80,000 ducats a year. The Church as a whole had an annual income of over 6 million ducats, of which 2 million belonged to the regular clergy, and 4 million to the secular. These were enormous figures, especially in view of the fact that tithes (which were traditionally paid in kind) had been widely impropriated by laymen in return for fixed payments in a depreciated currency.

The privileges of the clergy were formidable. The regular and secular clergy shared with *hidalgos* the privilege of exemption from the taxes levied by the Crown, and they were more successful than the *hidalgos* in evading the payment of municipal dues. They accumulated large quantities of property in mortmain, and made strenuous attempts to extend their privileges to their servants and dependents. Moreover, bishops, abbots, and cathedral chapters owned large demesnes, over which they exercised full temporal jurisdiction.

The bishops of fifteenth-century Castile were not slow to exploit these advantages. Members of aristocratic families, and sometimes themselves the sons of bishops, they were a warrior race who found themselves perfectly at home in the struggles that surged round the throne. They had their own fortresses and private armies, and they were not unduly reluctant to lead their own troops into battle. The formidable primate of Spain, Don Alfonso Carrillo (1410–82), who helped Ferdinand forge the papal dispensation which made possible his marriage, changed sides and took the field with the Portuguese against Isabella at the battle of Toro in 1476; while the great Pedro González de Mendoza, Archbishop of Seville, faced him in the opposing camp.

The activities of these bellicose prelates perhaps not unnaturally suggested to Ferdinand and Isabella the desirability of a counter-offensive by the Crown as soon as the War of Succession was brought to an end. The Church was far too powerful to give them any hope of being able to strip the bishops of their temporal powers, but they compelled Carrillo and his colleagues to place their fortresses in the hands of royal officials, and insisted (although never with complete success) that the Crown's right to superior jurisdiction throughout the realm extended even to the lands of the Church. But the key to any lasting success was clearly to be found in the vexed question of appointments to bishoprics, and it was to this in particular that they addressed their attention.

The position over the filling of ecclesiastical benefices in fifteenth-century Castile was delicate and involved. While the right of patrons to present to the lesser benefices was by now well established, presentation to the more important benefices was a source of constant dispute. Cathedral chapters, which traditionally enjoyed the right to elect bishops of their choice, had for long been fighting a losing battle to preserve this right in the face of challenges by the Papacy on the one hand and the Crown on the other. During the years of anarchy of the mid-fifteenth century the Papacy had made frequent attempts to appoint its own candidates to bishoprics – a practice that Isabella was determined to resist, as she made clear when the Archbishopric of Zaragoza fell vacant in 1475. She based her resistance to the papal policy of provisions on 'ancient custom', whereby the Crown in Castile allegedly possessed the right of 'supplicating' in favour of its own candidate, whom the Pope would then duly appoint. If Ferdinand and Isabella were to challenge the Papacy successfully over the question of papal provisions, they needed the full support of the Castilian Church, and this led them in 1478 to summon an ecclesiastical council at Seville, which proved as important for the definition of the Crown's ecclesiastical policy as the Cortes of Toledo of 1480 were important for the definition of its administrative intentions. The programme laid before the council for discussion made it clear that the Crown was determined to secure control over all benefices in Castile, and that it expected clerical ratification for its defiance of Rome. The council duly agreed to intercede with the Pope, but the delegation which it sent to Rome met with no success. A vacancy in the see of Cuenca in 1479, however, gave Ferdinand and Isabella a chance to insist on their alleged royal prerogatives; but while Sixtus IV eventually capitulated in the bitter dispute which followed, he made no concessions which would prejudice future papal action on the fundamental issue of provisions.

The very limitations of the agreement negotiated between Crown and Papacy in 1482, over the Cuenca dispute, suggested the need for an alternative line of approach. The opportunity came with the near-completion of the *Reconquista*. The Spanish Crown surely deserved some signal reward for its untiring efforts to expel the Infidel, and what more fitting reward could be imagined than a royal *Patronato* – patronage – over all the churches to be established in the reconquered kingdom of Granada? This was now the prime object of the Crown's ecclesiastical policy – an object which was triumphantly achieved in 1486. By a papal bull of 13 December 1486, Innocent VIII, who needed Ferdinand's help in furthering the Papacy's Italian interests, gave the Spanish Crown the right of patronage and presentation to all the major ecclesiastical benefices in the newly conquered kingdom.

The securing by the Crown of the Granada *Patronato* was a momentous achievement, because it provided not only an ideal solution which Ferdinand and Isabella hoped to extend by degrees to all their dominions, but also a practical model for the Church in the New World. In the twenty years after the discovery of America, Ferdinand manoeuvred with extraordinary skill to obtain from the Papacy absolute royal control over all ecclesiastical foundations in the overseas territories. Exploiting to the full the alleged or real similarities between the recovering of South Spain for Christendom and the conquest of the Indies, he first proceeded to obtain from Alexander VI, in the bull *Inter caetera* of 1493, exclusive rights for the Spanish Crown in the evangelization of the newly discovered lands. This was followed in 1501 by a further bull conceding the Crown in perpetuity all tithes levied in the Indies. The climax came in the famous bull of 28 July 1508 by which Julius II (who, like his predecessors, urgently needed Ferdinand's help in Italy) gave the Spanish Crown the coveted universal *Patronato* over the Church in the New World, which included the right of royal presentation to all ecclesiastical benefices. The *Patronato*, rounded out by further concessions in the following years, conferred on the Spanish monarchy a unique power over the Church in its American possessions. Outside the kingdom of Granada, nothing comparable existed in Europe. It was true that, following on the concordat between France and the Papacy in 1516, Charles V obtained from Adrian VI in 1523 the right to present to all bishoprics in Spain, so that the major object of Ferdinand and Isabella's ecclesiastical policy was at last achieved in the peninsula itself; but disputes over non-consistorial major benefices and over simple benefices continued until the concordat of 1753. In the New World, on the other hand, the Crown was absolute master, and exercised a virtually papal authority of its own. No cleric could go to the Indies without royal permission; there was no papal legate in the New World, and no direct contact between Rome and the clergy in Mexico or Peru; the Crown exercised a right of veto over the promulgation of papal bulls, and constantly intervened, through its viceroys and officials, in all the minutiae of ecclesiastical life.

Even if Ferdinand and Isabella never secured in Spain as absolute a control over the Church as was eventually secured in America, they still obtained in practice, if not in theory, a large part of what they wanted. By the exercise of diplomatic pressure they ensured that Spanish benefices were no longer given to foreigners and that the Papacy agreed to appoint the Crown's own nominees to bishoprics. They were successful, too, in preventing the sending of appeals in civil suits from the Valladolid *chancillería* to Rome. Above all, they obtained for the Crown in perpetuity a sufficient degree of control over the wealth of the Church to deprive their successors of any financial inducement to follow the example of a Gustavus Vasa or a Henry VIII and break violently with Rome. Contributions by or through the Church came, in fact, to constitute an extremely important part of the Crown's income during the sixteenth century. Of these contributions, two became regular sources of revenue under the Catholic Kings. The first consisted of the *tercias reales* – a third of all the tithes paid to the Church in Castile. For centuries these had been paid to the Crown, but merely on a provisional basis, and it was only by a bull issued by Alexander VI in 1494 that the *tercias reales* were vested in the Crown in perpetuity. The other, and much more valuable, contribution was the *cruzada*. Bulls of the *cruzada* had originated in the need to finance the *Reconquista*: indulgences were sold at a fixed rate to every man, woman and child willing to buy one. In spite of the fact that the *Reconquista* was completed during the reign of the Catholic Kings, Ferdinand contrived to secure the perpetuation of the bulls of the *cruzada* as a source of royal income, and one which, in the nature of things, came to be diverted to purposes far removed from those originally intended.

The interest displayed by the Catholic Kings in the Church was not, however, confined to its financial resources, attractive as these were. Isabella's faith was fervent, mystical, and intense, and she viewed the present state of the Church with grave concern. It suffered in Spain from the abuses commonly ascribed to it throughout fifteenth-century Europe: pluralism, absenteeism, and low standards of morality and learning in secular and regular clergy alike. Concubinage in particular was accepted as a matter of course, and was no doubt further encouraged by a practice apparently unique to Castile, whereby the child of a cleric could inherit if his father died intestate. In some sections of the Church, however, and especially in the Religious Orders, there was a deep current of discontent at the prevailing laxity; in particular, the Queen's Jeronymite confessor, Hernando de Talavera, constantly urged upon her the need for total reform. Under Talavera's guidance, the Queen devoted herself wholeheartedly to the work of raising the moral and intellectual standards of her clergy. As effective nomination to bishoprics came to be increasingly exercised by the Crown, the morals and learning of candidates ceased to be regarded as largely irrelevant details, and high social rank was no longer an essential passport to a diocese. As a result, the standard of the Spanish episcopate rose markedly under the Catholic Kings, although some of Ferdinand's own appointments still left a good deal to be desired. Cardinal González de Mendoza, who succeeded Carrillo at Toledo in 1482, hardly conformed to the model of the new-style prelate; but the remarkable munificence of his patronage no doubt did something to atone for the notorious failings of his private life. In 1484 he founded at Valladolid the College of Santa Cruz, which set the pattern for further foundations designed to raise educational standards and produce a more cultivated clergy; and he probably did more than any other man to foster the spread of the New Learning in Castile.

While the Queen and her advisers worked hard to raise the standards of the episcopate and the secular clergy, a movement was gaining ground for reform of the Religious Orders. The Franciscan Order had long been divided between *Conventuales* and Observants, who wanted a return to the strict simplicity of the Rule of St. Francis. Among the Observants was the austere figure of Francisco Jiménez de Cisneros, whom the Queen regarded as a providential substitute for her confessor Talavera, when the latter became first Archbishop of Granada in 1492. Already in 1491 Alexander VI had authorized the Catholic Kings to take in hand the reform of the monastic orders, and two years later Cisneros launched himself with characteristic energy into the work of reform, and continued to direct it with unflagging vigour after his appointment to Cardinal Mendoza's see of Toledo on the cardinal's death in 1495. Starting with his own Order, the Franciscans, he set about imposing a strict observance of the Rule in face of the most intense opposition. The Franciscans of Toledo, expelled from their convent, came out in procession beneath a raised cross, intoning the Psalm *In exitu Israel Aegypto*, while four hundred Andalusian friars preferred conversion to Islam and the delights of domesticity in North Africa to a Christianity which now suddenly demanded that they adandon their female companions. Slowly, however, the reform advanced. It spread to the Dominicans, the Benedictines, and the Jeronymites, and by the time of Cisneros's death in 1517 not a single Franciscan 'conventual' house remained in Spain.

While differing profoundly from his predecessor in the conduct of his personal life, Cisneros was a worthy successor to Mendoza in his patronage of learning. His determination to raise cultural standards in Castile gave rise to two great achievements, neither of which Isabella herself was destined to see: the founding in 1508 of the university of Alcalá for the promotion of theological studies, and the publication of the great Complutensian Polyglot Bible, in which the Greek, Hebrew, and Latin texts were printed in parallel columns. These achievements emphasized one of the most important characteristics of the Isabelline reform movement: its willingness to adapt itself to contemporary requirements. Cisneros, if not himself strictly a humanist, at least grasped the urgent need to harness the new humanistic studies to the service of religion. Under his leadership, the reformers, instead of rejecting the New Learning, used it to further the work of reform.

Admittedly the reform movement under Ferdinand and Isabella was no more than a beginning, and there seems to have been a decline in the standards of the episcopate during the second and third decades of the sixteenth century, but at least something of permanent importance had already been achieved. Moreover, the timing of the reform was perhaps more important than its extent. Cisneros helped give the Spanish Church a new strength and vigour at the very moment when the Church was everywhere under heavy attack. At a time when the desire for radical ecclesiastical reform was sweeping through Christendom, the rulers of Spain personally sponsored reform at home, thus simultaneously removing some of the worst sources of complaint and keeping firm control over a movement which might easily have got out of hand. Here, as in so many of their governmental activities, Ferdinand and Isabella displayed an uncanny ability to take the initiative and give visible shape to their subjects' ill-defined aspirations.

But if the Catholic Kings usually contrived to retain the leadership, they were subject to strong pressures, and the routes they followed took some strange and unexpected turnings. They ruled a country whose religious sensibilities had been heightened almost to fever pitch by the miraculous achievements of recent years. As the Castilians saw the kingdom of Granada crumble before them, and the hopes of centuries realized at last, it was natural that they should think of themselves as entrusted with a holy mission to save and redeem the world, threatened as it was by the new advance of Islam from the east. But to be worthy of their mission they must first cleanse the temple of the Lord of its many impurities; and of all sources of pollution, the most noxious were universally agreed to be the Jews. The reign of the Catholic Kings was therefore to see the final act in a tragedy which had begun long before – a tragedy in which the sovereigns themselves both led, and were led by, their people.

During the Middle Ages the Jewish community had played an outstanding part in the cultural and economic life of both Castile and the Crown of Aragon. Where other west European states had expelled their Jews, they continued to be tolerated in Spain, partly because they were indispensable, and partly because the existence of a tolerant Moorish kingdom on Spanish soil would have reduced the effectiveness of any general measure of expulsion. During the plague-stricken and insecure years of the mid-fourteenth century, however, their position began to grow difficult. Popular hatred of them was fanned by preachers, and mounted to a terrible climax in anti-Jewish riots which swept Castile, Catalonia, and Aragon, in 1391. To save their lives, many submitted to baptism; and, at the end of the fourteenth century, these converted Jews – known as *conversos* or *marranos* – equalled and perhaps outnumbered those of their brethren who had survived the massacres and remained true to the faith of their fathers.

In the first decades of the fifteenth century the *conversos*, or New Christians, led uneasy, but not unprofitable, lives. Their wealth gave them an entry into the circle of Court and aristocracy; contending political factions jostled for their support, and some of the leading *converso* families intermarried with those of the high Castilian nobility. But their very power and influence as financiers, administrators, or members of the ecclesiastical hierarchy, naturally tended to breed resentment and suspicion, for the rise of a rich *converso* class seemed to threaten the whole social order of Castile, based on hereditary status and on the possession of landed wealth. While churchmen questioned the sincerity of their conversion, aristocrats expressed resentment at finding themselves dependent on the loans of wealthy *conversos*; and the populace at large, especially in Andalusia, hated them for their activities as tax-collectors or as fiscal agents of the nobility. Anti-semitism, fanned by social antagonisms, was therefore dangerously close to the surface, and occasionally erupted in savage outbursts, like the Toledo riots of 1449. These riots had the most sinister consequences, for they provoked the first decree of *limpieza de sangre*, or purity of blood, excluding all persons of Jewish ancestry from municipal office in Toledo.

During the first years of the Catholic Kings the Court maintained its traditionally tolerant attitude to the Jews. Ferdinand himself had Jewish blood in his veins, and the Court circle included not only *conversos* but also a number of practising Jews, like Abraham Senior, the treasurer of the *Hermandad*. A growing number of *conversos*, however, were now reverting to the faith of their fathers, and their defections were a source of deep concern to the genuine converts, who were afraid that their own position would be jeopardized by the back-sliding of their brethren. It may therefore have been influential *conversos* at Court and in the ecclesiastical hierarchy who first pressed for the establishment of a tribunal of the Inquisition in Castile – a tribunal for which Ferdinand and Isabella made formal application to Rome in 1478. Permission was duly granted, and a tribunal of the Holy Office was established in Castile. Placed under the direct control of the Crown, it was run from 1483 by a special royal Council – the *Consejo de la Suprema y General Inquisición* – and its task was to deal not with the Jews, nor with the Moriscos, but with New Christians who were suspected of having covertly returned to their old beliefs.[8]

This formidable body was in fact created to solve a specifically *Castilian* problem. While there were many *conversos* also in the Crown of Aragon, they were not a source of concern to the authorities like their brothers in Castile. But in spite of this, Ferdinand insisted on extending the Castilian-style Inquisition to the Levantine states, which, ever since the Albigensian crusade, had possessed a rather somnolent Inquisition of their own. His efforts provoked bitter opposition. In Aragon the inquisitor Pedro de Arbués was murdered in Zaragoza Cathedral, and in Catalonia both lay and ecclesiastical authorities resisted the proposal on the grounds that it would be economically disastrous, and that it would prejudice the Principality's laws and liberties. In 1487, however, Ferdinand won

8. For the methods of the Inquisition, see below, pp. 218-20.

his way. An inquisitor was installed in Barcelona, with all the consequences that had been prophesied. Frightened *conversos* – anything
from six hundred to three thousand – fled the country, taking their
capital with them. Many of these men were big merchants or
administrators, whose presence could ill be spared if Barcelona were
ever to recover its former commercial pre-eminence.

The imposition of the new-style Inquisition in the Crown of
Aragon as well as in Castile is often regarded as a move by Ferdinand
to increase his *political* control over his Aragonese possessions. It is
true that the Inquisition was the one institution, apart from the
monarchy itself, common to the possessions of Spain, and that in
this sense it did to some extent serve as a unifying organ. But it has
yet to be proved that Ferdinand saw in it a weapon for destroying
local autonomy and furthering the process of centralization. The
conventional emphasis on Isabella's piety makes it easy to overlook
the strong religious strain of her husband, a fervent devotee of the
Virgin, an ardent supporter of ecclesiastical reform in Catalonia, and
a man whose messianic brand of religion gave him many of the
attributes of the *converso*.

Yet while the establishment of the Inquisition was primarily a
religious measure designed to maintain the purity of the faith in the
dominions of the kings of Spain, its importance was by no means
restricted to an exclusively religious sphere. In a country so totally
devoid of political unity as the new Spain, a common faith served
as a substitute, binding together Castilians, Aragonese, and Catalans,
in the single purpose of ensuring the ultimate triumph of the Holy
Church. Compensating in some respects for the absence of a Spanish
nationhood, a common religious devotion had obvious political
overtones, and consequently a practical value which Ferdinand and
Isabella were quick to exploit. There was no sharp dividing-line
between religious and political achievements, but, rather, a constant
interaction between the two, and every political or military triumph
of the new dynasty was raised to a new level of significance by a
natural process of transmutation into a further victory for the Faith.

In the constant interplay between politics and religion, the establishment of an Inquisition throughout Spain had obvious political
advantages, in that it helped to further the cause of Spanish unity
by deepening the sense of common national purpose. The same was

true of the conquest of Granada and its aftermath. The holy war ended in 1492 with the achievement of Spain's territorial integrity; this in turn forged a new emotional bond between the peoples of Spain, who shared a common sense of triumph at the downfall of the infidel. But, as a great religious achievement, the triumph naturally demanded a further act of religious dedication. The Moors had now been defeated and stripped of their power. But there still remained the Jews and the crypto-Jews, ensconced at the very heart of the body politic, and purveying their pernicious doctrines throughout its length and breadth. Since the Inquisition had failed to obliterate the sources of contagion, more drastic measures were clearly required. The conquest of Granada, while glorious and triumphant, had also depleted the resources of the treasury. What more natural than to celebrate the triumph and remedy the deficiency by expelling the Jews? Local edicts, like that of 1483 in Seville, had already banished them from certain areas. Finally, at Granada on 30 March 1492, less than three months after the surrender of the Moors and less than three weeks before the signing of the capitulations with Columbus, the Catholic Kings put their signatures to an edict ordering the expulsion of all professed Jews from their kingdoms within the space of four months.

The edict of expulsion was the logical culmination of the policy that had begun with the introduction of the Inquisition; and it represented the last, and greatest, triumph of the zealous *conversos*. The departure of the Jews from Spain would remove temptation from all those New Christians who still looked back uneasily to their abandoned faith. They must now decide which master they would serve. Many *conversos* did, in fact, choose to leave the country in the company of the practising Jews. Figures are unfortunately highly unreliable, but the Hebrew community at the beginning of the reign is thought to have been some 200,000 strong, of whom 150,000 lived in Castile. Some, particularly from the Crown of Aragon, had left before the edict of expulsion. Others had been converted. On the publication of the edict, perhaps 120,000 to 150,000 people fled the country. These included some influential but half-hearted *conversos* – men of standing in the Church, the administration, and the world of finance. There were several last-minute conversions, including that of Abraham Senior, and a great effort

was made to keep indispensable Jewish physicians in Spain. This
meant that a new group of dubious converts was now added to the
converso ranks, although, on the other hand, all the inhabitants of
Spain – except, for a few years more, the Moriscos – were now
nominally Christian. As such, they were subject to the jurisdiction of
the Holy Office, which found its task considerably eased by the
disappearance of a practising Jewish community that served as a
standing temptation to the converts, and was outside inquisitorial
control.

The conquest of Granada and the expulsion of the Jews had laid
the foundations for a unitary state in the only sense in which that was
possible in the circumstances of the late fifteenth century. At least in
the minds of Ferdinand and Isabella, they helped impose a unity
which transcended administrative, linguistic, and cultural barriers,
bringing together Spaniards of all races in common furtherance of
a holy mission. The gains seemed great – but so also was the cost.
Even a divine mission is liable to require some human agency, and
to this the Spanish mission was no exception. The resources for
accomplishing the great enterprises that lay ahead were none too
plentiful in fifteenth-century Spain, and they were inevitably
diminished by the expulsion of the Jews. The year 1492 saw the
disappearance from Spain of a dynamic community, whose capital
and skill had helped enrich Castile. The gap left by the Jews was not
easily filled, and many of them were replaced not by native Castilians,
but by colonies of foreign immigrants – Flemings, Germans, Genoese
– who would use their new opportunity to exploit rather than to
enrich the resources of Spain. The effect of the expulsion was thus
to weaken the economic foundations of the Spanish Monarchy at
the very outset of its imperial career; and this was all the more
unfortunate in that the economic and social policies of Ferdinand
and Isabella proved in the long run to be the least successful part of
their programme for the restoration of Spain.

4. THE ECONOMIC AND SOCIAL FOUNDATIONS
OF THE NEW SPAIN

The Catholic Kings had revived the power of the monarchy, and, at
least in Castile, had laid the foundations of an authoritarian State,

galvanized into activity by a high sense of national purpose and by the glittering opportunities suddenly revealed by the overseas discoveries. Conscious of the need to organize the resources of the new State as well as to restore its administration, they were to be as active in legislating for the national economy as they were in religious and administrative reform. During Isabella's twenty-nine-year reign in Castile, no less than 128 ordinances were made, embracing every aspect of Castile's economic life. The export of gold and silver was forbidden; navigation laws were introduced to foster Spanish ship-building; the guild system was tightened up and re-organized; sporadic attempts were made to protect Castile's textile industries by temporary import prohibitions on certain types of cloths; and Flemish and Italian artisans were encouraged to settle in Spain by a promise of ten years' exemption from taxes. It would be misleading to describe these ordinances as constituent pieces of an economic programme, since this implies a coherent and logically developing design which did not, in fact, exist. The economic legislation of the Catholic Kings is best seen as their response to certain immediate and pressing fiscal or economic problems – a response which was consistently intended to increase the national wealth of Castile and the power of its kings.

In their economic as in their administrative ordering of Spain, Ferdinand and Isabella were content to accept and build upon already existing foundations. Their reign, so far from producing a significant change in the social organization of Castile, firmly perpetuated the existing order. Their attacks on the political influence of the magnates, and their employment of clerics and royal officials drawn from among the gentry and the *bourgeoisie*, have helped foster the impression that Ferdinand and Isabella were vigorous opponents of aristocracy. But, in fact, the assault on the political power of the magnates was not extended into a general assault on their economic and territorial power. It is true that the Act of Resumption of 1480 took a large slice out of their revenues; but the act dealt only with usurpations since the year 1464, and the bulk of the magnates' usurpations of Crown land and revenues had occurred before that date. All these earlier gains were left untouched, and the upper Castilian aristocracy remained an immensely wealthy class. The contemporary author Marineo Sículo provides the following list of

Castilian noble houses and their revenues, probably deriving from the early years of the reign of Charles V:[9]

DUKES (Total: 13)

Title	Family	Annual income ducats
Frías (Condestable de Castilla)	Velasco	60,000
Medina de Ríoseco (Almirante de Castilla)	Enríquez	50,000
Alba	Toledo	50,000
Infantado	Mendoza	50,000
Medina-Sidonia	Guzmán	55,000
Béjar	Zúñiga	40,000
Nájera	Manrique y de Lara	30,000
Medinaceli	La Cerda	30,000
Alburquerque	La Cueva	25,000
Arcos	León	25,000
Maqueda	Cárdenas	30,000
Escalona	Pacheco	60,000
Sessa	Córdoba	60,000
		565,000

MARQUISES (Total: 13)

Astorga	Osorio	25,000
Aguilar	Manrique	12,000
Cenete	Mendoza	30,000
Villafranca	Toledo	10,000
Priego	Aguilar y Figueroa	40,000
Ayamonte	Zúñiga y Sotomayor	30,000
Tarifa	Enríquez	30,000
Mondéjar	Mendoza	15,000
Comares	Córdoba	12,000
Los Vélez	Fajardo	30,000
Berlanga	Tovar	16,000
Villanueva	Portocarrero	20,000
del Valle	Cortés	60,000
		330,000

9. *Cosas Memorables de España*, op. cit., fs. 24–25v.

In addition, there were thirty-four counts and two viscounts in Castile, with a combined income of 414,000 ducats. Besides these sixty-two titled nobles in Castile, whose total rent-roll came to 1,309,000 ducats, there were a further twenty titles in the Crown of Aragon (five dukes, three marquises, nine counts and three viscounts) with a rent-roll of 170,000 ducats.

If anything, the reign of the Catholic Kings was characterized by an increase in the social and economic power of these great nobles. Some were able to benefit from the land distribution in the conquered kingdom of Granada. 'All the grandees and *caballeros* and *hijosdalgo* who served in the conquest of this kingdom,' wrote a contemporary chronicler, 'received *mercedes* – favours – each according to his status, in the form of houses, lands and vassals.'[10] All benefited from the legislation passed in the Cortes of Toro of 1505, which confirmed and extended the right to establish *mayorazgos* or entails, by which a great house could ensure that its possessions remained vested in it in perpetuity, passing undivided and intact from one heir to the next. The matrimonial alliances of the great Castilian families, which the Crown did nothing to check, still further helped to consolidate great blocs of land into the hands of a powerful few. As a result, the late fifteenth century sealed and confirmed the pattern of land distribution that existed in late medieval Castile. This meant in practice that 2 per cent or 3 per cent of the population owned 97 per cent of the soil of Castile, and that over half of this 97 per cent belonged to a handful of great families. Even if they had for the moment lost their former political predominance, houses like Enríquez, Mendoza and Guzmán therefore retained the vast economic resources and territorial influence acquired in earlier times.

The heads of these great houses were not transformed into Court nobles during the reign of the Catholic Kings. On the contrary, with the exception of a small group of magnates with posts in the royal household, the great aristocrats saw much less of Court life than they had in previous reigns, and preferred to live in their sumptuous palaces on their own estates than to dance attendance on a Court where they were excluded from political office. It was only in the

10. Quoted by Julio Caro Baroja, *Los Moriscos del Reino de Granada* (Madrid, 1957), p. 7.

years following the death of Isabella in 1504 that they made a bid to
recover their earlier position at Court and in the State, and their
success was short-lived. After that, there was no opportunity until
the reign of Philip III for them to obtain an influence at Court of the
kind to which they felt themselves automatically entitled. But, if
their political power was gone, their social predominance remained
unchallenged, and indeed was confirmed by the decision of Charles
V in 1520 to grade the Spanish aristocracy into a fixed hierarchy of
rank. At the top of the scale came the *Grandes de España* – twenty-
five grandees, drawn from the oldest families of Castile and Aragon.
These enjoyed the special distinction of being allowed to remain
covered in the presence of the King, and of being addressed by him
as *primos*, or cousins. Immediately below them were the other titled
aristocrats, known as *Títulos*, who in other respects were indistinguishable from the grandees.

Just under these two groups of magnates, who formed the élite of
the Spanish aristocracy, came a group which differed from them in
having no corporate entity of its own, but which none the less
enjoyed an acknowledged position in the social hierarchy. This
group consisted of the *segundones* – the younger sons of the great
houses. These possessed no title of their own, and were generally
victims of the *mayorazgo* system which reserved the bulk of the family
wealth for their elder brothers. Since their resources tended to be
limited, they were likely to devote themselves in particular to careers
in the Army or the Church, or to serve the Crown as diplomats and
administrators.

The remaining aristocracy in Castile was the lesser aristocracy,
whose members, distinguished by the coveted prefix of *Don*, were
known indifferently as *caballeros* or *hidalgos*. These varied enormously
among themselves. Some were rich, and some extremely poor; some
came from ancient families, while others were recently ennobled
bourgeois; many possessed rural estates and properties, with or without jurisdiction over vassals, but many also had town houses, and
lived similar lives to those of the upper class of citizens, with whom
they were usually closely interrelated. In Ávila, for instance, there
were numerous families of noble origin: families who transformed
the appearance of the city in the late fifteenth and early sixteenth
centuries by building themselves impressive town houses in the new

Renaissance style, and who played an essential part in the city's ceremonial life and in the control of urban government. Members of a society in which rank and family were of supreme importance, *hidalgos* were distinguished from the run of citizens by their possession of family coats of arms, which they emblazoned on houses and churches and convents and tombs with a profusion proper to a world in which heraldry was the indispensable key to all the subtleties of status.

The relationship of *hidalgos* to the world of business and commerce seems to have been somewhat ambiguous. Many of them were heavily engaged in financial administration, since only proven *hidalgos* could farm royal taxes. Many too, were involved in trade of one kind or another – a practice that does not seem, at least in the early sixteenth century, to have been regarded as incompatible with *hidalguía*, although an excessive concern with commercial affairs might cast a shadow over a family's reputation. Few, however, would be anxious to compromise too heavily a status which conferred on them not only great social prestige, but also important financial and legal advantages; for *hidalgos* shared many privileges with the magnates, of which the most important was exemption from payment of taxes to the Crown. They also enjoyed a privileged status before the law. In criminal cases they could be judged only by the *audiencias* or by special *alcaldes de Corte*, and all sentences upon them had to be confirmed by the Council of Castile. They could not be tortured or condemned to the galleys; they could not be imprisoned for debt; and in civil suits their houses, arms, and horses could not be sequestrated.

The social reputation and practical advantages attached to the possession of a privilege of *hidalguía* made it an object of universal desire. Vast quantities of time, and considerable mental gymnastics, were devoted to the construction, or fabrication, of genealogical tables which would prove the existence of aristocratic ancestors for the most unlikely families. In spite of the insistent emphasis on ancestry, however, the *hidalgos* did not by any means constitute a closed caste, nor was membership determined solely by the accident of birth. Ferdinand and Isabella, who depended on leading municipal families as well as on *hidalgos* for their lawyers, soldiers, clerics, and administrators, were so lavish in their bestowal of patents of nobility that the ranks of the *hidalgos* were constantly being refreshed by an infusion of new blood.Within a few years the Cortes of Castile were protesting at the number of new creations, but the extension of *hidalguía* to a wider and wider circle proved impossible to check. The intense, and growing, pressure from among the lower ranks of Castilian society for privileges of nobility, found in course of time an answering chord from an increasingly indigent Crown. From the 1520s privileges of *hidalguía* were being put up for sale as a means of bringing relief to a hard-pressed royal treasury. These privileges were apparently available to anyone with sufficient cash to spare, as the Cortes of 1592 complained: 'The sale of *hidalguías* is giving rise to numerous inconveniences, for they are generally purchased by wealthy persons of inferior quality. . . . This is hateful to all classes. Nobles resent finding people of inferior condition obtaining equality with them simply through the expenditure of money, to the consequent disparagement of nobility . . . while *pecheros* (tax-payers) are annoyed that people of no higher origin than themselves should secure precedence over them merely because of their wealth. . . .' But there was nothing to be done, and the flood of new creations continued unabated.

The effect of Ferdinand and Isabella's policies was therefore to confirm and consolidate the importance of rank and hierarchy in Castilian society, but at the same time to offer opportunities of social advancement to many who would have had much less hope of acquiring a privileged status in earlier reigns. One of the keys to advancement was education, which might eventually lead to a place in the royal service. The other was wealth, particularly urban wealth, which made possible the alliance between rich mercantile families (including those of Jewish origin) and families of respectable aristocratic lineage. The grandfather of St Teresa of Ávila, for instance, was a certain Juan Sánchez, a merchant of Toledo, who married into the aristocratic family of Cepeda. Penanced in 1485 for Judaizing practices, he moved with his family to Ávila, where, in spite of the fact that his experiences with the Toledo Inquisition were by no means unknown, he managed to marry all his children into families of the local nobility, and to continue his very successful career as a cloth and silk merchant. The family later switched from trade to the administration of rents and the farming of taxes, and St Teresa's father, Don Alonso Sánchez de Cepeda, was generally reputed both a rich and an honourable man, with a total estate in 1507 of a million *maravedís* (some 3,000 ducats), minus debts to the tune of 300,000 *maravedís* – at a time when a labourer's wages were some 15 to 20 *maravedís* a day, or 20 ducats a year.[11]

Activities of such families as the Sánchez de Cepeda of Ávila hint at the vitality of urban life in the reign of Ferdinand and Isabella, and at the considerable degree of social mobility to be found in the towns. If the cities were surrendering many of their most treasured privileges into the hands of royal officials, they were still intensely active communities, with an undeniable air of prosperity, and a vigorously independent existence of their own.

The picture of life in the countryside, however, is rather different. Unfortunately, little is known about Castilian rural life at this time, and in particular about the relations between vassals and their lords. A decree of 1480 released manorial tenants from the last traces of servile tenure, and left them free to sell their property and to move elsewhere at will. But they continued to be liable to seigneurial dues and subjected to seigneurial jurisdiction, which seems to have varied enormously according to the character of the lord; and any improvement in their legal position as the power of the Crown extended into the countryside, was not apparently matched by a comparable improvement in their economic status. There were, however, considerable gradations within a peasantry which constituted some 80 per cent of the population of Castile. There was a small peasant aristocracy – the 'rich labourers' who figure so prominently in Castilian literature, and who were the dominant figures in village life; and there was a considerable group of town-dwelling peasants, who combined the cultivation of their land with jobs as artisans or small traders in their home town. But the mass of the peasantry seems to have lived in a poverty-stricken state which could easily become acute. It is true that, except in some areas of Galicia, serfdom had disappeared, and that peasants who paid an annual *censo* for the rental of their land could feel reasonably secure before the law. It is also true that there was never a peasants' revolt in sixteenth-century Castile. But conditions, in some regions at least, were desperately hard, for the whole system of landed property was so arranged as to place upon the peasants the main burden of agricultural production without providing them with

11. See the extremely informative introductory section to the *Obras Completas de Santa Teresa de Jesús* (Biblioteca de Autores Cristianos), vol. 1 (Madrid, 1951).

the resources to work the land efficiently. Big landowners seem to have taken little interest in the direct exploitation of their estates. They were content, instead, to lease out much of their land. This land was worked by peasants who had probably been compelled to borrow in the first instance in order to secure a plot, and then found their meagre earnings drastically reduced by tithes, dues, and taxes. After this, it only needed one or two bad harvests to make them fall hopelessly into debt.

These troubles of the peasantry were particularly serious in that Castile's population was growing, and there were already moments when it was difficult to feed it. Agricultural techniques were extremely primitive; the soil, which was anyhow poor, was given too little rest, and the usual method of increasing production was to bring waste land under the plough – land which after a few seasons produced a rapidly diminishing yield. Traditionally, at least in good seasons, the Castilian *meseta* produced a certain amount of corn for export, but certain parts of the peninsula were incapable of feeding themselves – notably Galicia, Asturias, and Vizcaya, which were supplied from Castile by sea, and the Crown of Aragon, which imported grain from Andalusia and Sicily. But in years of bad harvests Castile itself was dependent on imports of foreign corn. The opening years of the sixteenth century in particular were years of serious harvest failures. Grain prices rose sharply from 1502, and remained high until 1509, when a spectacularly good harvest brought them down so drastically that many farmers were ruined.

The Government responded to the crisis by authorizing a massive importation of foreign grain in 1506, and by instituting in 1502 the so-called *tasa del trigo*, imposing a fixed maximum price for corn. This attempt at price-fixing, sporadically applied in the first decades of the century, was to become a permanent feature of the Crown's agrarian policy from 1539. Since it was designed to protect the interests of the consumer and not of the producer, it only served to add to the difficulties of an industry which already found itself in serious difficulties, and which – even more seriously – was consistently deprived of royal encouragement and support.

In spite of the increasingly grave problem of the national food supply, Ferdinand and Isabella adopted no vigorous measures to stimulate corn production. On the contrary, it was in their reign that the long-continuing struggle between sheep and corn was decisively resolved in favour of the sheep. The great expansion of the mediaeval wool trade had revitalized the economic life of Castile, but there inevitably came a point at which further encouragement of Castilian wool production could only be given at the expense of sacrificing agriculture. This point was reached in the reign of the Catholic Kings. The importance of the wool trade to the Castilian economy, and the value to the royal treasury of the *servicio y montazgo*, the tax paid the Crown by the sheep-farmers, naturally prompted Ferdinand and Isabella to pursue the policies of their predecessors and to take the *Mesta* under their special protection. As a result, a whole series of ordinances conferred upon it wide privileges and enormous favours, culminating in the famous law of 1501 by which all land on which the migrant flocks had even once been pastured was reserved in perpetuity for pasturage, and could not be put to any other uses by its owner. This meant that great tracts of land in Andalusia and Estremadura were deprived of all chance of agricultural development and subjected to the whim of the sheepowners. The aims of this policy were obvious enough. The wool trade was easily subjected to monopolistic control, and, as a result, it constituted a fruitful source of revenue to a Crown which, since 1484, had found itself in increasing financial difficulties, exacerbated by the flight of Jewish capital. An alliance between Crown and sheepowners was thus mutually beneficial for both: the *Mesta*, with its $2\frac{1}{2}$ to 3 million sheep, basked in the warm sunshine of royal favours while the Crown, whose control of the Military Orders gave it some of the best pasturing lands in Spain, could draw a regular income from it, and turn to it for special contributions in emergencies.

There were no doubt certain unintended advantages to Castile, in the intense royal encouragement of the wool industry. Sheep-farming requires less labour than arable farming, and the vast extent of the pasture-lands helped to produce a surplus of manpower which made it easier for Castile to raise armies and to colonize the New World. But on the whole the favouring of sheep-farming at the expense of tillage can only appear as a wilful sacrifice of Castile's long-term requirements to considerations of immediate convenience. It was in the reign of Ferdinand and Isabella that agriculture was confirmed in its unhappy position as the Cinderella of the Castilian economy, and the price which was eventually to be paid for this was frighteningly high.

Castile therefore began its imperial career with a distinctly unhealthy agrarian system. *Carestía*, or dearth, was always uncomfortably close, and too heavy a burden rested on the shoulders of an agrarian population which received neither adequate incentives nor adequate rewards for its labours. But the potential dangers of a shortsighted agrarian policy were easily ignored at a time when the Castilian economy appeared in other respects to be singularly prosperous. The late fifteenth century was a period of considerable economic expansion. Both internal and international trade were lively, and the restoration of peace after the long period of civil war had brought a new confidence and sense of security to the towns of Castile.

The economic achievement of Ferdinand and Isabella lay not so much in the making of something new as in the creation of conditions in which Castile's existing economic potential could be amply realized. In the peaceful climate of the late fifteenth century the seeds sown during the preceding hundred years came to fruition. The policies of the Catholic Kings were directed towards ensuring that the harvest should yield its maximum; they saw it as their task to regulate and organize, so that the vigorous but often confused and anarchical economic developments of earlier years should not be wasted or allowed to spoil. It was in this spirit, for instance, that they reorganized the fairs of Medina del Campo in 1483, and later attempted, although without success, to merge the fairs of Villalón and Medina de Ríoseco with those of Medina del Campo, to obtain at once both maximum efficiency and centralization. But it was above all to the regulating of the wool trade that they devoted their attention. Here, as elsewhere, there were obvious foundations on which to build. There was already a system of *flotas* or convoys for the shipment of Castilian wool to northern Europe; and Burgos, the centre of the wool trade, had a well-established merchants' guild with representatives in France and Flanders. The expulsion of the Jews in 1492 had dislocated the wool market, and it was to restore smooth working to the export system that the Catholic Kings created the famous *Consulado* of Burgos in 1494.

The *Consulado*, like many another institution introduced into

Castile under the government of Ferdinand, was Aragonese in origin. It combined the functions of a guild and of a mercantile court, and had existed in several towns of the Crown of Aragon since the late thirteenth century. A *Consolat de la Mar* had been set up in Valencia as early as 1283; Majorca had followed suit in 1343, and Barcelona in 1347, and by the mid-fifteenth century there were eight *Consolats* in the Levantine states. Burgos already had its merchant guild, but this lacked the powers of jurisdiction that belonged to a *Consulado*. The installation of a *Consulado* in Burgos was therefore as attractive to the local merchants as it was to Ferdinand and Isabella, who saw in it the ideal agency for encouraging a fuller exploitation of the wool trade and for bringing it under efficient centralized direction. Wool was prepared for the market in the interior of Castile, sold to merchants and exporters at the fairs, and then transported to Burgos, which served as a central depot. Burgos, however, was over a hundred miles from the nearest port, and pack mules carried the twelve to fifteen thousand woolpacks from Burgos to Bilbao, from where one or two fleets a year shipped the wool to Antwerp.

Burgos, although itself no port, thus acquired a complete monopoly in the organization of Cantabrian trade with the north. Acting as a natural link between the wool growers and the wool exporters, it alone could authorize the shipments of wool from the Cantabrian ports. In terms of increasing trade, the system seemed to work well. Wool exports continued to rise, and the Catholic Kings attempted to encourage the growth of a merchant fleet by offering subsidies to assist in the construction of ships of over 600 tons (a size more appropriate to a man-of-war than a merchantman) and by passing, in 1500, a navigation law, by which Castilian goods were to be exported in Castilian ships. But the monopoly enjoyed by Burgos also had its drawbacks, especially in that it sharpened the already bitter rivalry between Burgos and Bilbao. Bilbao possessed natural advantages denied to Burgos, and it was also the centre of the growing Vizcayan iron trade. Already by 1500 capital was migrating to Bilbao from Burgos, and finally, in 1511, Ferdinand yielded to the pressure of the Bilbao merchants, and authorized the creation in Bilbao of a special *Consulado* for Vizcaya.

For all its teething troubles, the *Consulado* system possessed such obvious convenience that it seemed natural to extend it also to the new trade with America. The *Consulado* de Burgos, itself inspired by the *Consolat* of Barcelona, was thus to provide the model for the famous *Casa de Contratación* – House of Trade – set up in Seville in 1503. Although the following decades were to see a number of experiments before the details of the system were finally settled, this represented the beginnings of that Sevillian monopoly over trade with the New World which was to last for two hundred years. Monopoly had come, almost imperceptibly, to seem the natural form of commercial organization in Castile.

The imposition of Aragonese institutions on the economic life of Castile was not exclusively limited to the creation of *Consulados*. It was also to be found in the reorganization of guilds in Castilian towns. During the Middle Ages the kings of Castile had not looked with favour on guilds, and these had largely remained charitable institutions, of little importance for the country's economic life. In the Crown of Aragon, on the other hand, they were highly organized corporations, meticulously regulating the life of their members, and insisting on high standards of workmanship by means of apprenticeship regulations, examinations, and close supervision. With the advent of Ferdinand to the throne, royal policy towards guilds in Castile was transformed. The Catalan-Aragonese guild system was introduced, and the towns were authorised to set up corporations for the various crafts.

At a time of economic expansion, therefore, the Catholic Kings had grafted on to the commercial and industrial life of Castile the rigid corporative structure which had already been showing signs of bankruptcy in the Crown of Aragon. It is difficult to determine the economic consequences of this policy, but it would seem on the whole to have been unfortunate that a full-blown guild system, with all its usual elaborate paraphernalia, should belatedly have been imposed upon Castile at a time when other parts of Europe were making tentative moves towards less rigid forms of industrial organization. Even the short-term consequences to Castilian industry of the tireless legislating activity of the Catholic Kings were not perhaps as favourable as it is sometimes assumed. The three leading industries of the Crown of Castile – iron manufactures in the north, the cloth manufactures of central Castile, and the Granada silk industry – need detailed study before judgment is passed, but the general impression is not at present one of startling progress. The Granada silk industry was temporarily dislocated by the revolt of the Alpujarras; the cloth industry was hampered by the import of foreign cloths in exchange for Castilian exports of raw wool. Moreover, the expulsion of the Jews had deprived Castilian industry both of skilled workers and of much-needed capital. Restriction and regulation may well have hindered more than they helped, and it is significant that those industries which appear to have thrived prove on inspection to be local domestic industries, or specialized luxury industries like Toledan jewellery and Sevillian ceramics – industries strictly limited in size, and not amenable to close control.

The obstacles to industrial advance were, however, formidable. Quite apart from the shortage of capital and of skilled workmen, distances were enormous and communications poor. Mule trains and ox-carts moved slowly and ponderously across the *meseta*, and the costs of transport added terrifyingly to prices: the cost, for instance, of carrying spices from Lisbon to Toledo was greater than the original price paid for the spices in Lisbon. Under Ferdinand and Isabella serious efforts were made to improve the country's system of communications. Roads were repaired, and certain new routes were constructed in the kingdom of Granada; and in 1497 Castile's wagoners and carters were grouped together into an organization known as the *Cabaña Real de Carreteros*, which enjoyed a privileged status on the Spanish highways and was exempted from local dues and tolls. Efforts were also made to create a national postal system with international extensions. During the Middle Ages the posts had been less well organized in Castile than in the Crown of Aragon, where the Confraternity of Marcús was responsible for a postal service which seems to have worked with considerable efficiency. Barcelona, which was the home of the Confraternity, became under the Catholic Kings the centre of an international postal network, radiating outwards to Castile and Portugal, Germany, France, and Italy. Meanwhile in Castile the postal system was entrusted to an official known as the *Correo Mayor* – an office which, from 1505, was held by succeeding generations of a family of Italian origin, the Tassis.

Improvements of posts and routes did something to bring closer together the different regions of the Spanish peninsula, but on the whole no more was done by the Catholic Kings to break down the economic barriers between their kingdoms than to break down the political barriers. The customs system continued untouched, so that all goods continued to pay heavy duties as they passed from one region to another. Nor was anything done to bring the different kingdoms into closer economic association. Instead, two separate economic systems continued to exist side by side: the Atlantic system of Castile, and the Mediterranean system of the Crown of Aragon. As a result of the expansion of the wool trade and the discovery of America, the first of these was flourishing. The Crown of Aragon's Mediterranean system, on the other hand, had been gravely impaired by the collapse of Catalonia, although there was some compensation for Catalonia's losses in the increased economic activity of late fifteenth-century Valencia. Ferdinand's pacification and reorganization of Catalonia, however, enabled the Principality at the end of the century to recover a little of its lost ground. Catalan fleets began to sail again to Egypt; Catalan merchants appeared once more in North Africa; and, most important of all, a preferential position was obtained for Catalan cloths in the markets of Sicily, Sardinia, and Naples. But it is significant that this recovery represented a return to old markets, rather than the opening up of new ones. The Catalans were excluded from direct commerce with America by the Sevillian monopoly, and they failed, for reasons that are not entirely clear, to break into the Castilian market on a large scale. They may have shown a lack of enterprise, but they also seem to have suffered from discrimination, for as late as 1565 they were arguing that the Union of the Crowns of 1479 made it unreasonable that Catalan merchants should still be treated as aliens in Castilian towns. As a result of this kind of treatment, it is scarcely surprising that Catalonia and the Crown of Aragon as a whole should have continued to look eastwards to the Mediterranean, instead of turning their attention towards the Castilian hinterland and the broad spaces of the Atlantic.

Castile and the Crown of Aragon, nominally united, thus continued to remain apart – in their political systems, their economic systems, and even in their coinage. The inhabitants of the Crown of Aragon reckoned, and continued to reckon, in pounds, shillings, and pence (*libras*, *sueldos*, and *dineros*). The Castilians reckoned in a money of account – the *maravedí*. At the time of the accession of Ferdinand and Isabella the monetary system in Castile was particularly chaotic.

The stabilizing of the coinage proved to be a difficult operation, but it was finally achieved by the pragmatic of 1497, which formed the basis of the Castilian coinage in the following centuries. This pragmatic established the following system:

Gold	*Excelente menor* (or ducat)[12]	375 *maravedís*
Silver	*Real*	34 *maravedís*
Vellón (silver and copper)	*Blanca*	½ *maravedí*

Meanwhile there had also been certain monetary innovations in the Crown of Aragon. In 1481 Ferdinand had introduced into Valencia a gold coin modelled on the Venetian ducat – the *excel·lent* – and an equivalent coin, the *principat*, was introduced into Catalonia in 1493. The Castilian reforms of 1497 meant, therefore, that for the first time the three principal coins of Spain – the Valencian *excel·lent*, the Catalan *principat*, and the Castilian ducat – were worth exactly the same. This represented the only measure of economic unification for their kingdoms which the Catholic Kings ever undertook. As such, it bore an odd resemblance to their achievements in the field of political unification. Just as the Crowns of Castile and Aragon were politically united only in the persons of their kings, so their monetary systems were similarly united only at the top, by a common coin of high value. Sole symbols of unity in a continuing diversity, the gold coins of early sixteenth-century Spain are at once a testimonial to the restored economies of the Spanish kingdoms and a mocking reminder that the policies of the Catholic Kings were no more than a faint beginning. Economically as much as politically, *Spain* still existed only in embryo.

5. THE OPEN SOCIETY

The reign of Ferdinand and Isabella was called by Prescott 'the most glorious epoch in the annals' of Spain. Generations of Spaniards, contrasting their own times with those of the Catholic Kings, would look back upon them as the golden age of Castile. The conquest of

12. In 1534 a new gold coin of less fineness, the *escudo*, was introduced, and gradually replaced the ducat, although this continued to be used in reckoning. Where the ducat was worth 11 reales and 1 *maravedí*, the *escudo* was worth 350 *maravedís*, or 10 silver *reales*. It was raised to 400 *maravedís* in 1566, and to 440 in 1609.

Granada, the discovery of America, and the triumphant emergence of Spain on to the European political stage lent unparalleled lustre to the new State created by the Union of the Crowns, and set the seal of success on the political, religious, and economic reforms of the royal couple.

Against the conventional picture of a glorious spring-time under Ferdinand and Isabella, too soon to be turned to winter by the folly of their successors, there must, however, be set some of the less happy features of their reign. They had united two Crowns, but had not even tentatively embarked on the much more arduous task of uniting two peoples. They had destroyed the political power of the great nobility, but left its economic and social influence untouched. They had reorganized the Castilian economy, but at the price of reinforcing the system of *latifundios* and the predominance of grazing over tillage. They had introduced into Castile certain Aragonese economic institutions, monopolistic in spirit, while failing to bring the Castilian and Aragonese economies any closer together. They had restored order in Castile, but in the process had overthrown the fragile barriers that stood in the way of absolutism. They had reformed the Church, but set up the Inquisition. And they had expelled one of the most dynamic and resourceful sections of the community – the Jews. All this must darken a picture that is often painted excessively bright.

Yet nothing can alter the fact that Ferdinand and Isabella created Spain; that in their reign it acquired both an international existence and – under the impulse given by the creative exuberance of the Castilians and the organizing capacity of the Aragonese – the beginnings of a corporate identity. Out of their long experience, the Aragonese could provide the administrative methods which would give the new monarchy an institutional form. The Castilians, for their part, were to provide the dynamism which would impel the new State forward; and it was this dynamism which gave the Spain of Ferdinand and Isabella its distinguishing character. The Spain of the Catholic Kings is essentially Castile: a Castile, overflowing with creative energy, which seemed suddenly to have discovered itself.

This self-discovery is nowhere more apparent than in the cultural achievements of the reign. After centuries of relative isolation, Castile had been subjected in the fifteenth century to strong and contradictory European cultural influences, out of which it would eventually fashion for itself a national art. Commercial contacts with Flanders brought northern influences in their train – Flemish realism in painting, the flamboyant Gothic style in architecture, and Flemish religion in the widely read manuals of popular devotion. At the same time, the traditional ties between the Crown of Aragon and Italy brought to the Spanish Court the new Italian humanism, and, belatedly, the new Italian architecture.

These foreign stylistic currents had somehow to be fused with the Jewish, Islamic, and Christian traditions of medieval Castile. The result was often an amalgam of warring influences; but in certain arts, particularly architecture, a genuine style emerged which came to be recognized as characteristically Spanish. This was the 'plateresque' – that strange blend of Moorish and northern, indiscriminately combining Gothic and Renaissance motifs to form fantastically ornamented surfaces. Equally remote from the purity of medieval Gothic and from the Renaissance ideal that detail should be subordinated to unity, the plateresque was a style which vividly suggested the exuberant and distinctive vitality of Isabella's Castile.

Like the other achievements of contemporary Castile, however, the creation of plateresque was dependent as much on the direction and impulse given by the rulers as on the creative vitality of the ruled. Plateresque was a rich and extravagant style requiring rich and extravagant patrons. Enrique de Egas built the hospital of Santa Cruz at Toledo for Cardinal Mendoza; Pedro de Gumiel was commissioned by Cardinal Cisneros to build the university of Alcalá. The Castilian grandees rivalled the great ecclesiastics as patrons, building themselves sumptuous palaces like that of the Duke of Infantado at Guadalajara, with its superbly elaborate ornamentation. But it is symptomatic of the newly acquired supremacy of the monarchy in Spain that many of the most lavish and impressive buildings were royal foundations – the Hospital de los Reyes at Santiago, the charterhouse of Miraflores, the royal chapel at Granada. Ferdinand and Isabella built and restored on an enormous scale, and they left on all their creations, by means of emblems and medallions, anagrams and devices, the imprint of their royal authority.

The Court was the natural centre of Castile's cultural life; and since Spain still had no fixed capital it was a Court on the move, bringing new ideas and influences from one town to another as it travelled round the country. Since Isabella enjoyed a European reputation for her patronage of learning, she was able to attract to the Court distinguished foreign scholars like the Milanese Pietro Martire, the director of the palace school. Frequented by foreign scholars and by Spaniards who had returned from studying in Italy, the Court thus became an outpost of the new humanism, which was now beginning to establish itself in Spain.

One of the devotees of the new learning was Elio Antonio de Nebrija (1444–1522), who returned home from Italy in 1473 – the year in which printing was introduced into Spain. Nebrija, who held the post of historiographer royal, was a grammarian and lexicographer, and an editor of classical texts in the best humanist tradition. But his interests, like those of many humanists, extended also to the vernacular, and he published in 1492 a Castilian grammar – the first grammar to be compiled of a modern European language. 'What is it for?' asked Isabella when it was presented to her. 'Your Majesty,' replied the Bishop of Ávila on Nebrija's behalf, 'language is the perfect instrument of empire.'[13]

The Bishop's reply was prophetic. One of the secrets of Castilian domination of the Spanish Monarchy in the sixteenth century was to be found in the triumph of its language and culture over that of other parts of the peninsula and empire. The cultural and linguistic success of the Castilians was no doubt facilitated by the decline of Catalan culture in the sixteenth century, as it was also facilitated by the advantageous position of Castilian as the language of Court and bureaucracy. But, in the last analysis, Castile's cultural predominance derived from the innate vitality of its literature and language at the end of the fifteenth century. The language of the greatest work produced in the Castile of the Catholic Kings, the *Celestina* of the *converso* Fernando de Rojas, is at once vigorous, flexible, and authoritative: a language that was indeed 'the perfect instrument of empire'.

A vigorous language was the product of a vigorous society, whose intellectual leaders shared the inquiring spirit common to so much of late fifteenth-century Europe. Humanism, patronized by the Court and popularized by the printing of classical texts, found enthusiastic adherents among the *conversos* and gradually gained acceptance in the universities of Castile. With the foundation of the university of Alcalá

13. Quoted by Lewis Hanke, *Aristotle and the American Indians*, p. 8.

and the publication of the Polyglot Bible, Spanish humanism came of age. Royal patronage had helped to make the new learning respectable, and the new learning proved in turn to be a useful key to royal favour. The Castilian aristocracy, like the aristocracy of other European states, was not slow to learn the lesson. Among the seven thousand students to be found at any one time in sixteenth-century Salamanca, there were always representatives of the leading Spanish houses, and some nobles themselves became distinguished exponents of the new learning, like Don Alonso Manrique, professor of Greek at Alcalá.

No doubt some of the manifestations of Spanish humanism were crude and jejeune, but even these were to some extent redeemed by the enthusiasm which characterized the cultural life of Castile under the Catholic Kings. There was a sense of intellectual excitement in the country, and a thirst for cultural contacts with the outside world. It is this, above all, which distinguishes the Spain of Ferdinand and Isabella from that of Philip II. The Spain of the Catholic Kings was an open society, eager for, and receptive to, contemporary foreign ideas. The establishment of the Inquisition and the expulsion of the Jews were steps in an opposite direction, but they proved at the time insufficient to deflect Spain from its voyage of discovery beyond its own frontiers. Under the government of the Catholic Kings, Castile – its most pressing domestic problems momentarily solved – was ready to throw itself into new experiences, cultural or political, with all the energy of a nation released from a long confinement. Ferdinand and Isabella, in giving Castile a new sense of purpose and direction, had released the springs of action. It was Castile, rather than Spain, which burst into life in the late fifteenth century – a Castile which had suddenly become aware of its own potentialities. Already, to the Castilians, Castile was Spain; and already it was being beckoned towards a still greater future, as circumstances both at home and overseas inexorably cast it for an imperial role.

4

The Imperial Destiny

I. THE FOREIGN POLICY OF FERDINAND

ISABELLA died on 26 November 1504. Her grandson, the Emperor
Charles V, was to be firmly established on the Spanish throne only in
1522. The intervening eighteen years, complex and confused, were
decisive in shaping the entire future of the Spanish Monarchy.
Against very considerable odds, the Union of the Crowns was somehow preserved during these years, royal authority over the nobles and
towns of Castile was confirmed, and Spain launched out on its
imperial course under the leadership of the Habsburgs. There was as
much of accident as of design in the final conclusion, but in so far as
it can be attributed to any particular policies, they were those of
Ferdinand and of Cardinal Cisneros.

The diplomatic involvement of Castile in the affairs of western
Europe, which was to culminate so unexpectedly in the placing of a
foreign dynasty on the Castilian throne, was the work of Ferdinand,
inspired in the first instance by the interests of Aragon. Louis XI's
intervention in the domestic troubles of Catalonia during the reign of
John II, and his seizure of the Catalan counties of Rosselló and Cerdanya in 1463, had exacerbated the traditional rivalry between the
Crown of Aragon and France. It was only natural that Ferdinand, as
the heir to this rivalry, should seek to induce his wife to abandon
Castile's traditional policy of alliance with France. Between 1475 and
1477 envoys were sent to Germany, Italy, England, and the Netherlands, offering them, as natural enemies of France, a Castilian alliance.
Here were the first steps towards the European involvement of
Castile, and towards that diplomatic isolation of France – later to be
reinforced by a series of dynastic marriages – which was to be the
permanent theme of Ferdinand's foreign policy.

During the following fifteen years, which were largely taken up
with the completion of the *Reconquista*, Ferdinand devoted himself in

particular to a tightening of the bonds between Spain and Portugal, in the hope of preparing the way for the ultimate unification of the peninsula. A marriage arranged between Isabella, the eldest daughter of the Catholic Kings, and Prince Alfonso of Portugal, eventually took place in 1490, but ended a few months later with the death of Alfonso. Isabella was remarried in 1497 to the new King Emmanuel of Portugal, but died the following year giving birth to the Infante Miguel, who himself was to die within two years. Distressed but undaunted, Ferdinand and Isabella married their fourth child, María, to Emmanuel in 1500. No opportunity could be neglected for ensuring the succession of a single ruler to the joint thrones of Spain and Portugal.

The fall of Granada in 1492 for the first time allowed Ferdinand to direct all his energies outwards in pursuit of a more active foreign policy. Two areas received his special attention: the Catalan–French border, and Italy. No true king of Aragon could resign himself permanently to the loss of the Catalan counties of Rosselló and Cerdanya. As the original homeland of the Catalans, they were considered as integral a part of the dominions of the kings of Spain as the kingdom of Granada, and their recovery was a prime object of Ferdinand's policy. His alliance with England at the Treaty of Medina del Campo in 1489 was intended to facilitate a Spanish invasion of France to recover the counties, by obtaining the assistance of an English diversion in the north. This particular project was unsuccessful, but a new opportunity shortly arose to acquire the counties, and this time without bloodshed. Charles VIII of France had conceived his idea of an Italian expedition, and in order to secure the quiescence of Spain while he was away on campaign, he agreed by the Treaty of Barcelona of January 1493 to restore Rosselló and Cerdanya to Ferdinand. For the next century and a half therefore, until the Treaty of the Pyrenees, the counties became once more a part of Catalonia, and Spain's frontier with France lay again to the north of the Pyrenees.

Satisfactory as was the bloodless reacquisition of Rosselló and Cerdanya, Charles VIII's invasion of Italy represented a new, and more serious, threat to the Crown of Aragon. Sicily was an Aragonese possession, while the kingdom of Naples belonged to a junior branch of the house of Aragon. A European coalition was needed to check the advance of Charles VIII; and the achievement of this coalition in 1495 in the shape of a Holy League between England, Spain, the Empire, and the Papacy, was one of the greatest triumphs of Ferdinand's foreign policy. In building up this coalition, Ferdinand laid the foundations of a diplomatic system that was to maintain and extend Spanish power throughout the sixteenth century. The success of the missions he sent to the various European capitals in pursuit of a Holy League had helped persuade him of the value of the resident ambassador – a figure increasingly employed by certain Italian states in the late fourteenth and fifteenth centuries. During the 1480s and 1490s, in his efforts to secure the diplomatic encirclement of France, Ferdinand established five resident embassies, at Rome, Venice, London, Brussels, and the migratory Austrian Court.[1] These resident embassies, which were to become permanent fixtures in Spain's diplomatic network, played a vital part in furthering the success of Spanish foreign policy. The men chosen to occupy them, like Dr Rodrigo de Puebla, the ambassador in London, were men of considerable ability, drawn from the same legally or clerically trained professional class which provided Ferdinand and Isabella with their councillors, judges, and administrators. Francisco de Rojas, who served in Rome and elsewhere, was a *hidalgo* of moderate means; de Puebla was a low-born *converso* with legal training, and a former *corregidor*. Both were Castilians, who were, in fact, much better represented in Ferdinand's foreign service than might have been expected in the light of the Crown of Aragon's much longer diplomatic tradition. They and their colleagues served Ferdinand with a loyalty that was by no means fully repaid. Invaluable as he found the reports of his resident ambassadors, he often failed to send them instructions, neglected to pay them, and not infrequently double-crossed them. There were, too, grave deficiencies in the whole organization of the Spanish foreign service. The absence of a fixed capital meant that diplomatic documents were scattered across Spain in a chaotic trail of papers which marked the route taken by Ferdinand on his travels. Letters went unanswered, treaties were lost. But the efficiency of the service increased as the reign went on, and if it was not yet as professional as that of some of the Italian states, it was far

1. See Garrett Mattingly, *Renaissance Diplomacy* (London, 1955), pp. 64–70 and 145–52.

superior to the diplomatic services of the majority of Ferdinand's enemies and allies.

With the entry of Charles VIII into Naples in 1495, however, it became clear that diplomacy must yield precedence to war. An expedition which had been sent to Sicily under the distinguished commander in the Granada campaign, the Great Captain Gonzalo de Córdoba, crossed over to Calabria in 1495. During his Italian campaigns of 1495–7 and 1501–4 Gonzalo was to show himself a commander of genius, quick to learn the lessons taught him by the enemy, and to apply them to his own troops. As a result, just as these years saw the creation of a professional diplomatic service that would serve Spain well for many years to come, so also they saw the creation of a professional army, whose skill and *esprit de corps* were to win Spain its great victories of the sixteenth and seventeenth centuries.

During the *Reconquista* the Castilians had tended to develop their light cavalry at the expense of their infantry. Light cavalry, however, proved unsuitable for bearing the brunt of the war in Italy; and after his defeat at Seminara, the first battle of his Italian campaign, Gonzalo began to search for new formations capable of withstanding the assault of Swiss pikes. It was clearly necessary to build up the infantry arm and to increase the number of arquebusiers. Borrowing both from the Swiss and the Italians, Gonzalo managed to revolutionize his army by the time of his triumphant battle of Cerignola in 1503, turning it essentially into an infantry army. In the Granada campaign the Spanish infantrymen, although still despised, had already shown their individual valour and their capacity for rapid movement, but against the French and Swiss they were far too lightly armed and inadequately protected. It was necessary to provide them with better protection, while somehow at the same time allowing them to maintain the speed and suppleness which could give them superiority over the more cumbersome ranks of the Swiss. This was finally achieved by equipping them with better protective armour – light helmets and cuirasses – and better offensive weapons, so that half were equipped with long pikes, a third with short sword and javelin, and the remaining sixth with arquebuses. At the same time the formations were entirely reorganized. The ancient units, the companies, too small for modern warfare, were now grouped into *coronelías* of perhaps four companies, each *coronelía* being supported by cavalry and artillery.

It was this organization, devised by the Great Captain, which provided the basis for the further development of the Spanish army during the sixteenth century. In 1534 the army was grouped into new model units called *tercios*, about three times the size of the *coronelías*. The 'sword and buckler men' of the Italian wars had now disappeared, and the *tercios* were composed only of arquebusiers and pikemen. A *tercio* generally consisted of twelve companies of about 250 men each, so that it was about 3,000 men strong, and it proved to be an extremely effective fighting force. It was less wasteful of manpower than the Swiss system, had greater fire-power, and was superb in defence, since attacking cavalry would break on the phalanx of pikes, which was deep enough to face an attack from every side. As a formation it dominated the battlefields of Europe for over a century, and its very success helped to reinforce the self-confidence of a fighting force which was, and knew itself to be, the best in the world.

Renaissance Italy therefore proved to be an ideal testing-ground both for Spanish diplomacy and for the Spanish military system; and if these were still imperfect instruments in the reign of Ferdinand, they none the less between them won him striking successes. Not only were the French defeated on the battlefield, but a combination of guile and diplomacy enabled Ferdinand to ease the Neapolitan dynasty off its throne. In 1504 the defeated French recognized the Spaniards as the lawful possessors of Naples. Naples thus rejoined Sicily and Sardinia as an Aragonese possession, and was brought, like them, under the government of viceroys and the jurisdiction of the Council of Aragon.

The winning of Naples was a triumph of the first magnitude for Ferdinand's 'Aragonese' foreign policy, in the furtherance of which he successfully engaged the resources of Castile. But the diplomatic manoeuvres which preceded and accompanied it were to have, for Spain in general and Castile in particular, consequences both unforeseen and unwanted. In the customary manner, Ferdinand had sealed his alliances with dynastic marriages. In order to reinforce the English alliance, a marriage was arranged between Catherine of Aragon and Arthur, Prince of Wales; and in 1496–7 the alliance between Spain and the Empire was solemnized in a double marriage between their two royal houses. The Infante Juan, the only son of the Catholic Kings and heir to the Spanish throne, married Margaret, daughter of the Emperor Maximilian, while their daughter Juana married Maximilian's son, the Archduke Philip. Juan, however, died six months after his marriage, and when Margaret was delivered of a still-born child any hope of a direct succession from Ferdinand and Isabella in the male line was destroyed. The succession would now devolve upon their eldest daughter Isabella of Portugal and her children by Emmanuel of Portugal, but Isabella's death in 1498, followed by that of her son Miguel in 1500, put an end also to this possibility. This meant that, from 1500, the succession, in a manner totally unforeseen, would go to the Infanta Juana, and eventually to her eldest son Charles, who would inherit both Spain and the Habsburg hereditary possessions.

The Union of Spain and the Habsburg lands was the last thing that Ferdinand and Isabella would have wished, but there now seemed no possibility of averting it. When Isabella died in November 1504 it was in the bitter knowledge that the government of her beloved Castile would go to a mentally unstable daughter, and to an incapable son-in-law who knew nothing of Spain and its ways, and showed no desire to learn. Ferdinand's foreign policy, which had begun by attempting to win allies for Spain in its struggle with the French, had ended by placing the Spanish inheritance in the hands of a foreign dynasty.

2. THE HABSBURG SUCCESSION

The twelve years separating the death of Isabella in 1504 from that of her husband in 1516 are incomprehensible in terms of purely Spanish history. From the moment of Isabella's death the fate of Spain was intimately connected with events in the court of Burgundy, where Juana and the Archduke Philip were waiting to take up their Spanish inheritance. During the following years there was a constant traffic between Castile and the Netherlands – a traffic of place-hunters and secret agents, participators in a squalid drama whose outcome determined the future of Spain.

Ferdinand himself, although not always the leading actor, was never

Table 2 THE SPANISH HABSBURGS (Names of Emperors in small capitals)

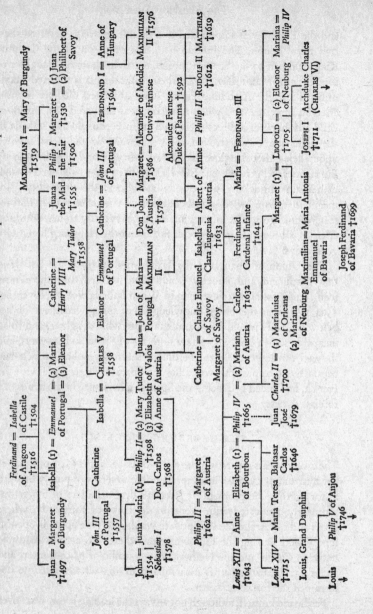

far from the centre of the stage. The 'old Catalan', as his enemies called him, had been placed in an unenviable position by his wife's will. Deprived of the rank and title of King of Castile, he was graciously permitted to govern the country during the absence of the new 'Queen Proprietress' Juana, or, in the event of her unwillingness to govern it herself, until her son Charles should reach the age of twenty. His new position as a mere administrator was not one to which Ferdinand could easily reconcile himself, and although he was prepared to give Philip the style of king in his correspondence, he none the less had Castilian coins stamped with the legend 'Ferdinand and Juana, King and Queen of Castile, León and Aragon'. But Philip, infirm in almost every purpose, was at least determined not to let his new inheritance go by default, and he could count on the support of many Castilian nobles, who hated Ferdinand as a strong ruler and also as a Catalan, and hoped to see him replaced by the compliant Philip. These nobles had valuable allies at the Burgundian Court, well placed to bring heavy pressure to bear on the Archduke. Juana's marriage, in particular, had brought to the Court several members of influential Spanish families, like her maid of honour, María Manuel, whose brother, Juan Manuel, related to great Castilian families like the Córdobas, the Silvas and the Mendozas, acted as the go-between for Philip's Burgundian advisers and the Castilian grandees.

While aristocratic intrigue was active in promoting the effective succession of Philip and Juana, there was, however, another, and perhaps more potent force operating in favour of a closer association between Castile and the Habsburgs' Burgundian possessions. The development of the Castilian wool trade had made the economies of Castile and the Low Countries mutually interdependent: indeed, by the middle of the sixteenth century nearly half of Spain's export trade was with the Netherlands, which in turn sent a third of its exports to Spain. The discovery of the Indies made the Spanish connexion all the more valuable to Netherlands merchants, in that colonial products and American silver were now added to the traditional Spanish exports of wool, wine, and oil. Economic considerations thus joined aristocratic ambition in producing a movement for closer Spanish–Habsburg ties.

Ferdinand was well aware of the danger, but could do little to avert it. The voice of aristocratic faction was being heard again in Castile, and the supporters of Ferdinand were few. While he persuaded the Cortes of Toro in January 1505 to ratify his title to the regency, his position was becoming increasingly insecure and would be untenable if ever Philip and Juana set foot on Castilian soil. In an effort to ward off the moment of disaster, he now totally reversed his traditional foreign policy, and made a bid for French support, which led to the treaty of Blois with Louis XII in October 1505. By this treaty, Ferdinand was to marry Louis's niece, Germaine de Foix. Ferdinand's remarriage, while part of the diplomatic game, had also a deeper purpose. If Germaine were to produce an heir, the whole question of the succession would be dramatically reopened. It might be possible to put forward the child as a rival to the Habsburg candidature for the throne of a united Spain; and if this manoeuvre should prove unsuccessful, at least the Crown of Aragon could be saved from the hands of a foreign dynasty. While the crown of a united Spain was naturally a much more desirable prize, Ferdinand was perfectly capable, if circumstances required it, of turning his back on his life's work and dissolving a union between Castile and Aragon which had always been purely personal in character. But, in the event, neither the hopes nor the fears aroused by Ferdinand's remarriage were to be realized. Germaine did, in fact, bear a son in 1509, but he lived only a few hours. With the death of this child the last real possibility of a new fragmentation of Spain was effectively removed. The Union of the Crowns was, after all, to be permanent.

Ferdinand's second marriage merely strengthened the ties between the grandees and the Archduke Philip, who had now decided to make the journey to Spain. In preparation for his arrival he patched up a compromise with Ferdinand in November 1505, for a tripartite government of Ferdinand, Juana, and himself. Leaving Guillaume de Croy, Sieur de Chièvres, to govern the Netherlands in his absence, he sailed from Flanders on 10 January 1506, only to be wrecked off the coast of England. It was not until 21 April that he was able to set sail again, and in the meantime the Castilian nobility had profited from the weakness of government to reopen its old feuds. In spite of the agreement between the two rulers, neither had the slightest confidence in the other's promises, and Philip seems to have toyed with the idea of landing in Andalusia and summoning the nobles to take up arms against Ferdinand. But second thoughts prevailed, and he chose instead to land at Corunna and to seek a peaceful agreement with his father-in-law. Ferdinand for his part was preparing for armed resistance, but as soon as Philip landed on 26 April almost the entire higher nobility went over to him, leaving Ferdinand bereft of influential supporters. There was nothing for it now but to play for time. The two men met on 20 June 1506, and signed an agreement seven days later at Villafáfila, whereby Ferdinand handed over the government of Castile to his 'most beloved children', and promised to retire to Aragon. At the same time Philip and Ferdinand agreed that Juana's mental infirmities made her incapable of government, and signed a second treaty excluding her from it. The same afternoon Ferdinand announced that he refused to recognize the validity of the agreements, and that his daughter should never be deprived of her rights as Queen Proprietress of Castile. A fortnight later, having won complete freedom of action to interfere in the Castilian succession question whenever he wished, he left Castile, to await better times.

By September he was in Naples, where he relieved the Castilian officials, including the viceroy, Gonzalo de Córdoba, of their offices. But if he thought that his long association with Castile had finally ended, he was soon proved wrong. On 25 September the Archduke Philip suddenly died. His death pushed his grief-stricken widow over the brink into open insanity, and left his six-year-old son, Charles of Ghent, who was still in Flanders, as heir to the Spanish throne. A regency council was set up under the presidency of Archbishop Cisneros, but in face of the growing public disorder in Castile, Cisneros and others appealed to Ferdinand to return. The old King was careful to bide his time. Nearly a year elapsed before he came back to Castile, where he moved with great care, slowly consolidating his position before rounding on factious nobles like the Marquis of Priego. In 1509 his daughter, now utterly mad, retired with her husband's corpse to Tordesillas, where she was to pass the remaining forty-six years of her life in a state of deep deranged melancholy shot through with sudden moments of lucidity – Queen of Castile to the end of her days. In view of her obvious unfitness to govern, the Cortes of Castile named Ferdinand administrator of the kingdom in 1510.

Any satisfaction that Ferdinand may have felt at his re-establishment in the government of Castile is likely to have been mitigated by rue-

ful contemplation of the future that awaited his kingdoms. He may
have cherished hopes that his grandson Ferdinand, who was being
educated in Spain, would somehow eventually assume the government instead of his elder brother Charles of Ghent, to whom Ferdinand had transferred the animosity he had previously felt for Philip.
But short of an act of providence – of which there had admittedly
been a singular number in his lifetime – the prospects appeared unfavourable. Perhaps despairing of the future, he chose to leave the
government of Castile largely in the hands of Cisneros, and to devote
himself instead to foreign policy, and in particular to the perennial
Italian question.

During the last years of his life, Ferdinand's diplomatic ability was
revealed at its greatest, and won further advantages for a Spain he had
already served so long and so well. As always, his aim was to preserve
the Aragonese possessions in Italy and to prevent any further expansion of French power, but he also seems to have looked beyond this
to the establishment of a general European peace which would enable
him to undertake a crusade for the conquest of Egypt and the recovery
of Jerusalem. This perhaps rather unexpected ambition remained un-
fulfilled, and was transmitted, along with the rivalry with France, to
the Flemish grandson whom Ferdinand so heartily disliked.

He did, however, achieve a more restricted, and perhaps more use-
ful, ambition in these final years. He had long wanted to round off his
conquests with the acquisition of the little independent kingdom of
Navarre, of which his father, John II of Aragon, had once been king.
Since then, Navarre had passed in turn to the families of Foix and
Albret. Claiming that a secret alliance between the Albrets and France
included a provision for a joint French-Navarrese invasion of Castile,
Ferdinand sent an army into Navarre under the command of the
Duke of Alba in July 1512. The country was occupied without difficulty, and Ferdinand made use of his alliance with the Papacy to
obtain the formal deposition of the Albrets and the removal of their
sovereign rights.

The acquisition of Navarre was a source of enormous satisfaction
to Ferdinand on sentimental grounds, but he can hardly have been
unaware of the other advantages of its possession, which were listed
by the Florentine Guicciardini, then on an embassy to Spain. According to Guicciardini, Navarre was a fine state, not so much for its

revenues, which were relatively small, but for the 'conformity' which it had with Ferdinand's other kingdoms. It was valuable, too, because it closed the passage into Spain, while allowing the Spaniards entry into France.[2] Here were the defensible frontiers and the relative uniformity of customs and language, which were increasingly being regarded as desirable features for a prince who was bent on extending his dominions. Politically, however, the uniformity was no greater than that which existed between Castile and the Crown of Aragon. The kingdom of Navarre possessed, and was allowed to retain, its own customs, coinage, and institutions, including a Cortes and a *Diputación*. As might have been expected from Navarre's past associ-ation with the Aragonese dynasty, it was joined on its annexation to the Crown of Aragon; but three years later Ferdinand changed his mind, fearing perhaps, as the chronicler Zurita suggests, that union with the Crown of Aragon would encourage the Navarrese to extend their liberties and exemptions. Perhaps also because he wished to commit Castile to the protection of Navarre, he arranged in 1515 for its definitive incorporation into the Crown of Castile, although its semi-autonomous government continued to remain untouched.

If Ferdinand hoped to placate his enemies in Castile by the gift of Navarre he was to be disappointed. His government, dominated by Aragonese officials, was becoming increasingly unpopular, and Castil-ian nationalist sentiment – briefly disillusioned by the behaviour of the Archduke Philip – was again turning to the Burgundians for help. The Great Captain, the Marquis of Priego, and other leading nobles were all planning in 1515 to leave Spain and take service with their new hope, Charles of Ghent. But this proved to be unnecessary. Ferdinand was ailing, and he died at the village of Madrigalejo in

2. Francesco Guicciardini, *Legazione di Spagna* (Pisa, 1825), pp. 61–2 (letter xvi, 17 September 1512). The word 'conformità' used by Guicciardini remains vague, but it would seem not unreasonable to assume that he was thinking of language as well as of habits and customs. Machiavelli is more explicit in the third chapter of *The Prince*, where he says that conquered states are easier to hold when they are of the same 'language, customs, and laws' as the country which conquers them. The 'conformity' of Navarre to Ferdinand's other kingdoms, while by no means complete, was certainly no less close than that of Brittany and Gascony to France, which Machiavelli adduces as examples of his maxim. [While the southern part of Navarre went to Spain in 1512, the northern, French, part remained an independent state until the accession of Henry of Navarre to the French throne as Henry IV.]

Estremadura on 23 January 1516. The man who had achieved so much – the Union of the Crowns, the annexation of Navarre, the ordering of Spain and its promotion to the ranks of the great European powers – died embittered and resentful, cheated not by his opponents, all of whom he had outwitted, but by a malignant fate which had placed his masterwork in the hands of alien descendants.

On his death-bed Ferdinand had been reluctantly persuaded to rescind a previous will in favour of his younger grandson Ferdinand, and to name Charles of Ghent as his heir. He also arranged that, until Charles should come to Spain to take up his inheritance, his bastard son Alonso de Aragón should act as regent of Aragon, Catalonia, and Valencia, while the government of Castile should be entrusted to Cardinal Cisneros. The Cardinal ruled Castile with all the authoritarianism of the humble cleric elevated to a high secular command, but nothing less could have saved the country from anarchy. Even if death opportunely removed the Great Captain and the Duke of Nájera, there were still many dangerous nobles whose feuds and ambitions were a constant threat to public order. Not only were there fierce faction struggles, like those between the Duke of Infantado and the Count of La Coruña, but the grandees were determined to discredit Cisneros in the eyes of Charles's advisers in Brussels. Failing this, they planned to proclaim the Infante Ferdinand king. A group of nobles, including the Duke of Alburquerque, the Count of Benavente, and Don Pedro Girón, met at the Duke of Infantado's palace in Guadalajara to plot the overthrow of the Cardinal, but Cisneros was too quick for them. The Infante was separated from his closest adherents, and, in order to forestall an aristocratic attempt to seize control of the government, a volunteer militia was raised in Castile, known as the *gente de la ordenanza* and inspired by the old *Hermandad*.

This militia of some 30,000 well-equipped men was a kind of standing army, and offered a foretaste of arbitrary power that was by no means to the liking of nobles or towns. Cisneros was too inflexible, his hand too heavy; and the mounting complaints against his government found answering echoes in Brussels. But the death of Ferdinand had to some extent modified the relationship between the leaders of Castilian discontent and Charles's Flemish advisers. As long as Ferdinand lived, the more intransigent Castilian nationalists, exasperated by the Aragonese characteristics of his régime, could turn to the Flemings for sympathy and support. But Ferdinand's death made Charles the ruler of Aragon as well as of Castile – a fact that Ferdinand's former servants were quick to appreciate. As soon as their old master was dead, they flocked to Brussels – men like Lope Conchillos, Ferdinand's principal secretary; the Aragonese secretaries, Pedro de Quintana and Ugo de Urríes; Antonio Agustín, vice-chancellor of the Council of Aragon; and a non-Aragonese official, Francisco de los Cobos, chief assistant of Lope Conchillos. On arriving in Brussels, most of these men were confirmed in their offices, to the deep distress of Cisneros, who sent constant warnings to Flanders against the employment of Ferdinand's former servants, many of them notoriously corrupt.

There was, then, constant friction between the government of Cisneros and the growing circle of Spanish officials around Charles. But the Castilian aristocracy, which loathed the government of Cisneros, was equally finding Charles's circle of Spanish advisers increasingly unpalatable. Many of them came from the Crown of Aragon, 'and it would be better for the kingdom that its affairs were entrusted to the purest-bred Frenchman than to an Aragonese'.[3] Even worse, most of them were *conversos*. A future Government of Flemings, Aragonese, and Jews was the last thing the Castilians had envisaged when they originally placed their hopes in Charles of Ghent.

Yet such a government was becoming increasingly possible, for the moment of Charles's long-awaited visit to Spain was at last approaching. On 4 July 1517 Charles and his suite arrived at Middleburg, where the fleet awaited them, but it was held up for two months by contrary winds, and was unable to leave until the second week of September. Even then, instead of landing at Santander according to plan, Charles was forced by bad weather to disembark on a wild stretch of the Asturian coast. The days that followed his landing had a curious dreamlike quality, and must have seemed to Charles a strange introduction to his new dominions. With his suite of 200 ladies and gentlemen, inadequately supplied with horses, mules, and ox-carts that had been hastily gathered together to meet the emergency,

3. Jorge Varacaldo to Diego López de Ayala, 27 September 1516, *Cartas de los Secretarios del Cardenal . . . Jiménez de Cisneros . . .*, ed. Vicente de la Fuente (Madrid, 1875), p. 29.

he was led along the winding mountain routes of north Spain, through a barbarous countryside totally unprepared to receive him. To make matters worse, he fell ill on the journey, and his physicians insisted that the party move inland, away from the dangerous sea air. Through fog and drenching rain it moved slowly southwards. At last on 4 November it arrived at Tordesillas, where Charles and his sister had a brief meeting with a mother whom they could scarcely remember. The real purpose of this meeting was to secure from Juana the necessary authorization for Charles to assume royal power; once this was given, Charles could act as King of Castile.

The first move of Charles's principal adviser, Chièvres, was to send a letter to Cisneros instructing him to meet the King, and advising him that in future his services would no longer be required. Cisneros was now gravely ill, and on the very day the letter arrived – 8 November 1517 – he died at Roa near Valladolid. The old tradition that the arrival of the letter hastened the Cardinal's death is unlikely to be true, but there could be no doubt of the significance of Chièvres's letter. For the past two years Cisneros and the Castilians had been struggling to wrest Charles from the hands of his Burgundian advisers, and had planned to secure control of his government as soon as he arrived in Spain. Cisneros's letter of dismissal showed that this plan had failed. The Castilians had been worsted by Chièvres and his Flemings, and had seen all their forebodings confirmed. The alien Habsburg had assumed the government of Spain – and assumed it with alien ministers.

3. NATIONALISM AND REVOLT

The new King, a gawky, unprepossessing youth with an absurdly pronounced jaw, did not make a favourable impression on his first appearance in Spain. Apart from looking like an idiot, he suffered from the unforgivable defect of knowing no Castilian. In addition, he was totally ignorant of Spanish affairs, and was surrounded by an entourage of rapacious Flemings. It was natural to contrast him un-favourably with his brother Ferdinand, who enjoyed the supreme advantage of a Castilian upbringing – a background that seemed to Charles's advisers to be so fraught with danger for the future that they shipped Ferdinand off to Flanders a few months after his brother's arrival in Spain. His departure, which (as was intended) deprived the grandees of a potential figurehead and the populace of a symbol, merely increased the discontents of a disaffected nation.

The principal complaint of the Castilians was directed against the Flemings, who were alleged to be plundering the country so fortuitously inherited by their duke. Castilian allegations of Flemish rapacity have sometimes been treated with scepticism, on the grounds that the information about the iniquities of the Flemings comes overwhelmingly from humanist writers like Pietro Martire, who hated the aristocratic world of Chièvres and his friends, or from royal officials like Galíndez de Carvajal, disappointed in their hopes of the new régime. But there is sufficient evidence to suggest that, even if the Castilians exaggerated the failings of foreigners whom they neither liked nor understood, the alleged rapacity of the Flemings is firmly rooted in fact. Charles was a pawn in the hands of his Grand Chamberlain Chièvres, and offices and honours went to Chièvres's friends. Charles's tutor, Adrian of Utrecht, who had been in Spain since 1515 as his special agent, received the bishopric of Tortosa. Chièvres himself was given the lucrative post of *contador mayor* of Castile, which he sold to the Duke of Béjar for 30,000 ducats, while his sixteen-year-old nephew, Guillaume de Croy, was appointed to the Archbishopric of Toledo itself. Chièvres's wife, and the wife of Charles's chief equerry, Charles de Lannoy, were each given passports to take out of Spain three hundred horses and eighty pack-mules laden with clothes, bullion, and jewellery. The Governor of Bresse, Laurent Gorrevod, was granted the first licence to ship negroes to the Indies – a privilege calculated to be worth 25,000 ducats when he sold it to the Genoese. No doubt the stories about the 'plundering' of Castile by the Flemings were magnified in the telling, and were deliberately distorted for purposes of propaganda, but at least enough was taken to give point to the little rhyme composed by the Castilians in honour of the occasional ducat that had not yet gone to Flanders:

> Doblón de a dos, norabuena estedes
> Pues con vos no topó Xevres.[4]

When the Cortes were held at Valladolid in January 1518 to swear allegiance to the new King and vote him a *servicio*, the *procuradores*

4. 'Congratulations, double doublon, on not falling into Chièvres's hands.

seized the opportunity to protest against the exploitation of Castile by foreigners; and they found some outlet for their indignation in addressing Charles only as 'su Alteza', reserving the title of 'Magestad' exclusively for his mother, Juana.

After the conclusion of the Castilian Cortes, Charles left for the Crown of Aragon, arriving at Zaragoza on 9 May. During the seven months spent by the Court at Zaragoza, where the Cortes showed themselves a good deal more obdurate than those of Valladolid, the highly unpopular Grand Chancellor, Jean Sauvage, died, and was replaced by a much more cosmopolitan character, Mercurino Gattinara. The change of officers fittingly preceded by a few months a total change in Charles's affairs. News reached Charles as he was on the road to Barcelona at the end of January 1519 of the death of his grandfather Maximilian; five months later, after long intrigues and the expenditure of vast sums of money, he was elected Emperor in his grandfather's place. Gattinara, a man whose broad imperial vision was inspired by a cosmopolitan background, an acquaintance with the political writings of Dante, and, most of all, by the humanist's longings for a *respublica christiana*, showed himself fully prepared for the change. Charles was no longer to be styled 'su Alteza', but 'S.C.C.R. Magestad' (Sacra, Cesárea, Católica, Real Magestad). The Duke of Burgundy, King of Castile and León, King of Aragon and Count of Barcelona, had now added to his imposing list of titles the most impressive of all: Emperor-elect of the Holy Roman Empire.

Charles's election as Emperor inevitably altered his relationship to his Spanish subjects. It did much to increase his prestige, opening up new and unexpected horizons, of which the Catalans – as a result of his residence among them at this moment – were probably the first to become aware. Charles himself was changing, and beginning at last to acquire a personality of his own; he seems to have established an easier relationship with his Catalan subjects than with the tightly suspicious Castilians; and Barcelona for a glorious six months revelled in its position as the capital of the Empire. If a foreign ruler had obvious disadvantages, there might none the less be compensations, as yet barely glimpsed.

It was the disadvantages, however, which most impressed the Castilians as Charles hurried back across Castile in January 1520 to embark for England and Germany. If the King of Castile were also to be Holy Roman Emperor, this was likely to lead to two serious consequences for Castile. It would involve long periods of royal absenteeism, and it would also involve a higher rate of taxation in order to finance the King's increased expenditure. Already, at the news of Charles's election, voices were raised in protest against his impending departure. The protests originated in the city of Toledo, which was to play the leading part in the troubles of the next two years, for reasons that are not yet fully clear. The city seems somehow to have exemplified, in heightened form, all the tensions and conflicts within Castile, offering an illuminating example of the constant interaction of local and national affairs.

Like Córdoba, Seville, and any other large town in Castile and Andalusia, Toledo was torn by the feuds of great noble houses, whose rivalries reached back far into the past. Inevitably, rival families had ranged themselves on different sides during the civil wars of the fifteenth century, and the pattern was repeated in the succession struggles that followed the death of Isabella. Toledo itself was divided into two principal factions: the Ayalas, led by the Count of Fuensalida, and the Riberas, headed by Don Juan de Ribera. The Riberas had supported Ferdinand in 1504, while the Ayalas, and their friends the Ávalos, had thrown in their lot with the Archduke Philip. They duly reaped their reward after Philip's arrival in Castile with the appointment of Hernando de Ávalos as *corregidor* of Jérez de la Frontera, but Ávalos was relieved of his post on Philip's unexpected death. Until 1516 the Riberas were in the ascendant, but, with the death of Ferdinand, the fortunes of the rival families were once again reversed, and Cisneros restored Ávalos to office. The triumph of the Ayala faction, however, was short-lived, for it fell victim to the new political feuds generated during the Cisneros régime of 1516–17. As former supporters of the Archduke Philip, the Ayalas might reasonably have expected to continue in favour after the arrival of his son Charles in Spain; but so bad were the relations between the Cisneros group and Charles's Flemish advisers, that Chièvres removed many of the Cardinal's supporters, including the unfortunate Hernando de Ávalos, from office.

By 1519, therefore, there had been a strange reversal of roles. The Ribera faction, the old supporters of Ferdinand against a Habsburg succession, now found themselves favoured by the Chièvres régime,

THE FOUR INHERITANCES
OF CHARLES V

from his paternal grandfather
Maximilian of Austria
from his paternal grandmother
Mary of Burgundy
from his maternal grandfather
Ferdinand of Aragon
from his maternal grandmother
Isabella of Castile

DENMARK

D

Lübeck
Hamburg

Leipzig
Cologne
Erfurt
EMPIRE
Prague
SILESIA
BOHEMIA
Nuremberg
MORAVIA
Ulm
Vienna
Augsburg
AUSTRIA
STYRIA
Basle
Innsbruck
CARINTHIA
ZERLAND
TYROL
Villach
REPUBLIC
OF
VENICE
Trieste
va
DUCHY OF
MILAN
Milan
Venice
Pavia
Mantua
Genoa

Mühlberg

KINGDOM
OF
HUNGARY

OTTOMAN
EMPIRE

Nice

PAPAL
STATES

CORSICA
Rome
Ragusa

KINGDOM
OF
NAPLES
Naples
CORFU

SARDINIA
Lepanto

Messina
Palermo

SICILY

RANEAN
Bona
Tunis
La Goletta
SEA
GERIA

Map 4

and became loyal supporters of the dynasty they had formerly mistrusted. The Ayalas, on the other hand, disillusioned by the treatment they had received at the hands of a dynasty they had originally supported, now openly identified themselves with the anti-Flemish, Castilian nationalist sentiments of which their patron Cardinal Cisneros had been the symbol.

Family feuds, while crucially important, cannot, however, explain in every instance the alignment of two opposing factions – for and against the Emperor – that was now taking place in Castile. Hernando de Ávalos, the real leader of the Ayalas, found an influential ally in another *caballero* of Toledo, Juan de Padilla, who by origin was a member of the rival faction of the Riberas, and had married a Mendoza – a family loyal to Charles. Padilla was a disgruntled and embittered man, who felt himself to have been slighted in the distribution of favours; and if he was hardly the man to turn spontaneously from indignation to action, his ambitious wife María Pacheco suffered from no such inhibitions. Padilla and his friends now took it upon themselves to voice the discontents of Castile. In November 1519 they wrote to the leading cities, pointing out that Charles had spent much longer in Aragon than in Castile, and proposing a meeting of municipal representatives. These were to make certain demands: that Charles should not leave the country; that no more money should be allowed to go abroad; and that foreigners should not be appointed to offices in Spain.

In an atmosphere of impending crisis, Chièvres and Gattinara pressed ahead with their plans for Charles's departure. These plans included another session of the Castilian Cortes to vote a further *servicio*. The subsidy of 600,000 ducats voted at Valladolid in 1518 was intended to cover a period of three years; but money was needed at once for the Emperor's journey, since the sums granted by the Cortes of the Crown of Aragon had proved insufficient. Charles's advisers, however failed to prepare Castilian public opinion or to mollify bruised feelings by tactful concessions. They hoped to weaken the opposition by disregarding precedent and summoning the Cortes to Santiago, a remote town convenient only for Charles, who was to embark at the nearby port of Corunna. They also insisted that the *procuradores* to the Cortes should come armed with full powers. This itself was not a novel demand, for the Crown had insisted on full powers being given both in 1499 and 1506. Since then, however, its authority had been undermined by the succession struggles, and both the demand for full powers and the choice of Santiago as the site of the Cortes merely added to the anger of the towns. When the Cortes opened at Santiago on 1 April 1520 it was found that Salamanca had flatly defied the royal order, and that other towns had prepared secret instructions for their *procuradores*. In fact, only Burgos, Granada, and Seville, whose town councils were dominated by Charles's adherents, had given their representatives the full powers requested by the Crown.

The *proposición real* read at the opening session by Ruiz de la Mota, Bishop of Palencia, elaborated on the imperial theme on which he had already expatiated, as Bishop of Badajoz, in the Cortes of 1518. He had explained on the earlier occasion how the Empire had turned to Spain for its Emperor. While still insisting on the universalism of the Empire and the absolute necessity for Charles's departure from Spain, he and the Emperor were now especially careful to emphasize that Spain itself was the foundation of the Empire and that Charles would be back in three years at the most. Even the idea of a Spanish-based Empire, however, did nothing to placate the Cortes. The *procuradores* refused to believe that Charles would ever return, and the majority were not prepared to vote a subsidy until their grievances had been considered. On 10 April, hoping to gain time which could be used to put pressure on individual *procuradores*, Gattinara transferred the Cortes from Santiago to Corunna. The interval was obviously used to some effect, for a majority eventually approved the subsidy, although six towns still stubbornly resisted. Having obtained what he wanted (although the subsidy was, in fact, never collected), Charles nominated Adrian of Utrecht as regent, and set sail on 20 May to take up his inheritance. But he left behind him a nation in revolt.

The revolt of the *Comuneros*, which began in the last week of May 1520 and continued until the defeat of the *Comuneros* at the battle of Villalar on 23 April 1521 was a confused affair, lacking in cohesion and a sense of positive purpose, but at the same time expressing, however inarticulately, deep-seated grievances and a burning sense of national indignation. Essentially it was a movement *against*, rather than *for*, any particular object: in so far as the *Comuneros* were animated by any constructive ideals, these consisted in the preservation of the old Castile – a Castile untouched by the dangerous winds that were beginning to blow so strongly from abroad. In spite of the determination of nineteenth-century historians to depict the revolt as liberal and democratic, it was in its origins fundamentally traditional, as the demands of the *Comuneros* themselves suggested.[5] The revolt had been sparked off by the attack on the independence of the Cortes; and the desire of the rebels to preserve that independence gave it, at least in part, the character of a constitutional movement. But there was little that was radical in their constitutional demands, other than the request that the towns should have the right to assemble Cortes on their own initiative every three years. No attempt was made to secure for the Cortes the right of legislation, nor was any attempt made to strengthen it by the inclusion of new towns. The prime concern of the Cortes was to preserve intact its traditional rights, and it therefore concentrated on demanding that the *procuradores* should be paid by the cities rather than the Crown, and that they should not be told to come with full powers.

There was, then, no attempt to set up the Castilian Cortes as a partner of the Crown in the work of government, let alone to promote the idea of the Cortes as a possible alternative government. However radical may have been the action of the rebels in forming a revolutionary Junta, they remained conservative in intention. Theirs was constitutionally a movement on the defensive – a movement of angry reaction to a long period in which royal government, whether exercised by the Catholic Kings or by Cardinal Cisneros, had eroded away many of the traditional powers and prerogatives of the Castilian towns. It was significant that one of the demands sent to the Emperor by the revolutionary Junta of Tordesillas on 20 October 1520 was that no *corregidor* should in future be appointed, except at the specific request of the town concerned. However sudden and complete the collapse of royal authority in 1520, it was clear that the hand of government had lain heavy on the towns in the none too distant past.

The essentially moderate character of the rebels' constitutional demands hardly suggested the depth of feeling behind the revolt, nor the violent form that it was shortly to assume. For all the importance

5. The demands are printed in Prudencio de Sandoval, *Vida y Hechos del Emperador Carlos V*, vol. 1 (Pamplona, 1614), pp. 304–38.

of the constitutional grievances of the municipalities, these were heavily outweighed among the mass of the Castilian populace by other complaints of more general appeal. It was well known that the King had asked for money, not once but twice in the space of three years. It was universally assumed that the country was being stripped bare by foreigners, who were sending shiploads of its wealth abroad. The behaviour of the King's Flemish suite had made an indelible impression on the minds of those who had seen it – which meant, in practice, the towns of north and central Castile. A sermon preached by a Dominican at Valladolid in the summer of 1520 forcefully expressed their feelings: 'It is of these realms that Your Majesty is true sovereign and proprietor, and you have bought with money the Empire, which ought not to pass nor be transmitted to your heirs; and Your Majesty has reduced the realm to the poverty in which it stands, and your followers have enriched themselves excessively.'[6] The real spur to revolution was thus a burning hatred of the foreigners and of a foreign rule which was stripping the country of its wealth; and this nationalistic indignation was reflected in the demands of the Junta of Tordesillas that the King should live in Castile, that he should bring no 'Flemings, Frenchmen, nor natives of any other country' to fill the posts in his household, and that in everything he should conform to the customs of the 'Catholic Sovereigns Don Fernando and Doña Isabel, his grandparents'.

It does not seem to have occurred to the rebels that there might be a certain incompatibility between their anxiety to return to the days of Ferdinand and Isabella and their desire to loosen the tight grasp of the Crown. The Catholic Kings were already passing into history – symbols of a golden age to which Castile would for ever aspire to return. The rebels remembered Isabella's piety and wisdom, not her zealous concern to extend her royal powers. They remembered the 'secure liberty' she had given them, and forgot its authoritarian overtones. Measuring the present against an idealized past, when a Castile ruled by a truly Castilian sovereign had wrought great things, they raised the banner of revolt in a gallant but hopeless attempt to prove to themselves that, although everything was different, it could still be the same.

Since they championed at the outset a cause with wide general

6. Quoted by H. L. Seaver, *The Great Revolt in Castile* (London, n.d.), p. 303.

appeal, the rebels secured a great body of support that appeared at first to ignore the sharp social divisions within Castile. Although agricultural labourers fought in the *Comunero* army, the revolt was essentially an urban revolt, confined at first to the towns of north Castile, which had first-hand experience of Charles's Flemish following. But within the towns the movement seems, at the beginning, to have been general. The clergy, monks, and friars, were violent partisans of the revolt, partly perhaps out of mistrust for the new ideas entering Spain from Flanders and the north. Many urban nobles and gentry, like the Maldonados of Salamanca, also showed themselves sympathetic to the rebels. The grandees on the whole behaved with extreme caution. While they sympathized with many of the aspirations of the rebels, they chose to play a waiting game, like the Duke of Infantado, hoping to see which way the battle would go before taking sides.

The movement began in the towns with popular risings against royal officials: *corregidores* were forced to flee for their lives. The populace would then turn for leadership to some members of a distinguished local family, as in Toledo, where the royal administration was replaced by a commune headed by Pedro Laso de la Vega and Juan de Padilla. During the summer of 1520 other towns followed Toledo's example and set up communes of their own. It was essential to co-ordinate the activities of these communes, but the traditional rivalry of the towns of Castile made the task a difficult one, and when the Toledo leaders summoned a congress of *Comunero* representatives at Ávila in July, only delegates from Segovia, Salamanca, and Toro appeared. But at the moment when enthusiasm seemed to be flagging Adrian of Utrecht and his regency council played into the hands of Padilla and his friends by ordering an attack on Segovia. Unable to press home its assault, the royalist force moved to the great arsenal town of Medina del Campo in search of siege artillery, only to be met with fierce resistance by the townspeople. In the street fighting that followed a number of houses were fired, the flames took hold and a large part of the city was burnt to the ground.

The burning of Medina del Campo on 21 August 1520 transformed the situation in Castile. The destruction of the greatest financial and commercial centre in the country provoked a wave of indignation which for the first time stirred the cities of the south, brought Jaén into the *Comunero* movement, and induced the defaulting towns of the north to send their representatives to the Junta at Ávila. But it was ominous that the new-found unity of the *Comuneros* was the product only of a fresh upsurge of indignation. The fundamental problem of finding a common programme of action remained unsolved, and it was in an attempt to resolve this problem that the leaders of the Junta turned to the one source of authority in Castile potentially higher than that of Adrian of Utrecht – the mad Queen Juana. If they could once secure her written recognition of the legality of their cause, their triumph would be complete. At Tordesillas in September Padilla managed to elicit from the Queen expressions of sympathy for his aims, but Juana stubbornly refused to sign any documents. Although Adrian and his council were chased out of Valladolid shortly afterwards, and the Junta prepared to assume the government of Castile, Padilla, in fact, had shot his final bolt.

Away in the Netherlands the Emperor's advisers, already distracted by the problem of Luther, decided after much discussion that certain concessions should be made. They agreed to suspend the collection of the *servicio* and to appoint no more foreigners to offices in Castile, and they also decided to associate the two most important grandees, the Admiral and the Constable of Castile, with the regency government of Adrian of Utrecht. Their bid to win back the great nobility to active loyalty to Charles proved to be well timed. Since the interviews with Juana in the autumn of 1520, the *Comunero* movement had been running into trouble. The Flemings were now far away, Adrian was at the worst but a pallid replica of Chièvres, and time and distance were beginning to blunt the indignation that had given impetus to revolt. In the towns the rising was rapidly degenerating into civil war between traditional enemies, and in the Junta of the *Comuneros* itself, where opinions were divided on the next step to be taken, power was falling into the hands of the more extreme. Voices were now beginning to be raised against the power of the nobles and the rich. A movement which had begun as a national rising against a foreign régime was assuming some of the aspects of a social revolution.

This could not but affect the attitude of the nobles, whose tacit approval, if not active encouragement, was essential if the revolt were to win lasting success. The dangers to the aristocracy inherent in any general revolution were already at this very moment being vividly illustrated by events in Valencia. Here, curiously divorced from events in Castile, another revolutionary drama had been unfolding on its own. Discontent had begun to flare up in Valencia as early as the summer of 1519, while Charles was in Barcelona. This time it had nothing to do with the behaviour of the Flemings, of which the Valencians had seen nothing: indeed, if there was any cause for political discontent it lay in the absence, not the presence, of the King and his Court. The prime motive for unrest, however, was not political but social. Orders had been given for the arming of the guilds against possible raids on the Valencian coast by Turkish galleys. At this moment, in the summer of 1519, the city of Valencia was struck by plague, which a preacher in Valencia Cathedral pronounced to be a divine chastisement for the prevailing immorality. If this was so, it seemed particularly unjust that the most immoral of all – the nobles and the rich – should escape its consequences by fleeing the city. Feelings were running high, all those in authority had fled, and the armed artisans in the guilds banded together in a *Germanía* or brotherhood, which took over control of the city and then began to extend its power into the countryside. This was an urban movement – a movement of middling burgesses, of weavers, spinners, artisans – and it was led in its first months by a Catalan weaver resident in Valencia, Juan Llorenç, who hoped to turn Valencia into a republic like Venice. But extremists like Vicenç Peris wrested control of the movement from the hands of Llorenç (who died shortly afterwards); and they turned it against the nobles and their Morisco vassals, whom they forcibly baptized.

While the *Comuneros* were rising in Castile, therefore, the rebel *Germanía* of Valencia had become a violently radical social movement. Although its aims had been curiously vague since the death of Llorenç, it clearly constituted a grave threat to aristocratic power and to the whole hierarchical order. It is difficult to determine what repercussions this had on the nobility in other parts of Spain. It is perhaps significant that the Aragonese nobility, unpleasantly close to the movement in Valencia, showed no sympathy for the *Comunero* cause. There are also signs that the Valencian troubles had an impact farther afield. In Murcia, for instance, Don Pedro Fajardo, first Marquis of los Vélez – whose former tutor, the great humanist Pietro Martire, had written him scathing descriptions of the behaviour of the Flemings – had at first supported the *Comuneros*. But when the revolt of the communes in Murcia came to be infected by the more extreme spirit of the *Germanías*, los Vélez prudently changed sides and raised his own army against the Valencian rebels.

As the Castilian nobility, affected either by events in Valencia or by the growing radicalism of the movement nearer home, gradually retreated from their earlier sympathetic attitude into strict neutrality or outright hostility, the *Comuneros* in turn became increasingly anti-aristocratic in their pronouncements and actions. During the winter of 1520 and the early spring of 1521 the revolt of the *Comuneros* began to turn into a social struggle against the nobility, as the extremist faction in the Junta, led by Gonzalo de Guzmán of León, defeated Laso de la Vega and his moderates. Towns under seigneurial jurisdiction, like Nájera and Dueñas, renounced obedience to their lords; and anti-aristocratic sentiments reached their climax in the Junta's announcement of 10 April 1521 that war would in future be waged with 'fire, sack, and blood' against the estates and properties of 'grandees, *caballeros*, and other enemies of the realm'. The revolt of the *Comuneros* had been transformed into a social revolution.

As such, it was doomed. It forfeited the assistance of the aristocracy, which was indispensable for any permanent success, and it alienated the more moderate rebels, who ceased to attend the Junta. Adrian of Utrecht and his advisers had managed to win back Burgos into the royalist camp during the course of the winter, and, as fear of social upheaval spread, one after another of the towns of Castile and Andalusia followed Burgos's lead. The *Comuneros*, however, found some compensation for these losses in the adherence of a disgruntled noble, Don Pedro Girón, and in the vigorous support of Antonio de Acuña, Bishop of Zamora, who came to their help with a private army over two thousand strong. Acuña was the last of the warrior-prelates of Castile, and the most formidable of them all. A member of the family of Acuña, one of the great houses of central Castile, he had found favour with Ferdinand and Isabella, who made him their diplomatic agent in Rome. On Isabella's death he deserted Ferdinand for Philip the Fair, and continued in Rome until 1507, when he persuaded Julius II to appoint him Bishop of Zamora by promising that he would do everything possible to further the Papacy's interests in Castile. When the Council of Castile objected to his appointment, he seized his bishopric by force, and successfully held it against the attempts of the *alcalde* of Zamora, Rodrigo Ronquillo, to evict him. Although he managed to work his way back into the good graces of Ferdinand, and to obtain royal confirmation of his appointment, he was never entirely secure in his hold over his diocese. Zamora was the scene of unending faction struggles, and these merged into the struggle of the *Comuneros* as Acuña, expelled from the city by his enemies, put himself at the head of the rebels of Zamora, while the *alcalde* Ronquillo, his implacable enemy, became one of the leading royalist commanders. Now, in the early months of 1521, Acuña led his troops across northern Castile, joined the council of war of the *Comuneros* at Valladolid, conducted a few spirited forays into the surrounding countryside, and then took it into his head to march on Toledo, where he induced the populace to proclaim him Archbishop, in place of the recently deceased Guillaume de Croy.

The revival of *Comunero* fortunes under the fiery leadership of the Bishop of Zamora proved, however, to be no more than a passing phenomenon. The *Comunero* army, composed of local militia, rural labourers, and a handful of gentry, was unlikely to be a match for the royalist army marching southwards under the Constable of Castile. On 23 April 1521 the two armies met in the fields of Villalar, outside Toro. The *Comunero* infantry offered little effective resistance, most of the army scattered in confusion, and Padilla and the Segovian *Comunero* leader Juan Bravo were captured, and executed the following day.

The revolt of the *Comuneros* was now virtually at an end. Toledo, the first Castilian city to rise, was the last to yield, thanks to the heroism and determination of Padilla's widow, María Pacheco. The Bishop of Zamora fled in disguise to join the French troops who were at this moment invading Navarre, but he was caught on the way, and imprisoned in the castle of Simancas. Here, five years later, his career came to a suitably stormy close. In attempting to escape, the Bishop was rash enough to kill his jailer, and Charles V sent his old enemy, the *alcalde* Ronquillo, to investigate. Ronquillo, ignoring a clerical immunity which seemed in this instance peculiarly inappropriate, sentenced Acuña to be tortured and garrotted. The Bishop's body was strung up from one of the turrets of Simancas – a gruesome warning that had lost its point, for open defiance of the King and his ministers was already a thing of the past. After the defeat at Villalar, the rebels had melted away, and the nobles and gentry most implicated in the troubles found in the French invasion of Navarre a convenient opportunity for an ostentatious parade of their loyalty to the Crown. In Valencia, too, the rebellion was crushed. Peris was defeated outside the city of Valencia in October, and was finally captured and executed in March 1522. When Charles landed at Santander on 16 July 1522, he returned to a Spain once more at peace. By October he felt strong enough to issue a general pardon for the *Comuneros*, although nearly three hundred of the rebels were specifically excluded from its provisions. The authority of the Crown had prevailed, and the king had returned as absolute master to a cowed and subdued Castile. But this time he had taken the precaution of coming with 4,000 German soldiers at his side.

4. THE IMPERIAL DESTINY

The defeat of the *Comuneros* and the *Germanías* was crucial for the future of Spain. It meant that the Habsburg succession was now firmly established both in the Crown of Aragon (where, in any event, Catalans and Aragonese had failed to come to the help of the Valencians), and in Castile, where it had previously been resisted, or, at the most, grudgingly accepted by aristocracy and towns. The royalist triumph closed in Castile a chapter that had opened with the death of Isabella in 1504. During the intervening seventeen years all the achievements of the Catholic Kings had been jeopardized – the Union of the Crowns, the curbing of the aristocracy, the imposition of royal authority on the country at large. With the victory of Charles's supporters at the battle of Villalar, these achievements were finally secured. There were no more revolts in Castile against the power of the Crown.

Against the obvious gain to Castile in the restoration of firm government must be set other consequences of the defeat of the *Comuneros*, more difficult to assess. The revolt of 1520–21, while nominally a rising against an unpopular and alien government, had also displayed many of the characteristics of a civil war; and, like all civil wars, it left deep scars. The family feuds and vendettas, while momentarily curbed by the restoration of royal authority, were far from being exorcised from the body politic of Castile. Traditional enmities continued to be handed on from generation to generation, and *Comunero* and anti-*Comunero* families, no longer able to meet in open conflict, carried their obscure vendettas to the Court of the new dynasty, where, in the corridors and the council chambers, they pursued their struggle for power.

It is difficult to determine how far there was any ideological content in these struggles, but there are signs that the *Comunero* families like the Zapatas continued to regard themselves as the upholders of that fervent nationalist tradition which had been defeated at Villalar. For Charles's victory was much more than the triumph of the Crown over its traditional enemies, or of the forces of order over those of anarchy. It represented also something larger – the momentary triumph of Europe over Castile.

The *Comuneros* had fought to save Castile from a régime whose character and policies seemed to threaten that sense of national identity achieved amid such turmoil only a generation before. Their failure meant the definitive establishment of an alien dynasty with an alien programme, which threatened to submerge Castile in the larger entity of a universal Empire. The imperial tradition was foreign to medieval Spain, and the imperialism of Charles V awakened no ready-made response in the Castilian population at large. Ferdinand had already dragged Castile behind him into great European enterprises in support of Aragonese interests. Now, with Charles V, Castile was subjected to a fresh set of European ideas, preconceptions, and values, many of which it found hard to accept. The signs of change were everywhere. Already in 1516 the Burgundian Order of the Golden Fleece had been enlarged to include ten places for Spaniards, and at Barcelona in 1519 Charles held his first Spanish investiture. In 1548 the traditional Court ceremonial of the kings of Castile was replaced, to the Duke of Alba's chagrin, by the far more elaborate ceremonial of the House of Burgundy, and the Royal Household was reorganized on the Burgundian model. These changes were symbolic of the closer association between Castile and the outer world implicit in the succession of Charles of Ghent to the Spanish throne.

In spite of the strong anti-Flemish, anti-imperial sentiments to be found in Castile, there were at least some circles in Castilian society ready to accept and welcome foreign ideas. The Court and the universities had been exposed to foreign influences during the reign of Ferdinand and Isabella, and Spanish humanism and culture had developed under the stimulus of ideas from both Italy and Flanders. Similarly, Spanish religion had been invigorated by the spiritual currents that had come to it from the Netherlands. During the 1520s the Spanish public, which in previous decades had devoured with such enthusiasm the works of devotion of the Netherlands mystics, was to turn with no less enthusiasm to the works of the greatest of all exponents of the pietist tradition of the Netherlands – Desidèrius Erasmus.

The Erasmian invasion of Spain is one of the most remarkable events in sixteenth-century Spanish history. In no other country of Europe did the writings of Erasmus enjoy such popularity and so widespread a diffusion. In 1526 the *Enchiridion* appeared in a Spanish translation, and the translator was able to write proudly to the author: 'At the Court of the Emperor, in the towns, in the churches, in the monasteries, even in the inns and on the roads, everyone now has the *Enchiridion* of Erasmus. Hitherto it was only read in Latin by a few scholars, who did not always understand it; now it is read in Spanish by men of all conditions, and those who had previously never heard of Erasmus now know him through this one book.'[7] Erasmus's enormous popularity in Spain, which reached its peak between 1527 and 1530, seems in part attributable to the large *converso* element in Spanish society. The 'new Christians', recent converts from Judaism, were naturally attracted to a religion which had little regard for formal ceremonies, and which placed the weight of its emphasis on moral and mystical tendencies in the Christian tradition. But, beyond the appeal to the *conversos*, Erasmus's doctrines had the potent attraction perennially exercised on Spaniards by the north – a north which had now given Spain its king.

Since the Imperial Court in the 1520s was also Erasmian in its outlook, finding in the universalism of Erasmus a valuable reinforcement of the Imperial idea, a natural bond of sympathy developed between some of the leading Spanish intellectuals and Charles's régime.

7. Quoted by M. Bataillon, *Érasme et l'Espagne* (Spanish translation, *Erasmo y España* (Mexico, 1950), vol. 1, p. 326).

Erasmian humanists like Luis Vives and Juan de Valdés were close to the Emperor's associates or held office in the Imperial chancery. These men saw in the government of Charles an opportunity for the establishment of a universal peace which, as Erasmus insisted, was the necessary prelude to the long-awaited spiritual renovation of Christendom.

It would be absurd, however, to assume that Erasmianism reconciled the mass of the Castilians to the Imperial régime and the Imperial mission. Not only was Erasmianism itself soon to wither in the harsher religious climate that prevailed after 1530, but even in the days of its greatest influence it appealed to no more than a select minority. The highly influential Imperial secretary Francisco de los Cobos, for instance, knew no Latin, never showed any concern for the intellectual interests of his age, and always displayed a marked lack of enthusiasm for the whole concept of empire.

Castile as a whole came to reconcile itself to the government of Charles V for other, less intellectual, reasons. The Emperor employed an increasing number of Spaniards in his service, and over the years he came to acquire a deep sympathy for the land and the people of Castile – so much so, that Castile eventually became a natural choice for his final retreat. At the same time, the Castilians began to discover in the doctrines of empire some features which they could usefully turn to account. Cortés's conquest of Mexico, completed a few months after the defeat of the *Comuneros*, had opened up unlimited possibilities, as Cortés himself was quick to appreciate. In his second letter to the Emperor, of 30 October 1520, he wrote that the newly discovered territory was so large and important that Charles could reasonably assume for his new domain a fresh Imperial title, as fully justified as his existing title of Emperor of Germany. While neither Charles nor his successors acted on Cortés's suggestion that they should style themselves Emperors of the Indies, the fact remained that a new empire had appeared in the western hemisphere, and that the existence of this empire offered an incentive to Castilian nationalism to extend its boundaries and to aim at the world hegemony to which its possession of vast overseas territories would seem naturally to entitle it. Consequently the transition was easily made from the medieval concept of empire, which held little appeal for the Castilians, to a concept of Castilian hegemony under the leadership of a ruler who himself was already the most powerful sovereign in Christendom. But even the crudest nationalism requires a mission, and this again was ready to hand in the double task that had devolved upon Charles in his capacity as Emperor: the defence of Christendom against the Turk, and the preservation of Christian unity in the face of the new Lutheran heresy. Thus equipped with both a mission and a leader, the Castilian nationalism that had been defeated at Villalar arose phoenix-like from the ashes to greet the glittering opportunities of a new, imperial age. But a certain irony attended its resurrection, for something else had been defeated at Villalar which would not rise again: Castilian liberty, crushed and defenceless in face of the restored royal power.

5

The Government and the Economy in the
Reign of Charles V

I. THE THEORY AND PRACTICE OF EMPIRE

THE Emperor Charles V ruled Spain, as King Charles I, from 1517 until his abdication in January 1556 in favour of his son, Philip. Of his nearly forty years as King he spent just under sixteen in Spain itself. These sixteen years were made up of one long stay of seven years, and five shorter visits:

> September 1517 to May 1520
> July 1522 to July 1529
> April 1533 to April 1535
> December 1536 to Spring 1538
> July 1538 to November 1539
> November 1541 to May 1543

After 1543 he was not seen again in Spain until September 1556, when, having renounced the throne, he returned to take up residence in a small palace adjoining the monastery of Yuste. Here he died in September 1558.

In this bare list of Charles's visits to Spain lies one of the essential clues to the character of his empire and to the pattern of Spanish history during the years of his government. The fears of the *Comuneros* were largely fulfilled: Spain's first Habsburg sovereign was an absentee king. Moreover, he was a king with numerous other commitments, which would always make it necessary for him to weigh up against Spain's national interests the wider interests of Imperial policy. In spite of the great, and growing, importance of Spain in the balance of Charles's empire, it always took second place in any conflict of interest, yielding precedence to considerations of Imperial prestige and authority which the majority of Spaniards found it difficult to grasp.

The necessary absenteeism of Charles, the number of his dominions and the extent of his commitments, all posed enormous problems to which solutions had somehow to be found. There was the immediate question of who was to rule Spain during Charles's frequent absences, and, beyond this, the more difficult question of Spain's status and its obligations in relation to the various territories which together composed the Imperial patrimony. Whatever answers were found, they were bound to demand administrative and fiscal readjustments, which in turn reacted upon the whole structure of Spanish society and the Spanish economy.

During Charles's long stay in Spain from 1522 to 1529, his principal adviser, at least in name, was the Imperial Grand Chancellor the Piedmontese Mercurino Gattinara. As Grand Chancellor, however, Gattinara would naturally accompany the Emperor on his travels, acting in particular as his chief adviser in matters of foreign policy. The revolt of the *Comuneros* had made it quite clear that Spain could not be governed from elsewhere, but Juana was obviously unfit even to take nominal charge of the country's government in the absence of her son. In 1526, however, Charles married his cousin Isabella, the daughter of Emmanuel of Portugal. The marriage, which was a logical continuation of the policy pursued by the Catholic Kings to bring about a closer association of Castile and Portugal, gave Charles a son, Philip, in the following year. It also gave him, in Isabella, the perfect Empress, a magnificently regal figure, who acted as Regent in her husband's absence, until her early death in 1539.

The effective government of Spain, however, lay for twenty years or more in the hands of a man of humble origins from the Andalusian town of Úbeda – Francisco de los Cobos. Cobos had originally secured a post in the royal secretariat through the patronage of the Queen's secretary, Hernando de Zafra. After rising slowly, but steadily, in the service of Ferdinand, he took the crucial decision of his career in 1516, when he left Spain for Flanders on Ferdinand's death. A competent, extremely industrious man, more distinguished for his general affability and good humour than for any very striking traits of personality, he arrived in Flanders with the recommendation of Cisneros and the additional advantage of being one of the very few royal officials arriving from Spain who had no taint of Jewish blood. With his usual capacity for pleasing the influential, he managed to secure the favour of Chièvres, who appointed him secretary to the

King. From this moment his career was made. His experience in the various departments of the government of Castile stood him in good stead when the Emperor came to Spain, and the fact that he was steadily gaining in royal favour marked him out as an increasingly obvious rival to the Grand Chancellor Gattinara. The year after 1522 saw a struggle for power between the two men to secure control of the machinery of government – a struggle that had already been won by Cobos when Gattinara died in 1530. Between 1529 and 1533 Cobos travelled abroad with the Emperor, acting as his principal adviser along with Nicholas Perrenot de Granville; but later, his expertise in financial affairs, and perhaps also his lack of sympathy for Imperial policies, caused him to remain in Spain, where he enjoyed great power and influence until his death in 1547.

The government of Spain ran so smoothly under the gentle guidance of Los Cobos that it almost seems as if for twenty or thirty years the country had no internal history. The terrible storms that had shaken it in 1520 and 1521 had all died away. An almost unnatural calm descended upon the political life of Castile, where the reiterated complaints of the Cortes about the long absences of the Emperor and the heavy expense of his policies were almost the only outward signs of that deep uneasiness about the future which had originally inspired the revolt of the *Comuneros*.

While the country's tranquillity can partly be attributed to the skill of Los Cobos in the handling of a nation weary of civil war, it is also to be ascribed to the essentially static character of Charles V's imperialism. The Empire consisted of a number of hereditary possessions – Habsburg, Burgundian, and Spanish – acquired by the dynasty at different periods and governed by it under conditions that varied greatly from one country to the next. Charles's concept of his numerous and widespread territories was patrimonial. He tended to think of each as an independent entity, governed by its own traditional laws in its own traditional manner, and unaffected by the fact that it was now only one among many territories ruled by a single sovereign. His territories themselves also tended, by their own attitude, to reinforce this concept. None wished to be considered of merely secondary importance just because its king happened also to be Holy Roman Emperor and the ruler of other states: Spain, for instance, extracted from Charles in September 1519 the promise that 'the placing of the title of Emperor before that of King of Spain was in no way to be understood as prejudicing the liberty and exemptions of these kingdoms'.

The association of Charles's various territories was therefore similar in character to the association of territories that together formed the medieval federation of the Crown of Aragon. Each continued to enjoy its own laws and liberties, and any alteration in those laws to bring the constitutional systems of the differing territories into closer conformity to each other would be regarded as a flagrant violation of the ruler's hereditary obligations to his subjects. The traditional view was well expressed by a seventeenth-century jurist: 'the kingdoms must be ruled and governed as if the king who holds them all together were king only of each one of them'.[1] The king of all remained primarily the king of each, and was expected – in cheerful disregard of all the formidable obstacles imposed by space and time – to behave in accordance with this principle. To the Aragonese, Charles was King of Aragon; to the Castilians, King of Castile; to the Flemings, Count of Flanders; and if they occasionally allowed themselves a certain feeling of pride that their King was also the ruler of many other territories, this was generally outweighed by annoyance at the demands made upon him by those territories, to the consequent neglect of their own particular interests.

Two important consequences followed from this concept of Charles's empire as a mere aggregation of territories almost fortuitously linked by a common sovereign. In the first place, it led to the 'freezing' of the various constitutional systems in these territories. Each was alert to any real or implied threat to its traditional status, and this in turn inhibited the development of any common institutional organization for the empire as a whole, such as Gattinara would probably have liked, but which Charles himself seems never to have considered. Secondly, it prevented the growth of a closer association of the various territories for either economic or political purposes, which might in time have helped to produce an imperial mystique, a sense of participation in a common enterprise. In the absence of any such mystique, Charles's dominions continued to think exclusively in terms of their own interests, and to resent their

1. Juan de Solórzano Pereira, *Política Indiana* (Madrid, 1647; reprinted Madrid, 1930), book iv, chap. xix, §37.

involvement in wars which seemed to be little or no concern of theirs.

So far as Castile was concerned, many of Charles's policies seemed to Castilians to deviate sharply from the traditional policies pursued by his predecessors. His feud with the King of France, his war against the Protestant princes of Germany, appeared to have little or nothing to do with the promotion of Castilian interests, and hardly seemed to justify the use of Castilian manpower and the expenditure of Castilian money. Even his Italian policy, culminating in the acquisition of the duchy of Milan[2] and the winning of Spanish dominance over the peninsula, had strong critics among those Castilians like Juan Tavera, Cardinal Archbishop of Toledo, who looked back to the days of Isabella and Cisneros. To Tavera and his friends, Spanish involvement in Italy was a perpetuation of the 'Aragonese' foreign policy of Ferdinand, and was bound to lead Castile into European conflicts, whereas Castile's interests required peace in Europe and a continuation of the crusade against the infidel along the shores of Africa. It remained for the no less 'Castilian', but more realistic, Duke of Alba to grasp the fundamental strategic importance of Italy for the preservation of one of Castile's primary spheres of interest – the central and western Mediterranean basin, increasingly threatened by the Turkish advance.

The growth of the Turkish threat to the western Mediterranean was, in fact, to have a decisive impact on the character and development of sixteenth-century Spain. The Europe of Charles V found itself confronted by a powerful State specifically organized for war – a State possessing resources of money and manpower on an imperial scale. The threat to Spain was open and obvious. Its coasts were exposed to pirate attacks; its grain supplies from Sicily could easily be cut; and it had, in its large Morisco population, a potentially subversive element, well placed to aid and abet any Ottoman attack on Spanish soil. Spain therefore found itself in the front line of the battle, a natural bastion of Europe against a Turkish assault. It was at this point that Charles's imperialism came into its own. An empire was wanted to meet the attack of an empire. The States of the Crown of Aragon by themselves would have been too weak to prevent and

2. Milan reverted to Charles V as an Imperial fief on the death of its last Sforza duke in 1535. Charles conferred it on his son, Prince Philip, in 1540, and thereafter it remained attached to the Spanish Crown.

throw back a Turkish attack, while Castile also required a line of defence beyond its own borders. Charles's imperialism provided exactly this. He could draw on the financial and military resources of his widespread dominions, on the naval power of his Genoese allies, and on the loans of his German bankers, to defend Italy and Sicily, and hence Spain itself, against the onslaught of Ottoman imperialism. However weak the links between his various territories, they none the less formed a sufficiently solid mass to impede the further advance of the Turk, and to provide between them the resources for a successful defence such as they could never have mustered on their own.

There were, however, counterbalancing disadvantages for Spain in Charles's domination of half the Continent. In particular, he was too absorbed in the German problem and in his wars with France to be able to pursue a consistently offensive policy against Ottoman power. The capture of Tunis in 1535 thus remained an isolated incident, and, in the end, Charles's Mediterranean policy came to be limited to a mere holding operation. In this respect especially, Charles's Castilian and Aragonese subjects found their ruler's possession of the Imperial title a constant liability, requiring frequent diversions from a strictly Mediterranean policy, and demanding of them large and continuing sacrifices for causes that appeared to them unnecessary and remote. It was true that Spain enjoyed under Charles V and his successor the inestimable blessing of peace on its own soil, at a time when large regions of Europe were the scene of constant warfare; but while it escaped the ravages of war, Castile in particular was almost permanently on a war footing, fighting battles sometimes for itself, but no less frequently for others. Charles always insisted that these battles ultimately redounded to the benefit of his Spanish subjects, and he succeeded in making many Castilians identify themselves and their country with his crusade against the Turk and the heretic. In perpetuating Castile's crusading tradition, and giving it a new sense of purpose and direction, he undoubtedly met a psychological need. But there was a high price to be paid, for the perpetuation of a crusade entailed the perpetuation of the archaic social organization of a crusading society. It also meant that the institutions and economy of sixteenth-century Spain and its empire were formed, and deformed, against the sombre background of incessant war.

2. THE ORGANIZATION OF EMPIRE

If warfare was a dominant theme in the history of Spain under Charles V and Philip II, bureaucratization was another. In order to govern Spain and its overseas possessions, and to mobilize their resources for war, a large number of officials were required. Charles was, and remained, an old-style ruler who liked to lead his armies in battle and to govern his subjects personally, and there remained to the end of his life an element of the improvising amateur about his manner of government. But all the time the sheer physical problems involved in ruling large territories spread over vast distances were imposing new bureaucratic methods and administrative procedures, which came gradually to replace government by the spoken word with government by the written word – government by paper. Already by the reign of Philip II it seemed unbelievable that Charles V should once have called for pen and ink only to find that there was none in the palace (or so at least the story went). The replacement of the warrior-king Charles V by a sedentary Philip II, who spent his working day at his desk surrounded by piles of documents, fittingly symbolized the transformation of the Spanish Empire as it passed out of the age of the *conquistador* into the age of the Civil Servant.

The character and timing of the transformation were determined by the constitutional characteristics of the Spanish kingdoms, by the conquest of an American empire, and also by the demands of war. As early as 1522 it had become clear that the existing system of government was inadequate for the new demands that were being imposed upon it, and the Grand Chancellor Gattinara set about rationalizing and improving Spain's administrative machinery. Between 1522 and 1524 he reformed the Council of Castile, founded a Council of Finance, reorganized the government of Navarre, and established a Council for the Indies. With these reforms of the early 1520s, the pattern was set for the government of the Spanish Monarchy throughout the sixteenth century. It was elaborated in 1555 by the removal of Italian affairs from the province of the Council of Aragon and the creation of a special Council of Italy to handle them, but the basic system remained untouched.

The system was essentially conciliar in character, along the lines already established during the reigns of Ferdinand and Isabella. (See Table 3.) Such a system was well suited to the particular needs of an empire as geographically dispersed and constitutionally diversified as that of Spain. Any effective system of government for the Spanish Monarchy clearly had to take into account both the prolonged absences of the Emperor from his various dominions, and the insistence of those dominions on the scrupulous observation of their laws and customs. At the same time it had to provide at least some central direction for the co-ordination of policies. The organization of the Councils adequately met these various needs.

The immediate purpose of a Council was to advise the monarch. This meant that the Councils must be attendant upon the person of the King, or, if he were out of the country, of the regent. The fact that the Court was frequently on the move and that there was no fixed capital until Philip II's selection of Madrid in 1561, made it difficult to accomplish this without loss of efficiency, and Valladolid seems increasingly to have become the administrative capital of the realm in these years. At the same time Cobos took steps to combat the lack of continuity in the administrative system by planning the establishment of an archive of official documents. Hitherto, some State papers had been kept in Segovia Castle, others at Medina del Campo, and still others in the chancellery at Valladolid. The increasing number of official documents made it essential to set up some central repository, and Charles V and Cobos finally selected as the most suitable site the fortress of Simancas, which was conveniently close to Valladolid. Between 1543 and 1545 orders were issued for the transference to Simancas of all State papers and for the turning over by officials of all documents in their possession to the newly appointed keepers of the archive. Simancas was to suffer many vicissitudes, and government officials (especially in the seventeenth century) would frequently ignore, or obtain exemptions from, the orders to hand over their papers on leaving office, but at least Spain now possessed a central archive worthy of the new bureaucratic State.

The Councils themselves can be divided broadly into two classes: those that concerned themselves with advising the monarch on general or departmental questions relating to the Monarchy as a whole, and those responsible for the government of the individual territories within it. Of the more generalized advisory Councils, the

Table 3 THE CONCILIAR SYSTEM

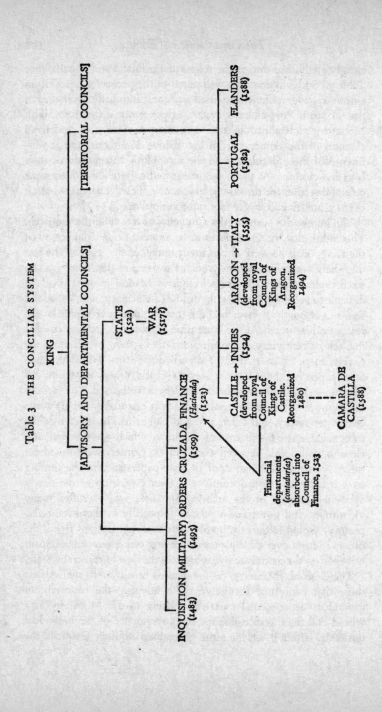

best known in the later years of Habsburg rule, but the most indeterminate in composition and functions under Charles V, was the *Consejo de Estado* – the Council of State. This was in theory a Council to advise the monarch on matters of general policy 'concerning the government of Spain and Germany', and consisted in 1526 of the Archbishop of Toledo, the Dukes of Alba and Béjar, the royal confessor, and the Bishop of Jaén, together with Gattinara and Count Henry of Nassau. But there was jealousy among those who were excluded, and Charles chose to avoid trouble by dispensing with the Council's advice and largely confining its functions to those of an official nature. More active was another Council closely associated with the Council of State and sharing some of its councillors: the Council of War, which was responsible for the military organization of the Monarchy. The first reference to this body as an independent Council dates from 1517, but it was remodelled in 1522 to make it a more effective instrument in the new circumstances created by Charles's succession to the Imperial title.

The most important of Gattinara's reforms, however, was the creation of a Council of Finance – the *Consejo de Hacienda*. The need for a financial organization better than that provided by the two *contadurías mayores* of Castile was borne in upon Gattinara as he surveyed the grim picture of royal penury that greeted him on his arrival in Spain. There was a convenient model to hand in the *Conseil des Finances* of Flanders, of which the nominal head, Count Henry of Nassau, had accompanied Charles to the peninsula. Orders were therefore given in February 1523 for the establishment of a Council of Finance, including Nassau among its members. Cobos was the secretary of the new Council, and although it was Gattinara who had originally proposed the Council, it was the protégés of Cobos who were favoured in the appointments.

The Council had originally been designed to deal with the Castilian finances, but inevitably it came to be concerned with the Crown's finances in general. Meeting daily to examine estimates of income and expenditure, it largely superseded the old *contaduría de hacienda*. The other *contaduría*, however – that of accounts – acquired a fresh lease of life as a dependent organ of the Council, responsible for dealing with the Crown's growing expenditure and with the vital task of organizing the large-scale credit operations essential to keep it solvent.

While Castile's financial system required, and obtained, a radical overhaul, the rest of the country's administrative machinery continued to function very much as it had in the reigns of Ferdinand and Isabella. The Council of Castile, reduced in size by Gattinara's reforms, remained the principal organ of government, but, by decrees of 1518 and 1523, there developed out of it a small cabinet council known as the *Consejo de la Cámara de Castilla*, which only attained proper conciliar rank in 1588. This cabinet council was simply a body of three or four councillors of the Council of Castile, who were entrusted with the special task of advising the King on all matters arising out of the royal *Patronato* of the Spanish Church, and on judicial and administrative appointments.

Outside the realm of the royal finances, the greatest administrative challenge to Gattinara lay not in Spain itself, but in Spain's new overseas possessions. In the first years after the discoveries, all business connected with the Indies passed through the hands of a legally-minded cleric, Juan Rodríguez de Fonseca, the Queen's chaplain and later Bishop of Burgos. Although commercial affairs were to become the particular province of the *Casa de Contratación* which had been established at Seville in 1503, Fonseca remained in supreme charge of all colonial matters, with occasional assistance from members of the Council of Castile. By the time of Charles's arrival in Spain it was already becoming clear that a more formal organization would be necessary, and this took shape in 1524, the year of Fonseca's death, when a special Council of the Indies was created.

This Council, consisting of a president and eight councillors, was the equivalent for America of the Council of Castile. It was entrusted with supreme control of all administrative, judicial and ecclesiastical matters relating to the Indies, and was the agency through which the Crown established its authority over its American possessions and developed a colonial administration. The organs of this administration were modelled on those of the peninsula, and gradually took over from the makeshift administrative system established by the *conquistadores*. Royal authority, instead of being temporarily exercised by individual *conquistadores* and by the *cabildos* (town councils), was now permanently vested in the twin institutions of *audiencias* and viceroyalties, both of which suffered a sea change as they crossed the Atlantic. The *audiencias*, of which six had been established by 1550, differed from those of the peninsula in acquiring political and administrative as well as judicial functions. The viceroys, on the other hand, were in some respects more restricted in the scope of their powers than their Aragonese equivalents. Where a viceroy in the Crown of Aragon was the *alter ego* of the King, entrusted with administrative and judicial powers, his equivalents in New Spain and Peru were primarily governors, enjoying enormous influence by virtue of their remoteness from the metropolis, but for this very reason carefully shorn of certain powers they would have expected to enjoy at home. The task of administering justice belonged not to them but to the *audiencias*, for although the divisions were often blurred in practice, it was the Crown's policy in the New World to separate government and jurisdiction wherever possible, so that the agencies responsible for them could each keep a constant check on the other. The Spanish Crown was quick to appreciate, here as elsewhere, that a system of checks and balances carefully distributed between a number of different institutions and social groups was the best, and possibly the only, hope of preserving its own authority in its dependent territories.

With the creation of the viceroyalties of New Spain and Peru, the number of viceroyalties in the Spanish Monarchy rose to nine – Aragon, Catalonia, Valencia, Navarre, Sardinia, Sicily, Naples, and the two American viceroyalties – and the Monarchy's administrative system was now established in the form in which it was to continue for the best part of two centuries. This system was in effect that of the medieval Catalan-Aragonese Mediterranean empire adapted and extended to meet the needs of a world empire. The vast distances in the empire – the eight months or more that were necessary to transmit messages from Castile to Peru – constituted a challenge to the Spanish Crown that was without precedent in European history. Inevitably the administrative system developed by Spain during the course of the sixteenth century had numerous defects, but its success in meeting the challenge was nevertheless remarkable.

The secret of this success lay in the skilful combination of effective regional government with the maximum degree of centralization possible in an empire of remote and scattered territories, some of which had never seen their King. The viceroys – the majority of them great Castilian nobles, like Antonio de Mendoza in New Spain, or Francisco de Toledo in Peru – enjoyed enormous powers, but yet at the same time found themselves closely tied to the central government in Spain. Each viceroy had to work in harness with the relevant Council at Court. The dispatches of the viceroy of Peru would be received and handled by the Council of the Indies; those of the viceroy of Catalonia by the Council of Aragon. A Council could be expected to keep a sharp look-out for any abuse of his powers on the part of the viceroy, since its own interests were at stake. Not only did any extension of viceregal power entail a proportional diminution of conciliar power, but a Council like the Council of Aragon consisted (apart from the Treasurer General) of natives of the territories concerned, who would be quick to react to any threat to the rights of their native land; for the Councils were much more than mere administrative organs in that they also fulfilled some of the essential functions of representative bodies. The original purpose behind them was to preserve a fiction central to the whole structure of the Spanish Monarchy – the fiction that the King was personally present in each of his territories.[3] A body of representative native councillors attendant on the person of the King could at least help to restrict the deleterious consequences of royal absenteeism, both by acting as the mouthpiece of provincial interests, and by seeing that the King's viceroy acted in conformity with a royal intention of which it considered itself the guardian.

The machinery for achieving this lay in the system of the *consulta*. A Council, meeting regularly – usually every working day by the later part of the century – would discuss the viceroy's latest dispatches and all matters of general significance in the territory under its jurisdiction. The results of its discussions would be embodied in documents known as *consultas*, which would summarize the views of the various members of the Council on a particular topic, so that the King would be sufficiently informed to make his decision. He might simply accept the majority recommendation; or, if the matter was a difficult one, he might pass the *consulta* to the Council of State, or to a special body of ministers, for further discussion. Their recommendations, also in the form of a *consulta*, would be referred back to

3. 'por lo qual se considera estar VM en cada reyno', Santiago Agustín Riol, 'Informe que hizo a Su Magestad en 16 de junio 1726', *Semanario Erudito*, vol. III (Madrid, 1787), p. 112.

him in due course for a final decision, which he would communicate by means of a written statement, often in his own hand, on the original *consulta*. Once the royal reply had been received by the Council, the secretary to the Council would draft the appropriate letters, to be signed by the King and dispatched to the viceroy for action.

The chain of communications that ran from viceroy to Council to King and back again to the viceroy ensured an exhaustive coverage of every item of importance in the government of the Spanish Monarchy. No States were more governed in the sixteenth century than those of the King of Spain, if government can be measured by the amount of discussion devoted to any individual problem and by the quantities of paper expended on its solution. The actual effectiveness of this government in terms of the governed is, however, much more difficult to determine. In many ways the Spanish administrative system paid a heavy price for its success. It solved the problem of maintaining central control over distant proconsuls, but only at the expense of stultifying prompt administrative action. Since everything had to be referred back to the Court for a decision, consultation tended to take the place of action, and government by discussion could easily mean no government at all. Moreover, with its own complicated built-in mechanism of an infinite series of checks and balances, the system distributed power so evenly among so many different bodies that each was ultimately reduced to powerlessness.

Many of the defects in the system were no doubt inevitable. Problems of distance were utterly insuperable, and distance not only imposed endless delays, but also prompted the need to create administrative machinery designed as much to restrict the powers of the governors as to attend to the interests of the governed. Many other defects, however, were capable of remedy, and if they were not remedied this was largely because of the character and the calibre of the men who ran the system.

The almost total absence of detailed studies of the Spanish bureaucracy in the sixteenth and seventeenth centuries means that very little is known of the thousands of officials of which it consisted. At the bottom of the scale were innumerable clerks and scribes, inspectors and tax-collectors, anonymous, unhonoured, and unsung. Above them, in ascending levels of importance, were the more senior officials of the viceregal administration, the members of the legal tribunals or *audiencias*, and the viceroys themselves, while at the Court were the royal secretaries, the members of the Councils, and the various secretarial officials.

From the days of Cobos the royal secretaries tended to form something of a class apart. Their duties were of the greatest importance, since they dealt with royal correspondence and acted as the links between the Councils and the sovereign. As early as 1523 Cobos himself was secretary of all the Councils except those of Aragon, Orders, and War; and he was to devote much energy to building up a trained professional staff for the secretariats, in the knowledge that they would be the nurseries of his successors. The team trained by Cobos included several names which were to ring down the corridors of the sixteenth century: Juan Vázquez de Molina, Cobos's nephew; Alonso de Idiáquez; Gonzalo Pérez; Francisco de Eraso. These men had much the same background as Cobos himself. They came from the class of small municipal gentry, and, apart from Pérez, had neither intellectual interests nor university training. Essentially they were professional civil servants, devoted to the interests of the Emperor and to their *patrón* Cobos, and held together by a strong *esprit de corps*. Their appearance of constituting a closed caste was reinforced by the frequent practice of passing on the secretaryships from father to son or uncle to nephew, so that such names as Pérez and Idiáquez constantly recur. This had the advantage of ensuring administrative continuity, but it also tended to perpetuate routine procedures which had outlived their usefulness, and to bring about the appointment of men who sometimes had nothing to recommend them other than a knowledge of the inner workings of the bureaucratic machine.

Members of the *audiencias* and the Councils had the same kind of social background as the royal secretaries. Charles V and Philip II were both careful to follow the practice of the Catholic Kings in restricting the higher nobles to army commands and viceroyalties, and in choosing for service at Court and in the legal tribunals men drawn from *hidalgo* families or from the *bourgeoisie*. Unlike the secretaries, however, these men had been educated at the universities, and had considerable experience in the Church or legal practice before they entered the royal service. Appointed to an *audiencia*, one

or two of the fortunate ones might hope eventually to be promoted
to one of the Councils at Court, with a place in the Council of Castile
as the pinnacle of their ambitions. This meant that they were already
relatively old men at the time of their appointment, anxious only to
enjoy in tranquillity the high office they had at last attained. Nor was
their considerable legal learning necessarily the best equipment for the
kind of problems that now confronted them. There was very rarely
an experienced man of affairs or a merchant in the Council of Finance,
and a legal or theological training was perhaps not the best preparation for struggling with the extreme complexities of the Castilian
economy.

Age, and a certain narrowness of background, were, however, the
least of the troubles that afflicted the Councils. There were constant
complaints of venality and corruption among royal officials, and not
least among the councillors. The scrutiny of an official's activities by
means of *visitas* and *residencias* imposed a certain check on corrupt
practices, but opportunities for gain were considerable, and the temp-
tations difficult to resist. Cobos, whom Charles V believed to accept
no bribes of importance, started life without a penny and ended it
with an annual income of some 60,000 ducats a year, which put him
on the same level as the richest nobles in Castile. Much of this wealth
came from grants made by the Emeror in gratitude for his services,
but it was easy enough for a man in Cobos's position to use his official
influence to swell his private income.

While the career of Cobos vividly illustrates the opportunities that
awaited a successful royal official, it also hints at some of the pressures
upon him. In the hierarchically-ordered societies of sixteenth-century
Europe the supreme aspiration was to find acceptance among the
ranks of the aristocracy. Even a man of the humblest origins might
eventually achieve this ambition through wealth and the King's
favour; and both might be acquired in the royal service, if not always
by strictly orthodox methods. Since the mark of a true aristocrat was
his display, there was a constant pressure on the ambitious royal
official to spend, which in turn produced a constant pressure to gain.
Cobos acquired land and built himself palaces. He bought tapestries
and pictures and jewels, and surrounded himself with all the appur-
tenances of aristocratic living; and in the end he secured the recognition he desired. His daughter married the Duke of Sessa, his son

became Marquis of Camarasa, and a new noble dynasty was founded. But it was a giddy spiral staircase he had climbed, and only a few would follow him to the top.

The temptation to mount was, however, irresistible. Yet the orthodox steps for mounting were few and far between. Cobos had been fortunate in that he was a constant recipient of royal favours, so that his upward path was relatively smooth. But the majority of officials were rarely singled out for special favours, and the salaries on which they were supposed to depend were absurdly small and very often in arrears. Although the smallness of official salaries was the inevitable result of the Crown's financial necessities, it was also the outcome of deliberate royal policy, since it was assumed that an official with a small salary would work all the harder in the hope of eventual *mercedes* or rewards. The theory was ingenious, but the practical results disastrous. Caught between his expensive social commitments and the impossibility of meeting them out of his salary, the official was compelled to have recourse to irregular money-raising methods, for which the Spanish administrative system made generous provision.

The opportunities for corruption among the members of the Councils reflect the character not only of the Spanish system of government, but also of the society that lay behind it – a society with many more resemblances to other sixteenth-century European societies than is often allowed. Organized in the form of a pyramid with the King at its apex, Spanish society looked naturally towards the King as the source of patronage, which would be percolated downwards through the various social layers by means of the usual clientage system. But a king with so many subjects in so many different territories could not confer his favours from the personal knowledge of the recipients to the extent that was still possible in a small society like that of Elizabethan England. It was at this point that the Councils had an exceptionally important function to fulfil. Innumerable petitions would flood in to the King from all those who, in the customary terminology of the age, claimed to have rendered him certain *servicios*, for which they duly requested *mercedes* or rewards. This concept of service and rewards – a survival from an age of much closer personal relations between a king and his subjects – had inevitably to be institutionalized in the changed conditions of the sixteenth century. This was done by channelling the petitions through the Councils, which would sift them and pass on their recommendations to the King.

Since the King would generally act on his Councils' advice, the councillors acquired enormous powers of patronage, which they naturally attempted to exploit to the full. Applicants for *mercedes* – for places of profit and honour and titles of nobility – would take certain obvious precautions to ensure that their petitions received prompt – and, if possible, favourable – consideration, and underpaid councillors were hardly likely to resist their overtures. There could be no better illustration of the kind of problem likely to arise from the grafting of a modern-style bureaucratic system on to a society that was still essentially medieval, for it was because the councils had inherited the mantle of medieval kingship, with its obligation to confer favours as well as to dispense government and justice, that the opportunities for corrupt practices were so great. Corruption itself, therefore, was only one further aspect of the enormous problem that confronted sixteenth-century Spain: the problem of constructing a modern state-system on economic and social foundations that were proving increasingly obsolete.

3. THE CASTILIAN ECONOMY

The hardest task facing sixteenth-century Spain was to adapt its essentially medieval political, social, and economic organization to the unprecedented demands made upon it by the responsibilities of world-wide empire. To a very considerable extent it was successful in meeting these demands on the institutional level, partly perhaps because of the experience gained by the Aragonese in tackling similar problems in the preceding centuries. But could it achieve a comparable success in meeting the economic challenge presented by the acquisition of potentially rich and productive overseas possessions? In other words, did the Castilians have the determination and the capacity to exploit their American conquests in such a way as to further the economic growth of their own country?

The New World could be a source of benefit to Castile as a supplier of commodities that were scarce or unavailable at home, and as a market for Castilian products. In the first flush of excitement caused by the discoveries, there was naturally much uncertainty as to the best means of exploiting the glittering opportunities of trans-atlantic trade. The first instinctive reaction to the discoveries was to treat the New World as an exclusive Castilian preserve, and in 1501 the passage of foreigners to the Indies was formally prohibited. Then in 1503, the famous *Casa de Contratación* was set up in Seville. This organization, which was probably inspired by the *Consulado* of Burgos and by the monopolistic trading system of the Portuguese, was designed to exercise absolute control over trade with the New World; but a few years later the principle of a Sevillian, and even of a Spanish, monopoly of the American trade came to be openly questioned. Already in the time of Cisneros it had become apparent that Spain would need foreign capital for its expensive colonizing ventures, and in the 1520s, in the first intoxicating years of Charles's imperialism, there occurred a passing phase of liberal legislation. In 1524 Charles V, under pressure from German banking houses, allowed foreign merchants to trade with the Indies, although not to settle in them. In 1525 and 1526 subjects from any of the Emperor's dominions were given the right of entry into America; and in 1529 the Crown went so far as to allow ten Castilian ports to trade directly with the New World, although their ships had to put into Seville for the registration of their cargoes on the return journey. But this decree, revoked in 1573, seems to have remained virtually a dead letter, possibly because the winds and currents were unfavourable to direct navigation between north Spain and the Indies. The earlier decrees also ran into trouble, as a result of growing indignation among Spanish merchants at the extent of foreign competition; and in 1538 the entry of all foreigners into America was again prohibited, although many would still continue to obtain passages, either by securing special licences or by acquiring naturalization as Castilian citizens.

In spite of various loopholes in the legislation, it is clear that, from the end of the 1530s, the principle of monopoly had triumphed: a monopoly favourable to the Crown of Castile, and most of all to the port of Seville. From now until 1680, when it yielded its primacy to Cadiz, Seville was the mistress of the Spanish Atlantic. At Seville would be congregated goods for shipment to the Indies from Spain and abroad, and back to Seville would come the galleons bearing the products of the New World. The most highly prized of the imports from America – which included dyestuffs, pearls, and sugar – were, of course, gold and silver. The quest for precious metals, of which Europe had run desperately short by the end of the fifteenth century, had been the principal driving force behind the colonial ventures, and in America the faith of the *conquistadores* was to be amply rewarded. In the very first years of the discoveries, small quantities of gold had been found in the Antilles – sufficient to whet the appetite for more. The conquests of Mexico and Peru brought in their train the discovery of gold and silver mines, culminating in 1545 in the finding of the fabulous silver mines of Potosí, to the south-east of Lake Titicaca. The exploitation of the enormous resources of Potosí on a really large scale only began, however, in the years around 1560, when a new method was invented for the refining of silver by an amalgam of mercury, of which the principal source of supply at this time was the Almadén mercury mines in Spain. From this moment, the production of silver far outran that of gold, and over the 160 years between 1503 and 1660 some 16,000,000 kilograms of silver arrived at Seville – enough to triple the existing silver resources of Europe – as against 185,000 kilograms of gold, which increased Europe's gold supplies by one-fifth.

The bullion consignments arriving at Seville belonged partly to the Crown and partly to private individuals. (See Table 4.) In accordance with laws of Alfonso X and Alfonso XI of Castile, any mines discovered in lands belonging to the king were considered to form a part of the royal patrimony; but the risks and difficulties inherent in the exploitation of the American mines induced the Spanish Crown to renounce its rights and to rent or dispose of the mines, in return for a proportion of the yield, finally fixed at one-fifth. The Crown's share of the bullion arriving at Seville, which seems to have averaged about 40 per cent of the total consignment, therefore consisted partly of this proportion, known as the *quinto real*, and partly of the sums sent back in payment of the taxes intro-duced by the Crown into the Indies. Of the private share of the consignment, part belonged to individuals who had made their fortune in the Indies and were bringing it back to Spain, but most of it was probably being remitted to Sevillan merchants by their American colleagues in order to pay for cargoes shipped to the New

Table 4

TOTAL IMPORTS OF TREASURE IN DUCATS
(375 *maravedís*) BY FIVE-YEAR PERIODS

(Based on the table, given in *pesos* of 450 *maravedís*, in Earl J. Hamilton, *American Treasure and the Price Revolution in Spain*, 1501–1650, Harvard University Press, 1934, p. 34.)

Period	Royal	Private	Total
1503–1505	116,660	328,607	445,266
1506–1510	256,625	722,859	979,484
1511–1515	375,882	1,058,782	1,434,664
1516–1520	312,261	879,575	1,191,836
1521–1525	42,183	118,821	161,004
1526–1530	326,485	919,640	1,246,124
1531–1535	518,833	1,461,445	1,980,277
1536–1540	1,621,062	3,104,408	4,725,470
1541–1545	909,346	5,035,460	5,944,806
1546–1550	1,911,206	4,699,247	6,610,453
1551–1555	4,354,208	7,484,429	11,838,637
1556–1560	1,882,195	7,716,604	9,598,798
1561–1565	2,183,440	11,265,603	13,449,043
1566–1570	4,541,692	12,427,767	16,969,459
1571–1575	3,958,393	10,329,538	14,287,931
1576–1580	7,979,614	12,722,715	20,702,329
1581–1585	9,060,725	26,188,810	35,249,534
1586–1590	9,651,855	18,947,302	28,599,157
1591–1595	12,028,018	30,193,817	42,221,835
1596–1600	13,169,182	28,145,019	41,314,201
1601–1605	7,823,863	21,460,131	29,283,994
1606–1610	10,259,615	27,426,634	37,686,248
1611–1615	8,655,506	20,778,239	29,433,745
1616–1620	5,217,346	30,917,606	36,134,952
1621–1625	5,869,387	26,543,427	32,412,814
1626–1630	5,542,561	24,402,871	29,945,432
1631–1635	5,680,589	14,852,435	20,533,025
1636–1640	5,629,564	13,947,959	19,577,522
1641–1645	5,723,394	10,944,169	16,516,563
1646–1650	1,998,135	12,126,521	14,124,656
1651–1655	2,686,654	6,065,867	8,752,520
1656–1660	727,829	3,305,515	4,033,339
Totals 1503–1660	140,863,304	396,521,815	537,385,119

World. For, in spite of the almost exclusive concentration of posterity on the spectacular bullion imports, Spain's trade with the Indies was at all times a two-way trade.

The first Spanish settlers in America needed almost everything from home: their arms, their clothes, their horses, their corn and their wine. Even after the colonists had become established in their new surroundings, they continued to remain heavily dependent on the metropolis for many of their essential supplies. Although European crops were rapidly introduced, agriculture in the Indies was slow to develop, and demand was outpaced by the growth of the white or partially coloured population. Figures are still largely a matter of guesswork, but there may have been some 118,000 colonists in the New World by 1570. These colonists clung nostalgically to Spanish ways of life; they wanted the luxuries of the Old World, its textiles, its books, its foodstuffs. Some of these would in time be produced in the New World itself, but meanwhile the ships would leave Seville laden with Castilian or Catalan cloth, and with wine, oil and corn from Andalusia, and would bring back silver and other desirable colonial produce in return.

The number of ships making the transatlantic crossing each year varied considerably, according to the economic and political circumstances of the moment, and ranged from sixty to over a hundred. From an early stage the majority of these ships were organized into convoys or *flotas*, on the Venetian and Portuguese model. There were various reasons for this. The transatlantic crossing, which took some two months, was dangerous, and skilled pilots were scarce; with the increasing quantities of bullion shipped back from the Indies, it was essential to provide a guard; and the registration of cargoes, which was necessary for checking the bullion and for levying the *almojari-fazgo* – the $7\frac{1}{2}$ per cent duty payable on goods imported into America from Europe – was more easily managed with a regular convoy system starting from Seville and Cadiz and making for one of the three chosen ports in the New World: Vera Cruz, Cartagena, or Nombre de Dios. In spite of these early attempts at control, which placed the organization of the *Carrera de las Indias* firmly in the hands of the *Casa de Contratación* and of the Indies merchants of Seville (who were organized into a *Consulado* on the Burgos model in 1543), the *flota* system only achieved its definitive form in the 1560s. From then on, in theory if not always in practice, two convoys would sail from Andalusia each year, one to New Spain and the other to Tierra Firme. The first of these, which later came to be known specifically as the *Flota*, would set sail in April or May for the Gulf of Mexico, while the other, which acquired from its escort of six or eight warships the collective name of the *Galeones*, would leave in August for the Isthmus of Panama, collecting ships from the northern coast of South America on the journey. Both fleets would winter in America, and would join forces at Havana in the following March for the return voyage to Europe. The convoy system was very expensive, but in terms of security it fully proved its worth. The only occasions on which the treasure galleons fell into enemy hands were 1628, when the Dutch Piet Heyn captured all but three of the vessels, and 1656 and 1657 when the fleet was destroyed by Blake.

The impact on the Castilian economy of this gradually developing trade between Seville and the New World remains extremely difficult to assess. Two problems are involved: how to measure the stimulus given to the economic life of Castile by the expanding American market, and how to gauge the consequences for Castile of the influx of American silver. The first of these problems requires much more study on a regional basis than it has so far received. Spain under Charles V had not one, but at least three economies, touching each other at various points but none the less distinct. There was Seville and its hinterland, facing towards America; there was northern Castile, traditionally orientated towards Flanders and northern Europe; and there was the Crown of Aragon, still largely concerned with its Mediterranean markets.

Of these three economic regions it was naturally the Andalusian that reacted first and most sharply to the conquest and colonization of the New World. Around 1500 the city of Seville had some 60,000 or 70,000 inhabitants. During the next two or three decades this figure was reduced by epidemics and by the emigration of ablebodied men to the Indies, but from the 1530s the the figures not only recovered, but began to increase dramatically, until they may have risen to as high as 150,000 by 1588. This spectacular increase made Seville one of the boom cities of the sixteenth century – larger than any other Spanish city, and surpassed in size only by Paris and Naples. It was a bustling, thriving city, with all the marks of the new prosperity that had come from its contact with the exotic world of the Indies; a city which as Guzmán de Alfarache said, had 'un olor de ciudad, un no sé qué, otras grandezas'. It was crowded with foreign merchants, Italians, Flemings, Portuguese, and it acted as an irresistible magnet to the inhabitants of northern and central Spain, who thought of it as an El Dorado in its own right and as the gateway to the untold riches of America.

During the course of the sixteenth century the inhabitants of northern Spain moved southwards in their thousands, travelling overland or by sea from Cantabria. This great movement of internal colonization, which gradually tilted the demographic balance of Castile away from the north towards the south and the west, was in a sense the final phase of the *Reconquista* – that long southward trek of the Castilians into Andalusia in pursuit of wealth. The migrants were coming to a land that had been touched by the brush of prosperity. The valley of the Guadalquivir as far as the Sierra Morena was being planted by Sevillian merchants with cereals, vines and olives for sale in Seville, and for export to northern Europe and to the Indies. Many Andalusian peasants were growing rich on the sales of their crops, and were becoming owners of extensive holdings of land. There were signs, too, of industrial as well as of agrarian vitality in the development of textile production in towns like Úbeda and Baeza, and in the increasing output of Granada silk, for which there was a growing demand in Flanders, France, and Italy.

The Crown of Aragon shared only marginally in this new-found prosperity. The Catalans unsuccessfully sought permission on several occasions during the reign of Charles V to establish consuls in Seville and Cadiz, and to obtain special privileges in connexion with the American trade. But they benefited indirectly from it in the increased sale of their cloths in the fairs of Castile – three-quarters of all these cloths being bought for shipment to the New World. On the other hand, the connexion between Seville and the north – as distinct from the east – of Spain were very close. Ships from northern dockyards played an important part in the *Carrera de las Indias*, and there was constant traffic and interchange between the three great commercial centres of Burgos, Medina del Campo, and Seville.

If the towns of northern and central Castile were so intimately associated with the life of Andalusia, this was primarily because of their own economic vitality, which made their co-operation essential to the merchants of Seville. Seville needed the shipbuilding skills and the navigational experience of the Basques, and it needed the

machinery of international credit that had been so elaborately constructed in the fairs of Castile – just as the fairs in turn needed the
silver that only Seville could supply. Medina del Campo later became
the slave rather than the partner of Seville, and an excessive dependence on the prompt arrival of the treasure fleet brought it to disaster;
but in the reign of Charles V, when financial transactions did not yet
monopolize its activity to the exclusion of all else, Medina could
draw upon the economic resources of the surrounding region to
assert its independence.

The prosperity of northern Castile in the earlier part of the sixteenth century, in fact, equalled or surpassed that of Andalusia. This
prosperity, while reinforced by the benefits that came from association with the developing economy of the Spanish Atlantic, was
essentially based on the solid foundations that had been laid during the
fifteenth century. The spectacular expansion of Castile's international
trade in that century had come largely from the Flemish demand for
Spanish merino wool – a demand that continued to grow in the early
sixteenth century. In the mid-1520s the flocks of the *Mesta* reached
their peak in a figure of some three and a half million head of sheep.
But there were other exports besides that of wool. There was a
considerable demand in France for the iron of Vizcaya, where the
metallurgical industry in the early sixteenth century seems to have
been technically advanced. There was a demand too, both in northern
Europe and Italy for the products of Spain's luxury industries –
ceramics, leather, silk, Toledo blades.

Castilian industry in the reign of Charles V was therefore bene-
fiting from an increased European demand in an age of international
economic expansion. But the most widespread industry was the
textile industry, particularly vigorous in Segovia, Toledo, Córdoba,
and Cuenca; and here the demand was largely Spanish and American.
Apart from what was exported to the Indies, most of Castile's cloth
went to supplying the home market. It seems probable that this home
market was growing: the population of Castile has been estimated at
some 6,270,000 for 1541, and this is believed to suggest some advance
since the late fifteenth century. An increase in population presented a
challenge to local industry and agriculture, and both showed some
signs of rising to the occasion. New land was brought under the
plough; new textile centres arose. In spite of the obvious signs of

expansion, however, both industry and agriculture suffered from internal weaknesses, and were exposed to external strains which slowed down their progress and partially crippled their performance.

Castilian agriculture, having been persistently disparaged by a royal policy which favoured the wool interest, was now called upon not only to meet the rising demand at home but also to supply the needs of the American market. The profits to be gained from the sale of wine and oil to the Indies tended to divert capital and resources in the south of Spain from corn-growing to the cultivation of vines and olives. This made the challenge all the greater to the corn-growers of Old Castile. But the majority of these were small peasants without either the resources or the technical skill to tackle the fundamental obstacle to a large increase in corn-production – the problem of drought. Irrigation schemes required capital, which at this time was heavily engaged in commercial projects; and the peasant, left to his own devices, increased his production by the only method he knew: the breaking of new soil. The new land might have to be rented from aristocratic proprietors, who leased it out, often for short periods, at rates which imposed a heavier burden on the peasant than the old feudal dues. Moreover, the money required to develop the land would have to be borrowed from some wealthy villager or townsman. This was done by means of the *censo al quitar*, a short-term loan at a rate of perhaps 7.14 per cent (one-fourteenth of the capital), guaranteed by a mortgage on the borrower's lands. In theory, the peasant should have benefited by the increase in agricultural prices and by the legal right conceded in 1535 to re-purchase the *censo* at any time. But in practice his profits were reduced by the *tasa* or fixed maximum, which was definitively re-established on grain prices in 1539, and he was usually in no position to re-purchase. If the Castilian peasant just managed to hold his own during the reign of Charles V, the increasing amount of peasant indebtedness suggested that future prospects were far from bright: one or two poor harvests or a fall in agricultural prices could all too easily lead to disaster.

The textile industry, while enjoying a boom similar to that experienced by Castilian agriculture, also rested on precarious foundations. There were, from the first, problems of quality. While the Castilian cloth industry was carefully – and indeed excessively –

regimented under guild control, little trouble was taken about the technical training of cloth-workers, and there was an endless stream of complaints about the low quality of home-produced wares. A further problem was that of labour. A young industry suddenly found itself flooded with an enormous home and American demand, which it was ill-equipped to meet. Failing to find sufficient labour among the urban artisans, it turned first to the peasants, and then to the army of vagabonds and beggars which tramped the Castilian roads. In 1540 the poor law of 1387 was renewed, imposing harsh penalties on vagrants and authorizing local authorities to set them to work without pay. The passing of the 1540 poor law was a victory for the school of the great humanist philosopher Juan Luis Vives, whose *De Subventione Pauperum*, published at Bruges in 1526, had demanded an absolute prohibition on begging and the close regulation of public charity. But while Crown and Cortes had come out in favour of the Vives approach to the problem of the idle poor, it was bitterly criticized by members of the Mendicant Orders, who did their best to reduce the effectiveness of the new legislation. The insistence of Fray Domingo de Soto and his colleagues that begging was a fundamental human right of which nobody should be deprived clearly aroused considerable public sympathy, for in 1552 the Cortes again had to insist that vagrants should be set to work, on the grounds that 'there is a shortage of workmen rather than of work to be done'. But although the legislation of 1540 continued to be the basis of government policy it seems to have remained virtually a dead letter. The vagrants continued to evade the half-hearted attempts to coerce them, and the persisting labour shortage undoubtedly contributed to one of the principal defects of Castilian cloths – their excessively high price.

Throughout the early years of Charles V's reign there had been a swelling chorus of complaints from the home market about the high price of Castilian manufactures, and in particular of home-produced textiles. This reached its climax in the Cortes of Valladolid of 1548, which attributed the high prices to the demand for Castilian cloths outside Spain, and proposed as a remedy that the import of foreign cloths into Castile should be permitted, while all exports of Castilian manufactures, even to the Indies, should be forbidden. The Crown responded by allowing the import of foreign textiles, but the Cortes remained dissatisfied. In 1552 they pressed again for a ban on exports to America. While the Crown again refused to accede to so drastic a proposal, it moved one step further in the direction desired by the Cortes by prohibiting all exports of Castilian cloth except to the Indies.

This remarkable legislation of 1548–52 was followed, as might have been foreseen, by a sharp depression in the Castilian textile industry, which suddenly found itself threatened by the competition of cheaper foreign products; and further legislation had to be hastily introduced in 1555 and 1558 rescinding the ban on exports. But ephemeral as was the legislation of 1548–52, its significance was enormous, for it marked the point at which the expanding Castilian economy was confronted by its first severe crisis – a crisis which, as the legislation showed, found the country groping in the dark for a way of escape from its dilemmas.

The nature of the crisis was obvious enough: Castilian goods were appreciably more expensive than goods imported from abroad. But the exact reasons for this were far from clear to contemporaries, and have remained a subject for vigorous, if inconclusive, debate into our own day. The Cortes attributed the phenomenon to the heavy foreign and American demand for Castilian goods. During the 1550s another possible explanation of the rise of prices in Spain was put forward by Martín de Azpilcueta, one of the members of the distinguished school of writers on economic and monetary matters which flourished at Salamanca University in these years. Writing in 1556, Azpilcueta listed a number of reasons why the value of money might change. His seventh reason was that 'money is worth more when and where it is scarce than where it is abundant', and elaborating on this he wrote: 'We see by experience that in France, where money is scarcer than in Spain, bread, wine, cloth, and labour are worth much less. And even in Spain, in times when money was scarcer, saleable goods and labour were given for very much less than after the discovery of the Indies, which flooded the country with gold and silver.'4 Here was the first clear exposition of the quantity theory in relation to the influx of precious metals from

4. The relevant passage is printed in full on pp. 91–96 of Marjorie Grice-Hutchinson, *The School of Salamanca. Readings in Spanish Monetary Theory, 1544–1605* (Oxford, 1952).

America – published twelve years before its exposition by the French Jean Bodin, who is usually given the credit for its discovery.

It was only in the present century, however, that an intensive effort was made to correlate Spanish prices with the figures for the import of American bullion. In 1934 the American economic historian Professor Earl J. Hamilton, after collecting and processing a vast amount of statistical information on American silver and Spanish prices, came to the conclusion that 'the extremely close correlation between the increase in the volume of treasure imports and the advance of commodity prices throughout the sixteenth century, particularly from 1535 on, demonstrates beyond question that the "abundant mines of America" were the principal cause of the Price Revolution in Spain'.[5] This explanation was readily accepted at the time, but in recent years there has been a growing awareness that acceptance of the theory in the form presented by Hamilton creates certain difficulties to which no solution has yet been forthcoming.

There is no dispute as to the existence of a sharp upward trend in Spanish price movements during the sixteenth century: Hamilton's figures suggest a fourfold increase between 1501 and 1600. Nor is there apparently any dispute that Spanish prices moved ahead of other European prices, and that the exchanges were usually unfavourable to Spain. The disagreement has come over the neat coincidence found by Hamilton between the rise in prices and the figures for bullion imports; and more recently it has extended to the whole question of the exact chronology of the price increases.

Hamilton's reading of his figures led him to conclude that Spanish prices passed through three stages:

1501–1550	a moderate rise;
1550–1600	the culmination of the price revolution;
1601–1650	stagnation.

This coincided very satisfactorily with the movements in the import of American bullion, which not only showed a remarkable agreement with the general price trend, but also could often be very closely correlated with many of the short-term price movements.

5. Earl J. Hamilton, *American Treasure and the Price Revolution in Spain, 1501–1650* (Harvard University Press, 1934), p. 301.

The correlation, however, eventually prompted certain embarrassing questions. Did Hamilton's figures, drawn from the official registers at Seville, really represent the total import of American silver into Spain? If, as seems probable, there was large-scale contraband, the figures lose much of their value. Still more important, what really happened to the silver when it reached Seville? Hamilton's thesis presupposes its steady injection into the Spanish economy, and a widening circle of rising prices as the silver moved outwards from Andalusia and spread through Spain and then through other parts of Europe. But this thesis ignores the question both of the ownership of the silver and the purposes to which it might be put. As regards the King's portion of the bullion imports, this tended to be mortgaged in advance to his foreign bankers, who might well transfer it abroad at once, without its in any way touching the Spanish economy. The private portion of the bullion imports could obviously be used for a wide variety of purposes – and not necessarily monetary purposes – depending on individual tastes. It would be reasonable to assume, however, that a large proportion of the silver remitted from America to Seville was intended to pay for goods sold in the Indies. If these goods were Spanish in origin, then the silver might well be expected to flow back into Spanish hands; but the extent to which they *were* Spanish in origin naturally depended upon the capacity of Spanish industry to meet the demands of the American market. Since there are many indications, especially in the second half of the sixteenth century, that Castilian industrial production was lagging badly behind the demand, it is natural to assume *an increasing share of foreign products* among the cargoes destined for America. In spite of the prohibitions on the export of precious metals from Spain, it is perfectly clear that the silver used to buy these foreign goods did not stay in the country, and that its registration at Seville was often a mere formality before its owners sent it abroad at the earliest possible opportunity. In view of this, the total quantity of silver registered at Seville and the total quantity entering Spain cannot safely be considered as automatically equivalent to each other. The close correlation between Spanish prices and bullion imports is therefore difficult to accept as it has so far been presented, since nobody knows what proportion of the bullion was actually imported into Spain.

While one side of the Hamilton equation – the amount of silver entering Spain – hardly seems to stand up to the criticisms that have been levelled at it, the other side of the equation – the price movements inside Spain – has also, more recently, come under critical scrutiny. A re-working of Hamilton's figures by Dr Nadal[6] would suggest that the greatest proportional increase in Spanish prices occurred in the first half rather than the second half of the sixteenth century, where Hamilton has his peak figures both for prices and for silver imports. On Dr Nadal's reckoning, there was a 2.8 per cent average annual increase in prices from 1501 to 1562, as compared with a 1.3 per cent average annual increase for 1562–1600. The rapid inflation of the first half of the century, with 1421–30 as the decade of the sharpest upward movement for the entire century, was thus followed by a slowing down of the inflationary movement in the last thirty years, after a further sharp upswing between 1561 and 1565.

The whole question of the exact origins of the price revolution is therefore once again reduced to a state of extreme uncertainty. If the sharpest price increase occurred in the first half of the century, this cannot be correlated with the maximum figures for the arrival of silver at Seville, which are to be found in the second half of the century. On the other hand, some correlation might still be found, if it were assumed – as is not unreasonable – that more of the American silver actually flowed into Spain in the first half than the second half of the century, when the share of Spanish products for the American market fell off. But even if no correlation were discovered, there can be not the slightest doubt that the influx of American silver played an important part in the raising of prices, although the exact nature of the part it played remains extremely difficult to assess. An attempt has recently been made by M. Chaunu to widen the Hamiltonian interpretation, by correlating Spanish prices not with the fluctuations in the imports of registered silver but with the fluctuations in Sevillian trade with the New World, as reflected in the figures for transatlantic shipping. This, however, is open to the objection that figures for shipping, while they can suggest much about the needs of the American market and about the general level of business confidence, cannot in themselves provide conclusive evidence about the level of production in Castile unless it is known – as it is not – what propor-

6. J. Nadal Oller, 'La Revolución de los Precios Españoles en el Siglo XVI', *Hispania*, vol. XIX (1959), pp. 503–29.

tion of the transatlantic cargoes consisted of specifically Castilian produce. Without this information, it is difficult to see that they provide any safer clue to the quantity of silver flowing back into the Spanish economy than is provided by Hamilton's Sevillian statistics. On the other hand, the Chaunu interpretation has the great merit of widening the scope of the discussion to suggest a much more subtle interrelationship between the Castilian economy and that of Castile's transatlantic possessions than has so far been assumed.

It seems clear at least that any satisfactory analysis of the causes of the price revolution will have to take into account many points beside the influx of precious metals. Debasement of the coinage, which pushed up prices in the England of Henry VIII and the France of Francis I, did not occur in the Spain of Charles V; but the Emperor's borrowings, which he partially financed by the creation of *juros*, or credit bonds, are likely to have had highly inflationary consequences. Similar results could have been produced by the lavish expenditure of the Spanish aristocracy on building, clothes, and jewellery, part of which may have been financed out of de-hoarded silver. Finally, and perhaps most important of all, there was the impact of a suddenly increased demand upon an undeveloped economy.

The demand came partly from the population increase at home, and partly from the expansion of traditional markets in Flanders and Italy, together with the creation of an entirely new market in America. While Castile made great efforts to meet this demand, the effectiveness of these efforts was restricted by the primitive character of its agrarian organization and also, in some spheres, by a shortage of labour. The inability of Castilian agriculture to feed a growing population at home while simultaneously supplying its new American market, pushed up food prices to a level which made it increasingly difficult for the ordinary Castilian to buy the necessities of life, and left him with little or nothing to spend on essential manufactured articles, of which the most important were textiles. The prices of these had themselves been forced up by the inadequate output of Castilian industry, much of which was in any event being sent to the profitable American market. The sales to America in turn brought into the country a sudden influx of silver, which raised the Spanish price level above that of other European states, and eventually led to an irresistible demand for the sale of foreign goods in Castile, on the grounds that they were appreciably cheaper. As soon as the Crown acceded to this demand Castilian industry found itself gravely threatened by foreign competitors, who not only broke into its home market but also prised their way into the hitherto exclusive American market, for which both the quantity and the quality of Castilian manufactures tended to be increasingly inadequate.

An interpretation along roughly these lines suggests explanations of the initial expansion of industry in sixteenth-century Castile, and of its consequent stagnation, which differ from those advanced by Professor Hamilton. For Hamilton, the principal stimulus to industrial advance was to be found in the lag of wages behind prices: prices rose faster than wages in the early part of the century, and this gave the Castilian industrialist a greater incentive than was enjoyed by his foreign counterparts. Conversely, as soon as salaries caught up with prices the incentive disappeared, and industrial expansion petered out. But in fact there is far too little evidence about Castilian wages in the sixteenth century to support this, or any other hypothesis, about the relation of prices and wages. The sharp rise in food prices suggests that the workman was an early victim of the price revolution, and that his living standards deteriorated over a considerable part of the century; but it is arguable that the principal beneficiaries of rising prices were not industrialists (who may soon have found themselves spending more on raw materials and on paying and feeding their employees), but those landowners who were in the happy position of being able to raise their rents.

In place of the Hamiltonian explanation in terms of the interrelationship of prices and wages, it might be more advisable to set an explanation in terms of expanding market possibilities, which served as an initial stimulus to economic expansion in Castile, but then came up against a series of difficulties – insufficient agricultural and industrial output, uncompetitive prices – which the country failed to surmount. The reasons for this failure would still have to be examined and analysed in detail, but it is only reasonable to take into account the fact that Castile found itself confronted in the mid-sixteenth century with problems of unprecedented complexity, and that if it tackled them in the wrong way, this was partly because there was no fund of previous experience on which to draw.

An admission of the complexity of the problems, however, should not preclude all consideration of the calibre of the men who had to wrestle with them, and of the degree of skill and determination which they displayed. These men were, first of all, the entrepreneurs themselves. Many of the merchants and businessmen in sixteenth-century Spain were foreigners: the Genoese in particular dominated the economic life of southern Spain, where many of them had been established since the *Reconquista*. Yet in spite of the large contingent of foreign merchants, and of the common assumptions about the Spanish lack of aptitude for business, there is a growing volume of evidence about the importance of native Castilian businessmen in Castilian economic life, especially during the earlier part of the sixteenth century.

Although the Genoese may have been predominant in the south, there was an active class of native merchants and financiers in the towns of north Castile in the reign of Charles V. The Venetian Andreas Navagero says as much in his account of the city of Burgos, which he visited during his travels in the peninsula between 1524 and 1526: 'The city is very populous and there are artisans of all kinds. Several gentlemen live here, and a number of nobles with fine palaces, like the Constable [of Castile] and the Count of Salinas. But the majority of its inhabitants are rich merchants, who travel on business not only throughout Spain but all over the world; they have very good houses and live very comfortably, and they are the most courteous people I have come across in Spain.' Burgos was, in fact, a city of merchant dynasties, like the families of Maluenda, Salamanca, and Miranda, and they had their counterparts in other north Castilian towns, including the most famous of all – the merchant banking family of Ruiz in Medina del Campo.

Many of these families were engaged in large-scale undertakings. Having originally made their fortune in the wool trade, they had then branched out into other commercial and financial transactions, including credit transactions for Charles V; and they had their agents in the banking houses of Seville, where there were several important native bankers such as the Espinosas, probably a *converso* family originating in Medina de Ríoseco. There is no reason to believe that these Castilian businessmen were in any respect inferior in commercial and accounting techniques to their counterparts elsewhere in Europe. The widespread use of Castilian for business transactions in commercial centres outside Spain suggests that there was nothing parochial about the Spanish merchant, and Simón Ruiz in particular can be regarded as the prototype of the sixteenth-century business-man.

It is not clear how far these men were interested in industrial enterprises, but at least they showed no inhibitions about exploiting the commercial and financial opportunities that had come with the country's growing prosperity in the early sixteenth century. There is indeed nothing to indicate that the sixteenth-century Castilian was congenitally unsuited to a business life; and if it seems ominous that the second and third generations of merchant dynasties should have preferred the pleasures of aristocratic existence to the tedium of the counting-house, this merely emphasizes their resemblance to their counterparts everywhere else in Europe. All the signs therefore seem to indicate that in the early sixteenth century there were very fair prospects for the development of a dynamic 'capitalist' element in Castile, which – like its equivalent in England or Holland – might gradually have imposed some of its ideals and values on the rest of society. The fact that these prospects were not realized would suggest that at some point adverse circumstances proved too strong, and that the enterprise of the north Castilian *bourgeoisie* failed to withstand a serious change for the worse in the country's economic and social climate.

It is clear that much of the responsibility for Castile's economic failure needs to be sought at a higher level than that of the entre-preneur – with the Government rather than with the businessman. Many of the Government's deficiencies are, in fact, to be found in the failings of the Council of Finance. Its members, almost all of whom had no personal experience of commercial and financial affairs, made no attempt to develop any coherent economic pro-gramme, or to think out the implications for the Castilian economy of the acquisition of an American empire. References are frequently made to the 'mercantilist' policies of sixteenth-century Spain, but it could be cogently argued that it was precisely because of the lack of any consistently pursued mercantilist policies (other than the Sevillian monopoly) that the country ran into such serious economic difficult-ies. There was no attempt at systematic exploitation of the resources of the New World other than those of the mines, and almost nothing was done to develop in the New World an economy which might complement that of Castile. It is true that the Government ordered the destruction of newly planted Peruvian vineyards and olive groves, for fear of their competing with the wine and oil exports of Andalusia; but colonial industries, on the other hand, were allowed to develop unchecked, and Charles V gave specific encouragements to the silk industry of New Spain, although this was an obvious competitor to the silk industry of Granada. The development of colonial industries was presumably allowed because of the inability of Castilian industry to supply all the needs of the American market, but it seems to have escaped the notice of the Government that a more logical method of dealing with the problem would have been to foster the growth of industry at home. Similarly, nothing was done to tackle the problem of the acute shortage of ships, which were urgently needed if an effective Spanish monopoly of trade with the New World were to be preserved. But the most serious failure of all was the failure to devise any scheme for using the supply of American silver for the benefit of the Castilian economy. While the responsibility for this failure lay immediately with the Council of Finance, it was ultimately bound up with the much wider question of the means employed by Charles V to finance his Imperial policies.

4. THE PROBLEMS OF IMPERIAL FINANCE

From the moment of his Imperial election Charles V found himself saddled with enormous commitments. The struggle with France in the 1520s, the offensive and defensive operations against the Turks in the 1530s, and then, in the 1540s and 1550s, the hopeless task of quelling heresy and revolt in Germany, imposed a constant strain on the Imperial finances. Always desperately short of funds, Charles would turn from one of his dominions to another in the search for more money, and would negotiate on unfavourable terms with his German and Genoese bankers for loans to carry him over the moments of acute penury, at the expense of mortgaging more and more of his present and future sources of revenue. This hand-to-mouth existence had prompted, in the very first years of the reign, gloomy prophecies about the certainty of financial shipwreck, but, in fact, it was not until 1557, when Philip II had succeeded his father, that the expected bankruptcy materialized. Until then, Charles's appeals to the generosity of his subjects and his constant recourse to loans from the bankers somehow managed to stave off the moment of disaster; but the price paid was a renunciation of any attempt to organize the Imperial finances on a rational basis and to plan a coherent economic programme for the various territories of the Empire.

The main cost of financing Charles's imperialism was borne by different territories at different times, depending on their presumed fiscal capacity and on the facility with which money could be extracted from them. The territories concerned were primarily European, for the part played by the new American possessions in financing Habsburg policies during the first half of the sixteenth century was relatively very small. Until the 1550s the Crown's revenues from America averaged only some 200,000–300,000 ducats a year, as compared with the 2,000,000 ducats a year of the later years of the reign of Philip II. This meant that the real entry of the New World into the Habsburg empire was delayed until the decade 1550–60, and that Charles V's imperialism, unlike that of his son, was essentially a European-based imperialism.

Among the European territories of Charles it was the Netherlands and Italy which bore the brunt of the Imperial expenditure during the first half of the reign. But as each in turn began to be squeezed dry Charles was compelled to look elsewhere for further sources of revenue, and by 1540 he was writing to his brother Ferdinand: 'I cannot be sustained except by my kingdoms of Spain.' Henceforth, the financial contributions of Spain – which meant essentially Castile – assumed a constantly increasing importance in relation to those of the Low Countries.

Within Spain there were several potential sources of revenue, both secular and ecclesiastical. The financial contribution of the Spanish Church to Habsburg imperialism in the sixteenth and seventeenth centuries still awaits an adequate study, but its importance would be difficult to overestimate. If the Lutheran princes of Europe were to gain great benefits from breaking with Rome and despoiling the Churches in their territories, the kings of Spain were to show that despoiling the Church was equally possible without going to the lengths of rupture with the Papacy, and that the long-term advantages of this method were at least as great, and probably greater. It was difficult for the Papacy to refuse new financial concessions when the, Faith was everywhere being endangered by the spread of heresy; and the Spanish Crown, by placing no restrictions on mortmain, could further the accumulation of property in the hands of the Church, where it was more readily available for taxation.

The direct revenues payable by the Spanish Church to the Crown in the reign of Charles V consisted of the *tercias reales*, or one-third of all the tithes collected by the Church in Castile, and the *subsidio*, a tax on clerical rents and incomes in all the Spanish kingdoms, fixed at a rate agreed between the Crown and the Papacy, but nominally dependent on regular votes by the clergy. To these would be added in 1567 the *excusado*, a new tax to help pay for the war in Flanders, consisting of the entire tithe of the most valuable piece of property in every parish. Besides these regular taxes, the Crown also enjoyed the revenues of vacant sees, and, most important of all, the lands and revenues of the Military Orders, which were permanently vested in it by Charles V's former tutor, Pope Adrian VI, in 1523, and were shortly afterwards assigned to the bankers as security for their loans. Finally, the kings of Spain received one very valuable tax which was granted them by papal concession and was payable by the laity as well as the clergy: the *cruzada*. This had originally been conceded as an emergency tax to help them in their struggle against the Moors, but became a regular source of royal revenue in the reign of Charles V, payable every three years by every man, woman and child anxious for a bull of indulgence. At a minimum rate of 2 *reales* a bull, this tax yielded during the Emperor's reign an average of some 150,000 ducats a year – not a great deal less than the Crown's income from America.

Of the secular taxes received by the Spanish Crown, those paid by the States of the Crown of Aragon constituted a relatively small share. In his eastern kingdoms the Emperor was entirely dependent for taxes on the subsidies voted by the individual Cortes of Catalonia, Aragon, and Valencia, which he made it a practice to summon together simultaneously to the town of Monzón. There were six sessions at Monzón during the course of the reign – 1528, 1533, 1537, 1542, 1547, 1552 – and the contributions varied from session to session, but they seem to have produced for the Emperor a total of only some 500,000 ducats for each five-year period. The Cortes were so powerful, and the conditions they imposed so stringent, that the chances of increasing the contributions were slight, and the Crown of Aragon was paying at the end of the reign no more than it was paying in the early years, in spite of the fact that prices had more than doubled in the intervening period.

The Emperor's failure to extract larger contributions from the Crown of Aragon inevitably made him increasingly dependent on the fiscal resources of Castile, where the Cortes were far less powerful, and where there were a number of important sources of revenue outside the Cortes's control. These extra-parliamentary taxes were known as the *rentas ordinarias*, and included customs dues (both external and internal), the *almojarifazgo* on the American trade, the *servicio* and *montazgo* on the transit of sheep and cattle, a tax on the Granada silk industry, and, above all, the famous *alcabala*. The *alcabala*, a tax on sales, had been collected by the Crown throughout the fifteenth century as a regular royal tax for which the consent of the realm was not required, although Isabella does seem to have had some scruples about its legality at the end of her life. As a tax, however, it was far too valuable to be allowed to pass under the control of the Cortes for the sale of a few conscientious scruples: at the beginning of the sixteenth century it probably accounted – together with the clerical *tercias reales*, with which it was traditionally associated – for some 80 per cent to 90 per cent of the Crown's entire income. But the Cortes did manage to obtain a veto over any increase in the tax assessments, and since it became a regular practice from 1515 for the towns to compound for the *alcabala*, paying a fixed sum known as the *encabezamiento*, the relative value of the *alcabala* decreased in proportion as prices rose. As a result, the Emperor was compelled to search for other sources of revenue to supplement a tax which, by the end of his reign, accounted for only a quarter of his income.

The only way of raising additional direct taxes was to secure them by parliamentary grant. For this reason the Castilian Cortes, after an erratic and undistinguished career in the later years of Isabella, recovered some of their former importance under Charles, and were summoned at least fifteen times in the course of the reign. The traditional grant voted by the Cortes was known as the *servicio*, and was regarded as a temporary subsidy granted for emergency purposes, as the Cortes were careful to remind Charles when he attempted in 1518 to continue the practice instituted by Ferdinand in 1504 of asking for a *servicio* every three years, whether or not there were an emergency. The decline in the value of the *alcabala* made it essential, however, that the *servicio* should become a regular tax. In spite of the defeat of the *Comuneros*, the Cortes summoned in 1523 were still sufficiently vigorous and independent to put up a strong resistance, but the *procuradores* were finally compelled to give way and vote a *servicio* of 400,000 ducats payable in three years. In the Cortes of Toledo of 1525 Charles attempted to sweeten the pill of defeat and simultaneously to free himself from dependence on corrupt and inefficient tax-farmers, by borrowing from the Crown of Aragon the idea of a permanent *Diputación* and allowing the *procuradores* of the Castilian Cortes to set up a permanent commission on the Aragonese model to supervise the collection of the tax and to see that the Emperor fulfilled his promises to the Cortes; but nothing could conceal the fact that the power of the Cortes had been broken, and that ordinary and extraordinary *servicios* would in future form a regular and essential part of the royal revenues.

As the yield of the *alcabala* declined, therefore, that of the *servicios* increased; and during the course of a reign in which prices doubled, the monetary yield of the *servicio* nearly quadrupled. While *servicios* of some 400,000 ducats a year helped to compensate the Emperor for the losses incurred through accepting the *encabezamiento*, and consequently meant no more for him than the partial replacement of one source of income by another, the effect of the change on Castilian society and the Castilian economy was very marked. The *alcabala*, defective as it was in many ways, had the great advantage of being a universal tax paid by members of every social order (except in certain circumstances, the clergy), in that it was a tax on everything bought and sold. The payment of the *servicio*, on the other hand, was customarily limited to one section of society, the *pecheros* or taxpayers, while all those enjoying privileges of nobility were exempt. Unfortunately, the figures for *pecheros* and *hidalgos* in the Castile of Charles V are extremely uncertain. One estimate suggests 781,582 *pechero* householders and 108,358 *hidalgo* householders, which would mean that some 13 per cent of the population was exempt from paying the *servicios*. In practice, the social distribution of the population varied enormously from province to province. In the province of León, for instance, there were as many *hidalgos* as *pecheros*; in Burgos, the *hidalgos* represented a quarter of the population; in Valladolid, an eighth; and the number of *hidalgos* decreased the further south one moved. As a result the incidence of the *servicios* was extremely unequal, both geographically and socially, but the general effect was everywhere to place the burden of taxation on the shoulders of those least able to bear it. Moreover, the *procuradores* who voted the tax were themselves drawn from the closed municipal oligarchies, most of whose members enjoyed, or were quick to acquire, privileges of *hidalguía*, and they consequently showed no great compunction in voting a tax which they themselves would not be called upon to pay.

The increase in the rate of the *servicios* therefore had extremely important social effects, in that it tended to widen the gulf between the exempt rich and the overburdened poor, and at the same time induced wealthy merchants and businessmen to abandon their businesses and buy privileges of *hidalguía* in order to escape the burden of taxation. Anxious to introduce a fairer system which would also enable him to draw upon the wealth of the rich, the Emperor attempted in the Cortes of 1538 to establish a tax on food-stuffs, known as the *sisa*, which would yield 800,000 ducats a year and would be paid by everyone, irrespective of social condition. Besides the representatives of the eighteen towns, Charles had summoned to these Cortes twenty-five archbishops and bishops, and ninety-five members of the aristocracy to advise him on methods of dealing with the acute financial emergency. The aristocratic estate, whose support was indispensable for the imposition of the *sisa*, showed itself bitterly opposed to a tax which would remove its traditional privilege of exemption. The Count of Benavente spoke for a class which already felt itself slighted and imperilled by the Emperor's habit of appointing the low-born to high secular and ecclesiastical office, when he said: 'The real need is to secure liberties and to recover those we have lost—not to give away those that we have.' The strength of the opposition finally compelled the Emperor to capitulate, and the *procuradores* responded to his appeals for assistance by falling back on traditional money-raising methods and voting an extraordinary *servicio*.

The outcome of the Cortes of 1538 was thus a victory for privilege – but a victory gained at what was finally to prove an immensely high price. The tax exemption of nobles and *hidalgos* had been preserved at the cost of destroying the last hopes of constitutionalism in Castile. After 1538 nobles and clergy were no longer summoned to meetings of the Castilian Cortes, where the representatives of the towns were compelled to fight single-handed a losing battle against the increasingly arbitrary demands of the Crown. While the Cortes continued to complain and remonstrate, they had sacrificed their last opportunity to make the grant of subsidies conditional on the redress of grievances, and in future the Crown was largely able to ignore complaints which threatened to encroach on its prerogative. At the same time, the refusal of the Cortes either to increase the *encabezamientos* or to sanction the imposition of new taxes like the *sisa*, compelled the Crown to look for alternative sources of income over which the Cortes had no control, and this naturally reduced the influence of the Cortes in the one field where it still enjoyed some power – that of finance. If the Castilian Cortes was from now on to be little more than a rubber stamp, this was primarily because of the short-sightedness and egoism of nobles and towns in the Cortes of 1538, where they threw away their last chance of exercising a veto over Governmental policies.

In spite of the Emperor's success in obtaining a regular tax from the Cortes in the form of the *servicio*, he only managed to raise the Government's revenues by 50 per cent during the course of his reign, whereas there was a 100 per cent rise in prices during the same period. With the population of Castile increasing, this meant in theory that the burden of taxation per head was decreasing, but in practice the re-distribution of taxes, as a result of the new importance of the *servicio* in relation to the *alcabala*, left the *pechero* in a worse position at the end of the reign than at the beginning. But this was not the only unfortunate result of the Emperor's fiscal policies. The relatively small increase in Castilian taxation under Charles V in fact gives a highly misleading impression of the economic consequences of his policies, since it diverts attention from one source of revenue that rose steeply throughout the reign – the revenue from loans.

It proved from the first quite impossible to meet the Government's rapidly increasing expenses out of the ordinary sources of revenue. The Crown's net income for 1534, for example, was estimated at some 420,000 ducats, whereas its anticipated expenditure was 1,000,000; and expenses had an unpleasant way of increasing, while income, no less unpleasantly, usually turned out to be less than expected. In order to meet the deficit the Emperor was compelled to resort to a number of expedients, such as appropriating the remittances of American silver to private individuals – as happened on no less than nine occasions during his reign – and 'compensating' the victims with *juros*, or Government bonds. But confiscations of silver remittances, or the sale of privileges of nobility, were emergency measures which might fill a sudden immediate need, but which were quite inadequate for dealing with the problem of a permanent deficit.

A regular system of deficit financing had somehow to be evolved, and this was achieved by the employment of bankers and by the sale of *juros*. Over a period of thirty-seven years, Charles V, whose normal annual revenue as King of Spain was about 1,000,000 ducats a year, rising to 1,500,000 after 1542, was able to borrow 39,000,000 ducats on the strength of the credit of Castile. Until the disastrous years after 1552, when the Emperor's credit was fatally shaken, a variety of bankers, German, Genoese, Flemish, and Spanish, were prepared to advance him money on the understanding that they would receive payment from the next treasure-fleet or from future Castilian tax revenues. This understanding took the form of a written contract, known as the *asiento*, which was prepared by the Council of Finance. The purpose of an *asiento* was to stipulate the times and places for the bankers to deposit their loans, together with the terms of interest and the methods of repayment. As the *asiento* system became regularized and the Emperor's needs increased, one after another of the Crown's sources of income came to be alienated to the bankers, and a larger and larger share of its annual revenues was diverted to debt financing.

The sale of *juros* had similar consequences. *Juros* were originally annuities granted by the Crown out of State revenues as a special token of favour, but considerable numbers were sold by Ferdinand and Isabella to help finance the Granada war. Charles V continued and extended this practice on such a scale that it reached mammoth proportions. *Juros*, which yielded an interest of up to 7 per cent, depending upon the type of *juro* bought, were assigned in turn to each of the *rentas ordinarias*, with the result that by 1543 65 per cent of these ordinary revenues were devoted to the payment of annuities. Apart from the fact that the Crown was steadily mortgaging away its future revenues, so that annual estimates of income from ordinary sources lost all real meaning, the enormous increase in the number of *juros* during the reign of Charles V had incidental economic and social consequences of very great importance. *Juros* were bought by foreign and native bankers, by merchants and nobles, and by anyone with a little money to spare. The result was the growth of a powerful *rentier* class in Castile, investing its money not in trade or industry but in profitable Government bonds, and living contentedly on its annuities. If ever a suggestion was made, as it was in 1552, that the Government should undertake a gradual redemption of the *juros*, there was an immediate outcry from all the holders of *juros*, who saw no safe alternative for their investments except in the purchase of land, the price of which would rise sharply if the *juros* were redeemed.

Charles V's fantastically expensive foreign policies and his dependence on credit to finance them therefore had disastrous consequences for Castile. The country's resources were mortgaged for an indefinite number of years ahead in order to meet the Emperor's expenses, a large proportion of which had been incurred outside Spain. His reliance on credit contributed sharply to the prevailing inflationary trends. Above all, the lack of provision in the Crown's financial policies – its inability to devise any coherent financial programme – meant that such resources as did exist were squandered, while the methods used to extract them might almost have been deliberately designed to stunt the economic growth of Castile. The reign of Charles V, in fact, saw three dangerous developments that were to be of incalculable importance for sixteenth- and seventeenth-century Spain. In the first place, it established the dominance of foreign bankers over the country's sources of wealth. Secondly, it determined that Castile would bear the main weight of the fiscal burden within Spain. In the third place, it ensured that within Castile the brunt of the burden was borne by those classes which were least capable of bearing it.

5. THE LIQUIDATION OF CHARLES'S IMPERIALISM

The Emperor's ministers in Spain were perfectly well aware of the grave effects of his policies on the country's life. During the 1530s the correspondence of the Empress had repeatedly urged Charles to return home for the good of the realm, and in the 1540s Cobos and Prince Philip did their best to impress upon Charles in their letters to him the terrible straits in which Castile now found itself. 'With what they pay in other ordinary and extraordinary dues,' wrote Philip to the Emperor in May 1545, 'the common people, who have to pay these *servicios*, are reduced to such utter misery that many of them walk naked. And the misery is so universal that it is even greater among the vassals of nobles than it is among Your Majesty's vassals, for they are unable to pay their rents, lacking the wherewithal, and the prisons are full.'[7]

Cobos's despairing letters urging peace on the Emperor and protesting at the impossibility of raising new funds make it clear that ultimately it was not the financial ministers but the Emperor himself who was to blame. Cobos seems to have managed the royal finances as well as was possible in the circumstances. He successfully put an end to the raiding of the treasury by the great Spanish nobles, and he and his colleagues did their best to prepare estimates of income and expenditure as a basis for future policy. But the Emperor recklessly disregarded their advice, spending money on a lavish scale wherever he went, and urgently demanding large new remittances which Cobos could only raise by loans, often at very unfavourable rates of interest. If Cobos failed as a financial minister, this was largely because the Emperor demanded the impossible of him.

Cobos's constant financial preoccupations seem to have undermined his health, and he died in 1547, having driven himself hard to the end. His death removed one of the last of the Spanish ministers who had served Charles since the start of his reign and had helped to prepare Prince Philip to take up his inheritance. Cardinal Tavera had died in 1545; Charles's confessor García de Loaisa, Archbishop of Seville, in 1546, and Juan de Zúñiga, Philip's tutor and personal adviser, in the same year. The years 1545-7 thus saw the passing of

7. José M. March, *Niñez y Juventud de Felipe II*, vol. I (Madrid, 1941), p. 182.

a generation of ministers, and the emancipation of Philip from his tutelage. He had already married in 1543 his cousin, the Infanta María of Portugal, who died two years later in giving birth to a son, Don Carlos. In 1548, a widower of twenty-one, this prematurely aged young man was summoned by his father to join him in Brussels, leaving his sister María as regent in his place. The experience he had gained in the government of Spain was to be supplemented for the first time by some knowledge of the outside world.

Philip's journey to the Netherlands was intended to acquaint him with his Flemish subjects, but it was also to prove the first step in the gradual process by which the ageing Emperor divested himself of his crushing inheritance. Any hopes that Charles may still have entertained of placing Philip on the Imperial throne were to founder on the intransigence of his brother Ferdinand, who – together with his son Maximilian – was determined that both the Austrian lands of the Habsburgs and the Imperial title should remain in his own branch of the family. But the course of events in Germany, as much as Habsburg family squabbles, made an eventual division of Charles's inheritance unavoidable. In 1547 Charles won his great victory over the German Protestants at the battle of Mühlberg, and it seemed that Germany at last lay prostrate before him. But the very completeness of the Emperor's victory aroused deep anxiety among those German princes, like Maurice of Saxony, who had supported him at Mühlberg, and who now feared a consolidation of Imperial power in Germany at their own expense. In March 1552 Maurice broke with the Emperor and marched with his troops on Innsbruck, where Charles and Ferdinand were engaged in their consultations on the ultimate fate of the Empire. As Maurice entered the city by one gate Charles fled from it by another. Carried in a litter, and accompanied by only a small group of retainers, the ailing and gout-ridden Emperor continued his flight, over the Brenner, to reach safety in the Carinthian town of Villach. His German policy had collapsed in ruins about him, and heresy and rebellion had prevailed.

Charles's flight to Villach in 1552 symbolized the failure of his great Imperial experiment. The failure had been precipitated by the defection not only of Maurice of Saxony, but also of the Imperial bankers, who had finally lost confidence in the Emperor and had failed to advance the money that was needed to pay his troops. The bankers were correct in their assessment, for the claims on the Emperor had been too great and his resources ultimately too few. The Spanish royal finances, which had borne the full strain of the Imperial policies during the last reckless decade, were now moving inexorably towards bankruptcy, while the Empire itself was visibly splitting into two parts. Nothing now could keep the German lands under the control of the Spanish royal house, and Philip, who succeeded his father as King of Spain in 1556, would preside over an empire that was inevitably very different from that inherited by his father.

It was in the hope of making this new empire a viable unit that Charles married Philip to Mary Tudor in 1554. There was about the English match an imaginative boldness typical of the Emperor, coupled with a greater awareness of economic and strategic realities than had characterized some of his previous grand designs. In place of the vast and cumbersome geographical monstrosity that passed for an empire under Charles V, Philip II would rule an empire of three logical units: England and the Netherlands, Spain and Italy, and America.

Having arranged for his son an incomparably more manageable inheritance than he had ever obtained for himself, Charles removed himself to Spain, to spend his declining years in the land which had come to mean more to him than any of his other possessions. His retreat to Yuste, and the accession of his Spanish-born son, fittingly symbolized the hispanicization of the dynasty. The verdict of Villalar was at last reversed, and the Castile that had been threatened with foreign captivity had itself taken the foreigner captive. But Philip himself was still far from his native land, and his presence was needed in Castile to reassure his subjects that the cosmopolitan Imperial experiment of his father would never be repeated. His return, however, could only be a matter of time. The Emperor died on 21 September 1558. Less than two months later his daughter-in-law, Mary Tudor, died childless, and her death brought to an abrupt end any hope of the union of England, Spain, and the Netherlands beneath a single crown. In future, the Netherlands would be an isolated outpost of an empire whose heart would inevitably be Spain.

The peninsular kingdoms were now clamouring for Philip's return. The financial and economic situation had become increasingly precarious since Philip suspended all payments to the bankers in January 1557, and it was essential that the King come home. At last, in August 1559, he left Flanders for Spain. The King's anxiously awaited homecoming to Castile was something more than the return of the native. It symbolized the end of the universal imperialism of Charles V, and a turning-away from a Flemish-based central European empire to a Spanish-based Atlantic empire, with all the resources of the New World at its command. But the new Spanish-American empire of Philip II, which differed in so many ways from the European empire of his father, was never quite to break free from the circumstances of its origin; for it was under the double sign of bankruptcy and heresy that the empire of Philip II was born.

6

Race and Religion

PHILIP II returned in the autumn of 1559 to a restless and uneasy Castile. The desperate financial problems of the preceding years had compelled the Regency Government to resort to all manner of fiscal expedients which had tended to lower the standard of administration and weaken the royal authority. Municipal offices had been sold, and Crown lands and jurisdiction alienated. The nobles had attempted to turn the Crown's difficulties to their own advantage; and the populace, already subject to heavy taxation by the Crown, saw itself further threatened by the covert extension of aristocratic privilege.

The prevailing sense of unease was much increased by the discovery in 1558 of 'Protestant' cells in Valladolid and Seville. Was even Castile, the most Catholic land in Christendom, to be tainted by the Lutheran heresy? In the feverish climate of the 1550s the discovery of 'Protestants' in the heart of Spain seemed very alarming, threatening as it did new dangers at a time when the Church and the Inquisition thought themselves to have successfully barred the gates against the advance of heretical doctrines. But the alarm was, in fact, unnecessary. So far from being an ominous new development, the alleged heresy of the little communities in Valladolid and Seville was merely the rather pathetic finale to a story of heterodox practices which had begun many decades before.

As long ago as the closing years of the fifteenth century there had been hints in Spain, as in other parts of Europe, of certain deviations from the traditional stream of orthodoxy. The close contacts of late medieval Spain with the Netherlands and Italy had naturally introduced into Spain new ideas, not all of them in strict accordance with traditional canons of belief and behaviour. In the Netherlands, Christianity had developed a strong pietist strain, which tended to stress mental prayer at the expense of forms and ceremonies; and in

Savonarola's Florence it had acquired a visionary, apocalyptic character which made a deep appeal to a number of Spanish Franciscans at that time in Italy. Both these types of Christianity found their devotees in Spain, particularly among devout women (*beatas*) and among Franciscans of *converso* origin. It was only in the early years of the sixteenth century, however, that they began to inspire any form of religious movement. The decisive event appears to have been the conversion of a sister of the Franciscan Order, Isabel de la Cruz, who set about organizing devotional centres in such towns as Alcalá and Toledo. Under her influence the *Alumbrados* or Illuminists, as her followers were called, abandoned the visionary approach of Savonarola for a kind of mystical passivism known as *dejamiento*, which aimed at the direct communion of the soul with God by means of a process of inner purification which would end in total submission to the divine will. This brand of illuminism was in particular to triumph at Escalona, in the household of the Marquis of Villena, where in 1523 one of Isabel's disciples, Pedro Ruiz de Alcaraz, a layman of *converso* origins, succeeded in implanting the practice of *dejamiento* in place of the highly emotional Illuminism preached by a friar of the apocalyptic variety, Francisco de Ocaña.

The remarkable success of Isabel de la Cruz and Alcaraz, and the spread of Illuminism to many towns and villages of New Castile, soon became a source of concern to the Inquisition, which had recently emerged from a severe testing-time with its authority enhanced. As long as Ferdinand had lived, the Holy Office had been kept under strict royal control, but during the regency period it had managed, under the protection of Cardinal Cisneros, the Inquisitor General, to extend its hitherto limited powers and prerogatives, and to establish direct control over the local tribunals. The increase in the powers of the Inquisition and the extent of its abuses made it many enemies, who placed strong pressure on Charles V, while on his first visit to Spain, to authorize a drastic programme of reform. But he was dissuaded from immediate action by Adrian of Utrecht, the Inquisitor General of Aragon, and by the time of his second visit to Spain it was already too late. The intervening period had seen the rapid spread of Lutheranism in Germany, and an organization which at one moment seemed to have completed its task with the elimination of Judaism from Spain, now found in the rise of Lutheranism a potentially vast new field for its activities. The Emperor therefore decided, in spite of the continued complaints of the Cortes of Castile, to leave the powers of the Holy Office intact.

The fact that the inquisitors had at this time only the most shadowy ideas as to the nature of Lutheranism only served to make them the more zealous in their desire to uncover it in Spain. Chilled by the spectre of heresy and rebellion hovering over the German lands, they were determined to prevent its appearance at home. This entailed a more rigorous definition of orthodoxy than hitherto, and a greater degree of vigilance in detecting and following up the slightest hint of religious dissent. In these circumstances the Holy Office naturally turned its attention to the activities of the *Alumbrados*, and in 1524 arrested both Isabel de la Cruz and Pedro de Alcaraz for heresy. The arrests were followed in 1525 by the condemnation of forty-eight Illuminist propositions, and a decree was promulgated by the Inquisition of Toledo in the same year against the heresies of Luther. Even though a distinction was still being drawn between Lutheranism and Illuminism (and there were indeed fundamental differences between them), the Inquisition suspected that they were closely connected, especially as both movements emphasized internal religion at the expense of outward ceremonial. To leave Illuminism untouched would therefore be a grave danger to the Faith.

The Holy Office had little difficulty in dealing with the *Alumbrados*, most of whom were simple people without influential support. Anyone suspected of Illuminist practices was quickly taken into custody, and the net was thrown wide enough to ensnare even Ignatius Loyola, who was interrogated at Alcalá in 1526 and again in 1527, and forbidden to preach for three years. By these methods the Illuminist movement was effectively brought under control during the course of the 1520s, and the stamp of ecclesiastical disapproval was firmly placed upon it.

In the course of its campaign against the Illuminists, however, the Holy Office became aware that Illuminism had a far more sophisticated counterpart in the Erasmianism which had recently become so popular among the Spanish intellectuals. Technically, there was nothing heretical about the doctrines of Erasmus, whose many adherents at Court and in the Church included Alonso Fonseca, Archbishop of Toledo, and the Inquisitor General himself, Alonso

Manrique, Archbishop of Seville. Manrique and his friends could throw their protective mantle over the supporters of Erasmus, and encourage the printing of his books on the Alcalá presses, but even they could not make Erasmus respectable in the eyes of the narrowly orthodox. These feared and disliked Erasmianism on several counts. They believed that it gave aid and comfort to the Lutherans by emphasizing, as Illuminism emphasized, the inward aspects of religion at the expense of forms and ceremonies; and their suspicions were reinforced by the discovery of contacts between such Erasmians as Juan de Valdés and the Illuminist communities. Nor could an Inquisition dominated by the friars be expected to look with any approval on the doctrines of a man who devoted so much time and energy to denunciation of the Religious Orders.

It is also possible that there was another, partially subconscious, explanation of the bitter hatred felt for Erasmus in certain orthodox circles in Castile. Erasmianism was an alien doctrine enjoying support among the courtiers and the advisers of an alien Emperor. The driving-force behind the revolt of the *Comuneros* had been hatred of the foreigner and of foreign ways and ideas; and it does not seem altogether fanciful to see in the vendetta against the Erasmians in the late 1520s a continuation of the campaign against foreign influences which had characterized the Castilian revolt at the beginning of the decade. The monks and clergy who had thrown themselves with such energy into the struggle of the *Comuneros* were fighting for a cause that went beyond the mere preservation of Castilian liberties; they were fighting to preserve the Castile they had known, a Castile pure in faith, and uncontaminated by the taint of alien influences. Although the *Comuneros* were defeated, it was natural enough that many of the ideas which inspired them should live on, defended and upheld as they were by the more conservative members of the Religious Orders – immensely powerful bodies in the Spain of the sixteenth century. Against these traditionalists were ranged all those, whether in the universities, the Church, or the royal administration, who had been excited by a glimpse of the outside world as the shutters surrounding Castile were lowered one by one. Attracted by the Europe of the Renaissance, and recently encouraged by the arrival in their country of a cultured foreign Court, they were determined to keep the shutters down. To these, Erasmus was the symbol of a New

Learning that was all the more alluring for its cosmopolitan character.

The battle between Erasmians and anti-Erasmians may thus have been in some respects a conflict between opposing ideas about the future course to be taken by Spain. The concept of a perennial struggle between two Spains is perhaps too frequently invoked as an explanation of the tensions in Spanish history, but this does not necessarily mean that it lacks all value in relation to specific periods. If it is unwise to search too closely for a continuity extending over several centuries, it is still possible to see a recurrence of divisions of a kind common to all societies, but which have been particularly sharp at certain moments in the history of Spain. The peninsula's geographical position and historical experience periodically tend to make it divide in particular over the question of its relationship – whether political or cultural – with the other parts of Europe. One such moment of division was to be found in the middle decades of the sixteenth century. At a time of great religious and intellectual ferment throughout western Europe, it was natural that many should feel that Spain would only be safe if it remained true to its own secluded past; but it was no less natural that others should react with enthusiasm to new ideas from abroad, and see in them fresh hope for the regeneration of society. Since there was no obvious compromise between these two points of view at a time when the European situation was itself unfavourable to compromise, the struggle was likely to be long and arduous. It was, indeed, intensively fought from the 1520s to the 1560s, and it ended in victory for the traditionalists: by the end of the 1560s the 'open' Spain of the Renaissance had been transformed into the partially 'closed' Spain of the Counter-Reformation. In retrospect, the victory of the traditionalists appears inevitable; but at the time when the struggle opened, their eventual triumph seemed very far from assured. They were helped, no doubt, by the weaknesses and the failings of their opponents, but above all it was the change in the international climate from the 1530s, together with the very insolubility of Spain's own racial and religious problems, which brought them ultimate victory.

2. THE IMPOSITION OF ORTHODOXY

In 1527 Archbishop Manrique, hoping to draw the sting of Erasmus's opponents, summoned a conference at Valladolid to pronounce upon his orthodoxy. Although the conference ended inconclusively, Manrique hastened to forbid any more attacks on Erasmus, and it seemed that the Erasmians had triumphed. But the conservatives were not prepared to acknowledge defeat. By introducing an element of doubt about the orthodoxy of Erasmus they had already succeeded in putting their opponents on the defensive, and an opportunity soon presented itself for resuming the attack when Charles V – the great patron of the Erasmians – left for Italy in 1529. This time the anti-Erasmians adopted the device of accusing the Erasmians of Illuminism and Lutheranism. They received invaluable assistance from a certain Francisca Hernández, formerly the director of the *Alumbrados* of Valladolid, who turned informer after her arrest, and denounced, one after another, the leading Erasmians in Spain. Armed with this useful testimony the Inquisition felt itself strong enough to bring to trial certain influential Erasmians, including the famous Valdés brothers and Miguel de Eguía, the printer of Erasmus's works at Alcalá. The series of trials reached its climax in 1533 with that of the Greek scholar Juan de Vergara, a friend of Erasmus and a leading personality in Spanish humanist circles. Denounced as an Illuminist and a Lutheran by Hernández, Vergara was compelled in 1535 to abjure his sins publicly in an *auto de fe* and to spend a year in the seclusion of a monastery.

The campaign to smear Erasmianism by linking it with Lutheran and Illuminist heresies was brilliantly successful and the condemnation of Vergara virtually put an end to the Spanish Erasmian movement. Some Erasmians, like Pedro de Lerma, abandoned Spain, where they saw no future for scholarship and learning, while others were rounded up during the later 1530s. They, like their colleagues in other parts of Europe, were in effect victims of the times in which they lived – exponents of a tolerant humanist tradition which was everywhere collapsing before the advance of religious dogmatism. But they were also victims of the particular situation inside Spain, where the intermingling of Christians, Jews, and Moors had created religious and racial problems of unparalleled complexity and had prompted the organization of a tribunal dedicated to a solution along the only lines that seemed feasible – the imposition of orthodoxy. The Spanish Inquisition, operating in a land where heterodox views abounded and where the new heresies might therefore easily take root, was naturally terrified at the least hint of subversive practices, and dared not tolerate even the slightest deviation from the most rigid orthodoxy, in the fear that any deviation would open the way to greater heresies. For if the friars who ran the Inquisition were animated by hatred of alien beliefs, they also acted under the impulse of fear. The Holy Office was essentially the product of fear – and inevitably, being the product of fear, it was on fear that it flourished. In the 1530s and the 1540s it transformed itself into a great apparatus operating through delation and denunciation – a terrible machine that would eventually escape from the control of its own creators and acquire an independent existence of its own. Even if, as seems probable, most Spaniards had come by the middle of the sixteenth century to consider the Holy Office as a necessary protection – a 'heaven-sent remedy', as Mariana called it – this does not necessarily imply that they were not terrified of it. Fear bred fear, and it was a measure of the propaganda success of the Inquisition that it persuaded the populace to fear heresy even more than the institution which was designed to extirpate it.

The features of the Inquisition most notorious in popular accounts of its activities were often less exceptionable in the contemporary context than is sometimes assumed. Torture and burning for the sake of one's beliefs were not, after all, practices exclusive to Spain; and – even if this was scarcely a source of much consolation to the victims – the methods of torture employed by the Holy Office were on the whole, traditional, and did not run to the novel refinements popularly imagined. Great care was taken to ensure a 'just' verdict, and the death sentence appears to have constituted only a small proportion of the many sentences given. Unfortunately it is impossible to discover the total number of victims burnt for heresy. The figures were probably high for the first years of the tribunal's life – the chronicler of the Catholic Kings, Hernando de Pulgar, speaks of nearly 2,000 men and women – but seem to have dropped sharply in the sixteenth century.

While burning and torture were in no sense the exclusive prerogative of the Spanish Inquisition, the tribunal did, on the other hand, possess certain distinctive features which made it particularly objectionable. There was, first, the secrecy and the interminable delay of its proceedings: Fray Luis de León (1527–91) was kept for five years in the cells of the Inquisition awaiting his verdict. There was also the indelible stain which imprisonment inflicted not simply on the reputation of the accused himself, but on the reputation of his descendants also. Nor did he lose only his honour. One of the principal reasons for the fear of the Inquisition was to be found in its right to confiscate the property of those who were penanced. 'Reconciliation' therefore meant economic as well as social ruin – and consequently innumerable opportunities of blackmail for unscrupulous officials of the Holy Office.

Of all the obnoxious features of the Inquisition, however, perhaps the most obnoxious was its natural tendency to generate a climate of mistrust and mutual suspicion peculiarly propitious for the informer and the spy. There were some 20,000 familiars scattered through Spain, ever on the alert for manifestations of unorthodoxy; and their activities were supplemented by the unpleasant device known as the Edict of the Faith, by which inquisitors would visit a district at regular intervals and would have a list of heretical and obnoxious practices read to the assembled population. The reading would be followed by an exhortation to the hearers to denounce any such practices as had come to their knowledge, with severe penalties being threatened to those who kept silent. Since victims of the Inquisition were never informed of the identity of their accusers, the Edict of Faith presented an ideal opportunity for the settlement of private scores, and encouraged informing and delation as a matter of course. 'The gravest thing of all,' wrote Mariana, ostensibly reporting the opinion of others, but perhaps expressing his own, 'was that through these secret inquiries people were deprived of the liberty of listening and talking to one another, for there were in the cities, towns, and villages special persons to give warning of what was happening. . . .'[1]

In this climate of fear and suspicion, vigorous debate was checked and a new constraint made itself felt. Even if the Holy Office did not interfere directly with most secular works, the effects of its activities could not be confined exclusively to the theological sphere, which was technically its sole concern. Authors, even of non-theological

1. Quoted in Guenter Lewy, *Constitutionalism and Statecraft during the Golden Age of Spain; a study of the political philosophy of Juan de Mariana, S.J.* (Travaux d'Humanisme et Renaissance XXXVI, Geneva, 1960), p. 22.

works, would naturally tend to exercise a kind of self-censorship, if only to keep their writings free of anything that might mislead the ignorant and the uneducated, and furnish an additional weapon to enemies of the Faith. Consequently there was a new spirit of caution abroad, which inevitably inhibited the wide-ranging debate and inquiry that had characterized the reign of the Catholic Kings.

It would be wrong, however, to assume that the Inquisition was the sole source of constraint in sixteenth-century Spain, or that it introduced entirely new features into Spanish life. Indeed, it may have taken such firm hold of Spanish society precisely because it gave official sanction to already existing attitudes and practices. Suspicion of those who deviated from the common norm was deeply rooted in a country where deviation was itself more normal than elsewhere – and a man could be suspect for his race as well as for his faith. It is no coincidence that the rise of a tribunal intended to impose religious orthodoxy was accompanied by the growth of certain practices designed to secure racial purity, for religious and racial deviation were easily equated in the popular mind. Indeed, alongside the obsessive concern with purity of the faith there flourished a no less obsessive concern with purity of blood; both obsessions were at their most violent in the middle decades of the sixteenth century; both employed the same techniques of informing and delation; and both had the effect of narrowing the extraordinarily wide range of Spanish life, and of forcing a rich and vital society into a strait-jacket of conformity.

Even more than the development of the Inquisition, the development of the doctrine of *limpieza de sangre* – purity of blood – illustrates the tensions within Spanish society, and suggests how easily that society could fall victim to the uglier tendencies in its midst. During the fifteenth century the Jewish problem had become the *converso* problem, and it was probably inevitable that sooner or later attempts would be made to exclude *conversos* from public office. The first attempt of an official nature occurred at Toledo in 1449. In the later fifteenth and the earlier sixteenth century pure ancestry gradually became an indispensable condition for membership of certain Religious Orders, as also of the *Colegios Mayores* at the universities. The graduates of the *Colegios* naturally tended to carry with them the idea of discrimination as they attained high office in Church and State; and they no doubt derived encouragement from the fact that at the Court of Charles V, unlike that of Ferdinand and Isabella, there were few *conversos*, partly perhaps because the Emperor believed them to have been implicated in the revolt of the *Comuneros*.

While the Emperor was quite willing to give the force of law to local institutional statutes discriminating against those of Jewish origin (Moorish ancestry does not seem to have been of any moment), the movement in favour of racial purity only gathered real momentum as a result of certain events in the later 1540s. The scene of the new developments was the cathedral of Toledo, and the prime mover was Juan Martínez Siliceo, appointed Archbishop in 1546.

Both the place and the personality reveal a good deal about the origins and character of the movement for *limpieza de sangre*. Toledo, the home of the *Comuneros*, remained in the years after the revolt a bitterly divided city, in which the rival factions of the Ayalas and the Riberas continued to compete for civil and ecclesiastical office. Over the course of the years the question of ancestry had come to play a prominent part in these rivalries. The Ayalas, who had fought for the cause of Castilian nationalism against the Flemish Court, prided themselves on their purity of ancestry, and saw in *limpieza de sangre* a possible weapon for driving their rivals from office, since the Riberas, the Silvas, and the Mendozas were held to be tainted with Jewish blood. The Ayalas, however, seem to have made little progress, for at the time of the appointment of Siliceo to the see of Toledo the chapter and the cathedral benefices were alleged to be swarming with *conversos*.

Siliceo's appointment introduced a new and disturbing element into a troubled situation. It was the practice of Charles V, as of the Catholic Kings, to prefer the low-born to high office in Church and State, and Siliceo was a man of exceptionally humble origins. This was something which he was unable to forget, and which anyhow would have been very difficult to forget when he found himself among his canons of Toledo. The aristocratic families of Toledo had successfully acquired for themselves the best canonries and benefices, and, under the leadership of their dean, Pedro de Castilla – a man of royal, and Jewish blood – these aristocratic canons resented the appointment of an Archbishop of such inferior rank. Siliceo's birth may have been lowly, but he had one undoubted asset which many of his enemies lacked: his ancestry was pure. Naturally, he proceeded to make the most of this asset in his feud with Pedro de Castilla; and the dean in turn saw in the Archbishop's espousal of the cause of *limpieza* a conspiracy to introduce into the archdiocese more men of plebeian origin. The predictable clash came over the nomination to a canonry of a certain Fernando Jiménez. On inquiry, Jiménez proved to be the son of a *converso* who had recently fled the country after the Inquisition had begun inquiries into his alleged Judaic practices. Surely, argued the Archbishop, no one would accept a horse for his stable, even as a free gift, without being sure of the animal's pedigree. He therefore declined to accept this particular horse for his stable, and in 1547 forced through the chapter a statute of *limpieza* making purity of ancestry an essential condition for all future appointments to dignities and prebends.

The Toledo statute of 1547, although greeted with vehement protests, set a fashion which was imitated by one after another of the ecclesiastical and secular corporations in Spain. In 1556 Siliceo asked for, and obtained, royal ratification of the statute. It was particularly ominous that Philip II justified his approval with the remark that 'all the heresies in Germany, France, and Spain have been sown by descendants of Jews'.[2] In fact, orthodoxy in the Faith and purity of ancestry were now officially associated, and the stamp of royal approval was firmly set on a movement which was already beginning to get out of hand.

Although the Crown had at last placed itself squarely on the side of the statutes, the real pressure for statutes of *limpieza* came not from the top of Spanish society but from the bottom. The enthusiastic support of the doctrine of *limpieza* by such a man as Siliceo is itself symptomatic. Siliceo himself, while the villain of the piece, was also a victim – the victim of a social system which placed an exceptionally high value on birth and rank even for the Europe of the sixteenth century. The watchword of this society was *honour*, which implied to a Spaniard something external to his person – his worth as evaluated by other people. Honour was essentially an attribute of nobility, the

2. Quoted by Albert A. Sicroff, *Les Controverses des Statuts de 'Pureté de Sang' en Espagne du XVe au XVIIe siècle* (Paris, 1960), p. 138 n.

exclusive preserve of the high-born. It was natural enough that this code of aristocratic behaviour should be at once aped and resented by the more humble members of society, and especially by those who had risen to positions of eminence and yet saw themselves regarded as intruders in the world of privilege. The doctrine of *limpieza* provided men like Siliceo with a compensating code of their own, and one, indeed, which might effectively challenge the code of the aristocracy. Was it not preferable to be born of humble, but pure Christian parentage, than to be a *caballero* of suspicious racial antecedents? Pure ancestry thus became for the lower ranks of Spanish society the equivalent of noble ancestry for the upper ranks, since it determined a man's status among his fellow men. His honour depended on his ability to prove the purity of his ancestry – at first as far back as the fourth generation, and then, in Philip II's reign, from time immemorial. Once this was established he was the equal of any comer, irrespective of his rank, and this no doubt helped to give him that sense of equality which is, at first sight, one of the most paradoxical characteristics of the intensely hierarchical society of sixteenth-century Spain.

The growing insistence on purity of blood as a qualification for office placed the aristocracy in an embarrassing position. It was much easier to trace the ancestry of a noble than of a commoner, and there were few nobles without a dubious ancestor lurking somewhere in the background, as the famous family registers known as the *libros verdes* gloatingly proclaimed to the world at large. But popular sentiment was so strong and the religious implications of doubtful ancestry had been so widely insisted upon, that it proved impossible to check the mania for *limpieza*. As soon as purity of blood was made essential for office in the Inquisition and for entry into a religious community or a secular corporation, there was no escape from long and expensive investigations which might at any moment uncover some skeleton in the family cupboard. Since the testimony of even one malevolent witness could ruin a family's reputation, the effect of the statutes of *limpieza* was in many ways comparable to that of the activities of the Inquisition. They fostered the general sense of insecurity, encouraged the blackmailer and the informer, and prompted desperate attempts at deception. Names were changed, ancestries falsified, in the hope of misleading the *linajudo*, the professional who travelled around collecting oral evidence and scrutinizing pedigrees; and extreme care was taken to avoid matrimonial alliances which could contaminate a family with the taint either of *converso* blood or of penance by the Inquisition.

By the middle of the sixteenth century, therefore, orthodoxy in Spain was coming to mean not only the profession of a strictly orthodox faith, but also the possession of a strictly orthodox ancestry. Admittedly there were limits to the power of the *linajudo* – more, perhaps, than to those of the inquisitor. The test of *limpieza* was difficult to enforce in the upper reaches of society, and any family which had obtained a *hábito* of one of the Military Orders was automatically placed beyond the power of the investigator. But the obsession with a pure ancestry had the general effect of confirming in the popular mind the view expressed by Philip II that there was a correlation between heresy and a non-Christian background; and it helped to place power still more firmly in the hands of a narrow and exclusive class of traditionally-minded Old Christians, who were determined to bind the country close within the confines of a conformity which they themselves had defined. It was these men, highly influential in the Church, the Religious Orders, and the Inquisition, who had taken charge of the destinies of Spain by the fateful decade of the 1550s.

3. THE SPAIN OF THE COUNTER-REFORMATION

While the persecution of Illuminists and Erasmians, and the growing acceptance of the concept of *limpieza*, had set Spain on a particular course during the later years of the Emperor's reign, it was the events of the period between 1556 and the closing of the Council of Trent in 1563 which finally ensured that there would be no turning back. These were the years in which Renaissance Spain, wide open to European humanist influences, was effectively transformed into the semi-closed Spain of the Counter-Reformation. This was partly the outcome of the gradual transfer of power and authority to such stern characters as Hernando de Valdés (Inquisitor General from 1547) and Melchor Cano, the formidable Dominican theologian. But it reflected also a new bleakness in the spiritual climate of Europe. As Geneva became the centre of a new and more dogmatic Protestantism, so the last lingering hopes of a reconciliation between Rome and the Protestants vanished. Everywhere there was a new spirit of militancy abroad. Geneva prepared for battle with its printing-presses and its pastors; Rome, in process of reformulating its dogmas at the Council of Trent, prepared for battle with its Jesuits, its Inquisition, and its Index.

It was in this atmosphere of impending conflict that the spectacular discovery was made in 1557 and 1558 of 'Protestant' communities at Seville and Valladolid. Although these communities had certain contacts with Geneva, and might eventually have evolved into Protestant groups, they seem at the time of their discovery to have resembled the earlier *Alumbrado* communities. Their character is suggested by the fact that they included two well-known figures from among the cosmopolitan humanist circle around the Emperor: Dr Constantino Ponce de La Fuente (a former confessor of Charles V) and Dr Agustín Cazalla (one of the Emperor's favourite preachers). Twenty years earlier a man like Cazalla would probably have received little more than a brief penance. It was a measure of the change in the religious climate that he was now garrotted and burnt.

The violence of the Inquisition's reaction may partly be ascribed to its anxiety to improve its own standing with the Crown, but it also suggests a real alarm at the apparent advance of heresy in spite of all its efforts at repression. This time there could be no half measures. Not only must the heretical communities be liquidated, but greater efforts must be made to protect Spain from foreign contagion. On 7 September 1558, therefore, Philip's sister, the Infanta Juana, acting as regent for her brother, issued a pragmatic forbidding the import of foreign books and ordering that all books printed in Spain should in future be licensed by the Council of Castile; and another pragmatic in the following year forbade Spanish students to go abroad for study.

The law of 1558 was not in fact the first attempt at censorship in Spain. A pragmatic of 1502 had ordered that all books, whether printed at home or imported, should bear a royal licence, which could be conferred by presidents of the *audiencias*, and by the archbishops and certain of the bishops. In addition, there had also been periodic prohibitions of particular works. Ferdinand and Isabella had, for instance, forbidden the reading of the Scriptures in the vernacular, but their decree seems to have been directed principally against the *conversos*, and it was not until 1551 that the prohibition became both universal and definitive.[3]

In 1545 the Inquisition had drawn up what seems to have been the first Spanish Index, and this was followed by another in 1551. The Roman Index of 1559, however, enjoyed no authority in Spain; instead, the Inquisitor General Valdés followed up the censorship law of 1558 by publishing in 1559 a new Spanish Index, which considerably augmented that of 1551. The Index of 1559 was in many respects extremely severe: it banned the Enchiridion of Erasmus and many other religious works which enjoyed a wide popular appeal. Moreover, the Inquisition enforced its provisions with unprecedented severity. A methodical search was made for prohibited books, and the episcopate was entrusted with the task of organizing a systematic inspection of public and private libraries.

There seems no reason to doubt that the measures of 1558–9 administered a drastic shock to Spanish intellectual life. By cutting off the supply of foreign books, and imposing further restrictions on theological and devotional writings, they inevitably undermined the confidence of Spanish men of letters, and added one more set of barriers to the many barriers now being raised all over Europe to impede the free circulation of ideas. It is, however, difficult to determine how permanent were the consequences, especially as the replacement of Valdés as Inquisitor General by Cardinal Espinosa in 1566 led to some modification of the earlier severity. It is equally difficult to determine the extent to which Spain's relations with the European intellectual community were affected. The prohibition on

3. There was at this time no complete Spanish translation of the Scriptures in existence. Francisco de Enzinas, however, had published a translation of the New Testament from the Greek text of Erasmus in 1543 at Antwerp. In 1555 the Jewish press at Ferrara printed a Spanish version of the Old Testament from the Hebrew; and Juan Pérez de Pineda, a refugee monk from the convent of San Isidoro at Seville, produced his own translation of the New Testament and the Psalms at Geneva in 1556 and 1557 respectively. The first complete translation of the Bible into Castilian was the work of Casiodoro de Reina, another refugee from the convent of San Isidoro, and appeared at Basle in 1569. Passages from the Scriptures were, of course, included in many books that circulated freely in Spain, and Spanish authors continued to quote extensively from the Bible. (See the pages by Professor E. M. Wilson on Spanish versions of the Bible in *The Cambridge History of the Bible*, ed. S. L. Greenslade, Cambridge, 1963), pp. 125–9.)

Spaniards studying abroad obviously restricted one fruitful source of contact with foreign ideas; but it seems that the prohibition was never total, and distinguished Spaniards were still to be found in the second half of the sixteenth century in the universities of Italy and Flanders, and even those of France. Intellectual contact with Flanders naturally remained close. The great scholar Arias Montano, for instance, went to Flanders on Philip II's instructions in 1568 to organize the preparation at Antwerp of a revised and improved edition of the Polyglot Bible of Cardinal Cisneros. Above all, there was no break in the close cultural relationship between Spain and Italy. From the fifteenth century onwards, Italy had been a constant source of intellectual and artistic inspiration to Spain, which in turn transmitted its own and Italian ideas to France and northern Europe. This northward flow of South European culture by way of Spain remained unaffected by the European religious crisis of the 1550s; and indeed Spanish influence on the cultural life of the north continued to grow, reinforced as it was by all the prestige of Spanish power and by the extraordinary quality and variety of Spain's literary and artistic achievements in the late sixteenth and early seventeenth centuries.

Yet the decrees of the 1550s inevitably meant a partial closure of Spain to ideas from outside. Religiously it remained part of the international community of Counter-Reformation Europe, but this was a community that embraced only half a continent. Europe was now divided within itself, each half barricading itself against the religious beliefs of the other. In this international conflict of the later sixteenth century, Spain's pre-eminent position and potential vulnerability made it acutely sensitive to the dangers of religious subversion, and it responded by becoming exceptionally selective in its approach to the products of foreign cultures, subjecting them to the minutest scrutiny before it allowed them entry.

While Spain was sealing itself off against the indiscriminate entry of foreign ideas, it was also in process of determining its relationship with the supreme head of Counter-Reformation Europe – a relationship which was bound to exercise an important influence on the outcome of the battle against international Protestantism. In the reign of Charles V, relations had been singularly unhappy between the Popes and an Emperor with important territorial interests in Italy; and during the pontificate of the fanatically anti-Spanish Paul IV

(1555-9) Spain and the Papacy actually went to war. On the death of Paul IV in 1559 Philip used his influence in the conclave to secure the election of a more amenable Pope, but the successful candidate, Pius IV, himself became involved in a controversy with Spain, which once again clouded the relations between Rome and its most powerful secular ally.

The dispute arose over a matter which is best seen as representing a further, and perhaps final, stage in the struggle of the conservatives to secure absolute control over Spain's religious and intellectual life. This was the affair of Cardinal Carranza. Bartolomé de Carranza was the son of poor, but *hidalgo*, parents. Born in Navarre in 1503, he was educated at Alcalá, and then joined the Dominican Order. After studying at the College of San Gregorio in Valladolid, where he became professor of theology, he was sent in 1545 as a delegate to the Council of Trent. Having gained a great theological reputation at Trent, he accompanied Philip to England in 1554 and became Mary Tudor's religious adviser and a ruthless suppressor of English Protestantism. In 1559 he returned to Flanders, where he investigated the clandestine trade in heretical literature with Spain. This early career would have seemed an ideal preparation for the post to which Philip now appointed him – that of Archbishop of Toledo in succession to Cardinal Siliceo; but in August 1559, after enjoying his archbishopric for less than a year, he was suddenly arrested by officers of the Inquisition. For seventeen years, first in Spain and then in Rome, he remained a prisoner, only emerging from prison in April 1576, a broken old man of seventy-three, to die a few days later.

The mystery surrounding the arrest of a man who might have appeared the ideal primate for Spain in the new age of open religious warfare, has never been fully dispelled; but Carranza, for reasons both good and bad, was a man with many influential enemies. He was perhaps unlucky in that he was appointed to his see at a time when the King was still abroad and had therefore been unable to consult either his usual advisers or the Council of the Inquisition. It was also unfortunate that Carranza, like his predecessor Siliceo, was a man of relatively humble origins. Twice running, prelates of a more aristocratic background had been disappointed of the rich see of Toledo. Among those who had hoped for promotion were two sons of the Count of Lemos – Don Pedro de Castro, Bishop of

Cuenca, and his brother, Don Rodrigo; and the Castro brothers found a powerful supporter in Valdés, the Inquisitor General, himself another disappointed candidate. Nor could Carranza expect much help from other Spanish prelates, since he had been rash enough to publish a book containing the most severe strictures on episcopal absenteeism. Even worse, he had long ago incurred the enmity of a fellow-Dominican, who was now Philip II's most trusted religious adviser. This was the theologian Melchor Cano. Cano had been a rival of Carranza at the College of San Gregorio in Valladolid, where the students had been divided into the rival factions of *canistas* and *carranzistas,* and his dislike of Carranza can only have been increased by Carranza's success at the Council of Trent.

Aristocratic and personal hatreds therefore played an important part in the conspiracy against Carranza, but it also seems likely that the Archbishop was a further casualty in the campaign of the Spanish traditionalists against allegedly 'liberal' theologians with foreign affiliations. For all his record as a persecutor of heretics, Carranza, having travelled round Europe with the Emperor, could himself easily be classed with the 'heretical' Dr Cazalla as a man contaminated by too frequent contact with the Erasmian Christianity of the north. While Siliceo, who had enemies enough, was so orthodox as to be untouchable, Carranza had published an enormous tome of Commentaries on the Catechism which left him dangerously exposed to the attacks of determined enemies. Cano and the Inquisitors now set to work; seeds of doubt were planted in Philip's mind; and the primate of Spain found himself arrested on suspicion of heresy.

Already a pawn in the feud between aristocrat and plebeian, between nationalist and cosmopolitan, the unhappy, if unsympathetic, Carranza now became also a pawn in the feud between the Spanish Crown and the Papacy. The King saw that he had in the Inquisition an admirable instrument both for extending his control over his dominions and for preserving them from heresy. He therefore proceeded to identify his own power with that of the Inquisition as Charles V had never done, and allowed himself to be pushed by the inquisitors into making the unprecedented claim that it was for the Inquisition and not for Rome to try prelates of the Church. The Pope contested the claim, but it was not until 1566 that he managed to secure the transference of the prisoner to Rome; and even then,

Spanish delaying tactics postponed for ten years a decision that was by no means so favourable to Carranza as many had expected.

The struggle between Philip II and the Papacy, exacerbated by the Carranza affair, served only to weaken the forces of the Counter-Reformation at a time when strength was imperative. Neither could afford an open break, for Rome needed Spanish military assistance, while Philip needed ecclesiastical revenues and the prestige that only the Pope could confer on his struggle against heresy. But there existed between the two a kind of undeclared war, in which Philip did everything possible to extend his control over the Spanish Church and to exploit its financial and political resources. The Inquisition was duly reduced to little more than a department of state; the enormous revenues of the see of Toledo were appropriated by the Crown during the seventeen years of Carranza's trial; the Tridentine decrees were finally published in 1565, but only with a proviso which guaranteed the Crown's continuing influence in ecclesiastical jurisdiction and episcopal appointments; and in 1572 papal briefs citing Spaniards to appear before foreign courts in ecclesiastical cases were declared null and void, and the King insisted on his right to scrutinize papal bulls, and if necessary to forbid their publication in his dominions.

Although Philip II's zeal for the preservation and extension of royal prerogatives was natural enough, his behaviour also suggests that in his heart he considered religion too serious a matter to be left to the Pope. Terrified of heresy, he would trust none but himself and his own chosen agents to eradicate it from his dominions. He would turn the Spanish Monarchy into an impregnable fortress, against whose walls the heresies that were sweeping Europe would batter in vain. While no fortress would be impregnable as long as there were traitors inside, it might at first sight seem difficult to justify the severity of the measures taken against those who were considered suspect in the faith. The rather pathetic handful of *Alumbrados* who found themselves in the cells of the Inquisition would hardly seem to have necessitated the mounting of so formidable a machine. But if, in retrospect, Philip and his agents would seem to have displayed an excessive alarm at the supposed dangers in their midst, their sense of insecurity is at least explicable in terms of both the domestic and the international situation at the time of the King's accession. By the 1560s it was becoming increasingly clear that the King was faced with war on two fronts, and the last thing he wanted was to be faced with a third front at home. The apparently panic measures of the first ten years of the reign were thus prompted by a genuine fear of imminent disaster, which, in the light of the events of the 1560s, seems by no means entirely misplaced.

4. THE CRISIS OF THE 1560s

The peace of Cateau-Cambrésis of 1559, ending the war between France and Spain, had come none too soon. Apart from the fact that the bankruptcy of 1557 made the continuation of the war virtually impossible, Philip, like the French King Henry II, could not fail to be concerned at the spread of the Protestant heresy in France. Besides this, there was the Turkish danger, now perhaps slightly abated, but none the less pressing. Rumours of a growing Ottoman weakness suggested that the moment might be propitious for an attempt to recover the initiative in the Mediterranean – something which had been impossible as long as the war with France continued. Philip therefore chose to rescind earlier orders for the opening of negotiations with the Turks for a ten- or twelve-year truce, and to conduct the war in the Mediterranean with all the resources at his disposal.

In the light of Spain's financial position, the decision was unwise. During the 1550s depression had hung over Seville's trade with the New World, keeping money tight and confidence low. The yield of taxes was totally inadequate for the Monarchy's heavy military commitments, and already in 1558 a heavy duty had been imposed on the export of Castilian wool. This was followed by the levying of customs along the Portuguese frontier, by increases in the *almojarifazgo* and the customs dues in the ports of Vizcaya, by the enforcement of the royal monopoly on playing cards, and the incorporation of the salt-mines into the royal domain. These measures greatly enlarged the yield of extra-parliamentary taxation, and the Crown's revenues were further increased in 1561, when the King induced the Cortes of Castile to agree to a large rise in the *encabezamiento* by promising to impose no new taxes without their consent (a promise that it was not difficult to evade).

The tax increases were very necessary if Spain was to mount a serious campaign in the Mediterranean. This had been clearly shown by the overwhelming defeat in May 1560 of a joint Spanish-Italian expedition to the isle of Djerba, which was intended as a base for the recovery of Tripoli. The Christian reverse – the most considerable since the failure of Charles V at Algiers in 1541 – encouraged the Turks to step up their pressure in the central and western Mediterranean, and even to approach the coast of Majorca in the spring of 1561. Spain urgently needed more ships, and the rise in royal revenues made it possible to launch a galley-building programme which might at least fill the gaps made by the losses of the previous years. But even now the Spanish fleet remained dangerously small. Although Don García de Toledo commanded a fleet of a hundred ships for his successful attack on the North African fortress of Peñón de Vélez in September 1564, many of these had been supplied by Spain's allies; and when, in the following year, a naval expedition was sent to relieve the beleaguered island of Malta, the entire southern coast of Spain was left undefended, and a party of corsairs from Tetuan landed at Motril and ravaged the coast.

While Spain in the early 1560s was slowly and painfully building up its strength in the Mediterranean, it was receiving a number of increasingly sharp reminders that Islam was not its only enemy, nor its eastern and southern coastlines the only frontiers open to attack. The spread of Calvinism and the outbreak of the French wars of religion in 1562 raised for the first time the spectre of a Protestant power on Spain's northern border. This itself was serious enough, but worse was to follow. Discontent was spreading in the Spanish Netherlands. Pressure from the Dutch nobility had induced Philip to remove Cardinal Granvelle from the government of the Netherlands in 1564; heresy was spreading among the inhabitants; and in August 1566 Calvinist mobs ran wild and sacked the churches. Philip, in fact, was faced with both heresy and rebellion in one of the most prized portions of his father's inheritance.

The grave news from Brussels confronted a congenitally indecisive monarch with the need to make a series of crucial decisions. Should he return to Flanders to re-impose his authority in person? Should he adopt a policy of moderation, as Cardinal Espinosa and the Prince of Eboli recommended in the Council of State, or should he order military action against the rebels, as urged by the Duke of Alba and the Count of Chinchón? Military action required money, but fortunately the Crown's financial position had recently begun to improve. During 1562 and 1563 the depression hanging over Seville's trade with the New World had gradually lifted, and the silver remittances for the Crown had started to rise. As fresh streams of silver were pumped into the system, Spanish power began to revive. With a new confidence born of new resources, the King decided in favour of repression. The Duke of Alba was ordered to the Netherlands with an army to suppress the revolt; and in spite of the success of the Governess of the Netherlands, Charles V's daughter Margaret of Parma, in restoring order among her rebellious subjects, the Duke was instructed to continue his march.

Before the departure of Alba there had been some uncertainty whether he was ostensibly going to the Netherlands to destroy heresy or to crush revolt. It was finally decided that the war in the Netherlands was best treated as a war against rebellious vassals; but in practice both Philip and his soldiers looked upon it as a religious crusade undertaken by a 'Catholic army' against a people whom Philip himself persistently described as 'rebels and heretics'. For Philip, heresy and rebellion were synonymous – and not without reason. Everywhere he looked, the Calvinists were subverting the established order. Calvinist preachers were stirring up the populace; Calvinist literature was poisoning men's minds. In the Netherlands, in France, the forces of international Protestantism were on the march. That it was an international conspiracy, Philip had no doubt, for each passing year showed more conclusively that the Dutch rebels were not alone. Behind them were the Huguenots, and the Breton seamen who were now waging war on Spanish shipping in the gulf of Gascony, and who were to cut Spain's maritime communications with Flanders in the winter of 1568–9. Behind them, too, were English privateers like Sir John Hawkins, whose raid into the Spanish Caribbean in 1568 brought Spain and England a step nearer to open war.

Already by 1568 it was clear that the struggle was spreading – spreading in particular to the sea, where the Protestants were at their strongest and where Spain was still weak. The war between Spain and international Protestantism was essentially a naval war, fought in the Bay of Biscay, the English Channel, and even, increasingly, in the hitherto exclusive preserve of the Spanish Atlantic. Spain's American possessions could no longer be regarded as safe. But for that matter it was questionable whether any part of the King's dominions was now immune from attack. Indeed, Spain itself was threatened, both by pirate attacks on its coasts, and by armed incursions across its frontier with France.

The acute sensitivity of Philip to the dangers from heresy is suggested by his behaviour in the Principality of Catalonia. The Principality was undoubtedly one of the weaker sections of the Spanish bastions, both because of its exposed position on the French frontier, and because the extent of its privileges made it little amenable to royal control. It was well known that there were Huguenots among the bandit gangs that were constantly passing to and fro across the border, and there was every reason to suspect that heresy had found converts among that steady stream of Frenchmen which had for some years been crossing the Pyrenees into Catalonia in search of work. If heresy were to take root in Catalonia, the position would be extremely grave, since the Principality had all the makings of a second Netherlands: a strong tradition of independence, its own laws and privileges, and a hatred of Castile that was accentuated by linguistic and cultural differences. Consequently, as the pressure mounted against the Catalan frontier, the King's fears grew. The viceroys were instructed to show the greatest vigilance in guarding the frontier, and in 1568 the situation appeared so alarming that severe new measures were decreed: a fresh prohibition on natives of the Crown of Aragon studying abroad; a harsher censorship in Catalonia; and a ban on all teaching by Frenchmen in Catalan schools. Then, in 1569, the Catalans refused to pay the new tax known as the *excusado*, which had just been authorized by Pius V. Convinced by their refusal that they were on the verge of going over to Protestantism, Philip ordered the Inquisition and the Viceroy to take action, and had the *Diputats* and a number of nobles arrested.

The King's vigorous action against the Catalan authorities is an indication of his deep anxiety about the course of events. As he himself later realized, the action was unwarranted: there was no breath of heresy among the Catalan governing class. But the situation seemed sufficiently dangerous to make action essential. The Protestant peril was growing hourly, and it was growing at a moment when the danger from Islam seemed also to be mounting to a climax. For Catalonia was not the only region of Spain where revolt and heresy threatened. On Christmas night of that terrible year 1568 – the year of the danger in Catalonia, of the cutting of the sea-route through the Bay of Biscay, and of the arrest and death of Philip's son and heir, Don Carlos – a band of Morisco outlaws led by a certain Fárax Abenfárax broke into the city of Granada, bringing with them the news that the Alpujarras had risen in revolt. Although the rebels failed to seize the city, their incursion signalized the outbreak of rebellion throughout the kingdom of Granada. Spain, which had surrounded itself with such strong defences against the advance of Protestantism, now found itself endangered from within; and the threat came not, as was expected, from the Protestants, but from its old enemies, the Moors.

5. THE SECOND REBELLION OF THE ALPUJARRAS (1568-70)[4]

While the converted Jews had for long been the object of inquisitorial attention, the Holy Office had been a good deal less worried about the converted Moors. This was largely because it despised them. The Moriscos were, by and large, humble men, occupying no positions of importance in the State; and while there was every reason to doubt the sincerity of their conversion, their beliefs no longer seemed likely to lead the faithful astray. On the other hand, there could be no doubt that the Morisco communities in Spain presented a difficult problem, both because they were an unassimilated racial minority, and because they were closely associated with Spain's greatest enemy – the Turk.

The savage outburst of racial and religious strife in Andalusia between 1568 and 1570 is an indication of the long-standing bitterness that had prevailed in the relationship between the Moors and the Christians of southern Spain, and of the deep resentment of the Moriscos at the treatment they had received. This revolt was, in

4. In writing this section I have drawn heavily on Dr Garrad's unpublished thesis on *The Causes of the Second Rebellion of the Alpujarras,* which he generously placed at my disposal.

fact, perfectly predictable, and had indeed been predicted, although the King chose to ignore the warnings he received. It was also a revolt that might have been avoided, if Philip II's own agents had not behaved with such folly. For the rebellion of the Alpujarras, although partially prompted by grievances that had for long been festering, was essentially a response by the Moriscos of Granada to a recent and drastic change for the worse in the conditions under which they lived.

For half a century after the first revolt of the Alpujarras in 1499 an uneasy balance had been preserved between the Old Christian authorities and the 'new Christian' population of Andalusia. Although pragmatics had been issued in 1508 prohibiting Moorish dress and customs, they had not been enforced, and the Moriscos had succeeded in preserving unbroken their links with their Islamic past. Few of them spoke any language but Arabic; they continued to wear their traditional dress, investing much of their wealth, as they always had, in the silks and jewellery worn by their women; they refused to abandon such practices as regular bathing, which the Spaniards regarded as a mere cover for Mohammedan ritual and sexual promiscuity; and they pursued with their customary savagery their family vendettas, although Spanish attempts at repression forced the participants to seek refuge in North Africa or to take to the mountains as outlaws.

The Spanish civil and ecclesiastical authorities in Andalusia continued to tolerate this state of affairs partly because there seemed to be no alternative, and partly because they were so at loggerheads with each other that combined action was impossible. Indeed, over the years a new balance of power had been evolved in Andalusia, to the very considerable advantage of the Moriscos. Throughout the early sixteenth century there existed a bitter feud over questions of jurisdiction between the *audiencia* of Granada and the Captaincy-General. The Captaincy-General had come in practice to be a hereditary office in the hands of a branch of the Mendoza family, and was held in turn by the first, second, and third Marquises of Mondéjar. The Mondéjars, in their struggle to maintain their position, had struck up a special relationship with the Moriscos, who found in them their most effective protectors against Church, *audiencia*, and Inquisition. As a result, the position of the Moriscos had become closely dependent on the ability of the Mondéjars to maintain themselves against an increasingly formidable array of enemies.

During the 1540s and 1550s, it became increasingly clear that the position of the Mondéjars was being undermined. Don Íñigo López de Mendoza, fourth Count of Tendilla, who had taken over the Captaincy-General in 1543 on the appointment of his father, the second Marquis of Mondéjar, to the viceroyalty of Navarre, found himself beset by enemies both in Andalusia and at Court. He had an influential ally at Court in the secretary Juan Vázquez de Molina, who kept him informed of his enemies' intrigues, and he gained additional support from the appointment of his father to the Presidency of the Council of the Indies in 1546. But in spite of this, his enemies gradually succeeded in reducing his power at Court by building up the position of the second Marquis of los Vélez, the head of the rival house of Fajardo.

During the 1550s, therefore, the decline in Tendilla's standing at Court left the Moriscos in an increasingly exposed position, while at the same time the whole administrative machine in Granada was so paralysed by the feuds and rivalries between Tendilla's supporters and enemies that it was in imminent danger of grinding to a standstill. But the most unfortunate feature of this breakdown of government was that it came at a moment when the Moriscos found themselves in increasing difficulties, both economic and religious.

The Morisco economy was based on the silk industry. This was badly hit, first by a ban on the export of woven silks in the 1550s, and then by drastic increases in the taxes on Granada silk after 1561. The decline in the prosperity of the silk industry occurred at a time when a land commission was busy investigating titles and recovering Crown property, and when the Inquisition of Granada was becoming increasingly active. Established at Granada in 1526, the Holy Office had been partially held in check by the Captains-General, who feared that the despoiling of the Moriscos by the Inquisition would make it impossible for them to pay the taxes that in turn were used to pay the troops. But during the 1550s, as the power of the Captain-General weakened, and negotiations between the Moriscos and the Holy Office for a general pardon finally broke down, the Inquisition intensified its activities, and confiscated an increasing amount of Morisco property in the course of 'reconciling' suspects.

In addition to the Inquisition, the unfortunate Moriscos found themselves confronted also by the Andalusian Church. Since the time of Archbishop Talavera, the clergy of Granada, left during long periods to their own devices as the result of episcopal absenteeism and the vacancies in the see, had merely succeeded in alienating the people they were supposed to convert. At once neglectful of their duties and intolerant in their attitude, they represented a major obstacle to the Christianization of the Moors. It was only in 1546 that Granada found, in Pedro Guerrero, a new Archbishop who appreciated that it was impossible to win over the Moriscos until he had first reformed his clergy. When he returned from the Council of Trent in 1564, he prepared plans for the implementing in his diocese of the Tridentine reforms, and summoned a provincial council in 1565 to consider his proposals. But, as might have been expected, the council's reaction was distinctly tepid, and it was only Guerrero's suggestions for a more effective policy towards the Moriscos that won immediate acceptance. Although, as Guerrero himself was the first to realize, any attempt to change the ways of the Moriscos without first changing the ways of the clergy was certain to lead to disaster, the recommendations for the reform of Morisco customs were duly embodied in a pragmatic, which was drawn up on 17 November 1566 and published on 1 January of the following year.

The pragmatic of 1566–7, which was the immediate prelude to the rising of the Alpujarras, was not, in fact, a particularly novel document. It tended, rather, to resume earlier decrees which had never been enforced: the prohibition of the use of Arabic, the orders that Moriscos should wear Castilian dress and abandon their traditional habits. This time, however, there was a real danger that the pragmatic would be enforced, and the Moriscos sent a deputation to Madrid to plead for its suspension. Their pleas were supported by the Count of Tendilla, who warned that enforcement of the pragmatic would have disastrous results; but his warning was ignored, and a lawyer called Pedro de Deza was appointed president of the *audiencia* of Granada to undertake the work of enforcement. The results were exactly as Tendilla had prophesied. The attempts to enforce the pragmatic were the immediate cause of the revolt.

Why, then, was the pragmatic issued and enforced? Three men

were particularly involved: Cardinal Espinosa (President of the Council of Castile), his henchman Pedro de Deza, and the King himself. As far as Deza was concerned, there were obvious advantages in the publication of the pragmatic. It would increase the jurisdiction of the Granada *audiencia*, at the expense of the Captain-General. This was something that he had every reason to welcome, for both professional and personal reasons. As president of the *audiencia*, he was heir to the tribunal's traditional vendetta with the Captaincy-General. In addition, there had apparently been a family feud between the Dezas and the Mendozas, stretching back to the time when an ancestor of Pedro de Deza supported Juana *la Beltraneja* in the civil wars of the fifteenth century. Deza could hardly fail to appreciate that a little trouble in Granada would redound to the discredit of the Count of Tendilla, whose leniency towards the Moriscos was well known.

Cardinal Espinosa, as President of the Council of Castile, had every reason to feel deeply concerned about the prospect of administrative breakdown in Granada. He distrusted the Count of Tendilla, partly no doubt because Tendilla's easy-going attitude to the Moriscos conflicted with his own rigorously orthodox views; and he had for some time been carefully placing his own men in the Granada administration in place of those appointed by the Marquis of Mondéjar, his predecessor as President of the Council, and the Count of Tendilla's father. The problem, in his eyes, was both religious and administrative, and the removal of Tendilla and the subordination of the Captaincy-General to the *audiencia* seemed the best way of solving it. He presumably succeeded in impressing this view on the King, over whom he exercised much influence at this time. The King was also moved by considerations of political and military security. The existence of numerous outlaws in the Alpujarras, the frequency of corsair raids, and, above all, the growing danger from the Turkish fleet in the western Mediterranean, made Granada particularly vulnerable. There was good reason to fear a Morisco rising in conjunction with a Turkish attack. Indeed, three Morisco spies arrested in 1565 had revealed a plot for the seizure of the Granada coast in the event of a Turkish success in the siege of Malta. Unless the situation was brought under control, therefore, Granada could easily become another battlefield in the war with the

Turk; the *Reconquista* would be undone; and the conflict would spread to the heart of Castile.

The publication of the pragmatic hardly seems in retrospect to have been the best method of preventing these disasters, but the grim picture in Philip's mind of a triumphant Islam raising the crescent once again on Spanish soil was by no means entirely fanciful in the circumstances of 1565 and 1566. The danger seemed very real, and the actual outbreak of the revolt in 1568 (although a surprise in that Philip believed he had successfully forestalled trouble) merely confirmed his forebodings. He was, in fact, more fortunate than he deserved to be, for the Turks unaccountably failed to exploit the Granada rebellion. As it was, the rising proved extremely difficult to crush, and would have been still more difficult if the Moriscos had succeeded in co-ordinating their plans and seizing the city of Granada. It could hardly have occurred at a more unfavourable moment for Philip. Andalusia and Castile had been drained of men by the levies for Alba's army, and recruits had to be brought from as far away as Catalonia. In addition, the terrain was ill suited to a swift campaign. The Count of Tendilla, third Marquis of Mondéjar since his father's death in 1566, knew the country well, and scored some brilliant successes in the opening months of the war. But, as so often happened, Philip's instinctive suspicion of the successful could not for long be held in check. Mondéjar was first ordered to share his command with his rival, the Marquis of los Vélez, and then to hand it over to the King's half-brother, Don John of Austria. The intrigues of Mondéjar's enemies, which had played so large a part in the origins of the revolt, therefore contributed also to the delay and expense incurred in its suppression, and it was not until the autumn of 1570 that the rising was finally crushed.

The revolt was over, but the problem remained. Philip chose to solve it in a manner that was logical but drastic. Since it was obviously dangerous to leave a defeated and sullen population heavily concentrated in one region of the peninsula, he ordered the dispersion of the Granada Moriscos throughout Castile. Considerable numbers of Moriscos did, in fact, contrive to remain in Andalusia – their numbers are estimated at anything from 60,000 to 150,000 – but much greater numbers were now let loose on the towns and villages of Castile, while 50,000 settlers were brought from Galicia, Asturias, and León to fill the gap left by their departure. In this way, the long-standing danger from Granada was at last removed, but only at the cost of creating a new, and even more complex, Morisco problem for succeeding generations.

6. THE FAITH MILITANT AND THE FAITH TRIUMPHANT

The revolt of Granada was suppressed none too soon. The Turkish fleet was out cruising again in the Mediterranean, and at one moment during the preparations in 1570 and 1571 for a Holy League between Spain, Venice, and the Papacy, the situation looked so menacing that Philip actually ordered the evacuation of the Balearic Islands. This remarkable order, which elicited the most lively protests from the city of Barcelona, was not in the end carried out, either because its execution was impossible or else because it had ceased to be necessary. The fleet of the Holy League was finally assembled at Messina in September 1571 under the command of Don John of Austria, fresh from his triumph in Granada; and, sailing into the Greek seas, it routed the Ottoman fleet at Lepanto on 7 October. Not only the Balearics but the entire western Mediterranean were safe from Islam at last.

The spectacular victory of the Christian forces at Lepanto in 1571 was to epitomize for contemporaries all that was most glorious in the crusade against Islam. It was an eternal source of pride to those who, like Miguel de Cervantes, had fought in the battle and could show the scar of their wounds, and of grateful wonder to the millions who saw in it a divine deliverance of Christendom from the power of the oppressor. Don John himself appeared as the resplendent image of the crusading hero, a man who had wrought great things in the Lord. The trophies of battle were proudly displayed, and the victory was commemorated in pictures, medals, and tapestries. But, in fact, the battle of Lepanto proved a curiously deceptive triumph, and the attempt to follow it up was peculiarly unsuccesful. Although Don John captured Tunis in 1573, it was lost again in the following year, and the Ottoman–Spanish struggle died away in stalemate.

The reasons for the strange anti-climax of the post-Lepanto years are partly to be found in the very nature of the Spanish victory. Stirred to their depths by the revolt of the Moriscos, and temporarily

Race and Religion

relieved by the apparent success of the Duke of Alba in repressing the Dutch, the Spaniards had for the first time committed their full strength to the Mediterranean struggle. This brought them victory at Lepanto; but an attack on this scale was likely by its very nature to elicit from the Turks a response on a similar scale. After Lepanto, the Ottoman Empire gradually mounted its counter-offensive, and this in turn demanded further large-scale preparations from Spain. Already by 1572 it was becoming questionable whether Spain could afford an all-out struggle in the Mediterranean, for on 1 April of that year the Dutch Sea Beggars had captured the port of Brill, and it became clear that the revolt of the Netherlands was very far from crushed.

There were obvious advantages to Spain, therefore, in disengaging in the Mediterranean. Fortunately, the Turks also had preoccupations of their own, and this made it possible to reach a tacit understanding. Slowly the two great empires, locked in combat for half a century, disengaged their forces; the Turks to deploy them eastwards against their Persian enemies, the Spaniards westwards towards the new Atlantic battlefield. The danger from Islam, which had dominated Spanish life for so long, was at last receding; and Spain became free in the 1570s and 1580s to concentrate its attention on the increasingly serious threat presented by the Protestant powers of the north.

At least the country was by now spiritually prepared for this new, and perhaps more difficult, conflict. All religious deviation within Spain had been successfully stifled. The frontiers had been closed against the indiscriminate entry of foreign ideas. Indeed, it was now possible to allow a certain relaxation. Under Cardinal Quiroga, who became Inquisitor-General in 1573 and replaced Archbishop Carranza as Archbishop of Toledo in 1577, both Church and Inquisition appear to have assumed a more moderate tone. Quiroga ordered the acquittal of Luis de León, who had been arrested by the Valladolid Inquisition in 1572, and he extended his protection to an important group of scholars – Arias Montano, Francisco Sánchez el Brocense, Francisco de Salinas – who had passed through difficult times in their attempts to introduce the methods of modern scholarship into Spanish intellectual life. It was Quiroga's Inquisition which allowed acceptance of the Copernican revolution in Spain – an acceptance so complete that Copernicus's work was recommended for study at Salamanca from 1594.

There was, then, a new confidence in the Castile of the later 1570s. The long years of ordeal seemed at last to be over, and the crusading spirit of an earlier generation had been resurrected by the triumph of Lepanto and by the challenge of the Protestant advance. This was a time of extraordinary intensity in Castile's spiritual life – an intensity which was apparent at many levels, and extended to many different spheres. It was reflected, for instance, in the reform movement within the Religious Orders. St Teresa, intent on returning to to the austerity of the primitive rule, founded the first house of Discalced Carmelites at Ávila in 1562; by the time of her death in 1582 there were fourteen priories and sixteen convents, and the grand total had risen to eighty-one by the beginning of the 1590s. Besides reforms in the existing Orders, new Orders made their appearance and established their houses – seventeen religious houses were founded at Madrid during the reign of Philip II. A great impetus was given, too, to charitable foundations. Many hospitals and alms-houses were established, and in the Hospitaller Brothers of St John of God there appeared a new religious congregation dedicated to the work of caring for the sick. St John of God (1485–1550) was a Portuguese who, after a dramatic conversion, found his true vocation when he set up a hospital for the poor sick at Granada in 1537. In 1572 his growing number of followers were organized by Pius V into a congregation under the Augustinian Rule. The Brothers enjoyed a remarkable success: by 1590 there were said to be 600 of them in Italy, Spain, and the New World, and they had seventy-nine hospitals containing over 3,000 beds.

The intense religious activity of the later sixteenth century, and the growth of a strong social conscience stirred by the sufferings of the sick and the poor, were in part a response to the programme formulated at the Council of Trent. As the Protestant challenge to Rome grew in strength and effectiveness, the need for reform came everywhere to be accepted as urgent. Quiroga, for instance, as Bishop of Cuenca before his elevation to Toledo, devised elaborate schemes for the promotion of charity and the advancement of learning in his diocese, and gave generous assistance to the poor. He was concerned, too, for the reform of his diocesan clergy, and as Primate of Spain he summoned in 1582 the twentieth Toledan Council, which was intended to initiate a movement for the reform of the clergy and laity, and to implement the Tridentine decrees. The extent to which the reform of the clergy was successful is difficult to gauge. There were probably some 100,000 religious in sixteenth-century Spain, with the numbers varying greatly from one region to another: in Galicia the regular and secular clergy represented 2 per cent of the population, in Catalonia 6 per cent. In some areas, notably Catalonia, parish priests were very poor, and standards of learning and morality were low, in spite of the earlier attempts at reform. It is probable, too, that as the century advanced and the numbers entering the Church increased, there were more priests incapable of being touched by any movement for reform. Against these, however, must be set an élite who represented the best ideals of Tridentine Catholicism; but there is no way of discovering what proportion this élite constituted of the clergy as a whole.

While the Council of Trent gave a powerful stimulus to religious activity, it must, however, be recognized that much of this activity derived from spiritual movements that existed in Spain long before the Council closed in 1565. It was true that Illuminism and Erasmianism had been formally suppressed, but the spiritual fervour which had originally inspired them forced its way irresistibly into new channels, and welled up afresh in the spiritual revival of the 1560s and 1570s. In particular, the neo-Platonic overtones of these movements, and their insistence on inward piety and the direct communion of the soul with God, had evoked a deep response among the inmates of monasteries and convents. In these institutions it found expression in the wave of mysticism which is one of the glories of later sixteenth-century Castile. The Inquisition first responded, in 1559, by placing a large number of mystical works on the Index. But if, as Melchor Cano believed, the tendency to an internal form of religion was the great heresy of the age, it was a tendency so deeply rooted that it proved impossible to dislodge. Moreover, monks and nuns could hardly be considered the natural allies of Erasmus, who had devoted his life to attacking them. Convinced, after all, that a mystical movement which could be kept well under control in the monasteries did not represent the great danger that had first been assumed, the Inquisition reversed its policy, and decided to tolerate the mystics. The result was a quite extraordinary outburst of mystical and ascetic literature. The climate was favourable, in that the reform movement was everywhere advancing, and the national crusade against Islam and the Protestants was mounting to its climax. In addition, there was the natural genius of St Teresa, who fired others with her example, and commended so enthusiastically the works of kindred spirits like Luis de Granada that the writings of the mystics achieved a certain fame. It was also peculiarly fortunate that mystical literature should have flourished at a time when the vernacular had attained an outstanding quality in literary expression, for the mystics were able to convey, both in prose and in verse, an extraordinary sense of personal immediacy when describing their arduous pursuit of the union of the soul with God.

The mystics found in personal religion a refuge from the confusions and disorders of the world, but others preferred to confront directly the intellectual and religious problems of the age. The most pressing of all these problems in the world of the Counter-Reformation was the relationship of religion to the humanist culture of the Renaissance. In some fields, such as political thought, the challenge was obvious. Later sixteenth-century Spain produced a succession of writers, like Arias Montano and the Jesuit Pedro de Ribadeneyra, who were concerned to refute the teachings of a pagan Machiavelli, by reaffirming the scholastic tradition that all power is divinely derived and that its exercise should conform to the dictates of a Natural Law implanted in men's hearts. In other fields, however, the challenge was more subtle and less easily met, although the ultimate response was perhaps more satisfying than that of the political theorists. Renaissance humanism had found its philosophical expression in neo-Platonism, to which earlier sixteenth-century Spanish writers were strongly attracted. This was especially obvious in the vogue of the pastoral novel, with its idealized vision of an earthly paradise – a vision difficult to reconcile with the Christian doctrine of man's fall. This fundamental incompatibility meant that sooner or later there was likely to be a reaction both against the idealism of Renaissance culture and against its anthropocentric emphasis. As the campaign against the Erasmians had shown, there were many conservatives in Castile ready to reject the entire Renaissance tradition; but against these were ranged others, like Luis de León and Alonso Gudiel, anxious to preserve what they could of

Renaissance ideals and to fuse them with the reinvigorated Roman Catholicism of the post-Tridentine age.

The fusion of Renaissance and Counter-Reformation ideals was the work of the later decades of the sixteenth century. It had begun already in philosophy, in the revived and renewed scholasticism of the school of Salamanca. In literature, it took the form of a gradual shift from idealism to realism – a realism preoccupied with a world that had been corrupted by the sinfulness of man, whose redemption could come only through the performance of good works and an absolute trust in the saving grace of God. While the famous picaresque novel *Lazarillo de Tormes*, published in 1554, was already realistic in tone, it remained for Mateo Alemán, in his *Guzmán de Alfarache* of 1599 to transform the memoirs of a *pícaro* into the mordantly realistic autobiography of a converted sinner: a book in which the sense of sin is overpoweringly strong. Not only was there a new awareness of man's inherent sinfulness in the masterpieces of Spanish literature of the late sixteenth and early seventeenth centuries, but also a new preoccupation with human psychology, which perhaps owed something to the mystical movement of the preceding decades. But one further element was needed to complete the transition to the harsh realism of the late sixteenth century. This was the ability to set the moral and material problems of the individual against his social background. It was the misfortunes that overcame Spain in the last ten or fifteen years of the century which somehow suddenly brought the picture into focus, and gave to Spanish authors their acute realization of the unutterable complexity of existence, as they watched with disillusionment and incomprehension the shipwreck of a nation that appeared to have been abandoned by its God.

There can be no doubt that the international religious conflict of the later sixteenth century acted as a sharp incentive to Spanish religious and intellectual sensibility, posing challenges which were often triumphantly met. But it would also seem that the cost was high, for individual scholars had been harassed and persecuted, and fresh constraints had been imposed on the expression of ideas. There is something stifling about the atmosphere of later sixteenth-century Spain, as if the religious life of the country had become too intense, and the ways of escape too few. In a citadel so barred against the outer world it was perhaps natural that feuds and rivalries should abound. These were years of bitter dissension between the different Religious Orders, and also of feuds within the Orders themselves, as the conservatives and the progressives battled for control. The Jesuits, especially, came under heavy attack from the secular clergy and from the other Orders – particularly the Dominicans – who suspected them of harbouring Illuminist and heretical tendencies in their midst. Philip II himself, under the influence of Melchor Cano and Arias Montano, distrusted them deeply, and made several attempts to prevent the Papacy from conferring further privileges upon an Order which was already far from amenable to control by the Inquisition and the Crown. As the Jesuits, undeterred by royal coldness, successfully consolidated their position, the temper of religious controversy became increasingly bitter, and mounted to a climax with the publication by the Spanish Jesuit Luis Molina at Lisbon in 1588 of his *Concordia Liberi Arbitrii* – a book which initiated a violent debate between the Jesuits and the Dominicans on the problems of grace and free will.

Within the Orders also there was acrimonious controversy. Rivalries among the Augustinians played their part in the arrest by the Inquisition of Luis de León; the reform of the Carmelites by St Teresa was checked in the 1580s by a revolt from within the Order, led by the conservative Nicolás Doria. These feuds, exacerbated by personal enmities, were in reality a reflection of the continuing struggle between Renaissance and anti-Renaissance, between those who accepted certain elements of the humanist tradition and those who did not.

Enormous energy was consumed in this struggle, and if a spirit of defeatism pervaded later generations, this may well have been because the strain of conflict was ultimately too much to bear. The Spain of the mid-sixteenth century had not only been fighting Moors and Protestants, but had also been attempting to resolve the inner tensions created by the presence of *conversos* and Moriscos; and at the same time it had been confronted with the enormous task of determining its relationship to a Europe which attracted and repelled it in equal degrees. In these circumstances, it was not surprising that it faltered. For a moment it had seemed that the solution was simple, and the enemy plain. While Valdés and Cano crusaded to impose Spanish on Erasmian Christianity at home, the Duke of Alba crusaded to

impose Spanish on Erasmian Christianity in the rebellious Netherlands. But a crusade tends, by its very nature, to be an oversimplifica-
tion, and it sometimes creates more problems than it solves. As long
as the crusaders could believe in their crusade, Spanish religion burnt
with a special intensity. But the faith militant could not always be
sustained at a white heat; and already by the 1570s it was becoming
apparent that, along with heresy, something of inestimable value
had perished in the flames.

7

'One Monarch, One Empire, and One Sword'

I. KING AND COURT

IN a sonnet addressed to Philip II, the poet Hernando de Acuña looked forward to the imminent arrival of the promised day on which there would be but one shepherd and one flock in the world, and 'one monarch, one empire, and one sword'. This sentiment was well calculated to appeal to a king who saw in unity beneath his own personal direction the sole hope of salvation in an embattled and heresy-ridden world. There was no particular arrogance in this belief. It sprang, rather, from Philip's sense of the mission conferred upon him by his Maker. As King he had to exercise a double trusteeship, first for God, and secondly, through God's appointing, for his subjects, whose humble servant he was: 'for the people was not made for the sake of the prince, but the prince was instituted at the instance of the people.'[1] The King must 'work' for the people – *'trabajar para el pueblo'* – who had been committed to his charge. It was his task to protect them from foreign enemies and to dispense justice among them, for the essence of good government was that it should be *just* government, in which the King rewarded the good, punished the wicked, and saw that all men, irrespective of rank, remained in undisturbed possession of their rights and property.

The man upon whom this task devolved had been carefully trained for his office. Charles V had impressed upon his son his own high sense of duty, as expressed in the famous confidential instructions which he prepared for him before leaving Spain in 1543. Philip was advised to keep God always before his eyes, and to listen to the advice of good counsellors; he must never give way to anger; he must never do anything 'offensive' to the Inquisition; and he must see that justice was dispensed without corruption. These instructions

1. Quoted from Philip II's instructions to the Viceroy of Naples (1558), by Charles Bratli, *Philippe II, Roi d'Espagne* (Paris, 1912), appendix VII, p. 234.

were carefully followed, for Philip entertained for his father a respect amounting to veneration. He was for ever measuring himself against his father, desperately attempting to live up to the idealized model of the great Emperor; and this in turn made him acutely conscious of his own shortcomings. His feelings of inadequacy only increased this indecisiveness which appears to have been a hereditary characteristic of the Habsburgs. Always in need of advice, and yet intensely suspicious of the motives of those who proffered it, he would endlessly procrastinate as he struggled to reach his decision. Himself a weak man, he tended to shun strong personalities, whose resolution he envied and whose strength he feared; instead he would turn for counsel to the faceless men, to a Ruy Gómez or a Mateo Vázquez – supple characters who would insinuate where an Alba would command. Distrustful and yet too trusting, Philip felt completely safe only among his State papers, which he would tirelessly read, mark, annotate, and emend, as if hoping to find in them the perfect solution to an intractable conundrum – a solution which would somehow dispense him from the agonizing duty of making up his mind.

Yet against the hesitation and the uncertainties must be set an iron sense of duty to God and to his subjects, and a passionate desire to live up to the high moral obligations inherent in a concept of kingship, the roots of which were deeply embedded both in the scholastic tradition and in the Castilian popular consciousness. The king who disregarded the moral law and transgressed the bounds of justice was a tyrant, and it was universally held that the people could refuse to obey the commands of such a ruler:

> En lo que no es justa ley
> No ha de obedecer al Rey.
> (Calderón, *La Vida es Sueño*, Act II)

The King's confessors and the Court theologians therefore had a positive role to play in advising the sovereign on all questions which appeared to pose problems of conscience, just as the King in turn had a certain moral obligation to follow their advice. It was in accordance with this tradition that Philip consulted his theologians in 1566 on the legitimacy of his religious policy in the Netherlands, and summoned in 1580 a Junta consisting of Fray Diego de Chaves, Fray

Pedro de Cascales and the royal chaplain, Arias Montano, to advise him on whether the use of force would be justified in securing for himself the Portuguese succession.

Since all power derived from God, the King was morally bound to maintain justice and to right wrongs. Philip II took this duty with intense seriousness. There are several instances of his intervening in cases of an alleged miscarriage of justice, as when an *oidor* from the *chancillería* of Valladolid treated in a high-handed manner the *corregidor* of Madrigal de las Altas Torres; and in 1596 the King found time to write to the President of the Valladolid *chancillería* about the case of a soldier who had been whipped without having first been given the opportunity to exonerate himself. He considered it morally incumbent upon him to be scrupulous in his regard for special liberties and *fueros*, but here again, in cases of a conflict between two laws, the higher law must prevail. This meant that *fueros* could not be employed as a mere pretext for committing disorders, as the students of Salamanca discovered to their cost in 1593, when they resisted arrest by royal officials on the grounds of their privileged status, and the King ordered that they should be punished 'in conformity with the laws of our kingdoms, in spite of the said privileges of exemption conceded by us'.

Contemporaries were impressed above all by the King's readiness to allow justice to take its course, even at the expense of his own private interest and comfort. Baltasar Porreño, who collected innumerable anecdotes about Philip II in his *Dichos y Hechos del Rey Don Felipe II*, constantly insists upon this trait, and quotes the King's words to a councillor about a doubtful case in which the Crown's financial interests were deeply engaged: 'Doctor, take note, and inform the Council, that in cases of doubt the verdict must always be given against me.' But the supreme example of the King's ruthless subordination of all personal considerations to the public welfare is to be found in the terrible and grotesque affair of the arrest and death of Don Carlos.

Don Carlos, the child of Philip's first wife, María of Portugal, had grown up to be an abnormally vicious creature of uncontrollable passions, totally unfitted for the government of an empire. Added to this was a deep hatred for his father, and an unmeasured ambition which may have led him into making sympathetic overtures to the

Dutch rebels. At eleven o'clock on the night of 18 January 1568 a strange procession, consisting of the King, the Duke of Feria, Ruy Gómez, and other members of the royal council, made its way downstairs to the bedroom of the 23-year-old Prince. As they opened the door, the ministers rushed forward to seize the dagger and arque-bus which the Prince always kept at the head of his bed. After a painful scene, in which Philip announced to his frightened son that he would treat him no longer as a father but as a king, the chamber was barred, guards were placed outside the door, and Don Carlos found himself in permanent confinement. Four days later the King wrote to the President of the Valladolid *chancillería* informing him of the Prince's arrest – a measure which had become necessary 'for the service of Our Lord and for the public welfare'.

The King's action was openly criticized by his subjects. The Prince, whatever his failings, had committed no criminal offence, and the royal justice was held to be excessively rigorous. Perturbed by the groundswell of opposition, Philip wrote to the grandees, the bishops, and the town councils explaining that the Prince's arrest was a matter of absolute necessity, and making it clear that he wanted no represen-tations made about the matter. This did not prevent the States of the Crown of Aragon from sending embassies to Madrid to request an explanation, which was not forthcoming. The King preserved an icy silence on the subject, partly, no doubt, because the misfortunes of his son touched him very deeply. The fate of the heir to the Spanish throne was, however, a matter of universal interest, and nothing could prevent the most intense gossip and speculation both inside and outside Spain. In consequence, when the wretched Don Carlos died on on 24 July, after having wrecked his always precarious health by a combination of hunger-strikes and violent remedial measures, the worst was at once assumed: the King had poisoned his son. For years afterwards the most sinister rumours travelled round Europe, until they came out at last into the open when William of Orange, in his famous *Apology* of 1581, levelled a formal accusation against the King.

There seems no reason to doubt either that the Prince's arrest was a necessity, or his death an accident. But there is something rather terrible about the picture of a king whose sense of duty was so rigid that he could not bring himself to visit his son in his last hours of agony. This was not for want of feeling. The death of Don Carlos moved his father deeply, and left a gaping void in what was to be a year of fearful bereavement. Philip's third and much-loved wife, Elizabeth of Valois, died in the autumn of 1568, having borne him only daughters, Isabella Clara Eugenia and Catherine. In 1570 he married his fourth wife, Anne of Austria, the daughter of his sister María and of his cousin, the Emperor Maximilian II; but of the five children she bore him before her death in 1580, only one, the future Philip III, lived beyond the age of eight. Through the life of Philip II there filed an endless succession of funeral cortèges, tragic reminders of the mortality of princes; and the King, to conceal his sorrows, taught himself to maintain an icy self-control, and devoted himself with redoubled energy to his solitary labours.

It was, then, as a professional ruler that Philip surveyed the world, sometimes wistfully sighing for the quiet life of a gentleman with an income of 6,000 ducats a year, but ruthlessly suppressing personal joys and sorrows when they threatened to interfere with his duties as a king. He did, however, manage to secure some private life by building for himself the Escorial – part-mausoleum, part-monastery, and part royal residence – where he could retreat from the public gaze and devote any leisure hours to his library and his pictures. He was a great connoisseur, and a generous patron of artists; and he took a deep personal interest in the building of the Escorial by Juan Bautista de Toledo and his disciple Juan de Herrera. The outcome of their labours, began in 1563 and completed in 1584, effectively epitomized the man and his times. In the Escorial, with its frigid façade, the exuberant plateresque of the early Spanish Renaissance is gone for ever, replaced by the cold symmetry of a constricting classicism, imperial, dignified, and aloof – a fitting symbol of the triumph of constraint in the Spain of the Counter-Reformation, and of the triumph of authoritarian kingship over the disruptive forces of anarchy.

The principles of mathematical harmony that obtained in the architecture of the Escorial were also applied to the selection of a capital. In 1561 the Spanish Court, which was still peripatetic, moved from Toledo to Madrid. It seems that the move was not, at the time, intended to be permanent, but Madrid was conveniently close to the new palace of the Escorial, and it gradually came to be recognized as the capital of the Monarchy. The town's only real claim to this particular honour lay in its geographical position as the mathematical centre of Spain, and somehow this conferred upon its choice a kind of inevitability; for, in the words of the chronicler Cabrera, 'it was right that so great a Monarchy should have a city which could function as its heart – a vital centre in the midst of the body, which ministered equally to every State in time of peace and war'.[2]

In spite of the selection of Madrid as a permanent capital, Philip did not entirely cease to travel. Apart from frequent visits to Toledo, to Aranjuez and to his hunting lodge of El Pardo, he visited Barcelona in 1564, Córdoba in 1570, Lisbon in 1582–3, the capitals of the three States of the Crown of Aragon in 1585, and Aragon again in 1592. But, unlike that of Charles V, the government of Philip II was essentially a fixed government – a fact with enormous implications for the future of his territories.

The choice of a capital at once central and remote contradicted one of the fundamental assumptions on which the Spanish Monarchy rested. If the many territories that together constituted the Monarchy were regarded as independent units of equal rank, then they were all entitled to an equal degree of consideration. The development of a conciliar system represented an attempt to deal with this problem, but Charles had always supplemented conciliar government by repeated visits to his various kingdoms. The establishment of a permanent capital meant in effect the renunciation of the Emperor's practice of peripatetic kingship – a practice which, for all its drawbacks, had the very great advantage of giving his peoples occasional visual proof that their King had not forgotten them. Admittedly a fixed capital was not in itself inconsistent with frequent royal visits, but as soon as the Court was organized on the assumption that it would not be permanently on the move, it tended to develop an inertia of its own arising from the trouble and expense of frequent upheavals.

In assuming that he could acquaint himself intimately with the needs and problems of his territories from an observation-post in the geographical centre of Spain, Philip tended to overlook the fact that this solution to the problem prevented his territories from acquainting themselves with *him*. Perhaps because of his own sense

2. Luis Cabrera de Córdoba, *Filipe Segundo, Rey de España* (ed. Madrid, 1876), vol. I, p. 298.

of unease among the crowd, which can only have been increased by his unhappy experiences in the Netherlands, he tended to underestimate the magical effects of the royal presence, and to neglect those little personal gestures in which his father excelled. As a result, he allowed a barrier to grow up between him and his subjects, which his constant but solitary concern for their interests was insufficient to surmount.

Philip was equally mistaken in assuming that residence in the mathematical centre of the peninsula would foster the impression of absolute impartiality in the treatment of his subjects. The first to complain were the Italians, who found themselves part of a Monarchy that was acquiring an increasingly Spanish colouring; for the King, having settled in Spain, had also chosen to dispense with the assistance of several of his father's non-Spanish advisers. It was true that in the new Council of Italy, created in 1555, there were three places reserved for Italians, but its first president was a Spaniard, the Duke of Francavilla. 'The King,' reported the Venetian ambassador, 'has no regard but for Spaniards; with these he converses, with these he takes counsel, with these he rules.'

But the Monarchy of Philip II was not even in the full sense a really Spanish Monarchy. As time went on, it became increasingly Castilian in character. Even if Philip had no such intention, the very selection of a capital in the heart of Castile naturally gave his government a Castilian complexion. The King had established his residence in a stridently Castilian environment; he was surrounded by Castilians and was dependent on Castilian resources for the overwhelming proportion of his revenues. In these circumstances it was natural enough that viceroyalties and other lucrative offices at Court and in the Monarchy should be bestowed on Castilians. But it was no less natural that this trend towards the Castilianization of the Monarchy should have been watched with the deepest concern by Catalans and Aragonese. Where Charles V had managed to hold general Cortes for the Crown of Aragon almost every five years, Philip II held them twice only, in 1563 and again in 1585. The infrequency of the sessions is almost certainly to be explained by the fact that the small subsidies eventually voted by the Aragonese kingdoms were simply not worth the heavy expenses of the journey and the large political concessions required before the money was forthcoming. But Cortes which to the King were merely an occasion for the extraction of money, were looked upon by the peoples concerned as primarily an opportunity for seeing their King and obtaining redress of their grievances. The virtual abandonment of the Cortes of the Crown of Aragon therefore seemed to Aragonese, Catalans, and Valencians to represent an abandonment of themselves, and they came to look upon this neglect as part of a Castilian plot to deprive them first of their King and then of their liberties.

The effect of the isolation of the King in the heart of Castile was therefore to reinforce the latent suspicions of the non-Castilian regions of the peninsula about Castilian intentions. The mutual antagonism of Castilians and Aragonese, which had so chequered the reigns of Ferdinand and Isabella, had already developed by the end of Charles V's reign into an undisguised contempt for the Aragonese among the Castilians, and a corresponding anxiety about Castilian intentions in the Crown of Aragon. As seen by the Aragonese and the Catalans, the spectacular success of Castile had merely added to the already unbearable arrogance of its inhabitants, who 'want to be so absolute, and put so high a value on their own achievements and so low a value on everyone else's, that they give the impression that they alone are descended from heaven, and the rest of mankind are mud'.[3] Castilian aristocrats had openly expressed their hatred of Aragonese institutions, and had given the impression that the time would come when the Crown of Aragon would be ruled by the laws of Castile. It was therefore easy enough for Catalans and Aragonese to see the policies of Philip II as one further stage in an elaborate conspiracy to Castilianize the Monarchy.

There is no clear evidence that Philip himself entertained any such design. He had been instructed by his father to treat the States of the Crown of Aragon with the utmost circumspection in view of their extreme sensitivity about their laws and liberties; and the revolt of the Netherlands no doubt gave extra point to this advice. Moreover, Philip had inherited the Emperor's patrimonial concept of his dominions as independent units, all with their own individual laws, which he was under conscience bound to observe. While he may have hoped to reduce their mutual isolation by intermarrying the

3. Cristòfol Despuig, Los Col·loquis de la insigne Ciutat de Tortosa, ed. Fidel Fita (Barcelona, 1877), p. 46. A series of imaginary dialogues by a Catalan gentleman, first published in 1557.

various provincial aristocracies, he does not appear to have grasped, any more than his father, the concept of the Spanish Monarchy as a living organism with an existence of its own, over and above that conferred upon it by its subordination to a single ruler. Indeed, perhaps precisely because he looked upon himself as the only link between his various territories, Philip found it difficult to conceive of them as possessing any unity, real or potential, other than that provided by his own person.

So personalized a concept of the nature of the Monarchy naturally tended to endow it in the King's mind with a purely static character, whereas in fact, like all constitutional organisms, it was inevitably subject to change. The very choice of Castile for the establishment of a capital, and the consequent process of gradual Castilianization, was itself bound to introduce changes by modifying the constitutional position of the provinces and their relationship to their King. Exaggerated as the immediate fears of the provinces may have been, they were not far wrong in suspecting that the Monarchy was being set on a path which would lead inexorably to a specifically Castilian solution of its constitutional problems. For this was, after all, one possible answer to the problem of the Monarchy's diversity. There was at least the logic of simplicity in the Castilian demand that the various states of the Monarchy should be stripped of their tiresome laws and privileges, and be governed instead by the laws of Castile.

Against the Castilian answer to the problems of the Monarchy there was, however, a possible alternative answer which possessed a greater appeal for the non-Castilian provinces. This was to be found in the work entitled *El Concejo y Consejeros del Príncipe*, published at Antwerp in 1559 by the Valencian humanist Fadrique Furió Ceriol. As might have been expected of a Valencian, Furió's proposals stemmed from the Aragonese tradition of empire, in which each territory preserved its own constitutional structure and kept its own laws and liberties. The empire for him seems to have been a kind of federal organization, with the King drawing his councillors equally from all his States.

In the very first years of Philip's reign, therefore, two possible solutions to the problem of imperial organization – a Castilian and a federalist – stood face to face. The problem itself, which had already begun to acquire a new importance as Philip assumed the guise of a

Castilian monarch, became urgent with the revolt of the Netherlands in 1566. On the King's treatment of the Dutch rebels depended
much more than the fate of the Netherlands alone. If the Castilian
extremists were to win the day, then the Neapolitans, the Aragonese,
and the Catalans would have cause to fear that their turn would come
next. If, on the other hand, the problem of the Netherlands could be
solved in such a way as to keep the Netherlands a contented member
of the Spanish Monarchy, the non-Castilian provinces would be
better able to withstand the pressure of an over-mighty Castile.
From the 1560s, then, the problem of the Netherlands hovered over
all the deliberations in Madrid, urgently requiring an answer and
yet too complex to allow of any clear-cut solution. For the problem
of the Netherlands was ultimately the problem of the Spanish
Monarchy as a whole – of its future direction and constitutional
structure.

2. THE FACTION STRUGGLES

The method by which the debate on the Netherlands was conducted
is only understandable in terms of the governmental system of
Philip II. The essence of this system was the combination of conciliar
advice with royal action – or inaction. The King himself was the
executive officer, personally attending to all matters of government,
however trivial. It was he who studied the dispatches, drafted the
orders, and carefully supervised the labours of his secretaries.

To some extent, indeed, Philip was his own secretary. Certainly
he had many of the secretary's characteristics: 'no secretary in the
world uses more paper than His Majesty,' Cardinal Granvelle acidly
remarked.[4] In spite of this, even Philip needed considerable secretarial
assistance. The sixteenth century was for many countries the great
age of the secretary, who was becoming an important officer of state
with discretionary powers. This rise of the secretary had partly
occurred under the influence of Spain, for the French secretaries of
State appointed by Henry II in 1547 to some extent modelled themselves on their Spanish colleagues. In Spain itself, however, the
further development of secretarial power was inevitably checked by

4. Quoted by M. Van Durme, *El Cardenal Granvela* (Spanish translation
from the Flemish, Barcelona, 1957), p. 357.

the King's personal bureaucratic proclivities. None the less, the secretaries remained indispensable, and their indispensability gave them a great, if shadowy, influence in the management of government. Always close to the royal person, and intimately acquainted with the contents of his dispatches, they could not but be powerful figures, assiduously courted by the many pressure groups within the Spanish Monarchy.

Of the secretarial officials trained by Los Cobos, almost the only experienced survivor on the accession of Philip II was Gonzalo Pérez. Originally recommended to Cobos by the Emperor's secretary Alonso de Valdés, just before Valdés's death in 1532, Pérez was an excellent Latinist and a man of considerable erudition. Having entered the Church without apparently possessing any deep sense of vocation, he rose to eminence on his appointment as secretary to Prince Philip in 1543. From this time onwards he was in Philip's constant service, minuting his correspondence and deciphering his confidential dispatches. As sole secretary of State, Pérez enjoyed enormous influence – perhaps too much for one man, for on his death in 1566 the secretaryship was divided into two, along geographical lines. *Norte*, the northern department, went to a Basque, Gabriel de Zayas, while *Italia*, the southern department, was entrusted to Gonzalo's illegitimate son, Antonio Pérez.

While the executive part of the government consisted of the King and his secretaries, the advisory part remained the various councils, organized largely as they had been in the reign of Charles V. Philip was extremely careful to continue his father's practice of excluding great nobles from office in the central government, and reserving their services for viceroyalties, embassies, and military commands. But in a hierarchically ordered society it was impossible to overlook the claims, the aspirations, and the feuds of the magnates; and although many of them chose to live like kings on their estates rather than pass their days in attendance on an uncongenial monarch in an uncongenial Court, it was essential to provide opportunities for them to make their voices heard. Philip was from the first acutely aware of the fact that he ruled a deeply divided land, in which the control of such cities as Toledo and Seville was disputed by rival aristocratic factions organized on a basis of family relationships and an elaborate clientage system. The only way to neutralize these dangerous feuds was, as he appreciated, to give them an outlet at Court, providing in one of the Councils a forum in which the partisans could express their rival views.

The obvious forum for discussion was the Council of State, which acquired under Philip a spurious glitter that helped to hide the fact that the King and not the Council was the real source of power. During the 1560s and 1570s the Council of State was turned into the battleground of two opposing factions, each struggling to obtain sole influence with a king who delighted in the art of playing off one against the other. The exact significance of these factions is extremely difficult to determine, but it is probable that much of their antagonism derived from family rivalries whose origins are lost in the shadowy regions of Spanish local history, but which had been exacerbated by the civil wars of the fifteenth century and by the succession struggles of the early sixteenth. For instance, the rival Toledo families of the Ayalas and the Riberas, which had come into conflict during the revolt of the *Comuneros*, and then again over the statutes of *limpieza* in the cathedral chapter, were each linked by ties of blood and clientage to the great families which clashed at Court. The Ribera faction at Toledo included the Silvas, and the Silvas in turn were close adherents of the enormously powerful house of Mendoza, which comprised twenty-two heads of families of the high aristocracy. Their rivals, the Ayalas and Ávalos, on the other hand were members of another aristocratic network, including the houses of Zapata and of Álvarez de Toledo, and headed by the great Duke of Alba himself.

There are several indications that even in Philip II's reign the Castilian aristocracy still lived beneath the shadow of the hatreds generated during the revolt of the *Comuneros*. As late as 1578 Don Luis Enríquez de Cabrera y Mendoza, second Duke of Medina de Ríoseco and Admiral of Castile, indignantly declared to the Imperial ambassador that the King's government was not a government of justice but of tyranny and revenge, since power now lay in the hands of those whose fathers had been *Comuneros*, and who sought to avenge themselves on their former opponents. The full significance of this remark is not yet clear, although a study of the family background of the councillors and officials at the Spanish Court would no doubt help to elucidate it. But there are enough signs of *Comunero* and anti-*Comunero* affiliations among the two Court factions of the 1560s and 1570s to suggest that the Admiral's assertion provides at least one important clue to the bitterness of their struggles.

While it is true that the Duke of Alba's family played no significant part in the revolt of the *Comuneros*, its allies, the Zapatas, had been enthusiastic partisans of the rebels. On the other hand, the Duke of Infantado, head of the Mendozas, had (after some prevarication) come out in support of the Emperor. If post-*Comunero* Castile was divided between those who supported an 'open' Spain and those who stood for 'closed' Castilian nationalism as represented by the *Comuneros*, then the Mendozas, cultured and cosmopolitan, represented the first, and Alba the second. But it is impossible to say how far these positions were consciously held, and how far 'ideological' as distinct from family disagreements determined the respective alignments.

In the early years of Philip II the Mendoza faction at Court was headed by the King's favourite and confidant Ruy Gómez de Silva, Prince of Eboli. The son of an aristocratic Portuguese family, he had come to Spain as a child with his maternal grandfather, *mayordomo mayor* to the Empress Isabella, and had grown up in the palace with Philip. Appointed a Councillor of State on Philip's accession, he married in 1559 Doña Ana de Mendoza, indiscreet, ambitious, capricious and volatile. Ruy Gómez's ascendancy with the King, whom he treated with exactly the right touch of smooth deference, made him an extremely influential character at Court, and the natural leader of all those who disliked the Duke of Alba. Among these was the secretary Antonio Pérez, who formed an easy alliance with the Prince of Eboli, and was to succeed him as leader of the faction on Eboli's death in 1573. It was natural that Antonio Pérez should join this camp, for there had been a feud between his father and the Duke of Alba; and, in addition, his wife was a member of the Coello family, violent anti-*Comuneros* whose residence in Madrid had been destroyed during the revolt by the *Comunero* Zapatas.

The Eboli and the Alba factions were fighting primarily for power – for ascendancy with the King and the consequent control of patronage. But beyond this, they represented, either by tradition or by force of circumstance, or both, differing points of view which were crystallized in the discussions over the revolt of the Netherlands.

Where Alba and his friends were advocates of a ruthless repression of the revolt, the Eboli faction entertained a discreet sympathy for the rebels and was anxious for a negotiated settlement. It is true that the choice of Alba to crush the revolt firmly committed his supporters at Court to a policy of repression, but there is every indication that this policy accorded with Alba's own inclinations and with his views about the proper organization of the Spanish Monarchy. Many years later, in a discussion in the Council of State about certain difficulties with Aragon, Alba said that, given three or four thousand men, he would wipe out Aragon's liberties; to which the Marquis of los Vélez, a member of the Eboli group, replied that this was not the advice to give the King if he wished to see him retain his territories, but that the way to preserve them was to respect their *fueros* and observe the conditions under which they had been inherited.[5]

This clash at the council table suggests that the two factions stood for two opposing solutions to the problem of the Monarchy: the Alba faction for the Castilian nationalist solution, involving the destruction of provincial liberties, and the Eboli group for the 'Aragonese' federalist solution, as outlined by Furió Ceriol. In sending Alba to the Netherlands, the King had come down in favour of the 'Castilian' approach, but his willingness to stand by it would clearly depend on the extent of Alba's success. By 1573, after six years of terror, it was obvious that Alba had failed, and he was accordingly relieved of his post.

The failure of Alba left the way free for the Eboli faction, but in the intervening period it had fallen into a state of some disarray. The president of the Council of Castile, Cardinal Espinosa, who had supported Eboli on the specific issue of the Netherlands, lost the King's favour and died immediately afterwards (allegedly of mortification) in September 1572. More serious, Eboli himself died in July 1573. The effective leadership of the truncated party now devolved upon Antonio Pérez. Pérez acquired a useful if politically inexperienced ally in Bishop Quiroga, Espinosa's successor as Inquisitor-General; but the faction needed an aristocratic figurehead, and one was not found until 1575, when Pérez did a deal with a former enemy of the Mendozas, the third Marquis of los Vélez (son of the commander in the Granada campaign who died in 1574) and

5. *Las Obras y Relaciones de Antonio Pérez* (Geneva, 1631), pp. 205–6.

secured his appointment to the Council of State. The faction did, however, have a coherent policy to set before Philip as an alternative to that pursued by Alba – a policy formulated by none other than Furió Ceriol. Furió's 'remedies' of 1573 for the troubles in the Netherlands[6] consisted of a number of measures aimed at pacification and conciliation. These included the dissolution of the Council of Troubles and the abandonment of the Tenth Penny, together with certain positive constitutional proposals which were fully consistent with the 'Eboli' approach to the government of the Monarchy: a guarantee by the King to preserve the traditional laws and liberties of the Netherlands, and the appointment of Netherlanders to offices in 'the Indies, Italy, Sicily' and the various other provinces.

The man chosen by Philip to carry out this policy of pacification in the Netherlands was Don Luis de Requesens, at that time Governor of Milan, a member of one of the most distinguished families of Catalonia and father-in-law of Don Pedro Fajardo, who would shortly become third Marquis of los Vélez. Requesens, who left for the Netherlands in the autumn of 1573, prided himself on being independent of both the factions at Court. But an 'Aragonese' solution to the problem of the Netherlands, if such was intended, was to prove no more practicable than the 'Castilian' solution attempted by the Duke of Alba. A policy of pacification and reconciliation could only succeed if the army were kept under firm control, but the early 1570s – a period of recession in Seville's American trade – were a time of acute financial difficulty for Philip, and regular payment of the troops in the Netherlands was becoming increasingly difficult. In March 1574 the King agreed to offer the rebels a general pardon (containing many exceptions), to be drafted on the model of the pardon issued by Charles V after the revolt of the *Comuneros*. But in April the troops mutinied and marched on Antwerp, and although the mutiny was quelled, the incident caused such alarm that the proclamation of the pardon by Requesens in June fell flat.

No significant progress towards a general reconciliation was made during the following year, and the financial position was becoming acute. On 1 September 1575 came the second 'bankruptcy' of

6. They are included in the edition by Diego Sevilla Andrés of Furió Ceriol's *El Concejo y Consejeros del Príncipe* (Valencia, 1952), pp. 177–85.

Philip's reign, when the King suspended payments to the bankers. The suspension destroyed the delicate mechanism of credit by which remittances were made from Castile to Flanders; the Castilian fairs were temporarily paralysed, two Sevillian banks failed at the beginning of 1576, and the Genoese refused to undertake any more *asientos* until a settlement was reached. With its pay in arrears, the Spanish army in the Netherlands (which in 1575 consisted of only some 3,000 Spanish infantry, as against 25,000 Germans and 8,000 Walloons) grew increasingly restless. Requesens, whose health had long been poor, died on 5 March 1576, and his death removed the one figure of any authority in the crumbling Spanish régime. The troops, discontented and mutinous, were now without a master. As the months passed and no pay arrived, the predictable happened. On 4 and 5 November they ran wild, and sacked the city of Antwerp.

The 'Spanish fury' at Antwerp, which ended all chances of conciliation, occurred one day after the arrival in the Netherlands of a new conciliator, Don John of Austria. Don John's appointment in succession to Requesens is an indication of Philip II's continued support for the Eboli policy, for Furió Ceriol had suggested that Don John should be sent to the Netherlands if the King were unable to go himself, and the terms on which Don John accepted his appointment were very much in line with Eboli ideas. He asked for a free hand in the government of the Netherlands, and for permission to respect their laws and privileges. He insisted that all his correspondence should pass through the hands of Antonio Pérez, rather than those of the secretary of the northern department, Gabriel de Zayas, a protégé of the Duke of Alba. In addition, he requested authorization for an action consistently opposed by Alba, but supported both by the Papacy and by the Eboli faction – the invasion of England. Don John went to the Netherlands, therefore, enjoying the full confidence of Pérez and his friends, and with the intention of executing their policies.

Apart from the fact that Don John's temperament scarcely fitted him for the role of a conciliator, circumstances anyhow made his task impossible. The time for conciliation was in fact past, although the King was now ready to make certain concessions – including the withdrawal of all Spanish troops – which were embodied in the Perpetual Edict signed by Don John on 12 February 1577. Don John, who was anxious for a settlement that would leave him free to prepare an invasion of England, felt deeply the humiliation implied in these concessions. Already, on the very day that the Edict was signed, Antonio Pérez had written the King a note on behalf of Quiroga, los Vélez and himself, expressing alarm at the despairing tone of Don John's dispatches. While the King was anxious for peace in the Netherlands, he was not ready for war with Elizabeth. He therefore left Don John in a state of suspended animation – unable to conclude peace on satisfactory terms, but lacking the money to resume the war – and disconsolately watching the gradual blighting of the cherished ambition to conquer England and marry Mary Queen of Scots.

Increasingly frustrated by his enforced inactivity, Don John was now becoming convinced that a conciliatory policy was unworkable, and that the King must somehow be induced to authorize a full-scale resumption of the war. He was quite prepared, if necessary, to precipitate the renewal of a conflict which he anyhow considered unavoidable, and in late July 1577 he took the law into his own hands and seized the castle of Namur, from where he launched in August an impassioned appeal to the *tercios* to return to the Netherlands to wage war against the rebels. Meanwhile, he had sent his secretary Escobedo to Madrid to press the King for money. Escobedo, originally a protégé of Ruy Gómez and Antonio Pérez, had been appointed secretary to Don John at the instigation of Pérez in order to keep an eye on the activities of his mercurial master; but during his service in Flanders he had fallen under the spell of Don John and had become an enthusiastic supporter of his ambitious projects. By the time of Escobedo's return to Madrid, therefore, his devotion to Pérez had noticeably cooled – and all the more so since the ideas of Don John and the Pérez party no longer fully coincided.

The arrival of Escobedo in Madrid at the end of July was extremely unwelcome to Pérez. The two men – Escobedo dour and intransigent, Pérez vain, deceitful and sly – were natural rivals for power and influence. Moreover, Escobedo knew too much, and soon discovered more. Pérez, always greedy for money, was in the habit of selling State secrets – a fact of which Escobedo can hardly have been unaware, especially as Pérez had kept Don John fully informed of all that passed at the Council table in Madrid. Escobedo also seems to have stumbled on some extremely incriminating evidence about the close alliance that had developed between Antonio Pérez and the widowed Princess of Eboli, who had returned to Court in 1576 after three turbulent years in a nunnery and had plunged into a world of political intrigue. The exact character of her intrigues with Pérez remains a mystery, but it seems possible that, among various other private ventures, the Princess and Pérez were conducting secret negotiations with the Dutch rebels. In any event, Escobedo soon discovered enough to be able to ruin Pérez, and Pérez in turn realized that Escobedo must be promptly disposed of, if he himself were to survive.

Pérez's best hope lay with the King. Philip's natural distrust of his half-brother had been increased by Don John's recent behaviour in the Netherlands, and it was not difficult for Pérez to play upon the King's fears. Pérez apparently managed to persuade the King that Escobedo was Don John's evil genius; that the two men were plotting to secure for Don John the English – and perhaps even the Spanish – throne; and that Escobedo's removal would be fully justified on the grounds of reason of state. Once the King had been successfully convinced, it remained for Pérez to do the deed. Having failed in three attempts to kill Escobedo by poisoning, Pérez hired three assassins who duly murdered their victim in the street on the night of 31 March 1578.

The murder which Pérez believed would save him from disaster proved, in fact, to be the beginning of his downfall. Escobedo's friends were not prepared to let the matter be forgotten, and they found an ally in Mateo Vázquez, originally secretary to Cardinal Espinosa, and, since 1573, secretary to the King. Vázquez soon came to suspect at least part of the truth, and began to press the King for action. During the months that followed, Philip passed through agonies of indecision. Uneasily aware of his own complicity in Escobedo's murder, it began to dawn on him that Pérez might have trapped him into ordering the death of an innocent man.

It seems probable that these growing suspicions about the reliability of Antonio Pérez were reinforced by his behaviour during the summer and autumn of 1578. On 4 August the young King Sebastian of Portugal was killed in Africa at the battle of Alcázarquivir, leaving his aged uncle Cardinal Henry as heir to the Portuguese throne. Cardinal Henry's successor was likely to be one of three people: Don

Antonio, the Prior of Crato, an illegitimate member of the Portuguese royal house; the Duchess of Braganza; and Philip himself. The contest for the succession left the field wide open for intrigue, and there was no more zealous intriguer at the Spanish Court than the Princess of Eboli. There are indications, although no clear proof, that the Princess was working for the candidature of the Duchess of Braganza, whose son she hoped to marry to her own daughter; and it was natural for the Princess to turn for help to her old ally, Antonio Pérez, who, as secretary for Portuguese affairs, was naturally involved in all the negotiations over the succession.

Any hint of the intrigues of Pérez and the Princess over the Portuguese succession must have nourished the King's growing doubts about his secretary's activities. By the end of 1578 these doubts had grown sufficiently for him to withdraw his favour from Pérez's aristocratic ally, the Marquis of los Vélez, who had shared with the King and Pérez the secret of Escobedo's murder. Yet, curiously enough even the disgrace of los Vélez failed to convince Pérez that his own position was now in danger. Confident that the King's own complicity in Escobedo's murder would make it too damaging for him ever to take action, Pérez overlooked Philip's dogged determination to get to the bottom of an affair which touched his own kingship, at a most sensitive point. During all these long months the King was, in fact, carefully maturing his plans. His obvious need was to obtain new advisers. The Duke of Alba had been exiled to his estates; Pérez and his colleagues were utterly discredited. At this moment, when it was essential to prevent the Portuguese succession from slipping through his fingers, he turned to a statesman of great experience, well known for his capacity for quick thinking and decisive action – Cardinal Granvelle.

Since his dismissal from the government of the Netherlands in 1564, Granvelle had passed the years in Italy, a fading relic of an imperial past. On 30 March 1579 the King wrote asking him to come to Court at once, since he had the greatest need of his person. On 28 July Granvelle arrived at Madrid, in company with Don Juan de Idiáquez, whose father had been one of his most trusted colleagues in the Emperor's Government. The pair were greeted by Antonio Pérez. That same night, Pérez and the Princess of Eboli were taken into custody.

The arrest of Pérez and the Princess virtually put an end to the Eboli faction, which seemed to have obtained a permanent ascendancy at Court since the disgrace of Alba. In summoning Granvelle, Philip was turning his back on the immediate past: on a decade of intrigues which had culminated in his treacherous deception by a secretary in whom he had placed a totally unjustified confidence. But if the two factions had now disappeared, the ideas which they had championed still survived. The remaining years of the reign would show that new questions had an uncanny way of turning into old questions in a fresh guise, and in particular into the highly intractable question of the future organization of the Spanish Monarchy. But at least the questions would be tackled by new advisers – except that Granvelle was himself an older adviser than any he had come to replace.

3. THE ANNEXATION OF PORTUGAL

In many respects the years 1579 and 1580 represented not a break with the past but a return to it – to a more distant, and perhaps more glorious, past than the Eboli-Pérez era. At Court, an old councillor of Charles V, Cardinal Granvelle, was in the saddle. In the Netherlands, the Emperor's son Don John of Austria had died disillusioned and disappointed on 1 October 1578. Philip planned to replace him by appointing to the civil government of the Low Countries the Emperor's illegitimate daughter, Margaret of Parma, who had already acted as regent between 1559 and 1566 (although in the event Philip's plans were frustrated by the refusal of Margaret's son, Alexander Farnese, who had assumed the government on Don John's death, to share his power with his mother). This return at the end of the 1570s to figures from an imperial age was curiously appropriate, for these same years saw a radical change in the policies of Philip – a change to a policy of active imperialism, reminiscent in its scope of the imperialism of Charles V.

The first two decades of the reign had been years of great difficulty for Philip II. A succession of events in the 1560s – the revolt of the Granada Moriscos, the stepping up of the Turkish naval attack, the revolt of the Netherlands, and the outbreak of the French wars of religion – had kept him consistently on the defensive. Although the danger in the Mediterranean receded after the victory at Lepanto, the 1570s were also sombre years, overshadowed by the failure to subdue the revolt in the Netherlands, and by the royal bankruptcy of 1575–6. The Crown's financial difficulties had in turn compelled the King to ask the Castilian Cortes of 1574–5 for a further tax increase – a request to which the Cortes responded by raising the *encabezamiento* again, until it stood at four times its level in the early years of Charles V. In practice, the new figure proved to be quite unrealistic. Many towns reverted to the practice of collecting the *alcabala* instead of compounding for it, with extremely unfortunate results. At Medina del Campo, for instance, the tax on sales, which had previously stood at only 1·2 per cent rose to 10 per cent with serious consequences for trade at the fairs. In the end, the difficulty of collecting the tax at the increased rate forced the Crown to retreat, and in 1577 Philip reduced the *encabezamiento* by a quarter, to some 2,700,000 ducats a year – a figure at which it remained for the rest of his reign.

The inability of the Crown to extract more than some $2\frac{1}{2}$ million ducats from the *encabezamiento* suggested that the traditional sources of revenue in Castile had been extended to their limits, and that, unless alternative sources of supply could be found, the King would be compelled to remain on the defensive. At this moment, however, the wealth of the Indies came to his rescue. The introduction of the amalgam of mercury into the refining of Peruvian silver was by now beginning to yield results, and during the second half of the 1570s there was a dramatic increase in the supplies of silver reaching the King from the New World. During the 1580s and 1590s Philip could expect to obtain some two to three million ducats a year from the treasure fleets. Trade between Seville and the New World reached new heights; the bankers, partially satisfied by the *medio general* or debt settlement of December 1577, began to recover confidence; and the fairs of Castile, having miraculously survived the bankruptcies of 1557 and 1575, enjoyed in the 1580s an Indian summer.

This new *largueza* – abundance of money – gave Philip real freedom of manoeuvre for the first time in his reign. At last, after long years on the defensive, he could go over to the attack. It was because he had acquired this sudden accession of wealth that Philip was able

to embark upon the bold projects and imperial ventures of the
1580s and 1590s: the plans for the recovery of the northern Netherlands, for a moment so close to achievement under the brilliant
leadership of Alexander Farnese; the launching of the Armada
against England in 1588: the intervention in the civil wars in France
in the 1590s. These were the years of audacious enterprises, which
give the lie to the legend of the 'prudent' king; years of a spectacular
imperialism, which seemed for a moment as if it might make Philip
the master of the world.

While America provided the financial resources that subsidized
the new imperialism, it acquired its geographical orientation from
Philip's great success of 1580: the annexation of Portugal. The union
of Portugal with the Spanish Crown gave Philip a new Atlantic seaboard, a fleet to help protect it, and a second empire which stretched
from Africa to Brazil, and from Calicut to the Moluccas. It was the
acquisition of these possessions, together with the new influx of
precious metals, that made possible the imperialism of the second
half of the reign. But the two events were by no means unrelated;
for Portugal itself was won for Spain with American silver.

The disastrous outcome of King Sebastian's African crusade of
1578 demoralized a nation already afflicted by a profound unease.
Portugal under the House of Avis had achieved dazzling successes,
but by the middle of the sixteenth century the gilt was flaking off
the ornate edifice to reveal the flimsiness beneath. The Indian adventure had taken its toll of a nation with a population of only a
million; Indian riches had helped to enervate the Portuguese governing class; and the country was ruled with increasing incompetence
by a perennially bankrupt régime. But, beyond this, the economic
basis of the Portuguese empire suffered from certain structural weaknesses which became more apparent as the century advanced.
Essentially the Portuguese empire of the sixteenth century was an
Asian empire, with Brazil as little more than a stepping-stone to a
wealthy East. But in a world where Europe's trade balance with the
Far East was permanently unfavourable, the Portuguese needed
silver to purchase Asian spices. Unfortunately their empire, unlike
that of their Spanish neighbours, contained no silver-mines. Increasingly, therefore, Portugal was forced to turn to Spain for the
silver that the Spanish colonial empire alone could supply, and well

before 1580 the prosperity of Lisbon had come to depend very closely on that of Seville.

At a time when the country's economic future was already uncertain, its political future was hopelessly compromised by the disaster of Alcázarquivir. The King was dead and the dynasty threatened with imminent extinction; the nobility, which had followed Sebastian to the war, was either dead or held up to ransom for enormous sums which drained the country of its remaining stocks of silver; and the destruction of the army left the nation undefended. Cardinal Henry, aged and irresolute, was not the man to save his country in its hour of crisis. This was the moment for which Philip II had been waiting – a moment when he might at last hope to realize the old Trastámara ambition of unifying the entire peninsula beneath a single sceptre.

Philip's plans were laid with the utmost care. The immediate task must be to win over Cardinal Henry and the Portuguese ruling class to recognition of his rights. He chose for this purpose Cristóbal de Moura – a Portuguese who had come to the Court in the suite of John III of Portugal's widow, Philip's sister Juana, and had risen high in the favour of the king. With a liberal supply of Spanish silver at his disposal, Moura worked hard to undermine support for Philip's most dangerous rival, the Prior of Crato, and to dissipate aristocratic opposition to his master's succession.

A few months before his death on 31 January 1580 the Cardinal was at last induced to favour openly the candidacy of Philip, and agreement was reached between him and Moura on the conditions under which Philip should receive the crown. But valuable as was Cardinal Henry's uneasy approval, it was not of itself sufficient to ensure Philip's smooth accession to his throne. This had become clear when the representatives of the towns made known their support for the Prior of Crato in the Cortes summoned on 9 January. The Portuguese populace was, by tradition, bitterly anti-Castilian, as also was the lower clergy. The result was that, although a majority favoured Philip's claims in the regency council which assumed the government on Cardinal Henry's death, the council dared not openly proclaim the Spanish succession.

As soon as he heard the news of Henry's death, Granvelle realized that it was essential to act with speed, since there was a danger that

Table 5 THE PORTUGUESE SUCCESSION

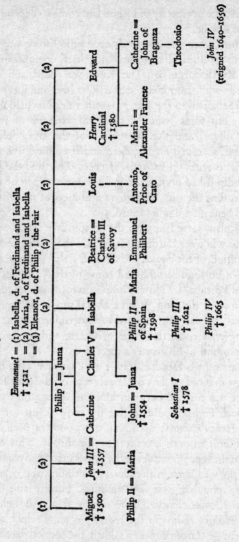

Emmanuel = (1) Isabella, d. of Ferdinand and Isabella
† 1521 = (2) Maria, d. of Ferdinand and Isabella
        = (3) Eleanor, d. of Philip I the Fair

the Pope might offer to mediate and the Prior of Crato secure assistance from England or France. Certain military preparations had already been made, and on Granvelle's insistence the Duke of Alba was summoned from his estates at Uceda to take command of the army for the invasion of Portugal. On the expiry of Philip's ultimatum to the Portuguese, the army was ordered to concentrate on the frontier near Badajoz, and it crossed into Portugal at the end of June. The supporters of Don Antonio put up some resistance, but Lisbon surrendered at the end of August, Don Antonio fled, and the Iberian peninsula was at last united beneath a single king.

While the union with Castile was accepted with a very bad grace by the Portuguese populace, the aristocracy and the upper clergy generally supported the claims of Philip II. So also did the Portuguese Jesuits – somewhat unexpectedly in view of the fact that Philip had always kept their Spanish brethren at arm's length. In addition, Philip appears to have enjoyed the support of the business and mercantile class in the Portuguese towns, anxious for the American silver that only union with Castile could bring. For economic reasons Portugal at this moment needed the political connexion with Spain, and it is significant that the connexion continued as long as – but no longer than – it brought tangible benefits to the Portuguese economy.

Yet while the economic advantages of a closer association with Castile may have helped to reconcile many influential Portuguese to the union, these advantages would probably have counted for little if Philip had chosen to disregard Portugal's traditional laws and system of government. This indeed is what Granvelle hoped the King would do. In Granvelle's opinion, Portugal's government and finances required drastic reorganization, and this could never be effected as long as the administration remained in native hands.

Once again, therefore, Philip was confronted with a problem which ultimately related to the whole constitutional ordering of the Spanish Monarchy – the problem of how to treat a state which had come by inheritance to the Spanish Crown. This time there was no Eboli faction to press upon the King the virtues of a 'liberal' solution; but in spite of this, Philip rejected Granvelle's ideas and settled the government of Portugal in a manner that would have earned him the wholehearted approval of the Prince of Eboli. Having duly assembled the Portuguese Cortes at Thomar in April 1581, he took the oath to observe all the laws and customs of the realm, and was recognized in turn as the lawful King of Portugal. The Cortes also asked him to ratify the twenty-five articles agreed between Moura and Cardinal Henry shortly before the Cardinal's death. These articles consisted of a wide range of concessions, which in effect preserved Portugal as a virtually autonomous state. The King was to spend as much time as possible in Portugal, and if forced to absent himself, he would confer the vice-royalty on a member of the royal family or on a native; a Council of Portugal conducting all its business in Portuguese was to be set up in attendance on the King's person; posts, both in Portugal itself and in its colonies, were to be given only to Portuguese nationals, and Portuguese were to be appointed to the royal households; while customs barriers between Castile and Portugal were to be abolished, Portugal was to keep its own coinage; and trade with its overseas territories was to remain exclusively in Portuguese hands.

These articles were accepted by Philip II and were to serve as the basis of the Portuguese governmental system during the country's sixty years of union with Castile. The fact that Philip was prepared both to accept them and (apart from the restoration of the customs barriers in 1593) to abide by them, is highly significant, for it shows that, in spite of the disappearance of the Eboli party, the King had not given way to the 'Castilian' solution to the problems of the Monarchy. Possibly because he had been shaken by events in the Netherlands, but more probably because of his inherited conception and innate sense of the proper relationship between himself and his peoples, he accepted the union of the Portuguese Crown to his own on terms that were essentially 'Aragonese' in spirit. Portugal was united to Castile in 1580 in exactly the same way as the Crown of Aragon had been united to Castile a hundred years before, preserving its own laws, institutions, and monetary system, and united only in sharing a common sovereign.

But this extension of the traditional method of union to yet another territory raised problems similar to those which had already been encountered in other parts of the Monarchy. If the King of each was also the King of all, how could his obligations to one individual kingdom be squared with his obligations to all the rest? The failure to solve this problem had played its part in the outbreak of the Netherlands revolt. There was no reason to believe that the Portuguese would find it any easier than the Dutch to reconcile themselves to the rule of an absentee and semi-alien King.

For a moment it seemed that this adjustment might not perhaps be required of them. During 1581 and 1582 Philip remained in Lisbon, leaving Granvelle to run the administration in Madrid. In many ways this was not a satisfactory division of power, for the separation of King and Minister merely widened the rift that was rapidly growing between them. Philip, as was natural, wanted to consolidate his position in Portugal. Granvelle, on the other hand, was anxious to press ahead with schemes for the recovery of the Low Countries. These, he believed, necessitated an immediate break with France and England, and a switch to a militantly imperial policy. The unpopularity of Granvelle's government among the Castilians, together with the policy disagreements between the King and his Minister, made it clear that Philip could not remain indefinitely in Portugal. Finally, in March 1583, to the chagrin of the Portuguese, he left Lisbon for Madrid, having appointed his nephew, the Archduke Albert, as Governor of the country.

To his great distress, Granvelle found that the King's return to Madrid failed to remove the differences between them. It had confidently been expected that the death of Granvelle's enemy, the Duke of Alba, in December 1582 would heal the breach between the Cardinal and the King, but between March and August 1583 Philip summoned Granvelle only twice to a private audience. The unfortunate Minister was beginning to discover for himself the truth of an assertion once made by his rival, Alba, that 'kings treat men like oranges. They go for the juice, and once they have sucked them dry, they throw them aside'.[7] Philip was now turning less and less to the Cardinal for advice. In 1583 he created a special new Junta to assist him in the task of government, which came to be known as the *Junta de Noche*. The Junta included Cristóbal de Moura (now the King's closest favourite), the Counts of Chinchón and Barajas, Mateo Vázquez, and Granvelle's colleague Juan de Idiáquez. The name of Granvelle was conspicuous by its absence.

7. Quoted from Antonio Pérez by Leopold Ranke, *The Ottoman and the Spanish Empires* (London, 1843), p. 41 n.

'I do not know what is going to happen,' wrote the disgruntled Cardinal to Idiáquez, 'but I have no wish to take part in the final ruin, towards which they are moving with their eyes closed. All business is left in the air; the administration is dominated by corrupt and dishonest officials who are not to be trusted, and the same is happening in judicial and financial affairs and in the running of the army and the fleet.'[8] Deeply disillusioned, he died on 21 September 1586, frustrated to the last in his desire to serve a Monarchy which to him was still the Monarchy of his revered master, the Emperor Charles V.

No doubt Granvelle had been a difficult and cantankerous character, too intransigent and authoritarian to preserve the favour of Philip II. No doubt, also, his mental outlook belonged to an imperial epoch remote from the very different epoch of the 1580s. Yet he possessed a breadth of vision and a capacity for general strategy which were badly needed at this juncture in the affairs of Philip II. Granvelle appreciated, for instance, that if the annexation of Portugal had created new difficulties for Spain, it also brought it unparalleled opportunities. It had given Spain a great accession of naval strength, making the combined Spanish and Portuguese merchant fleets the largest in the world: 250,000–300,000 tons, against the 232,000 tons of the Netherlands and the 42,000 of England. It had also given Spain a long Atlantic seaboard at a moment when the Atlantic was becoming the major battlefield between the Spanish Monarchy and the powers of northern Europe. Having providentially secured these wonderful advantages, it would be folly for Philip II to waste them.

Yet wasted they were. In 1585 Granvelle urged Philip to transfer his Government to Lisbon. Here, in Granvelle's view, was the perfect observation post for surveying the new Atlantic battlefield. From Lisbon, with its easy maritime communications to the nerve-centres of the world, Philip could have maintained effective control over the vast struggle now unfolding in western Europe and on the waters of the Atlantic. From here he could have directed the operations against England and the intervention in France. But the King elected instead to remain in the heart of Castile, far removed from the area of conflict; and by the middle of the 1590s it was already

8. M. Van Durme, *El Cardenal Granvela*, p. 366.

clear that Spain had lost the battle of the Atlantic. The 'final ruin' prophesied by Granvelle was approaching – a ruin precipitated by the victories of the Protestant powers of the north. The ruin might conceivably have been averted if the strategic opportunities that had come to Spain through the acquisition of Portugal had been more effectively exploited; but the opportunities were ignored, and it was not long before Portugal, with all that it had to offer, became little more than another burdensome addition to the increasingly unmanageable inheritance of the Spanish Habsburgs.

4. THE REVOLT OF ARAGON (1591–2)

When he recommended the removal of the Government from Madrid to Lisbon, Cardinal Granvelle may not have been exclusively influenced by strategic considerations. His experiences in Madrid had merely confirmed a long-standing uneasiness about the role of the Castilians in the management of the Monarchy. 'I recall having written to His Majesty more than once from Italy,' he wrote to Margaret of Parma in 1581, 'that the Castilians want everything, and I suspect they will end by losing everything.'[9] Unworthy heirs of the great imperial tradition, the Castilians, by their clumsiness and arrogance, were all too capable of shattering the fragile vessel which the Emperor had entrusted to his special care. Might not this danger perhaps be averted if the capital of the Monarchy were transferred from Castile to Portugal before it was too late?

Granvelle's distrust of the Castilians was widely shared throughout the Monarchy, although usually for other, less sophisticated, reasons. It was shared, for instance, by the upper classes of Aragon; and the Aragon of the 1580s and early 1590s was indeed to exemplify the fundamental problem of the Spanish Monarchy – the problem of the relationship between an increasingly Castilianized absentee monarch and subjects who clung to their traditional liberties with all the fervour of those who feared they were shortly to lose them.

By the 1580s, the kingdom of Aragon had become one of the most ungovernable of Philip II's possessions. Acutely suspicious of Castilian intentions, its governing class had barricaded itself behind the king-

9. M. Philippson, *Ein Ministerium unter Philipp II. Kardinal Granvelle am Spanischen Hofe* (Berlin, 1895), p. 231, n. 2.

dom's many *fueros*, which seemed to offer the best guarantee of immunity from royal and Castilian interference. Yet the very condition of Aragon in the later sixteenth century demanded royal intervention if a conflagration were to be avoided, for social tensions in the kingdom were becoming acute. Aragon, unlike Catalonia, had escaped civil war during the fifteenth century; but equally it had escaped a satisfactory agrarian settlement on the model of the *Sentencia de Guadalupe*. During the course of the sixteenth century the relations between lords and their vassals appear to have deteriorated. Some of the friction was caused by the presence of a Morisco population some 50,000 to 60,000 strong, a considerable proportion of which was employed on the estates of lay and ecclesiastical landowners. At a time of general population increase, the Old Christian population resented the favoured position enjoyed by the Moriscos both in the labour market and in the cultivation of the most fertile land, and there was a running war between the Moriscos who worked the rich lands along the banks of the Ebro and the Montañeses or Old Christians who came down with their flocks each winter from the Pyrenees. Seigneurial protection of Morisco labourers was thus an added irritant to a rural population which felt itself grievously burdened by feudal rights and exactions. Aragonese nobles were free to treat their vassals as they liked without fear of royal interference, and the Cortes of Monzón of 1585 actually increased their already very considerable powers by making any vassal who took up arms against his lord automatically liable to sentence of death.

While vassals could band together in self-defence against their lords, their only hope of permanent relief appeared to lie in recourse to the King. Consequently, they made great efforts during the course of the century to incorporate themselves into the royal domain. Some of these efforts met with success. At Monzón in 1585, for instance, Philip put an end to a ninety-five-year feud by agreeing to incorporate the vassals of the Barony of Monclús, and compensated the Baron with an annual pension of 800 *escudos* in perpetuity. But the really serious problem was presented by the county of Ribagorza, the largest barony in Aragon, which included seventeen towns and 216 villages, and extended from Monzón to the Pyrenees. From the strategic point of view its incorporation into the royal domain was extremely desirable; and the owner of the barony, the Duke of Villahermosa, was so exasperated by the rebelliousness of his vassals, that nothing would have pleased him better than a deal with the Crown. But unfortunately the incorporation of Ribagorza into the royal domain was endlessly delayed. The King was unwilling to pay a large sum by way of compensation, and a settlement was deliberately postponed by the machinations of the Treasurer-General of the Council of Aragon, the Count of Chinchón.

Chinchón's behaviour was motivated by a family feud which had arisen in the most extraordinary and terrible circumstances. In 1571 the Count of Ribagorza, the 27-year-old son of the Duke of Villahermosa, had formally sentenced his own wife to death on a charge of adultery, and the sentence was duly carried out. The victim of this judicial murder happened to be Chinchón's niece. The Count of Ribagorza, who fled to Italy, was caught and executed on the King's orders in the public square of Torrejón de Velasco, near Madrid, in 1573; but Chinchón was henceforth an implacable enemy of the house of Villahermosa. He pursued his vendetta both at Court and on Villahermosa's estates, where the Duke and his vassals were engaged in a regular war – the vassals, who enjoyed the assistance of a company of Catalan bandits, being covertly encouraged by Chinchón, while the Duke sought French help from Béarn.

A situation in which the King's principal minister for Aragonese affairs was personally involved in a feud on so large a scale with the most powerful noble in Aragon, was clearly fraught with the most explosive possibilities. But when the King at last decided to take remedial action, he only precipitated the disaster he had hoped to avoid. It seemed to him that the only way to bring Aragon under control was to fly in the face of tradition and appoint an 'impartial' viceroy who was not Aragonese by origin; and with his customary concern for legal niceties, he sent to Aragon in 1588 the Marquis of Almenara (who happened in fact to be a cousin of Chinchón) to secure a judgment on the legality of this procedure from the court of the Justicia of Aragon – the high official whose task it was to protect the kingdom's liberties. While the Justicia's judgment was favourable, the Aragonese ruling class as a whole was deeply perturbed at what appeared to be yet one more Castilian attempt to whittle away the Aragonese *fueros*. Anti-Castilian feeling among nobles, clergy, and the inhabitants of Zaragoza, was thus already reaching fever-pitch when the news arrived in the spring of 1590 that Almenara would be returning to Aragon with increased powers, which suggested that the viceroyalty would shortly be conferred upon him.

It was at precisely this moment, a few days before the arrival of Almenara, that a more unexpected figure suddenly turned up in Aragon – the King's ex-secretary, Antonio Pérez. For the last eleven years, Pérez had been kept in strict confinement under increasingly rigorous conditions. Finally, in February 1590, he was subjected to torture in an effort to make him produce vital information about the murder of Escobedo. Pérez still had his friends, and on the night of 19 April 1590 he managed to break out of his jail in Madrid, and, riding hard through the night, to reach safety across the border in Aragon. Here he availed himself of the traditional Aragonese privilege of *manifestación*, by which a man threatened by royal officials had the right to protection by the Justicia of Aragon, who would keep him in his own prison of the *manifestados* until sentence was pronounced.

The flight of Antonio Pérez came as a terrible blow to Philip. That Pérez, the repository of so many state secrets, should again be at liberty, was itself serious enough. But it was even worse that he should have fled to a kingdom in which the King's powers were so restricted, and most of all at a moment when discontent and unrest were rife. Pérez, whose family was Aragonese by origin, was perfectly informed of all the possibilities open to him under Aragonese law, and was well acquainted with the most influential figures of Zaragoza. When Philip (concerned, as always, to abide by the legal conventions) pressed his suit against his former secretary in the court of the Justicia, Pérez was able to publicize the King's complicity in Escobedo's murder with the evidence of documents he had secreted about his person. Realizing that he was hurting himself far more than he was hurting Pérez, the King halted the case and turned in desperation to his last hope – the tribunal of the Inquisition. This was the one tribunal in Aragon where the *fueros* lacked the force of law, and if Pérez once fell into the hands of the Inquisitors he was lost. But he managed to warn friends of his imminent transfer. On 24 May 1591, as he was being furtively moved to the prison of the Inquisition, the Zaragoza mob turned out with cries of 'Liberty' and 'Contra fuero', rescued Pérez from the hands of his jailers, stormed the palace of the Marquis of Almenara, and beat up the unfortunate Marquis so severely that he died a fortnight later.

The news of the Zaragoza riot brought Philip face to face with the problem he had long attempted to evade – whether to send an army into Aragon. The dilemma that confronted him was a serious one. Quite apart from his heavy commitments against the English and the Dutch, he was faced at this time with many domestic troubles. Not only was Aragon seething with rebellion, but the spirit of sedition was being fanned in Portugal by the irrepressible Prior of Crato; and even in Castile pasquinades were circulating about the tyranny of the King. At such a time there were obvious risks attached to sending an army into Aragon, especially since there was always the danger that the Catalans and Valencians might come to the help of the Aragonese.

The special Junta set up in Madrid to advise the King on the Aragonese question was sharply divided: the three members of the Council of Aragon who sat on the Junta all favoured leniency, as did the Prior of San Juan (Alba's natural son), while the rest of the Junta advocated repression. In spite of the disappearance of the Alba and Eboli factions, therefore, there was still a cleavage among the King's councillors on a problem relating to provincial liberties – a problem which bore an unpleasant resemblance to that of the Netherlands. This time, however, Philip had the disastrous failure of Alba's attempts at repression in the Low Countries to guide his decision. While arranging for troops to concentrate near the Aragonese frontier, he hoped to avoid the necessity of ordering them to cross it, and announced that his intention was only to 'preserve their *fueros* and not allow them to be abused by those who, under the guise of protecting them, are in reality the worst offenders against them'.

In practice, however, it proved impossible to avoid the use of force. Pérez had used all his arts to incite the Zaragoza populace, warning it that Philip planned to send an army to strip Aragon of its liberties. When a further attempt was made on 24 September 1591 to move him to the prison of the Inquisition, the crowd again came to his rescue, and this time Pérez broke free and fled from Zaragoza, intending to make for France. But he then changed his mind and returned in disguise to Zaragoza, planning now to lead a revolution which perhaps was intended to turn Aragon into a Venetian-style republic under French protection.

The events of 24 September finally convinced Philip that force would be necessary, and an army of some 12,000 men under the command of Alonso de Vargas crossed into Aragon at the beginning of October. In spite of the proclamation issued by the young Justicia, Juan de Lanuza, urging the country to rally to the defence of its liberties, the majority of the Aragonese showed no inclination to resist a royal army which many of the peasants may well have looked upon as an army of liberation from aristocratic oppression; nor did the Catalans show any inclination to come to the help of their brethren. Seeing that everything was lost, Pérez fled to France on the night of 11 November, and the following day the Castilian army made its entry into Zaragoza. Lanuza and his adherents, who had fled to Épila, were lured back to the capital; and in accordance with a secret order, which arrived on 18 December, Lanuza was seized and beheaded. A month later the King issued a general pardon. The pardon, however, excluded the Duke of Villahermosa and the Count of Aranda. Both these nobles were carried off to Castile where they died mysteriously in prison.

The revolt of Aragon was over, and Spanish unity preserved. The revolt had shown at once the weakness and the strength of the King of Spain. His weakness was revealed in the lack of any effective royal control over a kingdom enjoying as many liberties as Aragon; his strength in the social divisions within the country, which turned the revolt into little more than a movement by the city of Zaragoza and the Aragonese aristocracy to preserve laws and liberties which were too easily exploited by the few to the prejudice of the many. But there survived throughout the Crown of Aragon a sense of liberty which it would at this moment have been impolitic to flout. Moreover, as Philip has already shown in Portugal, he was deeply sensible of inherited obligation and of the bonds of legality. The revolt could easily have served as a pretext for acting as Alba had proposed thirty years before, and destroying the *fueros* of Aragon. But Philip chose instead to respect the laws. The Cortes of Aragon were summoned to meet at Tarazona in June 1592, so that any changes in the *fueros* would be legally procured. But such changes as were introduced were, in fact, remarkably moderate. The traditional requirement of unanimity in the votes of the four Estates of the Aragonese Cortes was altered to the requirement of a mere majority vote, although unanimity would still be needed for the voting of new taxes; the King was given the right to appoint non-Aragonese viceroys, at least until the next session of the Cortes; certain reforms were introduced into the management of the Aragonese *Diputación*; and, while the post of Justicia was allowed to survive, the official who held it was henceforth removable by the King.

It would hardly seem that the constitutional changes pushed through the Cortes of Tarazona under the shadow of the royal army were very far-reaching. In spite of the opportunity that had arisen for bringing the laws of Aragon into conformity with those of Castile, Philip decided instead to preserve the semi-autonomous political system of Aragon virtually unchanged. Both his handling of the annexation of Portugal and his response to the revolt of Aragon showed, therefore, that he remained dutifully loyal to his own sense of obligation and to his father's concept of a Monarchy of individual states each bound to their sovereign by their traditional legal ties, and continuing to lead independent lives according to their own historical systems of government. So far as Aragon was concerned, Philip's decision was to justify itself: the Aragonese never revolted again under the government of the House of Austria. But the fact remains that, under Philip II, the grievances of the non-Castilian States of the Monarchy were allowed to fester, and the fundamental constitutional problem of the Monarchy's organization was left unsolved. Portuguese and Aragonese continued to complain of neglect by a King who rarely visited them, who failed to grant offices and *mercedes* to their aristocracies, and who was so surrounded by Castilians that they could not but think of him as a Castilian King. With one of those compromises – so frequent with Philip II – which tended to make the worst of every world, the Aragonese federalist structure of the Monarchy was preserved, as the Prince of Eboli would have wished, but nothing was done to promote that spirit of mutual interchange which alone could make a federal system work. Instead, the Monarchy remained a Castilian-dominated Monarchy with an Aragonese political organization. Such a solution satisfied nobody. The Castilians resented having to bear the responsibility – and especially the fiscal responsibility – of empire without being able to enforce their will on provinces which sheltered behind 'archaic' laws and privileges; the non-Castilian provinces resented the Castilian monopoly of offices in the Monarchy and the Castilian domination of a King who had ceased to be their own. As a result, the unity which Hernando de Acuña had prophesied for the dominions of the King of Spain continued to elude them. Superficially there was, in the reign of Philip II, 'one monarch, one empire, and one sword'. But by the end of the reign it was apparent that one monarch remained too few; that the one empire was a divided empire; and that the sword was fatally blunted.

8

Splendour and Misery

I. THE CRISIS OF THE 1590S

DURING the 1590s there were numerous signs that the Castilian economy was beginning to crack under the relentless strain of Philip II's imperial adventures. The apparently inexhaustible stream of silver from the Indies had tempted the King to embark on vast enterprises which swallowed up his revenues and added to his mountain of debts: the Invincible Armada alone is said to have cost him 10,000,000 ducats, and in the mid-1590s he was probably spending over 12,000,000 ducats a year. How long he could continue to spend on this scale would ultimately be determined by the revenue-yielding capacity of his dominions both at home and overseas, and there is good reason to believe that by the 1590s this capacity was reaching its limits.

Less than a quarter of the King's annual revenues came from remittances of American silver; the rest was borrowed, or was paid for by taxes raised primarily by Castile. By 1590 it had become clear that, in spite of the large increase of 1575 in the figure for the *encabezamiento*, Castile's traditional sources of revenue were inadequate for the Crown's needs. Neither the *alcabala* nor the ordinary and extraordinary *servicios* were any longer sufficient, and it was found necessary to supplement them from 1590 by a new tax which was to bulk large in the fiscal history of seventeenth-century Castile. This new tax, which was voted by the Cortes, was in effect the excise which Charles V had vainly attempted to introduce in 1538. Called the *millones*, because it was reckoned in millions of ducats rather than in the traditional *maravedís*, it was first fixed at 8,000,000 ducats spread over a period of six years, the method of raising the money being left to the towns. On its prolongation in 1596, however, it was increased by a further 1,300,000 ducats a year to be collected in *sisas* on essential foodstuffs; and in 1600 the original and the supplementary levies were lumped together into a subsidy of 18,000,000 ducats payable over six years. This consolidated tax was levied on essential articles of consumption – notably meat, wine, oil, and vinegar – and its grant was made conditional by the Cortes on its being applied to certain specific purposes: the payment of the royal guard and royal officials, and the upkeep of frontier garrisons and the royal households, with any surplus being devoted to the reduction of royal debts by the redemption of *juros*.

In theory, the *millones* was a much more equitable tax than the *servicios*, from which anyone boasting a privilege of nobility was exempted; but in practice it was a good deal less egalitarian than it appeared, since landowners could supply themselves with most of the dutiable articles from their own estates. Once again, therefore, it was the poor who suffered. Inevitably a tax of this nature pushed up the cost of living in Castile. A tax-reformer in the 1620s calculated that, in a poor man's expenditure of 30 *maravedís* a day, 4 *maravedís* went in the *alcabala* and the *millones* alone, but the accuracy of the calculation was contested by his opponents, and at present it remains impossible to assess statistically the impact of taxation on individual Castilians or on the Castilian economy as a whole. What cannot be doubted, however, is the heaviness of Castile's fiscal contributions to the Crown in relation to those of other parts of the Monarchy. The Crown's principal sources of revenue in the late sixteenth century (excluding taxes raised in such territories as Naples and Milan, all of which were by now spent locally) were constituted as follows:

(1) Taxes paid by Castile

	Ducats p.a.
Alcabala	2,800,000
Millones	3,000,000
Servicios voted by Cortes	400,000
	6,200,000

(2) Dues collected in the Spanish Monarchy by papal concession

Cruzada	912,000
Subsidio	420,000
Excusado	271,000
	1,603,000

(3) American silver   2,000,000

Could Castile continue to bear a burden of this nature without being overtaken by economic disaster? Could America continue to supply this quantity of silver? And, in any event, were even these large sums from the New World and the Old sufficient to pay for Philip II's imperial adventures? These were the questions that pressed themselves with increasing urgency on the Spanish Crown and its bankers during the 1590s.

The last question was the first to be answered – and answered in the most brutal manner. On 29 November 1596 Philip followed his procedure of 1575 and suspended all payments to the bankers. The Crown had gone bankrupt again. On this, as on previous occasions a compromise was finally reached with the bankers: by the so-called *medio general* of 1597, it was agreed that outstanding debts would be repaid in the form of *juros*, which meant in effect the transformation of a floating into a consolidated debt. But, as in all operations of this sort, there were inevitable casualties, and the most important victims of the bankruptcy proved to be the fairs of Medina del Campo. The fairs, which had recovered from the royal bankruptcy of 1575, and had functioned with considerable regularity since reforms in 1578 and 1583, were now once more interrupted; and when they started operations again in 1598 it soon became clear that their great days were past. The financial capital of Spain was to shift definitively in the early seventeenth century from Medina to Madrid, and such payments as were made in Medina del Campo during the course of that century were no more than sad reminders of a departed age. The towns of north Castile were fading into history, their streets still walked by the ghosts of Simón Ruiz and his friends – figures from a time when Spain basked in the *largueza* that came from abundance of silver, and when Castile could still provide financiers of its own.

But the bankruptcy of 1596 meant more than the end of northern Castile's financial pre-eminence: it meant also the end of Philip II's imperial dreams. For some time it had been apparent that Spain was losing its battle against the forces of international Protestantism. The first, and most crushing, blow was the defeat of the Invincible Armada in 1588. The enterprise of England had come to mean everything both to Philip and to Spain since the Marquis of Santa Cruz first submitted to the King his proposals for the great design in 1583. To Philip it seemed that an invasion of England, which Santa

Cruz believed could be successfully undertaken for the cost of little more than 3,500,000 ducats, offered the best, and perhaps the only, hope of bringing the Dutch to their knees. While the King pored over his plans day after day in the Escorial, and the elaborate preparations moved slowly to their climax, the priests from their pulpits whipped up the nation to a frenzy of patriotic and religious fervour, as they denounced the iniquities of the heretical Queen of England and vividly evoked the glories of Spain's crusading past. 'I consider this enterprise the most important undertaken by God's Church for many hundreds of years', wrote the Jesuit Ribadeneyra, the author of a moving exhortation to the soldiers and captains engaged in the expedition. 'Every conceivable pretext for a just and holy war is to be found in this campaign. . . . This is a defensive, not an offensive, war: one in which we are defending our sacred religion and our most holy Roman Catholic faith [*fe católica romana*]; one in which we are defending the high reputation of our King and lord, and of our nation; defending, too, the land and property of all the kingdoms of Spain, and simultaneously our peace, tranquillity and repose.'[1]

Only a few months later Ribadeneyra was writing a mournful letter to 'a favourite of His Majesty' (probably Don Juan de Idiáquez), attempting to explain the apparently inexplicable: why God had turned a deaf ear to the prayers and supplications of His pious servants. While Ribadeneyra found sufficient explanation in Spain's sins of omission and commission, and full consolation in the very trials sent by the Almighty to test His chosen people, the psychological consequences of the disaster were shattering for Castile. For a moment the shock was too great to absorb, and it took time for the nation to realize its full implications. But the unthinking optimism generated by the fantastic achievements of the preceding hundred years seems to have vanished almost overnight. If any one year marks the division between the triumphant Spain of the first two Habsburgs and the defeatist, disillusioned Spain of their successors, that year is 1588.

The material effects of the defeat of the Armada were, however, much less striking. Out of an original total of 130 ships, as many as two-thirds managed to limp home. Moreover, the Spanish fleet not

1. Pedro de Ribadeneyra, S. I., *Historias de la Contrarreforma* (Biblioteca de Autores Cristianos, Madrid, 1945), pp. 1331 and 1333.

only made up its losses with remarkable speed, but actually became a more formidable fighting force than it had been before. In a letter addressed to Sir Francis Walsingham just after the news of the defeat of the Armada had arrived, the Huguenot commander François de La Noue wrote that Philip II's power was founded on his possession of the Indies, and this in turn depended on his control of the sea. 'Spain wanted to take Flanders by way of England, but you will be able to take Spain by way of the Indies. It is there that it must be undermined . . .'[2] But it soon became clear that this was not easily achieved. Hawkins, Drake, and the Earl of Cumberland made daring attacks on Spain's overseas possessions and on its transatlantic shipping; a costly expedition was sent to Lisbon in 1589; but the Spanish coasts could not be effectively blockaded, and year after year the silver fleets – too well defended for a successful frontal attack – came safely home to port. Not only this, but Philip himself was soon strong enough to resume the offensive, and, goaded by the attack of Essex on Cadiz in 1596, sent another Armada against England in the following year, only to see it dispersed by the storms.

Yet, if the contest on the high seas remained undecided, the defeat of the Armada had in other ways tilted the balance of power against Spain. La Noue had said in his letter to Walsingham: 'In saving yourselves you will save the rest of us.' His prophecy proved correct. Spain's great crusade against the Protestant powers of the north had ended in failure. The news of the defeat of the Armada gave Henry III of France the courage to shake off his humiliating dependence on the Roman Catholic fanatics of the Ligue, and to organize the assassination of the powerful Duke of Guise. This event, and the succession to the French throne of the Protestant Henry of Navarre after Henry III's own assassination seven months later, compelled Alexander Farnese to turn his attention from the Netherlands to France. When he died in December 1592 he left the Dutch still unconquered, and his two French campaigns of 1590 and 1591 had brought Spain no compensating success.

The conversion of Henry of Navarre to Rome in 1593 effectively destroyed any prospect of a successful Spanish candidacy to the throne of France. It was true that France itself had not gone Protestant,

2. Letter of 17 August 1588 reproduced in the appendix to Henri Hauser, *François de la Noue, 1531–1591* (Paris, 1892), pp. 315–19.

but otherwise Philip's northern policy had failed. The bankruptcy of 1596 set the seal on this failure, and made a return to peace imperative. Painfully aware that his days were numbered and that his inexperienced son would succeed to an empty treasury, Philip set about reducing Spain's enormous commitments. The first step towards the liquidation of the costly imperialism of the 1580s and early 1590s was the dispatch of the Archduke Albert to the Netherlands. His arrival in 1596 marked the beginning of a new policy towards the Low Countries, which were formally handed over in May 1598 to Albert and to the Infanta Isabella Clara Eugenia, who became his wife. It was true that Albert and Isabella, although nominally sovereign princes, were still closely tied to Spain, and that the Low Countries would revert to Spain after their death, if their marriage proved to be childless. But at least the ties between Spain and the Netherlands had been loosened, and it would consequently be easier for Spain to call a halt to the war in Flanders without excessive loss of prestige.

The old King could not bring himself to make peace with England: this would come only in 1604. But on 2 May 1598 he concluded with Henry IV the treaty of Vervins, which brought the Franco-Spanish war to an end. At the time when he signed the treaty, Philip was reported to be so 'withered and feeble' that it was thought impossible for him to live much longer; and he died on 13 September 1598, after months of excruciating illness which he bore with his accustomed fortitude.

Philip's death, after forty years as King of Spain, changed everything and yet changed nothing. As the policies of his last years had shown, even the will of the King of Spain had to bend before the harsh realities of an empty treasury and an exhausted nation. His successors, however, had still to learn this lesson for themselves. The new régime of Philip III ordered a fresh military effort to be made in Flanders at the start of the new century and sent a half-hearted expedition to Ireland in 1601, but war could not be fought without resources, and the resources were draining away. In 1607 – a mere ten years after the decree of suspension of payments of 1596 – the Spanish Crown was forced to repudiate its debts once again, and two years later Spain signed its twelve-year truce with the Dutch. The new rulers of Spain had belatedly discovered, as Philip II had himself discovered, that there were certain forces beyond their control, and that a withdrawal from the aggressive imperialism of the later sixteenth century had become both necessary and inevitable.

The circumstances which compelled Spain's phased withdrawal from its imperial adventures during the last decade of the sixteenth century and the first decade of the seventeenth were both global and national. The national, Castilian, crisis was the one which forcefully attracted contemporary attention. Behind this, however, was a less obvious crisis of still wider dimensions, which inevitably reacted upon the fortunes of Castile. This was a crisis brought about by a gradual but profound change in the character of the economic relationship between Spain and its overseas empire.

The imperialism of Philip II's reign had been based on a Spanish-Atlantic economy, in that it was financed out of the resources of America and of a Castile which itself received regular injections of silver from the silver-mines of the New World. During the last decade of the sixteenth century American silver was still reaching Spain in very large quantities, and the port of Seville had an undeniable air of prosperity; but the comforting appearances masked the beginning of a radical change in the structure of the entire Spanish-Atlantic system.

This change was, in part, a direct result of Spain's war with the Protestant powers of the north. In the first two decades after the outbreak of the Netherlands revolt, the Dutch had continued to trade with the Iberian peninsula. Spain was dependent on northern and eastern Europe for its supplies of grain, timber, and naval stores, a large proportion of which were transported in Dutch vessels. Irked by Spain's continuing dependence on the Dutch, and anxious to strike a blow at the Dutch economy, Philip II placed an embargo on Dutch ships in Spanish and Portuguese ports in 1585, and again in 1595. The Dutch appreciated as well as Philip II that any interference with their peninsular trade threatened them with disaster. They needed Spanish silver and colonial produce, just as they also needed the salt of Setúbal for their herring industry. Faced with embargoes on their peninsular trade, they therefore reacted in the only possible way, by going direct to the producing areas for the goods they needed – to the Caribbean and Spanish America. From 1594 they were making regular voyages to the Caribbean; in 1599 they seized the salt island of Araya. This intrusion of the Dutch into the Caribbean disrupted the pearl fisheries of Santa Margarita and dislocated the system of maritime communications between Spain's colonial possessions. For the first time, Spain found itself heavily on the defensive in the western hemisphere, its overseas monopoly threatened by increasingly audacious Dutch and English attacks.

The presence of northern interlopers in the American seas was a serious danger to the Spanish commercial system; but potentially even more serious was the simultaneous transformation in the character of the American economy. During the 1590s the boom conditions of the preceding decades came to an end. The principal reason for the change of economic climate is to be found in a demographic catastrophe. While the white and the mixed population of the New World had continued to grow, the Indian population of Mexico, scourged by terrible epidemics in 1545–6 and again in 1576–9, had shrunk from some 11,000,000 at the time of the conquest in 1519 to little more than 2,000,000 by the end of the century; and it is probable that a similar fate overtook the native population of Peru. The labour force on which the settlers depended was therefore dramatically reduced. In the absence of any significant technological advance, a contracting labour force meant a contracting economy. The great building projects were abruptly halted; it became increasingly difficult to find labour for the mines, especially as the negroes imported to replace the Indians proved to be vulnerable to the same diseases as those which had wiped out the native population; and the problem of feeding the cities could only be met by a drastic agrarian reorganization, which entailed the creation of vast *latifundios* where Indian labour could be more effectively exploited than in the dwindling Indian villages.

The century that followed the great Indian epidemic of 1576–9 has been called 'New Spain's century of depression' – a century of economic contraction, during the course of which the New World closed in on itself. During this century it had less to offer Europe: less silver, as it became increasingly expensive to work the mines, and fewer opportunities for the emigrants – the 800 or more men and women who were still arriving in the 1590s in each *flota* from Seville. At the same time, it also came to require less of Europe – or at least of Spain. European luxury products found themselves com-

peting with the products of the Far East carried to America in the
Manila galleon. But much more serious from the point of view of
Spain was the establishment in its American possessions of an economy
dangerously similar to its own. Mexico had developed a coarse cloth
industry, and Peru was now producing grain, wine, and oil. These
were exactly the products which had bulked so large in the cargoes
from Seville during the preceding decades. In fact, the staple Spanish
exports to America were ceasing to be indispensable to the settlers,
and in 1597 Spanish merchants found it impossible to dispose of all
their goods: the American market, the source of Andalusia's prosperity, was for the first time overstocked.

From the 1590s, therefore, the economies of Spain and of its
American possessions began to move apart, while Dutch and English
interlopers were squeezing themselves into a widening gap. It was
true that Seville still retained its official monopoly of New World
trade, and that Sevillan commerce with America reached an all-time
record in 1608, to be followed by a further twelve years in which
trade figures, while fluctuating, remained at a high level. But, as
an index to national prosperity, the figures are deprived of much of
their significance by the fact that the cargoes were increasingly of
foreign provenance. The goods which Spain produced were not
wanted by America; and the goods that America wanted were not
produced by Spain.

The changing demands of the American market presented the
Castilian economy with problems of readjustment which it was ill
equipped to tackle; for, during the preceding decades, there had been
a signal failure to reverse the economic trends apparent during the
later years of the reign of Charles V, and neither industry nor agriculture was in any state to meet the challenge of changing demand
and of increasing foreign competition. Indeed, Castile's economy was
showing every sign of stagnation, and even, in some areas, of actual
regression, as contemporaries themselves became increasingly aware
during the closing years of the century.

The first point to strike contemporary observers was the depopulation of Castile and the decay of agriculture. To some extent,
their observations were misleading. What passed for depopulation in
Castile during the second half of the sixteenth century may often have
been a redistribution of population as a result of internal migrations.

Of thirty-one towns in Castile, twenty, in fact, showed an increase of population between 1530 and 1594, and only eleven a decrease:

City	1530	1594
Valladolid	38,100	33,750
Córdoba	33,060	31,285
Medina del Campo	20,680	13,800
Alcázar de San Juan	19,995	10,285
Medina de Ríoseco	11,310	10,030
Santiago (1557)	5,380	4,720
Orense (1557)	5,290	3,500
Vigo (1557)	5,025	4,225
Túy (1557)	3,805	2,480
Corunna	3,005	2,255
Betanzos	2,850	2,750

It is noticeable that nine of these eleven towns with a declining population are in the northern half of Spain – the region likely to be most affected by the war with the Netherlands and by the spread of piracy in the Bay of Biscay. What contemporaries assumed to be a general depopulation may therefore have been a depopulation of the north – the most prosperous part of Castile in the earlier years of the century. The southwards migration of the inhabitants of this region could easily suggest a demographic disaster at a time when the population increase of the early sixteenth century may perhaps not yet have spent itself.

Apart from a shift of population from north to south, which was not necessarily inimical to economic advance, there was, however, another shift of population, the implications of which were very disturbing. This was the drift from the countryside to the towns. There are many indications that the position of the Castilian peasant and agricultural labourer was deteriorating in the second half of the sixteenth century. In the region of Valladolid, for example, there were increasing complaints after 1550 about peasant indebtedness and the dispossession of peasantry from their lands by creditors from the towns. It was all too easy for a small peasant to run into debt as the result of a succession of poor harvests. Even in good times his profits were limited by the *tasa del trigo*; and at all times he was liable to be subjected to the attentions of the tax collector, the billeting officer, and the recruiting sergeant.

The ordinary Castilian villager had few defences against these merciless agents of a higher power. There was, for instance, little protection to be had against the depredations committed by a licentious soldiery, and Calderón's *El Alcalde de Zalamea*, written around 1642, describes the kind of incident that was all too common in sixteenth- and seventeenth-century Spain. The soldiers despised the peasants in whose houses they were billeted, and treated them with mingled brutality and disdain. Military discipline, precarious at the best of times, seems to have declined sharply over the course of the years: captains tended to take the side of their soldiers in any incident that occurred between them and the civil population, and to see in the complaints of the civil authorities a threatened infraction of their jealously guarded *fuero militar*. As a result there were endless conflicts between civil and military jurisdiction, in which the municipal authorities were generally worsted, since military tribunals winked at the offences of their men, and the highest tribunal of all, the Council of War, could be relied upon to take the part of its captains and *maestres de campo*.

Calderón's rich peasant, Pedro Crespo, who took the law into his own hands and had the offending captain hanged, is at once the idealized symbol of a peasantry which had little effective legal protection against the provocations of the soldiery, and the expression of a spirit of resistance which, at least in Castile, was infrequent, partly because it had so little hope of success. Faced with a company of soldiers to be billeted in his village, and already crushed by the weight of royal taxes and seigneurial and ecclesiastical dues, the unfortunate peasant was liable to take the line of least resistance and to abandon his village, seeking shelter and safety with his family in the anonymous world of the town.

The exodus to the towns gradually transformed Castile into a land of deserted villages, with tragic consequences for the country's agrarian development. All over the Mediterranean region, the second half of the sixteenth century was a period in which local food production was proving increasingly inadequate for a still growing population. Castile, with its rural labour force dwindling, was no exception to this; and from about 1570 it began to be heavily dependent on grain supplies from northern and eastern Europe. After 1570, therefore, Castilian grain prices were rising; the fields were deserted; and the country was tied still more closely to a northern Europe from which it was already importing the manufactures that its own industries could no longer supply at competitive rates. While the Cortes of Castile constantly lamented the decay of agriculture, little was done to prevent it. The radical reforms that were really needed could be achieved only through a collective effort and a revaluation of national priorities so drastic as to appear inconceivable.

The physical and geographical obstacles to economic growth in Castile were admittedly exceptionally intractable. The soil was poor, the climate unfavourable, and internal communications hopelessly difficult. This meant that improvements – such as irrigation schemes or engineering projects – demanded a co-operative endeavour and the investment of considerable funds. The city of Toledo, for instance, with its thriving silk industry, had remained prosperous in spite of Philip II's transfer of the Court to Madrid in 1561; but continued economic expansion depended on its ability to improve its communications with the outside world. This could best be achieved by making the River Tagus navigable from Toledo to Lisbon – a difficult and expensive, but by no means impossible, enterprise. The work was begun with royal encouragement in the 1580s, and was completed, in accordance with the plans of an Italian engineer, in 1587. But the engineer died the following year; the engineering works proved insufficient on certain reaches of the river; and the navigation of the Tagus was eventually abandoned in the last years of the century.

The abandonment of the Tagus navigation scheme offers a striking local example of a national failure. It is true that the unexpected extent of natural obstacles in the river made the undertaking much more difficult than had originally been expected; but ultimately this was a human, rather than an engineering failure. The project was opposed by mill-owners along the river bank, and hampered by the imposition of tolls and dues on the traffic. But it seems that the decisive reason for the failure of the scheme was the constant opposition of the city of Seville, which saw in a navigable Tagus a serious threat to its own trade both with Toledo and with Lisbon. This was sadly typical of the reaction to any important project for the country's improvement. In Catalonia, for instance, plans for irrigating the plain of Urgel were sabotaged by merchants who were dependent for their livelihood on the continuation of grain imports from Sicily. Seville itself never built the bridge it so badly needed over the Guadalquivir, and it failed to tackle the increasingly serious problem of the silting up of the river, which was finally to destroy its commercial prosperity. The reasons were similar to those which had wrecked the Tagus navigation scheme: a reluctance to invest money in public works; personal and municipal rivalries; and, ultimately, a deadening inertia, which crippled both the capacity and the desire to act.

Although individual Spaniards showed both interest and proficiency in certain fields of scientific inquiry, and Galileo was invited to the Spain of Philip III, foreign travellers found the country as a whole backward, and uninterested in matters of scientific and technological concern. Already by the end of the sixteenth century many Spaniards seem to have been gripped by that sense of fatalism which would prompt the famous pronouncement of a Junta of theologians in the reign of Philip IV. Summoned to consider a project for the construction of a canal linking the Manzanares and the Tagus, it flatly declared that if God had intended the rivers to be navigable, He would have made them so. In the first instance, therefore, it seems to have been an attitude of mind, rather than any technical difficulty, which stood in the way of economic advance; and even if the attitude were not yet universal, real power in the country lay in such few hands, that one or two individuals could effectively prevent the implementation of schemes that could have been of benefit to many. This was particularly true in the realm of agrarian development. Much of the soil of Castile belonged either to magnates, who had accumulated large estates through the workings of the entail system, or to the Church, which had accumulated them through mortmain. Outside Andalusia, where the demands of the American market still offered some incentive to improve, these large landowners apparently showed no interest in irrigation projects, or in a more effective exploitation of the soil; and *bourgeois* landowners, who had acquired property from peasants, were either equally uninterested, or else lacked the resources to undertake improvements on their own. As a result, agriculture languished and the economy stagnated.

The return of peace towards the end of the century might perhaps have offered opportunities for economic recovery, on the assumption that the military budget could be cut. But given the will to reform – and this remained problematical – the prospects of success were drastically reduced by a sudden catastrophe. In the last years of the century, the harvest failed. The price of a *fanega* (1·6 bushels) of Andalusian corn rose from 430 *maravedís* in 1595 to 1,041 in 1598, and on the heels of dearth came plague. The epidemic made its first appearance in northern Spain in 1596, and moved steadily southwards, ravaging in its passage the densely crowded cities of Castile. The great plague of 1599–1600 wiped out at a single blow much of the population increase of the sixteenth century, and opened a new era in Castilian demographic history: an era of stagnation, and perhaps of demographic decline.

The economic consequences of the plague were to be seen in the labour crisis with which the new century opened, and can be traced in the 30 per cent increase in salaries in the three years that followed it. González de Cellorigo, an official in the chancellery of Valladolid who published in 1600, under the shadow of the plague, a brilliant treatise on the problems of the Spanish economy, accurately prophesied its effects: 'Henceforth we can only expect that everything requiring human industry and labour will be very expensive ... because of the shortage of people for tillage and for all the types of manufactures that the kingdom needs.' The acute labour shortage, and the consequent upswing of salaries, were, as González de Cellorigo appreciated, irreparable disasters for the Castilian economy, since they destroyed the possibility that the years of peace might be used to build up Castilian industry to a point at which it would again be able to compete with foreign industries in the home and overseas markets.

But the most serious long-term consequences of the plague may have been psychological rather than economic. Already, before it was struck by the plague, Castile was weary and depressed. The failures in France and the Netherlands, the sack of Cadiz by the English, and the King's request for a national *donativo* in 1596 as bankruptcy struck, completed the disillusionment that had begun with the defeat of the Invincible Armada. Then, to crown it all, came the plague. The unbroken succession of disasters threw Castile off balance. The ideals which had buoyed it up during the long years of struggle were shattered beyond repair. The country felt itself betrayed – betrayed perhaps by a God who had inexplicably withdrawn His favour from His chosen people. Desolate and plague-stricken, the Castile of 1600 was a country that had suddenly lost its sense of national purpose.

Castilians reacted to the moment of disillusionment in different ways. Optimism had gone, to be replaced by bitterness and cynicism, or else by the resignation of defeat. The new mood of fatalism and disillusionment naturally tended to reinforce certain latent tendencies that had already been encouraged by the unusual circumstances of the sixteenth century. During that century, events had conspired to disparage in the national estimation the more prosaic virtues of hard work and consistent effort. The mines of Potosí brought to the country untold wealth; if money was short today, it would be abundant again tomorrow when the treasure fleet reached Seville. Why plan, why save, why work? Around the corner would be the miracle – or perhaps the disaster. Prices might rise, savings be lost, the crops fail. There seemed little point in demeaning oneself with manual labour, when, as so often happened, the idle prospered and the toilers were left without reward. The events of the turn of the century could only increase this sense of insecurity and strengthen an already widespread fatalism. It was fatalism that characterized the outlook of the *pícaro*, and the seventeenth century was essentially the age of the *pícaro*, living on his wits – hungry today, well fed tomorrow, and never soiling his hands with honest work. 'Queremos comer sin trabajar': we want to eat without working.[3] The words could be applied to Castilians in many walks of life, from the townsman living comfortably on his annuities to the vagabond without a *blanca* in his purse.

It was in this atmosphere of *desengaño*, of national disillusionment, that Cervantes wrote his Don Quixote, of which the first part appeared in 1605 and the second in 1614. Here, among many other parables, was the parable of a nation which had set out on its crusade only to learn that it was tilting at windmills. In the end was the *desengaño*, for ultimately the reality would always break in on the illusion. The events of the 1590s had suddenly brought home to more thoughtful Castilians the harsh truth about their native land –

3. Lope de Deça, *Govierno Polytico de Agricultura* (Madrid, 1618), p. 23.

its poverty in the midst of riches, its power that had shown itself impotent. Brought face to face with the terrible paradoxes of the Castile of Philip III, a host of public-spirited figures – such men as González de Cellorigo and Sancho de Moncada – set themselves to analyse the ills of an ailing society. It is these men, known as *arbitristas* (projectors), who give the Castilian crisis of the turn of the century its special character. For this was not only a time of crisis, but a time also of the awareness of crisis – of a bitter realization that things had gone wrong. It was under the influence of the *arbitristas* that early seventeenth-century Castile surrendered itself to an orgy of national introspection, desperately attempting to discover at what point reality had been exchanged for illusion. But the *arbitristas* – as their name suggested – were by no means content merely to analyse. They must also find the answer. That an answer existed they had no doubt; for just as Sancho Panza had in him something of Don Quixote, so also even the most pessimistic *arbitrista* was still something of an optimist at heart. As a result, the Government of Philip III found itself bombarded with advice – with innumerable projects, both sensible and fantastic, for the restoration of Castile.

2. THE FAILURE OF LEADERSHIP

Absurd as were many of the *arbitrios* solemnly proposed to the ministers of Philip III, there were enough sane ideas among them to provide the basis of an intelligent programme of reform. The *arbitristas* proposed that Government expenditure should be slashed; that the tax-system in Castile should be overhauled, and the other kingdoms of the Monarchy be called upon to contribute more to the royal exchequer; that immigrants should be encouraged to re-populate Castile; that fields should be irrigated, rivers be made navigable, and agriculture and industry be protected and fostered. In itself there was nothing impossible about such a programme. The return of peace provided an admirable opportunity to embark upon it, and all that was needed was the will.

Much therefore depended on the character of the new régime. Philip III, twenty years old at the time of his accession, was a pallid, anonymous creature, whose only virtue appeared to reside in a total absence of vice. Philip II knew his son well enough to fear the worst:

'Alas, Don Cristóbal,' he said to Don Cristóbal de Moura, 'I am afraid they will govern him.' Philip's fears were to be fully realized. Well before his father's death, the future Philip III had fallen under the influence of a smooth Valencian aristocrat, Don Francisco de Sandoval y Rojas, Marquis of Denia. As soon as the old King died, Denia moved in to place his own friends and relations in the highest posts in the State. Don Cristóbal de Moura, the first minister during the last years of Philip II's régime, was moved out of harm's way to Lisbon as viceroy of Portugal; Rodrigo Vázquez de Arce was replaced as president of the Council of Castile by Denia's son-in-law, the Count of Miranda; and a convenient vacancy in 1599 enabled Denia to make his uncle Archbishop of Toledo.

It very quickly became clear that the régime of the Marquis of Denia was not likely to introduce the reforms that were so urgently required. Denia himself was an affable, easy-going man, whose prime concern was to enrich his family and to remain in power. He was singularly successful in both of these ambitions. A relatively poor man at the time he captured the King's favour, he soon became very rich indeed. Created Duke of Lerma in 1599, he accumulated offices and *mercedes* in rapid succession; the office of Comendador de Castilla, worth 16,000 ducats a year; a royal gift of 50,000 ducats in silver from the treasure fleet; another royal gift, this time diamonds to the tune of 5,000 ducats, to cheer him up when his health and spirits were low; and a profusion of baronies and lordships which helped to raise his annual income to 200,000 ducats by 1602, and enabled him in the same year to buy for 120,000 ducats the town of Valdemoro from the Marquis of Auñón.

Lerma had, in fact, succeeded in acquiring for himself a position in the State to which there had been no parallel since the time of Álvaro de Luna, the favourite of John II. More than a first minister, he was officially the *Privado* or *Valido* – the favourite of the King, and the first of a line of favourites which was to govern Spain during the course of the seventeenth century. It was difficult at first for Spaniards accustomed to the habits of Philip II to adapt themselves to a system in which the King merely reigned while the favourite ruled. In time, however, the *Privado* became an accepted feature of national life. Where the sixteenth century had produced innumerable 'mirrors' for princes, the seventeenth century devoted its attention to 'mirrors' for favourites, on the assumption that, since they could not be abolished, they might at least be improved. This rise of the favourite to an established position in government was partly the result of the personal characteristics of the descendants of Philip II – men who lacked both the ability and the diligence to govern by themselves. But it also reflected the growing complexity of government, which made it increasingly necessary to have an omni-competent minister, capable of extracting some decision from the mountain of *consultas* which piled up on the royal desk.

Already in the later years of Philip II attempts had been made to assist an ailing King in his administrative duties by the creation of the small *Junta de Noche* which acted as a clearing-house for the *consultas* of the various Councils. This Junta was abolished on the accession of Philip III, but Lerma soon had recourse to a similar device. No doubt this was partly because the death of the old King had led to an immediate weakening of royal power, and the magnates, so resolutely excluded from the Councils by Charles V and Philip II, were now pressing irresistibly for admission. Two *capa y espada* members were appointed to the Council of the Indies in 1604; and the Council of State, which came to consist of fifteen members, gradually fell into the hands of the grandees. The increasing aristocratic predominance in certain of the Councils made the recourse to a small Junta of his own confidants all the more desirable for the Duke of Lerma, if he were to retain power in his own hands. At the same time, certain aspects of government, like the state of the Crown's finances, required a detailed and expert study, such as they could not be given in full council, and this naturally led to the creation of special Juntas to deal with particular problems.

The trend in seventeenth-century Spanish government was therefore towards the creation of small committees of ministers, operating independently of the Councils. The régime of the Duke of Lerma saw only a tentative beginning in this direction, and the real establishment of government by Junta belonged to the 1620s and 1630s. But at last Lerma seems to have appreciated, as did his successor, the Conde Duque de Olivares, that the Councils were now so routine-ridden, and so consumed with concern for their own prestige and precedence, that they were becoming increasingly inadequate organs for the government of the Monarchy. The use of Juntas to by-pass the

Councils was an obvious way of escape from the dilemma, but their effectiveness would clearly depend on the calibre of the men appointed to sit in them. There were great opportunities to infuse fresh ideas into the government by selecting men from outside the usual *cursus honorum* that led to a seat at the council table. But whether the right men were chosen depended upon the Favourite.

Lerma's choice of confidants was uniformly disastrous. Easily deceived by plausible rogues, he elevated to positions of great importance the most unsavoury characters. In particular, his choice fell upon two adventurers who succeeded in insinuating themselves into his confidence – Don Pedro Franqueza and Don Rodrigo Calderón. Franqueza, the younger son of a Catalan gentry family, enjoyed a meteoric rise to power under Lerma's benign patronage. Entrusted with the task of reforming the royal finances, he managed to obtain the title of Count of Villalonga and an enormous fortune before his sins were found out. He fell from power in 1607 as dramatically as he had risen – arrested for malversation of funds, put on trial, and forced to disgorge some 1,500,000 ducats (about a fifth of the Crown's average annual expenditure). The career of his colleague, Calderón, was remarkably similar, although less abruptly terminated. Enjoying complete ascendancy over the Favourite, he succeeded in retaining his power as long as his master, and lost his position – and eventually his life – only with the coming of a new régime.

A Government which consisted of Lerma, Franqueza, and Calderón, hardly offered very hopeful prospects for that great campaign of reform and renovation for which *arbitristas* and country were clamouring, and it soon showed itself adept at shirking measures likely to antagonize the influential and the articulate. This was particularly obvious in its fiscal policies. One of the most important tasks facing the Government of Spain at this moment was to begin the delicate work of attempting to equalize the fiscal contributions of the different provinces of the Monarchy, in the hope of reducing the tax burden on Castile. It was true that Lerma managed to extract subsidies of 1,100,000 ducats from the Cortes of Catalonia in 1599, and of 400,000 ducats from those of Valencia in 1604, but so much of this sum was expended on bribes and *mercedes* in the two provinces that the Crown obtained virtually no benefit from the grants. The Government also attempted in 1601 to extend the payment of the *millones* to Vizcaya, but quickly abandoned the attempt in face of strong Vizcayan protests. The redistribution of the tax burden within the peninsula and the Monarchy was thus allowed to go by default at a moment when the improved international situation might have allowed a more resolute Government to embark on a more effective and equitable exploitation of its subjects' resources.

Having failed to spread more evenly the burden of taxation within the Monarchy, Lerma's Government also failed to redistribute the tax burden more equitably within Castile. Any fiscal measures which might help to reduce the gross inequalities between the exempt rich and the penalized poor was scrupulously avoided, and Lerma fell back instead on more comfortable expedients, such as the sale of offices and jurisdictions, the extraction of subsidies from the Portuguese Jews, and the manipulation of the Castilian coinage. A *vellón* coinage of pure copper was authorized in 1599, and was returned to the mints in 1603 to be stamped at double its face value. Although the Cortes of 1607 made their subsidy conditional on the suspension of *vellón* production, the temptation to make money out of money proved too strong for the perennially bankrupt Government, and minting was resumed in 1617, to be ended only in 1626 – by which time Castile was flooded with valueless coins.

Perpetually living on expedients, and anxious only for a smooth passage, the passive and negative régime of the Duke of Lerma was more remarkable for what it left undone than for what it actually did. Lerma himself was by nature indolent, and given to a resigned melancholy which kept him away from business for days on end. Hunting, the theatre, and lavish Court *fiestas* occupied the days of the King and his ministers, so that diplomatic representatives would constantly complain of the difficulty of obtaining audiences and transacting their affairs. Urgent problems, like the fiscal question in Castile, or the spread of banditry in Catalonia, were quietly shelved in the vain hope that they might in the course of time satisfactorily solve themselves; and the one positive action of the régime of real merit was the signing in 1609 of the Twelve Years' Truce with the Dutch – a settlement which Lerma steered through with some skill in the face of considerable opposition, but which was ultimately forced on him by the bankruptcy of the treasury. Otherwise the actions of his Government were ill advised and unfortunate, like the removal of the capital to Valladolid in 1601, which proved so unsatisfactory that it had to return again to Madrid in 1606.[4]

One action, however, the Government was to push through with a most uncharacteristic resolution: the expulsion of the Moriscos from Spain. There was a deliberate significance in the choice of the date on which the decree of expulsion was formally approved by the King – 9 April 1609, the day which also saw the signing of the Twelve Years' Truce. By the use of skilful timing, the humiliation of peace with the Dutch would be overshadowed by the glory of removing the last trace of Moorish dominance from Spain, and 1609 would be ever memorable as a year not of defeat but of victory.

The expulsion of the Moriscos, carefully prepared, and carefully executed between 1608 and 1614, was to some extent the act of a weak Government anxious for easy popularity at a time of widespread national discontent. But although the Government acted in response to pressures from beneath, there was a complexity about the whole Morisco problem which conferred a certain plausibility on the assumption that expulsion was the only remaining solution. Fundamentally, the Morisco question was that of an unassimilated – and possibly unassimilable – racial minority which had given endless trouble ever since the conquest of Granada. The dispersion of the Moriscos through Castile after the suppression of the second rebellion of the Alpujarras in 1570 had only complicated the problem by extending it to areas which had previously been free of Morisco inhabitants. From 1570 the Morisco problem was Castilian, as well as Valencian and Aragonese, although it varied in character from one region to another.

It was in Valencia that the problem appeared most serious. There were some 135,000 Moriscos in Valencia in 1609 – perhaps a third of the total population of the kingdom; and the proportion was increasing, since there had been a 70 per cent increase in the Morisco population between 1563 and 1609, against only a 45 per cent increase among the Old Christians. These Moriscos formed a closely

4. Lerma's principal reason for transferring the Court was probably to withdraw the King from the dangerous influence of his grandmother the Empress María, one of Lerma's most implacable foes. She had returned to Spain in 1576, after the death of her husband Maximilian II, to become a nun in the convent of the Descalzas Reales in Madrid.

knit community, significantly known as 'la *nación* de los cristianos nuevos de moros del reino de Valencia'. The very extent of their organization aroused widespread fears at a time when the danger of a Turkish attack on the Levantine coast still appeared very real. Nor did the discovery of links between the Aragonese Moriscos and the French Governor of Béarn do anything to diminish them. A Turkish-Protestant-Morisco conspiracy looked plausible enough to such a man as Archbishop Ribera of Valencia; and it could certainly be made to appear plausible to all those who were anxious to see the last of the Moriscos. These included Valencian lords whose vassals were Old Christians, and who envied the lords of Morisco vassals their greater prosperity; and it included, too, the lower class of the Old Christian population, hungry for the land which the Moriscos occupied. But the Valencian Moriscos had powerful protectors in the majority of the nobles, who were dependent on Morisco labour for their income. Equally, the townsmen who had lent money to aristocrats on the security of their estates were opposed to any sudden change that might reduce the rate of interest on their *censos*.

The balance of forces in Valencia suggests that, if the kingdom had been left to itself the Moriscos would have remained. But the presence of Moriscos in Castile had set up a whole new series of pressures which did much to strengthen the hand of those in favour of their total expulsion from the peninsula. The Castilian Moriscos, unlike their Valencian brethren, were rootless and scattered; and where the Valencian Moriscos were largely agricultural labourers, those of Castile had drifted to the towns and taken up a wide variety of fairly menial occupations, as carriers, muleteers, and small craftsmen. Since they were so widely dispersed, they hardly represented a very serious danger, but they were disliked by many Old Christians for spending too little, working too hard, and breeding too fast. In such a climate it was not difficult to whip up popular feeling by rhetorical arguments to the effect that Spain's recent misfortunes could be attributed to the continuing presence of unbelievers in a country that called itself Catholic.

Once the populace was aroused, the supporters of the Moriscos no longer dared raise their voices in protest, and the case against expulsion went by default. The vast bureaucratic machine was duly set in motion; the Moriscos were shepherded towards the frontiers and the ports, and the majority eventually found their way to North Africa, where many died of hunger and exhaustion, or were massacred by their unfriendly brethren. The total number leaving Spain is now reckoned at some 275,000 out of a probable Morisco population of rather over 300,000. The regional distribution of the emigrants was as follows:

Valencia	117,000
Catalonia	4,000
Aragon	61,000
Castile, La Mancha, Estremadura	45,000
Murcia	14,000
Andalusia	30,000
Granada	2,000

The economic consequences of the disappearance of the Moriscos from Spain are still by no means clear. A satisfactory evaluation would have to be undertaken on a regional basis, since the economic importance of the Moriscos varied from one area to another. Although industrious, they were neither wealthy nor economically enterprising members of the community, and to assume that their expulsion had economic effects comparable to those of the expulsion of the Jews in 1492 is absurd. But in some areas their departure left gaps which it proved difficult or impossible to fill. In the city of Seville for instance, there were some 7,000 Moriscos, occupied in humble but indispensable jobs as porters and carriers and dockyard hands, and the sudden removal of these men added to the many troubles of the port in the years around 1610.

In Castile the Moriscos had been too thinly scattered for their disappearance to have any drastic effect, but in Aragon and Valencia the story was very different. In Aragon, the fertile strip on the south of the Ebro was ruined. In Valencia, the consequences varied from one area to another, and in some places were modified by repopulation schemes which brought Old Christians to settle in abandoned areas; but the general effects on the Valencian economy were disastrous. Those who stood to lose most were the nobles who had employed Morisco labour on their estates, and depended for their income on the dues paid them by their Morisco vassals. Their losses were heavy, but to some extent they were mitigated by the policy of Lerma's government of shifting them on to the *bourgeoisie*. This was done by a pragmatic of 1614 which lowered the rate of interest on *censales* to 5 per cent, the losses being borne by the creditors – members of the Valencian *bourgeoisie*, and religious and charitable institutions – who had originally lent money to nobles on the security of their estates. Once again, therefore, the Lerma régime conformed to its usual practice of favouring the privileged at the expense of the less privileged, who lacked the influence to press their suit at Court.

In the national mood of euphoria created by the expulsion, its practical consequences were easily overlooked. It was only later, when Olivares and his colleagues attempted to mobilize the wealth, real or imagined, of the peripheral regions of the peninsula, that the real seriousness of the expulsion was brought home to the Government. In 1633 the royal confessor wrote: 'It is a very short time ago since the Moriscos were expelled – an action which did such harm to these kingdoms that it would be a good idea to have them back again, if they could be persuaded to accept our Holy Faith.'[5] But what was done could never be undone. The régime of the Duke of Lerma was never one to give much thought to the morrow, and the expulsion of the Moriscos aptly symbolized its general outlook in its total disregard for economic realities, its determination to adopt the easiest solution when confronted by admittedly intractable problems, and its tendency to give way before popular and sectional pressures. Here was a régime which, at a time when Castile stood most in need of government, was content merely to follow where others led; a government which preferred panaceas to policies, and which had nothing but high-sounding phrases and empty gestures to offer a society that desperately needed a cure for its many ills.

3. THE PATTERN OF SOCIETY

While it was relatively easy to expel the Moriscos from Spain, it was infinitely more difficult to expunge the traces of Moorish civilization from the soil of the peninsula. Moorish ways had profoundly influenced the life of Spanish society, and inevitably the processes

5. Elkan N. Adler, 'Documents sur les Marranes d'Espagne et de Portugal sous Philippe IV', *Revue des Études Juives*, vol. 51 (1906), p. 120.

involved in Spain's turning its back on Africa were painful and slow. It was something of a revolution when the new houses built in Seville during the course of the sixteenth century began to face outwards on to the street, instead of facing inwards as in Arab days. It was still more of a revolution when women started to appear at the windows, for it was in family life, and especially in the role of women in Spanish society, that Moorish habits were most deeply engrained. The Spanish upper classes had inherited the Moorish custom of keeping their womenfolk secluded, and the women themselves still retained many of their Moorish ways. They crouched on cushions instead of using chairs; in all Spain, except for the north and north-west, they remained semi-veiled, in spite of frequent royal prohibitions; and they had an extraordinary habit, which may perhaps have originated in Africa, of nibbling pieces of glazed pottery – a choice of diet which may account for their notoriously poor complexions. But the strongest reminder of the Moorish past was to be found in the extreme inequality between the sexes, which was much greater than in contemporary northern Europe, and which found its counterpart in extreme male gallantry towards the inferior sex.

Under the combined influence of Europe and America, habits slowly began to alter. The appearance in Seville of wealthy and dissolute creole women from the New World led to a gradual relaxation of manners and morals, and the veil was often retained as a convenient means of concealment instead of as a token of modesty. But, in spite of these changes, the position of the upper class Spanish woman seems to have altered far less between the Middle Ages and the seventeenth century than that of her foreign counterparts. Installed at the centre of the family unit, she remained the repository of traditional ideals and customs, many of which had been acquired from the Moors during the time when they were still the masters of Spain.

The survival of Moorish customs in seventeenth-century Spain vividly illustrates the enormous problems of adaptation which this society was called upon to make, and suggests something of the tensions to which it was subjected. If it tended to veer between two extremes – if, for instance, the extreme doctrine of *limpieza* appeared a natural solution to the problem of alien survivals – this was partly because the problems which faced it were themselves of such an extreme character. Castilian society, as the *arbitristas* never tired of pointing out, was a society based on paradox and contrast. The contrasts were everywhere: Moorish and Christian; devoutness and hypocrisy; fervent professions of faith and exceptional laxity of manners; vast wealth and abject poverty. There was no moderation here, no sense of proportion. The *Memorial de la Política Necesaria y Útil Restauración a la República de España* of González de Cellorigo is in practice one long text on the extremes of Spanish life and the paradoxes of its social and economic organization. For González, the greatness and perfection of a state were determined not by the extent of its possessions, but by a 'constant and harmonious' proportion between the different classes of its citizens. By this criterion Spain had reached the apex of its perfection in 1492. After the reigns of Ferdinand and Isabella it 'began to decline to our own days', when it seemed to be approaching its nadir. All proportion was now gone, and 'our republic has come to be an extreme contrast of rich and poor, and there is no means of adjusting them one to another. Our condition is one in which we have rich who loll at ease, or poor who beg, and we lack people of the middling sort, whom neither wealth nor poverty prevent from pursuing the rightful kind of business enjoined by natural law.'

It was precisely this absence of 'people of the middling sort', lamented by González de Cellorigo, which tended to differentiate the Spain of Philip III from other contemporary societies in western Europe (and conversely to approximate it to east European societies like Poland). Contrasts between wealth and poverty were not, after all, an exclusively Spanish phenomenon. The return of peace at the beginning of the seventeenth century had everywhere heralded the opening of an age of opulence characterized in the European capitals by a round of masques and fêtes, by lavish spending on building, costumes, and jewellery, and by a relaxation of moral standards which made courts the symbol of every kind of vice to the puritanically inclined. The uniqueness of Spain lay not so much in this contrast, as in the absence of a middling group of solid, respectable, hard-working *bourgeois* to bridge the gulf between the two extremes. In Spain, these people, as González de Cellorigo appreciated, had committed the great betrayal. They had been enticed away by the false values of a disorientated society – a society of 'the bewitched, living outside the natural order of things'. The contempt for commerce and manual labour, the lure of easy money from investment in *censos* and *juros*, the universal hunger for titles of nobility and social prestige – all these, when combined with the innumerable practical obstacles in the way of profitable economic enterprise, had persuaded the *bourgeoisie* to abandon its unequal struggle, and throw in its lot with the unproductive upper class of society.

Lacking a middle class which remained true to its own values, seventeenth-century Castile was sharply divided into the two extremes of the very rich and the very poor. 'There are but two families in the world,' as Sancho Panza's grandmother used to say, 'the haves and the have-nots' (*el tener y el no tener*);[6] and the criterion for distinguishing between them ultimately lay not in their rank or social position, but in whether they had anything to eat. Food, indeed, created new social classifications of its own:

> Al rico llaman honrado,
> Porque tiene que comer.[7]

The rich ate, and ate to excess, watched by a thousand hungry eyes as they consumed their gargantuan meals. The rest of the population starved. The endless preoccupation with food that characterizes every Spanish picaresque novel was no more than a faithful reflection of the overwhelming concern of the mass of the populace, from the impoverished *hidalgo* surreptitiously pocketing crumbs at Court, to the *pícaro* making a desperate raid on a market stall. 'Hermano, este día no es de aquellos sobre quien tiene jurisdicción la hambre' – 'hunger holds no sway today'.[8] But the days on which hunger held no sway were rare indeed; and the long weeks of emptiness were passed in scheming for a square meal, which itself would soon be consumed in an orgy of eating, and then forgotten as the pangs of hunger returned.

The best guarantee of a regular supply of square meals was, by tradition, service in *Iglesia, o mar, o casa real* – Church, sea (trade), or the royal service (at Court or in the army). By the seventeenth

6. *Don Quixote*, part II, c. XX.
7. From *Tratado espiritual de lo que pasa entre pobres y ricos*, an unedited contemporary poem, kindly shown me by Professor E. M. Wilson.
8. *Don Quixote*, ibid.

century the refrain had been narrowed down to *Iglesia, o casa real*. Castilians from all walks of life had come to look, as a matter of course, to the Church, Court, and bureaucracy to guarantee them the living which they disdained to earn from more menial occupations, at once despised and unrewarding.

The Church was both rich and welcoming. Although it suffered from heavy taxation, it had received over the years enormous gifts of money, jewels, and real estate. Bishoprics may have had heavy pensions charges against their revenues, but there were still fat benefices available, like the canonries of Seville, which had risen in value between the early sixteenth and the early seventeenth centuries from 300 to 2,000 ducats – a sixfold increase which shows that, at least in this diocese, the revenues of the cathedral chapter had risen faster than prices. The proliferation of new Religious Orders had opened up the possibilities of a religious life to large numbers of men and women whose anxiety for food and shelter tended to exceed their sense of religious vocation. A total figure of 200,000 regular and secular clergy has been suggested for the Spain of Philip IV, but there are no reliable statistics. A contemporary writer, Gil González Dávila, put the number of Dominicans and Franciscans at 32,000, and according to the Cortes of 1626 there were some 9,000 religious houses in Castile simply for men. 'I am a priest,' wrote González Dávila, 'but I confess that there are more of us than are necessary.'[9]

Alongside the Church stood the Court, with its glittering prospects of favour, position, and wealth. The Court of Philip III was very different from that of his father. The age of parsimony was over and the new King 'increased the service in his royal palace, and admitted many grandees as gentlemen of his household, departing from the style of his father'.[10] The break with the House of Austria's traditional practice of keeping the higher aristocracy away from Court came at a moment when the great Spanish nobles were in urgent need of help. The price rise, taken in conjunction with the general increase in expenditure that was expected of the aristocracy during the sixteenth century, had played havoc with the fortunes of the grandees. Since detailed studies of the higher Spanish aristocratic

9. Gil González Dávila, *Historia de la Vida y Hechos del Ínclito Monarca . . . Don Felipe Tercero* (ed. Madrid, 1771), p. 215.

10. Ibid., p. 45.

families do not exist, the changing pattern of their fortunes is still unknown, but a comparison of the annual incomes of thirteen ducal families between the early sixteenth century and 1600 (as given by Lucio Marineo Sículo and Pedro Núñez de Salcedo respectively)[11] gives some picture of what was happening:

Title	Early 16th century (ducats)	1600 (ducats)
Frías (Condestable de Castilla)	60,000	65,000
Medina de Ríoseco (Almirante de Castilla)	50,000	130,000
Alba	50,000	120,000
Infantado	50,000	120,000
Medina Sidonia	55,000	170,000
Béjar	40,000	80,000
Nájera	30,000	55,000
Medinaceli	30,000	60,000
Alburquerque	25,000	50,000
Arcos	25,000	80,000
Maqueda	30,000	50,000
Escalona	60,000	100,000
Sessa	60,000	100,000
	565,000	1,180,000

The figures show that the incomes of these thirteen families had barely doubled over a period when prices quadrupled, and it is not surprising that most of the families were heavily indebted by the end of the sixteenth century. While the entail system saved the great houses from having to sell off their estates, they were compelled to mortgage them in order to pay the interest on their debts. According to one of the Venetian ambassadors at the Court of Philip III, the grandees actually received no more than a fifth of their revenues, since the remaining four-fifths were being used to service their debts. This at least was the lot of the Dukes of Infantado, to judge from the will of the fifth duke, dated 4 March 1598. He explains his heavy debts by the failure of his parents to pay him the portion of an elder son, which had obliged him to mortgage his wealth in order to maintain his household; in addition he had been indebted by lawsuits, by marriage

11. For Marineo Sículo, see above, p. 112. The *relación* of Núñez de Salcedo is printed in *Boletín de la Real Academia de la Historia*, vol. 73 (1918), pp. 470–91.

settlements for his children, and by the expenditure of over 100,000 ducats on repairs and improvements to the ducal palace at Guadalajara. The Duke's successors met the challenge in the same way as other impoverished aristocrats. They left their 85,000 vassals and their 620 towns and villages to the care of stewards and administrators and transferred themselves to Madrid. Life at Court might be expensive (indeed, the Duke of Infantado is said to have spent more than 300,000 ducats in the course of the King's visit to Valencia in 1599), but the grandees expected to make up for their losses by plundering the royal treasury, just as their ancestors had plundered it when another favourite ruled Spain, in the reign of John II.

It was not only the grandees who benefited from the affluence of a generous King. The Spain of Philip III, like the England of James I, saw an inflation of honours. During the sixteenth century there had been a relatively moderate increase in the number of Spanish titles:

	Early 16th century	1600	
Dukes	17	21	(21 grandees)
Marquises	16	42	(8 grandees)
Counts	44	56	(3 grandees)
	77	119	

In the twenty-three years of his reign, Philip III created three dukes, thirty marquises, and thirty-three counts. This addition of new titles played its part in keeping a large share of the national wealth in aristocratic hands, in spite of the relative diminution of the wealth of the old grandee families. The combined rent-rolls of the aristocracy in the early sixteenth century totalled some 1,500,000 ducats; by 1630, when there were 155 titled nobles, their nominal combined incomes exceeded 5,000,000.

Although the real incomes of the nobles were far less than their nominal incomes, they still contrived to spend on a vast scale. Like the King, they had found it impossible to adjust their way of life to a new age in which prices were no longer automatically rising and debts were gratifyingly reduced by the process of inflation. At a time when less good money was entering Spain and more was leaving it, the King still managed to live beyond his means by striking a copper coinage for domestic use and then manipulating it at times of need;

and the nobles, paying their servants – as the King paid his – in debased *vellón*, followed the ways of their royal master and spent more
than they had. Their households grew larger and larger, swollen by
the Castilian custom of automatically re-employing all old servants
when the mastership of the house changed hands, even if the new
master already possessed a large household of his own. Thus the Conde
Duque de Olivares had 198 servants, the great Duke of Osuna 300,
and, in the later years of the century, the Duke of Medinaceli, heir to
an imposing array of estates, no less than 700. Royal pragmatics to
limit the number of lackeys and servants were useless, for domestic
service was one of the few important industries of Castile, and it
obeyed the laws of social custom and economic necessity rather than
those of the State. A large household enhanced the standing of its
owner; and service in a noble household, even when it entailed being
underpaid and underfed, was on the whole to be preferred to no
employment at all.

Inevitably, therefore, as grandees and lesser aristocrats drifted to
Court, they were followed by thousands who either possessed, or
aspired to, a place in their service. At a time when the population of
Castile had fallen, that of Madrid continued to grow: from 4,000 in
1530 to 37,000 in 1594, to anything between 70,000 and 100,000 in
the reign of Philip IV. The Court acted as a great magnet, drawing
to it from all over the country the rootless, the dishonest, and the
ambitious. Recognizing this, the Government ordered the great
nobles in 1611 to return to their estates in the hope of clearing the
Court of parasites, but the order suffered the fate of most of Lerma's
good intentions, and the *arbitristas* continued to fulminate in vain
against the unchecked growth of a monstrous capital which was
draining away the life-blood of Castile.

Younger sons and impoverished *hidalgos* flocked to the Court in
the hope of making or restoring their fortunes – a hope that did not
seem unreasonable when a Rodrigo Calderón could acquire the
marquisate of Siete Iglesias and an annual income of 200,000 ducats.
For the Court had much to offer: not only places in the households
of nobles, and even, with luck, in the palace, but places also in the
proliferating bureaucracy of the Spanish Monarchy. The only draw-
back to service as a royal official was that it required a modicum of
education; but, over the course of the years the expansion of the

educational establishments of Castile had amply catered for this need. According to one *arbitrista*, Fernández Navarrete, there were thirty-two universities and 4,000 grammar schools in Spain, turning out far more educated, or semi-educated, students and graduates than could ever hope to find employment in the professions. During the sixteenth century there had been a continuous foundation of universities and colleges – twenty-one new universities since 1516, and eighteen new colleges at Salamanca alone. Since the number of applicants for places in the administration far exceeded the number of places available, it became increasingly necessary for colleges to look after their own. Those in the best position to do this were the famous *Colegios Mayores*, like the four at Salamanca – *élite* establishments which had virtually acquired the status of independent republics within the universities. The *Colegios Mayores*, which had originally been intended for the aristocracy of talent, had provided Spain with many of its most distinguished scholars, clerics, and administrators: the *Colegio Mayor* of Cuenca at Salamanca, for example, produced over the space of fifty years six cardinals, twenty archbishops, and eight viceroys. But in the course of time poverty no longer became a necessary condition for entry, and standards slipped. The position of the *Colegios Mayores* was, however, impregnable. Their practice was to maintain at Court former pupils known as *hacedores* – men of rank and influence who would back members of their own colleges for official posts, on the understanding that the colleges would in return reserve places for their own friends and relatives. If no satisfactory position were available at the time, favoured students were installed by the colleges in special hostels, where they could pass the years – sometimes as many as fifteen or twenty – in great comfort, waiting for a desirable post to fall vacant.

Influence, favour, recommendation, were therefore essential passports. The more talented graduates had little hope of employment unless they could find an influential patron, and consequently a great army of students joined the ranks of the unemployed. Yet a degree conferred at least some status, and there was always the possibility of a lucky break: 'A man studies and studies, and then with favour and good luck he'll find himself with a staff in his hand or a mitre on his head when he least expects it.'[12] Everything, then, conspired to

12. *Don Quixote*, part II, c. LXVI.

attract the population to the economically unproductive occupations in society. There was always the chance of a sudden piece of good fortune to end the long years of waiting; and anyhow, what alternative was there? 'The number of religious, and clergy, and students, has doubled,' it was said in 1620, 'because they have no other means of living or maintaining themselves.' In fact, if Church, Court, and bureaucracy absorbed an excessive proportion of the potentially productive part of the population of Castile, this was not only because of their own innate attractiveness to a society which tended to despise the more menial occupations, but also because they offered almost the only prospect of remunerative employment in an underdeveloped economy.

Most of the *arbitristas* recommended the reduction of schools and convents and the clearing of the Court as the solution to the problem. Yet this was really to mistake the symptoms for the cause. González de Cellorigo was almost alone in appreciating that the fundamental problem lay not so much in heavy spending by Crown and upper classes – since this spending itself created a valuable demand for goods and services – as in the disproportion between expenditure and investment. 'Money is not true wealth,' he wrote, and his concern was to increase the national wealth by increasing the nation's productive capacity rather than its stock of precious metals. This could only be achieved by investing more money in agricultural and industrial development. At present, surplus wealth was being unproductively invested – 'dissipated on thin air – on papers, contracts, *censos*, and letters of exchange, on cash, and silver, and gold – instead of being expended on things that yield profits and attract riches from outside to augment the riches within. And thus there is no money, gold, or silver in Spain because there is so much; and it is not rich, because of all its riches. . . .'

The assumptions of González de Cellorigo about the way in which wealth was being used, or misused, find some confirmation in an inventory of the possessions of a wealthy royal official, Don Alonso Rámirez de Prado, a member of the Council of Castile arrested for corrupt practices in 1607. Besides his house, which he had bought from the Duke of Alba for 44,000 ducats, he possessed the following (figures being given in *escudos*, which consisted at this moment of 400 *maravedís*, against 375 *maravedís* to the ducat):

	Escudos
Silverware	40,000
Jewellery	40,000
Tapestries and hangings	90,000
Letters of exchange	100,000
Juros (in the name of himself and others)	470,000
Real estate	500,000
	1,240,000

Such an inventory gives force to González's constant insistence on the urgent necessity of redeeming *juros* and reducing the enormous burden on Castile of the Crown's debts, which lured away surplus wealth into unproductive channels.

The Castile of González de Cellorigo was thus a society in which both money and labour were misapplied; an unbalanced, top-heavy society, in which, according to González, there were thirty parasites for every one man who did an honest day's work; a society with a false sense of values, which mistook the shadow for substance, and substance for the shadow. That this society should also have produced a brilliant civilization, as rich in cultural achievement as it was poor in economic achievement, was no more than one among its many paradoxes. For the age of a copper coinage was the golden age of Spain.

The country's social and economic organization was by no means unfavourable to artists and writers. Among the upper classes of society there was money with which to assist them, and leisure to enjoy their works. Many nobles prided themselves on their patronage of the arts: the Counts of Gondomar and Olivares built up great libraries; the palaces of the Count of Monterrey and the Marquis of Leganés were famed for their picture galleries. The possibilities of building up collections were greatly enhanced by the frequency of auctions in Madrid, which enabled a connoisseur like Don Juan de Espina to gather together a remarkable collection of curiosities and works of art from the sales of great houses. Espina himself was an eccentric and something of a recluse, but among the upper classes of Madrid many kept open house for poets and painters.

On the whole, the wealth of the aristocracy seems to have been spent more on the patronage of literature and painting than on architecture. In the fifteenth and sixteenth centuries there had been much building of palaces, but in the seventeenth century the Church rather than the aristocracy was responsible for the most impressive edifices – innumerable churches and convents, in which the austerities of Herrera gradually yielded to a more ornate and theatrical style, culminating in the often frenzied convolutions of Churrigueresque baroque.

If the decline in aristocratic building is to some extent an indication of a decline in aristocratic wealth – at least in relation to that of the Church – the grandees still retained enough money to indulge in keen competition for the patronage of authors and artists. This was particularly true in Andalusia, where there was acute rivalry among the three great houses of Guzmán, Afán de Ribera, and Girón, for the patronage and friendship of the most distinguished talents. Moreover, the patronage was often well informed. Don Fernando Afán de Ribera, Duke of Alcalá (1584–1637) was an amateur painter, a great book collector, and a distinguished Latin scholar, who devoted his spare time to the investigation of Castilian antiquities; the Count of Olivares, after leaving Salamanca University, spent several years at Seville in the company of poets and authors, and tried his own hand at writing verse. When he became the Favourite of Philip IV – himself a great connoisseur, and a patron of art and letters – he made the Court a brilliant literary and artistic centre, famous for the theatrical presentations and literary *fiestas* in which such names as Lope de Vega and Calderón de la Barca figured prominently among the participants.

The climate was therefore propitious for literary and artistic production, although, as Cervantes was to discover by bitter experience, even genius did not guarantee a regular income. At the same time, the moral and emotional involvement of the intellectuals in the tragic fate of their native land seems to have provided an additional stimulus, giving an extra degree of intensity to their imagination, and diverting it into rewardingly creative channels. This was especially true of Cervantes, whose life – from 1547 to 1616 – spans the two ages of imperial triumph and imperial retreat. The crisis of the late sixteenth century cuts through the life of Cervantes as it cuts through the life of Spain, separating the days of heroism from the days of *desengaño*. Somehow Cervantes magically held the balance between optimism and pessimism, enthusiasm and irony, but he illustrates what was to be the most striking characteristic of seventeenth-century literature and artistic production – that deep cleavage between the two worlds of the spirit and the flesh, which co-exist and yet are for ever separate. This constant dualism between the spirit and the flesh, the dream and the reality, belonged very much to seventeenth-century European civilization as a whole, but it seems to have attained an intensity in Spain that it rarely achieved elsewhere. It is apparent in the writings of Calderón and the portraits of Velázquez, and it prompted the bitter satires of Quevedo. 'There are many things here that seem to exist and have their being, and yet they are nothing more than a name and an appearance,' Quevedo wrote at the end of his life.[13] Yet which was the real and which the illusory in González de Cellorigo's 'society of the bewitched, living outside the natural order of things'? Was the reality of Spanish experience to be found in the heroic imperialism of a Charles V or in the humiliating pacifism of Philip III? In the world of Don Quixote, or the world of Sancho Panza? Confused at once by its own past and its own present, the Castile of Philip III – the land of *arbitristas* – sought desperately for an answer.

13. Quoted by Gerald Brenan, *The Literature of the Spanish People* (Cambridge, 1951), p. 270.

9

Revival and Disaster

I. THE REFORM PROGRAMME

DURING the second decade of the seventeenth century it became increasingly obvious that the Government of the Duke of Lerma was living on borrowed time. Both at home and abroad the situation was deteriorating alarmingly. It was true that the murder of Henry IV in 1610 had opportunely removed any immediate danger of war with France, and that the double marriage treaty of 1612 between Louis XIII and the Infanta Ana on the one hand, and between Prince Philip and Elizabeth of Bourbon on the other, held out hopes of a new and happier chapter in the history of Franco-Spanish relations. But the *pax hispanica* never extended into the world overseas. The Dutch had used the years of peace since 1609 to consolidate and extend their gains in the Far East at the expense of the Portuguese empire. As the depredations of the Dutch continued, one minister after another came round to the view expressed in 1616 by Don Fernando de Carrillo, the President of the Council of Finance, that 'it has been worse than if the war had gone on'. The problem of the Dutch, unsolved and perhaps insoluble, was to dog the Spain of Philip III and IV as it had dogged that of Philip II, as if to confirm that the Spanish Monarchy would never shake itself free of the *damnosa hereditas* of the Netherlands.

At home, both the condition of Castile and the state of the royal finances gave rise to increasing concern. In spite of the return of peace, the Crown was still managing to spend some 8,000,000 or even 9,000,000 ducats a year – a figure quite without precedent, complained Carrillo (not entirely accurately) in 1615. If Philip II had managed to spend even more in the heyday of the 1590s, he had at least been able to draw on substantial revenues from the Indies. But in 1615 and again in 1616 the treasure fleet, which could be relied upon in the early years of the reign to bring the Crown 2,000,000 ducats a year, brought scarcely 1,000,000 ducats, and in the closing years of the decade the figure dropped to well below 1,000,000.

The gradual drying-up of the stream of silver from America – which is to be explained by the increasing cost of working the mines, by the growing self-sufficiency of the colonists, by heavier expenditure by the viceregal government in the New World, and perhaps by a fall in world silver prices – made it increasingly urgent to tackle the problem of financial and economic reform. To the voices of *arbitristas* and of *procuradores* of the Castilian Cortes were now added those of the Crown's financial ministers, urging Lerma to take action. In the early summer of 1618 he at last bowed before the storm. A special Junta, known as the *Junta de Reformación*, was created, and the Council of Castile was ordered to produce a report outlining possible remedies for Castile's present ills. But the Duke himself, who had sensibly taken out an insurance policy in the form of a cardinal's hat, was not to benefit from his belated piece of initiative. On 4 October 1618 he fell from power as the result of a palace revolution engineered by his own son, the Duke of Uceda, and his disgrace was followed by the arrest, in February 1619, of his henchman Don Rodrigo Calderón, who was later brought to trial on an imposing array of charges.

The Council of Castile duly produced its *consulta* on 1 February 1619. This was not, in fact, as impressive a document as it is sometimes made out to be, and its seven curiously assorted recommendations marked no advance on what the *arbitristas* had been saying for years. The misery and depopulation of Castile were ascribed to 'excessive taxes and tributes', and the Council proposed a reduction of taxes and reform of the fiscal system, which would partly be achieved by calling on the other kingdoms of the Monarchy to come to Castile's assistance. The Council also suggested that the King should curb his naturally generous instincts in the bestowal of *mercedes*. The Court should be cleared. New sumptuary decrees should be enforced, to curtail the fashion for expensive foreign luxuries. Deserted regions should be repopulated, and agricultural labourers be encouraged by the grant of special privileges. No more licences should be given for the establishment of new religious foundations. Moreover, the number of existing convents and grammar schools should be reduced and the hundred receiverships set up in 1613 be abolished.

Although these recommendations were curiously vague on exactly those points where it was most necessary to be specific, they were none the less important as representing the first real recognition by Philip III's Government of the gravity of Castile's economic problems. But the régime of the Duke of Uceda was no better equipped to transform policy into action than that of his father, and for two precious years the Council of Castile's proposals were quietly ignored. The days of the régime, however, were numbered. In the summer of 1619 Philip III made a State visit to Portugal, where the Cortes were assembled to take the oath of allegiance to his son. On the return journey he was taken ill, and although his condition improved shortly afterwards – thanks, it was said, to the intercession of St Isidore, whose remains were placed in his room – it soon became clear that he could not expect to live much longer. Full of contrition for a life which was as blameless as it had been unprofitable, he died at the age of forty-three on 31 March 1621, to be succeeded by his sixteen-year-old son, heir to a wasted estate.

Philip IV differed from his father in being quick-witted, intelligent, and cultivated, but resembled him in his absence of character. Quite without the animation of his younger brother Ferdinand (who, with singular inappropriateness, had been created Cardinal-Archbishop of Toledo in 1619 at the grave age of ten), he was inclined by temperament to depend on others who might stiffen his resolution and assist him in the formidable task of making up his mind. Born to rely on Favourites, he had already adopted – or, more accurately, been adopted by – his first and most influential Favourite before he came to the throne. This was a gentleman of his household, Gaspar de Guzmán, Count of Olivares. The Count was an Andalusian aristocrat, born in 1587 at Rome, where his father was Spanish ambassador. He was educated at the University of Salamanca and was intended for a career in the Church, but the sudden death of his elder brother made him heir to the family title and estates. Ambitious for office and advancement, he had to wait until 1615 before Lerma, naturally distrustful of so strong a personality, gave him office as a gentleman of the chamber to the young Prince Philip. Once in the royal household, Olivares worked hard, and eventually with success, to win the favour of the Prince. In the squalid intrigues of the last years of the reign he threw in his lot with the Duke of Uceda, and successfully manoeuvred for the recall to Madrid of his uncle, Don Baltasar de Zúñiga, who had been acting as ambassador at the Court of the Emperor. Being a man of ability and influence, Zúñiga would be more useful to his nephew at the Court of the King of Spain.

As Philip III lay on his death-bed, Zúñiga and Olivares moved fast to wrest control of the Government from the inept hands of the Duke of Uceda, and the favour of the new King carried them triumphantly to success. Until his death in October 1622 Zúñiga was nominally the first minister of Philip IV. But Zúñiga's ministry was in reality no more than a screen behind which Olivares groomed himself for the position of *Privado* that he held for twenty-two years, until his fall from power in 1643. A restless figure, never fully at ease either with others or with himself, Olivares was less one personality than a whole succession of personalities, co-existing, competing and conflicting within a single frame. By turns ebullient and dejected, humble and arrogant, shrewd and gullible, impetuous and cautious, he dazzled contemporaries with the versatility of his performance and bewildered them with his chameleon changes of mood. Somehow he always seemed larger than lifesize, bestriding the Court like a colossus, with state papers stuck in his hat and bulging in his pockets, always in a flurry of activity, surrounded by scurrying secretaries, ordering, hectoring, cajoling, his voice booming down the corridors of the palace. No man worked harder, or slept less. With the coming of Olivares, the indolent, easy-going days of the Duke of Lerma were gone for ever, and the stage was set for reform.

Olivares was, by nature and conviction, the heir of the *arbitristas*, determined to undertake with ruthless efficiency the reforms that had been so long delayed. But he was also the heir to another tradition which had found powerful advocates in the Spain of Philip III – the great imperial tradition, which believed firmly in the rightness, and indeed the inevitability of Spanish, and specifically Castilian, hegemony over the world. Under the government of Lerma this tradition had been muted in the capital of the Monarchy, where the eclipse of the crusading tradition had been curiously symbolized by the displacement in 1617 of St James from his position as sole patron of Spain. In future the warrior saint was to have a feminine partner in the person of a highly idealized St Teresa. But just as St James still had his fervent partisans, so also did the militant tradition of which he was the symbol. The supine policies of the Lerma régime were regarded with anger and contempt by many of its agents, who refused to reconcile themselves to the humiliating pacifism of Philip III's Government. Profiting from the weakness of the régime they despised, these agents – the great Italian proconsuls, like the Count of Fuentes, the Marquis of Bedmar, the Marquis of Villafranca, and the Duke of Osuna (viceroy of Sicily from 1611–16 and of Naples from 1616–20) – conducted over the years a militant and aggressive policy entirely at variance with that of Madrid. Although Osuna was re-called in disgrace in 1620 and later imprisoned on the orders of Zúñiga and Olivares, both ministers, in fact, shared many of his aims and aspirations. They believed, like him, that Spain could remain true to itself only if it remained true to its imperial tradition, and they despised the defeatist policies which had, in their opinion, brought it to its present miserable state.

Olivares therefore combined in himself the quixotic imperialism that belonged to the golden age of Charles V and Philip II, and the practical, down-to-earth approach of the *arbitristas*, for whom wind-mills remained windmills, whatever was said to the contrary. Throughout his career, the ideal and the practical, the crusading tradition and the reforming tradition, existed uncomfortably side by side, and it was oddly appropriate that the very first month of his ministry, when everything was set for reform, should also see the return of Spain to war. In April 1621 the truce with the Netherlands expired, and was not renewed. Apart from the fact that the triumph of the bellicose Orangist party in the United Provinces in any event made the renewal of the war virtually certain, there were powerful arguments in Madrid as well as in the Hague for allowing the truce to lapse. The Council of Portugal insisted on the irreparable harm done to Portugal's overseas possessions by the Dutch during the years of 'peace'; the Council of Finance tried to show that the cost of main-taining a standing army in Flanders in peacetime was not substantially less than in war. It was also argued that if the Dutch were once again engaged at home, they would be able to devote less energy to their pirate ventures, and a world-wide struggle could thus be localized. In addition, certain measures had already been taken which suggested that on this occasion there was a real chance of success against the Dutch. The revolt of the Valtelline in 1618 had provided a pretext for the Duke of Feria, Governor of Milan, to establish Spanish garrisons in this strategic valley linking Milan and Austria; and the revolt of Bohemia in the same year allowed Spain's best commander, Ambrosio Spínola, to occupy the Palatinate and secure control of the Rhine passages. These two actions, undertaken in the last year of the Uceda régime, had enabled Spain to consolidate its hold over the vital 'Spanish road', up which men and supplies could be sent from Milan to Flanders.

The success of the Spanish commanders helped to strengthen the hand of those who wanted a return to belligerent policies, and created a climate in which the renewal of war came almost to be taken for granted. So it was that in the very first month of its existence the new Government found itself committed to the continuation of war in the Netherlands and to the probability of its extension in central Europe. This immediately pushed up the figures for the anticipated expenditure of 1621. For years the Duke of Osuna had been insisting that the preservation of an empire as large and scattered as that of Spain depended on the possession of a first-class fleet. Under the Government of Philip III the Spanish fleet had been scandalously neglected, and ships had been allowed to rot in the dockyards for lack of money. But Olivares seems to have appreciated that a vigorous naval policy was essential for the success of Spanish arms, and by an order of November 1621 the Atlantic fleet was to be increased to a total of forty-six ships, and the sum allocated to its upkeep raised from 500,000 to 1,000,000 ducats a year.

By another royal order of the same month, the expenditure on the Flanders army was raised from 1,500,000 to 3,500,000 ducats a year. The Crown's anticipated annual expenditure was now over 8,000,000 ducats – and its annual deficit in the region of 4,000,000, with revenues being mortgaged for three or four years ahead. Since, as Olivares insisted in a memorandum he wrote at this moment for his royal master, 'kings cannot achieve heroic actions without money', the return to war itself gave extra urgency to the programme for reform. This was now begun with considerable vigour. As an earnest of the new ministry's intentions, the long list of royal favours and pensions was slashed, an inquiry was ordered into all ministerial fortunes acquired since 1603, and the hated Rodrigo Calderón was publicly executed. At the same time, new life was breathed into the

moribund *Junta de Reformación*, and the fruits of its labours appeared
in February 1623 in the publication of a series of twenty-three articles
of reform. These were a mixed series of ordinances, which draw their
inspiration from the writings of the *arbitristas* and from the Council of
Castile's *consulta* of 1619, and were infused by a conviction that
morals and economics were inextricably intertwined. There was to
be a two-thirds reduction in the number of municipal offices; strict
sumptuary laws were to be introduced to regulate the prevalent
excesses of dress; measures were to be taken to increase the population; prohibitions were to be imposed on the import of foreign
manufactures; and brothels were to be closed. Here at last was that
general reform of morals and manners which, it was assumed, would
bring about the regeneration of Castile.

Unhappily for Olivares's good intentions, the unexpected visit of
the Prince of Wales to Madrid the very next month threw austerity
to the winds; the origins of ministerial fortunes proved to be so
mysterious that the inquiry had to be abandoned; and the plan for
the reduction of municipal offices had to be jettisoned on the insistence of the *procuradores* of the Cortes, who found their municipalities
threatened with heavy financial loss. Within three years there was
nothing to show for the great reform programme except the modest
achievement of the abolition of the ruff. In the face of public inertia,
and the covert opposition of Court and bureaucracy, even the
reforming energies of an Olivares were doomed to frustration.

But if the reform of morals had to be postponed to a more propitious time, the reform of the finances could not afford to wait. The
financial situation confronting Olivares resolved itself essentially into
two separate but related problems. The Monarchy had run into
trouble in the reign of Philip III primarily because of the exhaustion
of Castile, which shouldered the principal burden of the Crown's
finances. The exhaustion of Castile, in turn, was principally attributed
to the weight of taxation that rested upon it, and bore specially hard
on its most productive citizens. Therefore the aim of Olivares's
financial policies must first of all be to redistribute more equitably the
incidence of Castilian taxation, and then to induce the other provinces
of the Monarchy to come to Castile's help, so that the disproportion-
ate burden borne by Castile could itself be lightened.

At the heart of Olivares's plans for Castile was a project for establishing a national banking system – a scheme proposed to Philip II by a Fleming, Peter van Oudegherste as early as 1576, and then intermittently considered during the reign of Philip III. A chain of banks would, it was believed, assist the Crown to reduce its debts, relieve it of dependence on the foreign *asentistas*, and, by placing a ceiling of 5 per cent on returns, drive much of the money invested in loan funds into direct investments in a search for higher rewards. This scheme was outlined in a letter sent in October 1622 to the towns represented in the Castilian Cortes, and was coupled with another proposal dear to Olivares's heart – the abolition of the *millones*. Instead of this tax on essential articles of consumption, which hit the poor hardest, and was anyhow increasingly unremunerative and difficult to collect, Olivares proposed that the 15,000 towns and villages of Castile should contribute, in proportion to their size, to the upkeep of an army of 30,000 men.

These projects ran into strong opposition in the Castilian Cortes. The *erarios*, or banks, were generally mistrusted – not without reason – and although there was a general desire to see the last of the *millones*, it proved impossible to agree on an alternative form of taxation. As a result, the banking scheme was abandoned in 1626, and the irreplaceable *millones* survived – to be extended to other commodities, and collected at the rate of not 2,000,000 but 4,000,000 ducats a year. Although Olivares had not yet given up all hope, and indeed made another attempt to abolish the *millones* in 1631, it was clear that powerful vested interests stood in the way of the radical fiscal reforms which he longed to introduce.

The plans for reforms in Castile, however, were only one part of an infinitely more ambitious reform programme for the entire Spanish Monarchy. During recent years, financial ministers and *arbitristas* alike had insisted that it was the duty of the other parts of the Monarchy to come to the relief of an exhausted Castile. But it was difficult to see how this could be achieved so long as the existing constitutional structure of the Monarchy was preserved. The privileges of such kingdoms as Aragon and Valencia were so wide, and their Cortes so powerful, that the chances of introducing a regular system of taxation on a scale approaching that of Castile seemed remote. Fiscal necessity, therefore, now came to reinforce the traditional Castilian nationalist arguments that provincial laws and liberties should be abolished, and the constitutional and fiscal organization of other parts of the Monarchy be brought into conformity with that of Castile.

At a time when statesmen all over Europe were attempting to consolidate their hold over their peoples and exploit national resources more effectively in order to strengthen the power of the State, it was natural that Olivares should see in the 'Castilianization' of the Spanish Monarchy the solution to many of his problems. If uniform laws were introduced throughout the Monarchy, the 'separation' between the various kingdoms, of which he was always complaining, would disappear, and it would be possible to mobilize effectively the resources of an empire which was potentially the most powerful in the world, but which at present was gravely weakened by its total lack of unity. Olivares thus became a partisan of the traditional 'Alba' approach to the question of imperial organization. But at the same time he seems to have had a real understanding of the grievances of the non-Castilian kingdoms, which protested at having to pay heavier taxes to maintain an empire of benefit solely to Castile. It is significant that one of his closest friends and advisers was a political theorist called Álamos de Barrientos, who had also been a friend and disciple of Antonio Pérez. It was, perhaps, under the influence of Álamos and of the political theories of the Pérez school that what otherwise might have been no more than a policy of 'Castilianization' at its most crude, was modified in Olivares's thought into a more generous and liberal programme. In a famous memorandum which he presented to Philip IV at the end of 1624, he admitted the many grievances of kingdoms which scarcely ever saw their King and which felt themselves excluded from offices in the empire and in the royal households. He therefore proposed that, while the laws of the various kingdoms should be gradually reduced to conformity with those of Castile, the character of the Monarchy as a whole should be made less exclusively Castilian, by means of more frequent royal visits to the various provinces, and by the employment of more Aragonese, Portuguese or Italians in important offices. If Olivares's Monarchy was therefore to consist of 'multa regna, sed una lex', it would also be a truly universal Monarchy, in which the many walls of partition between the 'multa regna' would be broken down, while their nationals were employed – irrespective of province of origin – in a genuine co-operative venture, of benefit to all.

Olivares himself realized that this grandiose vision of a unified and integrated Spanish Monarchy not could be achieved in a day, but he saw that it was important to 'familiarize' the various provinces with each other as quickly as possible, and to accustom them to the idea of thinking collectively instead of in purely individual terms. This meant, in effect, a reverse of the whole approach to the Monarchy that had been adopted by Charles V and Philip II, and had survived in default of any more positive vision. It seemed to Olivares that the process might start with the establishment of some form of military co-operation between the different provinces. This would not only have the merit of inducing the provinces to think of others beside themselves, but would also help to solve the problems of money and man-power which were at present threatening to overwhelm Castile. The long secret memorandum to the King of 1624 was therefore followed by a shorter memorandum, intended for publication, outlining a scheme to be known as the 'Union of Arms'. The Union was to be achieved by the creation of a common reserve of 140,000 men to be supplied and maintained by all the States of the Monarchy in fixed proportions:

	Paid men
Catalonia	16,000
Aragon	10,000
Valencia	6,000
Castile and the Indies	44,000
Portugal	16,000
Naples	16,000
Sicily	6,000
Milan	8,000
Flanders	12,000
Mediterranean and Atlantic islands	6,000

Any kingdom of the Monarchy which was attacked by the enemy would be immediately assisted by the seventh part of this reserve, or 20,000 infantry and 4,000 cavalry.

There were obvious practical difficulties in the way of this ingenious scheme. The States of the Crown of Aragon, for instance, had extremely rigid laws regulating the recruitment of troops and their use beyond the frontiers. It would not be easy to induce them to set aside these laws for the sake of helping a province like Milan, which was always liable to sudden attack. But the Conde Duque (as Olivares came to be known after being created Duque de Sanlúcar la Mayor in 1625) refused to be daunted. Determined to press forward with a scheme which offered real hope of relief for Castile, he and the king set out at the end of 1625 on a visit to the three States of the Crown of Aragon, whose Cortes were to be presented with the Union of Arms.

The Cortes of Aragon, Valencia and Catalonia, held during the spring months of 1626, proved to be even more unenthusiastic about the Union of Arms than the Conde Duque had feared. It was twenty years or more since the last Cortes had been held, and in the intervening years grievances had accumulated. Both Valencians and Aragonese objected to the novelty of the subsidy demanded by the King, and were adamant in their refusal to conscript men for foreign service. But the most recalcitrant of the Cortes were those of Catalonia, opened by the King at Barcelona on 28 March. The Catalans at this moment were more than usually touchy and disgruntled. Since the visit of Philip III in 1599 they had suffered a number of experiences which had made them particularly sensitive about the intentions of Castile. During the first decade of the century, the viceroys had shown themselves increasingly incapable of dealing with the bandits who had long troubled the peace of the mountainous frontier region, and who had recently taken to committing daring raids on the outskirts of Barcelona itself. The Government of the Duke of Lerma had shown an almost total lack of interest in the problem of preserving public order in the Principality – so much so, that during the feeble vice-royalty of the Marquis of Almazán from 1611 to 1615, it had seemed for a moment as if Catalonia would succumb to total anarchy. The situation was saved by the arrival in 1616 of a vigorous new viceroy, the Duke of Alburquerque. But Alburquerque and his successor, the Duke of Alcalá, only restored order by contravening the Catalan constitutions. Banditry in its worst form had been suppressed, but national susceptibilities had been gravely hurt in the process. When Alcalá finally left office in 1622 he had alienated every section of the community including the towns – the natural allies of the viceregal administration in its struggle against aristocratic disorder – by his contemptuous attitude to everything Catalan, and his high-handed treatment of the Principality's laws and privileges.

The Conde Duque's schemes therefore seemed to the Catalans to mark a further stage in a long-standing Castilian conspiracy to abolish their liberties, and their behaviour became increasingly unco-operative as the Cortes continued. At a moment when a trade recession in the Mediterranean had sapped the credit and confidence of their merchants, they were not to be tempted by Olivares's plans for the establishment of trading companies, including a Levant Company with its headquarters at Barcelona; and the Conde Duque's pleas for a generous co-operation in the military ventures of the Monarchy fell on deaf ears. The Catalans' prime concern was to secure redress for past grievances and security for the future, and rumours that Olivares's ultimate aim was the establishment of a Monarchy with *un rey, una ley, y una moneda* – one king, one law, one coinage – merely stiffened their determination to resist. Moreover, Olivares was in too much of a hurry, and made the mistake of trying to force the pace in an assembly whose procedural methods made it an infinitely slow-moving body at the best of times. As a result, one obstruction followed another, until the Conde Duque decided that further attempts to extract a subsidy were for the moment doomed to failure. On 4 May, before the Catalans realized what was happen-ing, the King and his party were gone from Barcelona, leaving the Cortes still in session.

On arriving back in Madrid, Olivares professed himself pleased with the result of the King's visit to the Crown of Aragon. He had, it is true, obtained a subsidy of 1,080,000 ducats from the Valencians, which the King accepted as sufficient to maintain 1,000 infantrymen for fifteen years. The Aragonese, for their part, had voted double this sum. This meant that, for the first time since the end of Charles V's reign, Aragon and Valencia would be making a regular annual contribution to the Crown's finances. On the other hand, both States had stubbornly refused to allow the conscription of troops for foreign service, so that the Conde Duque's plans for securing military co-operation between the provinces had been frustrated; and Cata-lonia, the wealthiest of the three States, had voted neither men nor money.

Undeterred by these setbacks, the Conde Duque published in Castile on 24 July 1626 a decree proclaiming the official inauguration of the Union of Arms. This explained that the King had undertaken his arduous journey to the Crown of Aragon in order to secure assistance for Castile, and that, as an earnest of the many benefits to come, the Crown itself would pay one third of Castile's contribution out of its own revenues. On 8 May, two months before the publication of this decree, the Government had suspended all further minting of *vellón* coins for Castile – a somewhat belated action, in view of the fact that, in a country flooded with *vellón* coins, the premium on silver in terms of *vellón* had reached nearly 50 per cent. These two measures – the inauguration of the Union of Arms and the suspension of *vellón* minting – seemed to symbolize between them the completion of the first stage of the Conde Duque's reform programme, and to hold out hope of relief for Castile and the restoration of the Castilian economy. They were followed on 31 January 1627, twenty years after the Duke of Lerma's bankruptcy, by a suspension of all payments to the bankers. Olivares hoped by this device to end the Crown's expensive dependence on a small group of Italian financiers – a move for which the times seemed propitious, since he had found a group of Portuguese businessmen both able and willing to undertake some of the Crown's *asientos* at lower rates of interest. With these measures successfully achieved, the King was able to announce to the Council of State in 1627 a long list of successes obtained by his ministry during the first six years of the reign: victories abroad, reforms at home, and a dramatic change for the better in the Monarchy's fortunes. If many of the achievements were illusory, and some of Olivares's most cherished projects had been frustrated, this was not revealed to the world. At least in the Conde Duque's eyes, the reform programme was slowly gathering momentum, and under his leadership the shape of the Monarchy would eventually be transformed.

2. THE STRAIN OF WAR

In spite of the vaunted success of the new régime, the fact remained that unless really effective measures could be introduced to relieve Castile, the Monarchy as a whole would be confronted with disaster. The Union of Arms in its early stages was not likely to make any very significant contribution to the problem of imperial defence; and although, as a result of remedial measures in America, the treasure fleets were again bringing some 1,500,000 ducats a year, the principal cost of the Crown's expensive policies was still being borne by

Castile. In 1627–8 the condition of the Castilian economy suddenly deteriorated. The country found itself faced with a startling rise of prices in *vellón* currency, and the Government was assailed with complaints about the high cost of living. It is probable that the inflation of these years was caused primarily by bad harvests and by the scarcity of foreign goods arising from the partial closing of the frontiers since 1624; but it was exacerbated by the recent monetary policies of the Crown, which between 1621 and 1626 alone had minted nearly 20,000,000 ducats' worth of *vellón* coins. Olivares had hoped to deal with the problem of inflation by relatively painless methods. But drastic action became essential after the failure of an attempt at price-fixing and of an ingenious scheme for the withdrawal of the *vellón* coins in circulation, and on 7 August 1628 the Crown reduced the tale of *vellón* by 50 per cent.

The great deflation of 1628 brought heavy losses to private individuals, but instant relief to the royal treasury. Taken in conjunction with the suspension of payments to the *asentistas* in the previous year, it might have served as the starting-point for a sounder financial and economic policy, aimed at clearing the Crown of some of its debts and reducing its annual budgets. In terms of the international situation, the moment was particularly favourable. Hostilities with England had petered out since the failure of the ludicrous English attack on Cadiz in 1625; Habsburg arms were victorious in Germany, and Richelieu was fully occupied with the Huguenots in France. The years 1627–8 probably offered the last real chance for a programme of retrenchment and reform in the Spanish Monarchy.

The chance was tragically missed as the result of a series of unfortunate events in Italy. In December 1627 the Duke of Mantua died. The candidate with the best claim to succeed him was a Frenchman, the Duke of Nevers. A French-controlled Mantua might endanger Spain's hold over north Italy and Milan, and the Spanish governor of Milan, Don Gonzalo de Córdoba, sent his troops into Montferrat in March 1628. Without publicly committing himself, Olivares gave the Governor tacit encouragement by sending him supplies; and, almost before he realized what was happening, he found himself engaged in war with the French in Italy.

The Mantuan War of 1628–31 seems in retrospect the gravest blunder made by Olivares in the field of foreign policy. It re-aroused all the old European fears of Spanish aggression, and brought French troops across the Alps in support of their candidate's claim. It failed in its object of keeping a Frenchman off the ducal throne of Mantua, and made it virtually certain that sooner or later France and Spain would again be involved in open war. From this moment, the chances of European peace were sensibly diminished. Although France did not declare war on Spain until 1635, the years between 1628 and 1635 were passed under the lengthening shadow of Franco-Spanish conflict as Richelieu consolidated his system of European alliances and laid his plans to free France from the long-standing threat of Habsburg encirclement.

The Conde Duque therefore found himself committed to heavy expenditure in Italy, and to further large subsidies to the Emperor, who was shortly to see all his victories of the early 1620s rendered nugatory by the advance of the Swedes. The immediate resources on which Spain could draw for the struggle in Italy and Germany were now slender. The Council of Finance reported in August 1628 that it was 2,000,000 ducats short on the year's provisions, and in the next month disaster came with the capture by Piet Heyn of the Nueva España treasure fleet – the first time that the American silver had fallen into enemy hands. These emergencies made it vital to discover and exploit new sources of revenue, and to mobilize the Monarchy more effectively for war.

For some years it had been obvious to the Conde Duque that the existing administrative system was inadequate for this purpose. The cumbersome machinery of the Councils merely obstructed his designs, and gave excessive powers to men who had no sympathy for his reforming policies. Over the years he had gradually been building up a nucleus of 'new' men in whom he could place absolute confidence – men like José González, his secretary, and Jerónimo de Villanueva, the Protonotario of the Council of Aragon. He made some progress in undermining the Councils by appointing his own chosen agents to them, but it became increasingly apparent that the whole conciliar system was so heavily committed to the maintainence of the *status quo* that he could never get from the Councils the swift and effective decisions he so badly needed for the promotion of his policies. He therefore turned more and more to the use of special Juntas, which rapidly proliferated under his Government, and took over from the Councils much of their most important work. This was especially true of the so-called *Junta de Ejecución*, which was set up in 1634 and replaced the Council of State as the effective policy-making body in the Spanish administrative system. Dominated by Olivares himself, and filled with his own friends and servants, the *Junta de Ejecución* was ideally placed to carry through the Conde Duque's designs for a more intensive exploitation of the resources of the Monarchy.

The new men of the Olivares régime displayed both zeal and ingenuity in their efforts to find new sources of revenue. Since administrative difficulties and the opposition of the Cortes prevented any radical reorganization of the tax system in Castile, it was necessary to devise supplementary means of raising money. The year 1631 saw the introduction of a tax on the first year's income from offices known as the *media anata*, and also of a salt tax, which provoked a rising in Vizcaya. In 1632 the Conde Duque obtained the Pope's consent to a special grant from the clergy, and appropriated a year's income from the Archbishopric of Toledo. He also ordered the collection of a voluntary *donativo* to help save Flanders and Italy, nobles being expected to give 1,500 ducats and *caballeros* 150. In 1635 he confiscated half the yield of all *juros* held by natives, and the entire yield of those belonging to foreigners – a device he continued to employ in succeeding years. In 1637 he imposed a new tax in the form of stamped paper, which became obligatory for all legal and official documents. In the same year he seized 487,000 ducats in American silver, and gave the owners 'compensation' in the form of unwanted *juros*; and two years later, ignoring the repercussions on Seville's trade, he appropriated a further 1,000,000 ducats by the same device. He sold Crown rents, titles, and offices, and revived the old feudal obligations of the aristocracy, who found themselves expected to raise and equip infantry companies at their own expense. In consequence, although the nominal distinction between *hidalgos* and *pecheros* remained as strong as ever, the practical distinction tended to disappear, as the aristocracy found itself mulcted of its money by a succession of fiscal expedients from which it could find no way of escape.

In spite of the success of the Conde Duque's efforts to squeeze more money from Castile, he was as well aware as anyone that there was bound to come a moment when Castile would be squeezed dry. This meant that the Union of Arms must be made effective, and in particular that Catalonia and Portugal, which were allegedly the two wealthiest States in the peninsula, must be induced to play a part commensurate with their presumed resources. Both of these States seemed to Olivares dangerously 'separated' from the rest of the Monarchy. The Portuguese had stood aloof while Castile prepared relief expeditions in 1634 and 1635 for the recovery of Portugal's own possessions in Brazil, which had been lost to the Dutch since 1630. The Catalans had shown themselves even more uncooperative, for they had again refused to vote a subsidy when the King and Olivares returned to Barcelona in 1632 to continue the interrupted session of the Cortes. Obstructions placed by the city of Barcelona had brought the Cortes to a standstill, for reasons that seemed to Olivares unbearably trivial. It was now thirty-three years since the Catalans had voted their last subsidy to the King, and since then the Principality had been nothing but a source of concern and annoyance to the Spanish Crown. If, as the Conde Duque believed, Catalonia was a rich province with a population of over a million (nearly three times the real figure), then it was high time that it should come to the assistance of Castile and to the rescue of the royal treasury.

Although the Conde Duque squeezed a certain amount of money out of the cities of Lisbon and Barcelona by bullying and blackmail, his real need was for regular financial and military assistance from Catalonia and Portugal. It was difficult to achieve this without reorganizing their Governments, but administrative reform was practically impossible in Catalonia because the constitutions forbade the appointment of Castilians to any offices other than the viceroyalty. There were similar difficulties in Portugal, but slightly more scope for manoeuvre. Under Philip III Portugal had been governed by viceroys, but the system had proved unsatisfactory, and in 1621 the viceroyalty had been replaced by an administration of governors. This, however, had led to constant dissension in Lisbon. In 1634 Olivares found, as he believed, the answer to these difficulties by appointing a member of the royal family, Princess Margaret of Savoy, as Governess of Portugal. The Princess's appointment had the merit of meeting Portuguese complaints about royal neglect, and also made it possible to infiltrate a number of Castilians into the Portuguese administration under the guise of advisers.

The scheme was not a success. The Government in Lisbon turned itself into two rival camps of Castilians and Portuguese, whose constant bickering made effective administration impossible. Moreover, the Lisbon Government's fiscal policies soon ran into trouble. The Princess had been sent to Lisbon with instructions to obtain from the Portuguese a fixed annual levy of 500,000 *cruzados*, to be obtained by the consolidation of existing taxes and the introduction of certain new ones. Although these taxes were to be used to equip expeditions for the recovery of Portugal's overseas territories, this did nothing to reconcile a populace which had always hated the union with Castile; and in 1637 riots broke out in Évora and other towns. Fortunately for the Conde Duque, the riots failed to flare up into nation-wide revolution, in spite of Richelieu's promises of help to the Portuguese. Although the lower clergy enthusiastically supported the rioters, the aristocracy, with the Duke of Braganza at its head, held aloof, and the risings petered out. But the Évora riots were an ominous indication that Portugal might one day attempt to break loose from the Castilian connexion. The upper classes might for the present remain loyal to Madrid, but their loyalty was being subjected to a growing strain. The aristocracy felt itself deprived o offices and honours, and neglected by the King. The commercial classes in Lisbon and the coastal towns were beginning to find that the Union of the Crowns had outlasted its economic value. They had found compensation for the loss of their Far Eastern empire under Philip III by building up for themselves a new sugar empire in Brazil, and by exploiting the resources of Castile's American territories. But in recent years there had been increasing discrimination against Portuguese merchants in the Spanish colonies, and the military and naval power of the King of Spain had proved insufficient to save Brazil from the Dutch. The bonds that tied Portugal to Spain were therefore being dangerously weakened at the very moment when Olivares was bringing Portugal under increasing pressure in order to make it an effective partner in the Union of Arms.

It was, however, in Catalonia, rather than in Portugal, that Olivares first came to grief. The outbreak of war with France in May 1635 greatly enhanced the strategic importance of the Principality of

Catalonia, since it guarded the eastern half of Spain's border with the enemy. This made it all the more unfortunate that relations between the Catalans and Madrid were so bad, and that Olivares had failed to obtain a subsidy from the Catalans before the war broke out. He was now in the delicate position of having to fight the war from a disaffected frontier province of whose loyalty he could no longer be entirely sure. At the same time, he needed the assistance of the Catalans to supplement the diminished manpower of Castile, and to contribute to the royal revenues. This was all the more necessary now that the war with France had again increased the Crown's expenditure. For the financial year October 1636 to October 1637, for instance, the Council of Finance had attempted to arrange the following provisions:

	Escudos
For Flanders	4,384,000
For Germany	1,500,000
For Milan	2,500,000
To be provided in Spain	2,000,000
For the fleet	500,000
For the royal households (in the event of a military expedition by the King)	64,000
For ambassadors	150,000

In addition to this, a further 2,000,000 *escudos* were required for the royal households, the ordinary expenses of the fleet, and the frontier garrisons.

These figures provide some indication of why it seemed impossible to Olivares to leave the Catalans alone: unable to raise more than half this sum from his ordinary and extraordinary revenues, he could afford to neglect no opportunity for attempting to extract a few more hundred thousand ducats wherever there seemed the remotest chance of success. Since all direct approaches to the Catalans had proved abortive, he began to toy with ideas of obtaining their assistance by more covert means. In 1637, when French troops crossed the Catalan frontier, the Catalans themselves had been slow in sending help; in 1638, when the town of Fuenterrabía in Guipúzcoa was besieged by the French, Catalonia alone of the States of the Crown of Aragon had refused all military aid. Determined to make the Catalans concern themselves, 'as up to now they have apparently not been concerned, with the general affairs of the Monarchy and of these kingdoms', he decided in 1639 that the projected Spanish attack on France should be undertaken from the Catalan border, so that the Catalans would find themselves involved in the war whether they liked it or not.

In the event, it was the French army which entered Catalonia in the early summer of 1639, capturing the frontier fortress of Salses on 19 July. The fall of Salses gave the Conde Duque a useful pretext for pushing the Catalans a little further into the Union of Arms. The Count of Santa Coloma, the native viceroy of Catalonia, was ordered by Madrid to mobilize the Principality for war, so that it could assist the royal army in Rosellón (Roussillon) to recover the captured fortress. During the autumn of 1639 the viceroy and the local ministers did their best to induce the adult male population of Catalonia to turn out for the war, and relentlessly harried the country into sending supplies to the front. For six long months the siege went on, amidst such foul conditions that many troops, both Catalan and non-Catalan, deserted the ranks. Furious at the desertions, Olivares ordered the royal ministers in the Principality to ignore the constitutions of Catalonia whenever the well-being of the army was at stake, on the grounds that the supreme law of defence outweighed all lesser laws. The unconstitutional proceedings of the ministers confirmed Catalan suspicions about the Conde Duque's ultimate intentions, and made the Principality more and more reluctant to co-operate in the Salses campaign. Hatred of Madrid, of the viceroy, and of the vice-regal administration mounted throughout Catalonia during the autumn and early winter of 1639, as royal orders became harsher and the country was constantly pressed to provide more men and more supplies for the Salses army. As a result, when the French finally surrendered the fortress on 6 January 1640, the Principality was in a dangerously explosive mood. The aristocracy, who had suffered heavy casualties during the campaign, hated and despised the Count of Santa Coloma for putting the orders of Madrid before the interests of his colleagues and compatriots. Barcelona and the towns had been finally alienated from a Government which had done nothing but attempt to extract money from them over a period of twenty years. The peasantry had suffered severely from the confiscation of their animals and crops. Increasingly, the Principality was listening to the appeals of the clergy to hold fast to its historic liberties, and was finding a responsive leadership in the Catalan *Diputació* headed by a vigorous cleric, Pau Claris, canon of the cathedral chapter of Urgel. By the beginning of 1640, therefore, Olivares, who had won a campaign, was on the point of losing a province – a danger of which he apparently remained unaware. For all his actions at the beginning of 1640 suggest that he believed himself to be close at last to the achievement of one of his most cherished ambitions: the establishment of the Union of Arms.

3. 1640

By 1640 the Conde Duque had come to see the Union of Arms as the best, and perhaps the only, hope for the Monarchy's survival. After early successes in the war with France, of which the most spectacular was the Cardenal Infante's invasion of France from Flanders in 1636, Spain had suffered a number of serious reverses. In 1637 the Dutch recaptured Breda, whose surrender to Spínola in 1625 had been immortalized by Velázquez. In December 1638 Bernard of Weimar took Breisach – a far more serious loss, since it meant that the Spanish road from Milan to Brussels was cut, and that the Spanish armies in the Netherlands could only be reinforced by sea through the English Channel. Then, in October 1639, Admiral Tromp defeated the fleet of Don Antonio de Oquendo at the Battle of the Downs, destroying at a single blow both the navy on which Olivares had expended so much effort, and the chances of sending relief to the Cardenal Infante in the Netherlands. On top of this came the failure of the combined Spanish-Portuguese armada which set out from Lisbon in September 1638 to attempt the reconquest of Brazil. After spending a fruitless year off Bahia, it was brought to battle by a considerably smaller Dutch fleet on 12 January 1640. At the end of four days of inconclusive fighting, its Portuguese commander, the Count of La Torre, abandoned his attempt to attack Pernambuco, and allowed the armada to disperse to the West Indies, leaving the control of the Brazilian seas in the hands of the Dutch.

These reverses filled the Conde Duque with gloom. For years he had been struggling to scrape together men, and money, and ships, and all his efforts seemed doomed to disappointment. He placed much of the blame for these defeats on the inadequacies of the Spanish commanders. Almost from the beginning of his ministry he had been complaining of what he called the *falta de cabezas* – the lack of leaders. It was because of his belief that the Spanish nobility was failing in its duties of leadership that he had sponsored the founding in 1625 of the Colegio Imperial at Madrid, an academy for the sons of nobles run by the Jesuits and designed to provide, in addition to a liberal education, practical instruction in mathematics, the sciences, and the art of war. But the Colegio Imperial failed in its principal aim. No new generation of military commanders appeared to take the place of Spínola and the Duke of Feria, and the higher Castilian aristocracy proved a constant disappointment to the Conde Duque. By 1640 he no longer bothered to conceal his contempt for the grandees, and they in response turned their backs on a Court where nothing awaited them but gibes from the Favourite and endless appeals to their pockets.

The absence of leaders was one of the principal reasons for Olivares's increasing anxiety to obtain a peace settlement. It was particularly with this in mind that he wrote in March 1640 in a memorandum for the King: 'God wants us to make peace, for He is depriving us visibly and absolutely of all the means of war.' But peace was not easy to obtain. As early as 1629 he had made moves for a truce with the Dutch, and by 1635 he was offering to close the Scheldt and hand over Breda, as long as the Dutch would give back Pernambuco. But the Dutch were adamant in their refusal to surrender their conquests in Brazil, and Olivares in turn could not afford to give up Brazilian territory for fear of the repercussions in Portugal. He had also begun secret negotiations with France almost as soon as the war broke out, but as long as Spain was winning victories he pitched his demands too high, while as soon as Spain began to suffer defeats and he moderated his demands, Richelieu lost interest in the immediate conclusion of a settlement.

Yet if peace was unattainable, it was becoming increasingly difficult to prosecute the war. Castile was by now so denuded of men that the levies were pitiful affairs, and it was becoming quite impossible to keep the armies up to strength. Moreover, the economic position was by now exceptionally grave, for Spain's last real source of economic strength – the trading system between Seville and

America – was failing. Olivares's repeated confiscations of silver remittances and his constant interference with the American trade had produced the inevitable result. The merchants had lost confidence; Sevillian shipping was in decay; and although the silver supplies were still coming regularly to the Crown – at least until 1640 when no silver fleet arrived – the whole system of credit and confidence by which Seville had for so long shored up the Spanish Monarchy was gradually crumbling. With Castile exhausted and America failing, the principal foundations of Spanish imperialism over the past hundred years were slowly giving way.

The gravity of the situation inspired Olivares with the boldness of despair. There was still, he believed, hope – not of out-and-out victory, but of a stalemate which would induce a no less exhausted France to come to terms. But this required an unrelenting pressure on the French, such as would only be possible if every part of the Monarchy – Catalonia and Portugal, Flanders, and Peru – joined forces in a supreme co-operative endeavour. The Catalans, for instance, must contribute troops for use in Italy, and they must prepare themselves for a fresh campaign along the French frontier. If the constitutions stood in the way of this, then the constitutions must be changed, and surely there could be no more favourable moment than the present, when a royal army was actually stationed in the Principality. The Conde Duque therefore arranged that the army which had been fighting the Salses campaign should be billeted in Catalonia until the next campaigning season; and under the shadow of the army he planned to hold a new session of the Catalan Cortes, which was to be used solely for the amendment of the more obnoxious constitutions.

The proposed Catalan Cortes of 1640 never met. The Catalan towns and peasantry were hardly in the mood to support the burden of billeting a foreign army, while the troops were in no frame of mind to put up with the second best. During February and March of 1640 troops and civilians clashed in many parts of the Principality, and the Count of Santa Coloma proved quite unequal to the task of keeping order. The Conde Duque responded to the situation as he had responded in the autumn of the previous year – by harsh threats and increasingly imperious orders to the viceroy to see that one of

Spain's last remaining veteran armies was properly billeted at whatever cost to the native population. At the beginning of March, on hearing that the clashes over billeting were continuing, he ordered Santa Coloma to arrest one of the *Diputats*, Francesc de Tamarit, and to have a secret inquiry made into the activities of Claris. But the arrest of Tamarit only made a serious situation worse. The peasantry were banding together against the *tercios*, and the towns and villages of northern Catalonia were in a highly inflammatory mood. At the end of April a royal official was burnt to death at Santa Coloma de Farnés, and the *tercios* were ordered to billet in the town and the surrounding countryside to punish the population for their crime. On reaching Santa Coloma de Farnés they could not be prevented from sacking it and setting it on fire. Their action roused the entire countryside to arms. Encouraged by the Bishop of Gerona's excommunication of the troops, a growing peasant army bore down on the *tercios*, which succeeded in making a skilful retreat towards the safety of the coast with the rebel forces following close on their heels. Finding themselves balked of their prey, the rebels then moved southwards, and on 22 May a group of them made an entry into Barcelona itself, headed straight for the prison, and released the arrested *Diputat*.

It was only when the news of the release of Tamarit reached the Conde Duque that he began to realize that he was faced with open rebellion. Until now he had tended to let himself be guided in his handling of the Principality's affairs by the Protonotario, Jerónimo de Villanueva, a character as antipathetic to the Catalans as they were to him. The Protonotario had encouraged him to believe that his Catalan policies were on the verge of success and that the Principality would shortly become a useful member of the Spanish Monarchy; but now he was suddenly confronted with evidence that the policies were leading to disaster. To some ministers it seemed that the rebels' entry into Barcelona provided Madrid with the necessary pretext for using the army to punish the Principality and to strip it of its obnoxious laws and liberties, but the Conde Duque realized that it was essential to set the problem of Catalonia into the wider context of the affairs of the Monarchy as a whole. He had to think of the repercussions in Aragon, Valencia, and Portugal of a frontal assault on Catalan liberties, and he had to bear in mind the gravity of the military situation in Germany and Italy, the exhaustion of Spain's armies, and the danger at such a time of holding down a province of the Monarchy by force of arms. Realizing that there could at this stage be no simple and clear-cut solution to the intractable problem of the Catalans, he reversed his policies of the preceding months, and ordered on 27 May that steps should immediately be taken to conciliate and pacify the Catalans before the situation got entirely out of hand.

The Conde Duque's change of policy came too late. The rebellion in Catalonia was rapidly acquiring a momentum of its own, inspired by hatred not only of the troops and the royal officials, but also of the rich and of all those in authority. The rebel bands moved from town to town, stirring up the countryside in their wake. Seeing that his authority was gone and that law and order were everywhere collapsing, the unfortunate Count of Santa Coloma begged the town councillors of Barcelona to close the city gates against the casual labourers who always flocked into the city at the beginning of June to hire themselves out for harvesting. But the councillors were either unable or unwilling to agree; the harvesters made their usual entry; and on Corpus day, 7 June 1640, they inevitably became involved in a brawl. The brawl soon acquired the dimensions of a riot, and within a few hours the mob was hounding down the royal ministers and sacking their houses. The viceroy himself had moved to the dockyards for safety, but a group of rioters forced its way in, and Santa Coloma was caught and struck down as he attempted to escape from his pursuers along the rocky beach.

The murder of Santa Coloma left such authority as remained in Catalonia in the hands of the *Diputació* and of the city councillors and aristocracy of Barcelona. Although they managed to shepherd the rebels out of Barcelona itself, it was impossible to maintain control over a movement which was spreading through the Principality, wreaking vengeance on all those of whom the rebels disapproved. Stunned as he was by the viceroy's murder, Olivares still seems to have hoped that the rebellion could be checked without recourse to arms, but the new viceroy, the Catalan Duke of Cardona, died on 22 July without being able to halt the drift to anarchy. Almost at the same moment the rebels gained control of the vital port of Tortosa. The loss of Tortosa made it finally clear that troops would have to be sent into Catalonia, in spite of the obvious risk of war in a province bordering on France; and Olivares pressed ahead with the formation of an army for use against the rebels.

The Conde Duque believed that the Catalans were still too loyal to call on the French for help, but he underestimated the determination and vigour of Claris, and the hatred of his Government and of Castile which his policies had inspired in every class of Catalan society. Some time before, Claris had already made tentative overtures to the French, and Richelieu, who had shown himself well aware of the possibilities of causing trouble both in Catalonia and Portugal, declared himself ready to offer help. During the autumn of 1640 Claris and Olivares stood face to face, Claris hoping to avoid the necessity of committing the Principality to an open break with Madrid, and Olivares equally hoping to avoid the necessity of using an army against the Catalans. 'In the midst of all our troubles,' wrote the Conde Duque to the Cardenal Infante in October, 'the Catalan is the worst we have ever had, and my heart admits of no consolation that we are entering an action in which, if our army kills, it kills a vassal of His Majesty, and if they kill, they kill a vassal and a soldier. ... Without reason or occasion they have thrown themselves into as complete a rebellion as Holland. ...'

But worse was to come. The revolt of the Catalans was bound to have its repercussions in Portugal, where there was a growing determination to cut the country's links with Castile. Uneasily aware that he could never be sure of Portugal as long as the Duke of Braganza and the higher Portuguese nobility remained at home, Olivares had ingeniously thought to kill two birds with one stone by ordering the Portuguese nobility to turn out with the army that was to be sent into Catalonia. This order meant that, if Portugal was ever to break free from Castile, it must act quickly before Braganza was out of the country. Plans for a revolution were laid in the autumn of 1640, probably with the connivance of Richelieu, who is believed to have sent funds to the conspirators in Lisbon. On 1 December, while the royal army under the command of the Marquis of los Vélez was gingerly advancing into Catalonia, the Portuguese conspirators put their plan into action. The guards at the royal palace in Lisbon were overwhelmed, Miguel de Vasconcellos – Olivares's confidant and principal agent in the government of Portugal – was assassinated, and Princess Margaret was escorted to the frontier. Since there were virtually no Castilian troops in Portugal, there was nothing to prevent the rebels from taking over the country, and proclaiming the Duke of Braganza king as John IV.

The news of the Portuguese Revolution, which took a week to reach Madrid, forced Olivares and his colleagues to undertake an urgent reappraisal of their policies. Simultaneous revolts in the east and west of the Spanish peninsula threatened the Monarchy with total disaster. Peace was essential: peace with the Dutch, peace with the Catalans. But although the Conde Duque now offered favourable terms to the Catalans, and the upper classes in Catalonia seemed predisposed to accept them as the army of los Vélez moved closer and closer to Barcelona, the populace was in no mood for surrender. It rioted in Barcelona on 24 December, hunting down 'traitors' with a savagery surpassing that of Corpus; and Claris, faced on one side with the fury of the mob, and on the other with the advancing Castilian army, took the only course open to him. On 16 January 1641 he announced that Catalonia had become an independent republic under French protection. Then on 23 January, finding that the French were not satisfied with this, he withdrew his plans for a republican system of government, and formally declared the allegiance of Catalonia to the King of France, 'as in the time of Charlemagne, with a contract to observe our constitutions'. The French were now prepared to give the Catalans full military support; the French agent, Duplessis Besançon, hastily organized the defence of Barcelona, and on 26 January a combined French and Catalan force met the army of los Vélez on the hill of Montjuich outside the walls of Barcelona. Los Vélez unaccountably gave the order to retreat, and the last chance of bringing the revolt of the Catalans to a speedy end was lost.

In September 1640, before the outbreak of the Portuguese revolt, Olivares had written in a long memorandum: 'This year can undoubtedly be considered the most unfortunate that this Monarchy has ever experienced.' The defeat of los Vélez at Montjuich set the seal on the disasters of 1640, confirming in the most conclusive manner that there could be no going back on the events of that fatal year. For 1640 had, in fact, marked the dissolution of the economic and political system on which the Monarchy had depended for so long. It had seen the disruption and decline of the Sevillian commercial

system which had given the Spanish Crown its silver and its credit;
and the disruption also of the political organization of the Spanish
peninsula, inherited from the Catholic Kings and transmitted unchanged by Philip II to his descendants. This political disruption was
itself the outcome of the crisis of the reign of Philip III – the crisis of
the Atlantic economy as the New World shrank back into itself, and
the crisis of the Castilian economy, undermined by long years of
abuse and by the strain of unending war. In attempting to exploit the
resources of the peripheral provinces of the peninsula, Olivares had
simply attempted to redress the balance that had been tilting more
and more against Castile, but he did it at a moment when the economies of Portugal and Catalonia were themselves being subjected to
growing pressure, and when Castile no longer had the strength to
impose its will by an assertion of military power. As a result, he had
imposed an excessive strain on the fragile constitutional structure of
the Spanish Monarchy, and precipitated the very disaster that it was
most necessary to avoid.

From the moment of defeat at Montjuich, Olivares knew that the
game was up. He had neither the money nor the men to prosecute
effectively the war abroad, while simultaneously attempting to
suppress two revolutions at home. But for all his despair, he was not
the man to surrender without a struggle, and he made superhuman
efforts to gather together fresh armies and to husband the Crown's
diminished resources. The unbroken succession of defeats, however,
had gravely weakened his position, and had given a new boldness to
his many enemies. Throughout Castile he was hated as a tyrant, but
the real danger came less from the populace than from the grandees.
In the summer of 1641 his agents unearthed a conspiracy by two great
Andalusian nobles, the Duke of Medina-Sidonia and the Marquis of
Ayamonte, both of them members of his own family of Guzmán.
Medina-Sidonia was the brother of the new Queen of Portugal, and
it seems that plans were being made not only to remove the Conde
Duque and to restore an aristocratic chamber to the Castilian Cortes,
but to follow the example of Portugal and turn Andalusia into an
independent State.

In spite of the failure of Medina-Sidonia's conspiracy, the nobles
continued to plot. Conditions in Castile were terrible, for in February
1641 the Conde Duque had begun tampering with the coinage, and

vellón prices rose to dizzy heights, with the premium on silver in terms of *vellón* reaching 200 per cent in certain instances before a deflationary decree in September 1642 again brought prices crashing down. Yet for all the misfortunes both at home and abroad, the King was still unwilling to part with his Favourite. In April 1642 he and the Conde Duque left for the front in Aragon, where the army met with no more success than before their arrival. During September French forces completed the conquest of Roussillon by capturing Perpignan, and in October the army commanded by the Conde Duque's cousin and close friend, the Marquis of Leganés, was defeated in its attempts to recapture Lérida. Back in Madrid, the Count of Castrillo, who had been entrusted with the government, was working away to undermine the Conde Duque's influence, and when the King returned to Court at the end of the year it was clear that the Conde Duque's days were numbered. On 17 January 1643 the King at last took the decision that had been so long awaited: Olivares was given leave to retire to his estates, and on 23 January he left Madrid for exile, never again to return to the capital where he had reigned for twenty-two years. Stunned by his dismissal, he still sought to vindicate his policies, which found an eloquent exposition in a tract entitled the *Nicandro*, written to his instructions and under his inspiration. But nothing now could set the clock back. Exiled farther away, to his sister's palace at Toro, he died on 22 July 1645 under the shadow of madness. So passed the first and the last ruler of Habsburg Spain who had the breadth of vision to devise plans on a grand scale for the future of a world-wide Monarchy: a statesman whose capacity for conceiving great designs was matched only by his consistent incapacity for carrying them through to a successful conclusion.

4. DEFEAT AND SURVIVAL

At the time of Olivares's fall from power the Spanish Monarchy seemed to have no future – only a past. But how much of the past could still be preserved was itself an open question. The death of Richelieu, two months before the disgrace of Olivares, had been followed by the death of Louis XIII early in 1643. These changes in France held out hopes of a general change for the better in the international situation, but it was doubtful whether Spain now had the strength to exploit the new possibilities offered by the advent of a regency government in Paris. The defeat of the Spanish infantry at Rocroi on 19 May 1643 seemed to symbolize the downfall of the military system which had sustained Spanish power for so long. The country now lacked both the armies and the leaders to turn the new international situation to account.

The years after 1643 saw a careful dismantling of the Conde Duque's system of government. The Juntas were abolished; the Councils recovered their powers; and the Conde Duque's principal lieutenant, Jerónimo de Villanueva, after steadily losing ground at Court, was arrested on suspicion of heresy by officers of the Inquisition in 1644. There was a general desire to forget the nightmare years of the Olivares régime, and Philip IV showed himself responsive to the mood of the moment by announcing that he intended in future to govern by himself without the aid of a *Privado*. The King did his best: he attended in person the meetings of the Council of State and dispatched business with commendable promptitude and efficiency. But although the spirit was willing the flesh was weak, in spite of the comfort and support which Philip derived in his solitary labours from the correspondence of a remarkable nun, Sor María de Ágreda, who gave him at once spiritual consolation and much sensible political advice; and gradually the power slipped from the King's hands into those of a discreet courtier, Don Luis de Haro, the nephew of Olivares.

It was typical of Haro that he succeeded in making people forget whose nephew he was. All things to all men, modest and friendly, Don Luis shunned the title of *Privado* while discreetly exercising its functions. A friend to the King where Olivares was his master, he had no difficulty in remaining in power until his death in 1661; and if his retention of power represented the triumph of mediocrity, this was perhaps not entirely unfortunate after two decades of heroics.

The immediate task of Don Luis was to steer the Monarchy back to peace, without letting it lose any more of its possessions in the process. During 1644 delegates for a peace conference had been arriving at the Westphalian towns of Münster and Osnabrück, but it was clear that the Spanish delegates were in a painfully weak position. The military situation continued to deteriorate, and at home Don Luis and his colleagues were struggling hard to avert another bankruptcy, which finally came twenty years after that of Olivares, in October 1647. But Spain's principal delegate at Westphalia, the Count of Peñaranda, was able to play on growing Dutch fears of the rising power of France, and succeeded in frightening the Dutch by revealing a secret offer made by Richelieu's successor, Cardinal Mazarin, to return Catalonia to Spain in exchange for Flanders. He also profited from the fact that the question of Brazil, which had always in the past prevented an understanding with the Dutch, had ceased to be of concern to Spain once Portugal was lost. By 3 January 1648 the general terms of a separate Spanish-Dutch treaty were agreed, and these formed the basis of the Treaty of Münster of 24 October 1648. By the Treaty, Spain recognized at last what had long been a fact – the independence and sovereignty of the United Provinces. After seventy years or more of conflict which, more than any other external event, had sapped the power and resources of Castile, the Government of Spain now bowed to the inevitable and accepted its inability to put an end to the revolt of the Netherlands. But the war with France continued.

The years 1647–8, which saw the completion of a peace settlement with the Dutch, saw also the narrow escape of the Spanish Monarchy from total dissolution. Once Catalonia and Portugal had revolted, there was every chance that the other provinces of the Monarchy would sooner or later make an effort to follow their example. As early as the autumn of 1640 the English ambassador at Madrid had written home that 'Aragon and Valencia begin to waver', but in spite of Catalan appeals for help, they were as reluctant to throw in their lot with the Catalans, as the Catalans had been to assist the Valencian *Germanías* in 1520, or the Aragonese in 1591. It was one of the greatest fortunes of the House of Austria that the States of the Crown of Aragon, while individually difficult and intractable, consistently failed to come to each other's assistance in emergencies, and to present a united front. This failure, which reflects the intense parochialism of Catalans, Aragonese, and Valencians in the years after the Union of the Crowns, was possibly the salvation of the dynasty in the most dangerous decade of the Monarchy's existence – the 1640s. Had Aragon and Valencia rallied to the help of the Catalans, the Iberian peninsula of the mid-seventeenth century would have reverted to its condition in the mid-fifteenth, divided between the three power blocs of Portugal, Castile, and the Crown of Aragon.

The danger in the mid-1640s came not from further movements in the Crown of Aragon, but from the former Aragonese possessions in Italy. In the summer of 1647 Sicily and Naples, exasperated by the constant stream of fiscal demands, revolted against the government of their Spanish viceroys. It seemed at this juncture that everything was lost, and that, with a little encouragement from the French, the Monarchy would in fact disintegrate into its component parts. Cardinal Mazarin, however, failed to exploit his opportunity to the full, and the Sicilian and Neapolitan movements were both suppressed. In August 1648 a plot was discovered which would have made the Duke of Híjar king of an independent Aragon with Mazarin's help, but by this time the chances of success were slight. The Monarchy had held together sufficiently during the crisis of 1647 for Híjar's conspiracy to seem no more than what in reality it was – a foolhardy adventure by a bankrupt grandee.

The ability of the Spanish Monarchy to weather the storm of the mid-1640s suggests that its structure possessed hidden reserves of strength which revealed themselves only in an emergency. On the whole, this is perhaps too flattering an explanation. By a paradox which would have delighted the heart of González de Cellorigo, such strength as it possessed derived from its weakness. As a result of the dynasty's consistent failure to establish throughout the Monarchy that unity and uniformity which it was Olivares's ambition to introduce, the provinces had retained under the government of the House of Austria a degree of autonomy far greater than the subordination of the viceregal governments to Madrid would suggest. Even if viceroys were expected to translate royal orders into action, they had to rely on provincial aristocracies and local governmental and municipal authorities to make the orders effective. Inevitably this meant that government consisted of a series of compromises, worked out between the provincial governing class, the viceroys, and the Councils in Madrid. As such, it may often have been inefficient and unsatisfactory, but only rarely was it actively oppressive. Viceroys came and viceroys went, but provincial aristocracies endured, yielding a little here, gaining a little there, and generally defending themselves with a considerable degree of success against any vigorous attempts by a viceregal government to extend the boundaries of royal power. Consequently, although Sicilian or Aragonese nobles might perpetually grumble about the extent to which they were neglected by the King, they were not on the whole prepared to translate words into deeds. Government by Madrid might seem intolerable, but the alternative could well be infinitely worse.

This was confirmed by the experience of Catalonia. The Catalan aristocracy was as discontented as the rest of the nation by 1640, and was duly swept into revolution along with everybody else. But it soon became clear that a revolution which had originally begun as a movement to free Catalonia from the domination of Madrid, possessed social overtones which threatened to subject the aristocracy to the rule of the mob. All the hatreds that had racked Catalonia in the preceding decades – the hatred of the poor for the rich, and of the unemployed rural population for the *bourgeois* and aristocratic landlord – came to the surface in the summer and autumn of 1640 as the traditional forces of order were weakened or removed. When Claris died shortly after the victory of Montjuich, no one remained with sufficient prestige to restrain the many anarchic elements in Catalan society. Under a French-controlled government, the Principality fell apart, split into warring factions by social antagonisms and family feuds; and one by one the nobles slipped over the border into Aragon, finding that the government of Philip IV was on the whole to be preferred to the government of a clique of politicians taking their orders from the King of France.

Don Luis de Haro was shrewd enough to turn Catalonia's internal dissensions to account, at a time when the French Government, under the impulse of the Italian-born Mazarin, was directing its attention away from Catalonia to Italy. As the French military effort in Catalonia weakened and the schisms in Catalan society widened, hope revived in Madrid that the Catalans could again be brought back into the fold. Slowly, the feeble armies of Philip IV advanced into the Principality whose powers of resistance were terribly weakened by hunger and then by plague. Mazarin, preoccupied with the Fronde, was unable to send adequate help, and by the beginning of 1651 the French position was everywhere crumbling. In July of that year the army of the Marquis of Mortara based on Lérida joined forces with the Tarragona army commanded by Philip IV's bastard son, Don Juan José de Austria, and the combined armies advanced on Barcelona. They were too weak to undertake a direct assault on the city, but the capital was invested and gradually starved out. Finally, on 13 October 1652, Barcelona surrendered. Three months later, Philip IV conceded a general pardon, and promised to observe all the Principality's laws and liberties as they had existed at the time of his accession to the throne. After twelve years of separation Catalonia was once again a part of Spain.

The failure of the Catalans to cut permanently loose from Madrid reflects both an original uncertainty in their aims at the start of the revolution, and a continuing failure to create a sense of national unity and purpose that transcended traditional social divisions. Their experience, which was shared by the Sicilians and the Neapolitans, does much to explain the unexpected resilience of the Spanish Monarchy at its moments of greatest peril. As long as the Spanish Crown left provincial liberties intact, and acted as a bulwark of the existing social order, loyalty to the King of Spain among the upper classes of provincial societies was not without its practical advantages. Once Olivares and the Protonotario had disappeared from the scene, and Philip IV had made it abundantly clear that the Principality could keep its old constitutional structure, the Catalan ruling class had little inducement to continue a rebellion which had weakened the barriers against social upheaval, and had exchanged the inefficient tyranny of Castile for the far more authoritarian government of the King of France.

The one exception to this picture of the meek return of a series of prodigal sons was Portugal. There were various reasons for the persistence and success of the Portuguese in their revolt. They had been united to Castile for only sixty years – too short a period for the population to reconcile itself to a permanent association with its traditional enemies, the Castilians. Moreover, Portugal had in the Duke of Braganza a ready-made king, whereas the Catalans, under the leadership of their *Diputació*, had a system of government which demanded a high degree of political maturity for effective functioning, and was too republican in character to inspire foreign confidence in an intensely monarchical age. Portugal also had geographical and economic advantages that Catalonia lacked. It was close enough to France to receive French help, while sufficiently far away to avoid falling under French domination. Where Catalonia remained confined to the world of the Mediterranean, Portugal belonged to the more dynamic world of the Atlantic, and had a vigorous mercantile community with strong business and financial ties with the countries of the north. It also had, in Brazil, the remnants of an empire, which, if it could once be recovered from the Dutch, might provide a firm basis for a new prosperity. Against all expectations, the Dutch failed to retain their hold on Brazil: after the departure of Prince John Maurice in 1644, the government of the country passed into less competent hands, the Dutch West Indies Company failed to mobilize adequate support in Amsterdam, and by 1654 Brazil was once again a Portuguese possession.

The recovery of Brazil was the salvation of Portugal. The sugar and slave trades provided it with resources for continuing the struggle with Spain, and helped to stimulate foreign interest in its survival as an independent State. In spite of the weakness of Castile, however, Portugal's survival by no means appeared at the time to be a foregone conclusion. Much depended on the international situation and the continuing help of France, and by the mid-1650s the Franco-Spanish war was at last drawing to a close. It would have been impossible for Castile to have continued the war for so long had not the revolts and disorders in France seriously weakened French arms and reduced the campaigns to military charades. As it was, the weakness of France gave Spain certain transient successes which seem so to have affected Don Luis de Haro that he unaccountably missed the opportunity to conclude a remarkably favourable peace treaty in 1656. The war therefore dragged on for another three years, during which the hostility of Cromwell's England again tilted the balance against Spain; and it was only in 1659, during protracted negotiations on the Isle of Pheasants on the River Bidasoa, that a Franco-Spanish peace settlement was finally agreed.

The terms of the Treaty of the Pyrenees were not as favourable as those which Mazarin had offered in 1656; but considering Spain's desperate weakness and the number of defeats it had suffered during the preceding twenty years it escaped surprisingly lightly. Its territorial losses were few: in the north, Artois; along the Catalan-French frontier, the county of Rosellón and part of Cerdaña – regions which Ferdinand the Catholic had recovered from France in 1493. Final arrangements were also made for the marriage of Philip IV's daughter María Teresa to Louis XIV: the dowry was fixed at 500,000 *escudos*, full payment being a condition of María Teresa's renunciation of all future claims to the Spanish throne. But if the terms of the peace settlement seemed remarkably moderate, the peace as a whole marks the formal passing of Spain's century-old pretensions to European hegemony. Already in 1648 it had made peace with the Dutch rebels, and had parted company with the Austrian branch of the Habsburgs, who had signed a separate peace with France. Now in 1659, in making its own peace with France, the Spanish Monarchy tacitly recognized the failure of its European ambitions, and turned its back on the continent whose destinies it had for so long attempted to control.

With the French war over, Philip IV could at last hope to realize his ambition of recovering Portugal for the Spanish Crown. But the Portuguese war was to bring the King nothing but further disillusionment during the last twilight years of his reign. With infinite labour, three Spanish armies were assembled under the command of Don Juan José de Austria, the Duke of Osuna, and the Marquis of Viana. Considering the disastrous financial circumstances of the Monarchy, this itself was no mean feat. The ability of the Spanish Crown to keep afloat financially during the second half of the reign of Philip IV is in fact something of a miracle at a time when miracles were so earnestly prayed for, and so disappointingly few. After the bankruptcy of 1647 only six years passed before the next bankruptcy in 1653. The bankruptcy itself was no cause for surprise. The Crown's expenses had been continuing to run at 11,000,000 or 12,000,000 ducats a year, of which half were in silver and the other half in *vellón*. José González, a survivor from Olivares's team of ministers and now president of the Council of Finance, returned to the Conde Duque's theme that the *millones* should be abolished, and proposed instead a flour tax, such as had been advocated in the 1620s. But again the opposition was too strong; the *millones* remained, and the Crown continued to employ the usual expedients like manipulation of the coinage and the sale of offices, which once again failed to produce the necessary income. The unfortunate bankers were, as usual, compensated in *juros*, and the dreary cycle began to repeat itself once more. In 1654 it was estimated that, out of the 27,000,000 ducats nominal annual income of the Crown, only 6,000,000 actually found their way to the treasury, 'and on many days the household of the King and Queen lack everything, including bread'. With the entry of England into the war, the Spanish coast was blockaded, the treasure fleet was captured in 1657, and for two years no silver arrived from the Indies. The Peace of the Pyrenees therefore came just in time, at a moment when it was possible to send only 1,000,000 ducats a year to Flanders instead of the usual 3,000,000, and when scarcely a banker remained who was willing to become involved in the financial affairs of the Spanish Crown.

The conclusion of peace with France brought some financial relief, but the new campaign in Portugal was expected to cost 5,000,000 ducats a year. There was no hope of raising this money from new taxes, since everything that could be taxed was already taxed, and further imposts were bound to be self-defeating. In the end, the Council of Finance solved its problem by issuing a new coinage known as *moneda ligada* whose silver content would give it a higher intrinsic value than *vellón*. By minting 10,000,000 ducats, it was hoped to have 6,000,000 free for the Portuguese campaign. This cynical monetary manoeuvre merely added to the instability of Castilian prices, and proved in the end to have been undertaken in vain. The Spanish armies in Portugal were badly equipped and badly led, and the Portuguese enjoyed the assistance of England and of France, which sent troops under the command of Marshal Schomberg. The army of Don Juan José was defeated by Schomberg at Amexial in 1663; and a new army, scraped together with enormous difficulty, was defeated at Villaviciosa in 1665.

At Villaviciosa Spain lost her last chance of recovering Portugal. Eventually, on 13 February 1668, she accepted the inevitable and formally recognized the country's independence. But Philip IV himself had not lived to see this final humiliation, for he died three months after the battle of Villaviciosa, on 17 September 1665. His later years had been as melancholy as those of his Monarchy, for whose misfortunes he considered his own sins to blame. His first wife, Elizabeth of Bourbon, had died in 1644, and his only son, Baltasar Carlos, in 1646. His second marriage in 1649, to his niece, Mariana of Austria, brought him two sickly sons, of whom the second, Charles, by some miracle survived to succeed his father at the

THE COLLAPSE OF
SPANISH POWER 1640-1714

Provinces in which there were
revolts
Provinces in which there were
conspiracies
Territories lost to Austria in 1714
Territories lost to France [Artois &
Rosellón 1659, Franche-Comté 1678]
Spanish military route
to Flanders

DENMARK

Stralsund

Münster

Cologne

Mainz

Magdeburg

SAXONY

Dresden

Prague

PALATINATE
burg

Vienna

BAVARIA

AUSTRIA
STYRIA
CARINTHIA

KINGDOM
OF
HUNGARY

SWITZERLAND

Innsbruck
TYROL

VALTELLINE

Geneva

DUCHY OF
MILAN Milan

Venice

Trieste

Turin

Mantua

Genoa

OTTOMAN EMPIRE

Nice
Marseilles

PAPAL
STATES

Ragusa

CORSICA

Rome

KINGDOM
OF
NAPLES
[1647]

Naples

SARDINIA
[1713]

Palermo

SICILY
[1647, 1674]
[to Savoy 1714]

Tunis

MEDITERRANEAN SEA

Map 5

age of four. This last pallid relic of a fading dynasty was left to preside over the inert corpse of a shattered Monarchy, itself no more than a pallid relic of the great imperial past. All the hopes of the 1620s had turned to dust, leaving behind them nothing but the acrid flavour of disillusionment and defeat.

10

Epitaph on an Empire

I. THE CENTRE AND THE PERIPHERY

THE Castile bequeathed by Philip IV to his four-year-old son was a nation awaiting a saviour. It had suffered defeat and humiliation at the hands of its traditional enemies, the French. It had lost the last vestiges of its political hegemony over Europe and seen some of its most valuable overseas possessions fall into the hands of the heretical English and Dutch. Its currency was chaotic, its industry in ruins, its population demoralized and diminished. Burgos and Seville, formerly the twin motors of the Castilian economy, had both fallen on evil times: the population of Burgos, which had been about 13,000 in the 1590s, was down to a mere 3,000 by 1646, and Seville lost 60,000 inhabitants – half its population – in the terrible plague of 1649. While the rival city of Cadiz gradually arrogated to itself the position in the American trade previously enjoyed by Seville, the trade itself was now largely controlled by foreign merchants, who had secured numerous concessions from the Spanish Crown. Castile was dying, both economically and politically; and as the hopeful foreign mourners gathered at the death-bed, their agents rifled the house.

Was there, then, no hope of resuscitation? Castile, which had lived for so long on illusions, still clung to the more potent of them with the tenacity born of despair. A Messiah would surely arise to save his people. But unfortunately, while there was no lack of candidates during the thirty-five years of the reign of Charles II, their qualifications proved on closer examination to be disappointingly meagre. The poor King himself, the centre of so many hopes, turned out to be a rachitic and feeble-minded weakling, the last stunted sprig of a degenerate line. His mother the Queen Regent Mariana, was totally devoid of political capacity. His half-brother, Don Juan José de Austria, Philip IV's illegitimate son, convinced himself and succeeded in convincing many others, that he was another

Don John for the salvation of Spain. His father knew better, and was careful to exclude him from the Government which he bequeathed to Charles II. This consisted of a carefully selected body of five ministers acting as a *Junta de Gobierno* to advise the Queen Regent until the King reached the age of fourteen. In this Junta, the balance both of personalities and nationalities was scrupulously maintained. One of its leading members was the wily Count of Castrillo, who had organized the overthrow of Olivares in 1642–3. Since the death of his nephew Don Luis de Haro in 1661, Castrillo had ruled Spain in partnership with a hated rival, the Duke of Medina de las Torres, who, however, was excluded from the Junta. The other members were the Count of Peñaranda, the diplomat who had negotiated the Treaty of Münster; Cristóbal Crespí, the Valencian Vice-chancellor of the Council of Aragon; the Marquis of Aytona, a noble with military experience from a distinguished Catalan family; a cleric, Cardinal Pascual de Aragón, the son of the Duke of Cardona, the Catalan grandee who had been Viceroy of Catalonia in the 1630s; and a Basque, Blasco de Loyola, to act as the Junta's secretary.

It is clear from the composition of this Junta that Philip IV had learnt the lesson of the Catalan Revolution and was determined to associate representatives of the various provinces of the peninsula in the delicate task of governing Spain during the royal minority. The days of Castilian hegemony were over, and even if Philip IV's Junta proved to be no more than an ephemeral institution which quickly lost its power to the Austrian Father Nithard, the Queen's Jesuit confessor, the principle of scrupulous regard for provincial rights which informed its composition was carefully maintained for the rest of the century. The weakness of Castile, in fact, made the reign of Charles II a golden age for the privileged classes in the various provinces of the Monarchy. In Spain and Italy, provincial liberties were given a fresh lease of life;[1] in America the colonial aristocracy was able to build up its great estates unchecked by interference from a central Government which had struggled so hard in the sixteenth century to retain effective control over its new domains. The half century which saw the consolidation of royal power in France was

---

1. The exception to this is Sicily, where the failure of a revolt in 1675 allowed the Spaniards to abolish the Senate of Messina and to extend the royal power.

thus for the Spanish Monarchy an age of continuing decentralization – a period during which the 'Aragonese' federal system was perhaps more wholeheartedly accepted than at any other moment during the government of the House of Austria.

This, however, was not federalism by conviction but federalism by default. The tranquillity enjoyed by the various provinces of the Monarchy was the direct outcome of Castilian weakness. Unable to tackle its own problems, and quite without the energy and the resources to repeat the centralizing experiments of the Conde Duque de Olivares, Castile allowed the other provinces to go their own way, and tacitly resigned itself to a constitutional formula which was in effect no more than a polite fiction for administrative and political stagnation in a changing world.

Spain's prospects as a European power clearly depended on Castile's capacity for recovery from the debilitating weakness of the middle years of the century. The immediate need was a long period of good government; but unfortunately there was no one capable of providing it. The Queen and Father Nithard, having reduced the Junta to impotence, had no conception of how to set about the task of restoring a land to which both of them were foreign. The Cortes of Castile, which might at this moment have come into its own, had long since shown itself to be little more than a forum in which the *procuradores* watched over the interests of their own privileged class; and there were no deep regrets when it ceased to be summoned after 1665. Nor was the aristocracy of Castile capable of filling the vacuum left by the decline of royal power. The great aristocratic houses had been able to weather the economic storms of the mid-century thanks to the possession of vast and inalienable estates; but with one or two distinguished exceptions, like the Count of Oropesa, their representatives were of such unmitigated mediocrity that they could contribute nothing to the salvation of their country. The moral and intellectual bankruptcy of the Castilian ruling class, which had so perturbed the Conde Duque a generation earlier, was now fully exposed at the moment when it could least be afforded.

While the Councils, lacking any firm direction from above, competed with each other for precedence and jurisdiction, political adventurers intrigued for favour at Court. Father Nithard had made numerous enemies, of whom not the least was Don Juan José de

Austria. Fearing imminent arrest, Don Juan fled in October 1668 first to Aragon and thence to Catalonia. During the winter months he managed to build up for himself an enthusiastic following in the Levantine kingdoms, and when he set out for Madrid early in 1669 with the intention of reaching a settlement with the Queen, he was greeted with acclamation all along the route. Looking increasingly like a conquering hero as he approached the capital, he felt strong enough by the time he reached Torrejón de Ardoz to demand the dismissal of Nithard. The following day, 25 February 1669, Nithard hastily left Madrid, and Don Juan's triumph appeared complete.

The *coup* launched by Don Juan José in 1669 had a certain symbolical significance, for this was the first occasion in modern Spanish history when an attempt was made from the periphery of the peninsula to seize control of the Government in Madrid. As such, it hints at a change of great importance in the balance of political forces inside Spain. Until 1640 it was always a question of Castile intervening in the life of the peripheral provinces; but now, for the first time, the peripheral provinces were themselves tentatively beginning to meddle in the affairs of Castile. Although Don Juan's *coup* was in fact badly bungled, a precedent had none the less been set; and in some ways it was a hopeful precedent, for it suggested that Aragon and Catalonia were beginning to emerge from their political isolation and to show that general concern for the welfare of the Monarchy which Olivares had demanded from them so insistently, and to such little effect.

Don Juan lacked the political skill to exploit a situation which seemed to have turned decisively in his favour. He duly obtained from the Queen the creation of a *Junta de Alivios* intended to introduce far-reaching reforms, but it succeeded in devising only minor improvements in Castile's fiscal system, and left the fundamental abuses untouched. While Don Juan hesitated to assume the supreme power, the Queen strengthened her position by creating a royal guard, known as the Guardia Chamberga, under the command of one of Don Juan's most determined opponents, the Marquis of Aytona. Either because he feared to plunge Castile into civil war, or because he doubted his own strength, Don Juan did nothing to force the issue. For a moment, there was a stalemate; and then Don Juan surprised everyone by accepting an offer from the Queen of the viceroyalty of Aragon, and conveniently removed himself from the neighbourhood of the capital.

After the failure of Don Juan's bloodless *coup*, power at Madrid fell into the hands of an Andalusian adventurer who had found favour with the Queen. This was Fernando de Valenzuela, the son of an army captain. Valenzuela managed to ingratiate himself with the populace of Madrid, for which he provided cheap bread and bull-fights, but he was faced with the hostility of Don Juan José and the opposition of the grandees, who resented his rapid climb into the ranks of the higher aristocracy. When Charles II was officially pro-claimed of age in 1675 it was expected that Valenzuela would be replaced by Don Juan José, but once again Don Juan allowed himself to be outmanoeuvred and the Queen Mother and Valenzuela man-aged to cling to power.

The political history of Castile now began to assume some of those characteristics of a comic opera, for which in a later age it was to become notorious. Indeed, it was at this moment that one of the essential ingredients of nineteenth-century Castilian politics first appeared – the *pronunciamiento*. As the grandees, exasperated by Valenzuela's accession to their ranks, banded together in December 1676 to demand the recall of Don Juan, the latter began to march on Madrid at the head of the army which had been fighting the French in Catalonia. The Queen took the only action open to her in the circumstances, and offered him the government. Valenzuela was arrested, and exiled to the Philippines. From there he later made his way to Mexico, where a throw from a horse brought his remarkable career to a fittingly spectacular conclusion.

The government of Don Juan José from 1677 until his unexpected death in 1679 was attended by disappointment at home and humilia-tion abroad. France and Spain had been at war since 1673, with Catalonia as the principal battlefront. Hopes of recovering Roussillon for Spain were dashed by the outbreak of revolt in Sicily in 1674, and it was necessary to abandon the offensive on the French frontier so that troops could be sent to crush the rising. Although the French were thwarted in Sicily, the Peace of Nijmwegen, which brought the war to an end in 1678, registered a further decline in Spain's international standing. It lost not only a number of important towns in the Netherlands, but also the entire Franche-Comté, that treasured survival from the Burgundian past, which had fallen into French hands in 1674. The empire that Charles V had governed was being shorn of its territories one by one, as Castile revealed itself too weak to come to their help; and Castile itself was sinking beneath the hopeless government of Don Juan. The expected saviour of Spain had shown himself, once power had been entrusted to his hands, to be totally incapable of exercising it. As he failed to tackle even the most obvious abuses, he forfeited in turn the support of the army, the Church, and the populace, and was mercilessly lampooned in the streets of the capital. His death in September 1679 came too late to save his reputation He died as he lived – the first of that long line of flashy leaders from whom the Castilians, expecting everything, obtained nothing.

It was in the years around 1680, between the death of Don Juan José and the fall of his mediocre successor, the Duke of Medinaceli, in 1685, that Castile's fortunes reached their nadir. The French envoy, the Marquis de Villars, was shocked at the change for the worse since his first mission to Madrid in 1668.[2] Although 'the power and the policy of the Spaniards' had been 'diminished constantly . . . since the beginning of the century', the change had 'become so great in recent times that one can actually see it occurring from one year to the next'. The feeble King and his feeble Minister, Medinaceli, were both reduced to a 'blind dependence' on the Councils, and particularly on the Council of State – 'an assembly of twenty-four persons without spirit or experience', like the Duke of Medina de las Torres, who had 'spent all his life in Madrid in total idleness, almost exclusively shared between eating and sleeping'. All important offices in the State and the army went solely to men of rank. Over the past forty years, tax collectors and tax tribunals had proliferated to an extraordinary degree. In conclusion, 'it would be difficult to describe to its full extent the disorder in the government of Spain', or, for that matter, the misery to which Castile had been reduced.

There is no reason to doubt the accuracy of Villars's description. The early 1680s were in fact, the years of Castile's total administrative and economic collapse. Apart from raw wool, as Villars pointed out, Castile had no exports with which to attract foreign wealth, and

2. Marquis de Villars, *Mémoires de la Cour d'Espagne de 1679 à 1681*, ed. A. Morel-Fatio (Paris, 1893). See especially pp. 1–10.

two-thirds of the silver in the treasure fleet went straight to foreigners without even entering Spain. Above all, the currency of Castile was now approaching the climax of its giddy career. In the last years of the reign of Philip IV, the premium on silver in terms of *vellón* rose to 150 per cent, and the last monetary measure of the reign – a deflationary decree in October 1664 – failed to reduce it for more than a few passing moments. By the middle of 1665 it was up again to 115 per cent; it reached 175 per cent by 1670 and 200 per cent by 1675. There was a sharp rise in Castilian commodity prices during the 1670s, and by the end of the decade a fresh attempt at deflation became inevitable. It came on 10 February 1680, when the 'good' *vellón* minted since 1660 was deflated by one half. The decree brought a violent collapse of prices, and produced a succession of bankruptcies from the Crown downwards. There was widespread recourse to barter; riots occurred in Toledo and Madrid; the royal family could not even raise sufficient funds for its annual trip to Aranjuez; and – more serious – the last remnants of Castilian industry were destroyed.

The economic paralysis of Castile in the 1680s was accompanied by the paralysis of its cultural and intellectual life. The depressing later years of Philip IV had at least been illuminated by the sunset glow of Castile's great cultural achievement. But Gracián had died in 1658, Velázquez in 1660, and Zurbarán in 1664. With the passing of Calderón de la Barca in 1681 and Murillo a year later, the last luminaries of the literary and artistic generation of the golden age disappeared. These men had no worthy successors. At a moment when inquiring minds in other parts of Europe were turning towards philosophical and scientific investigation, the spirit of inquiry was almost dead in Castile. There were still isolated groups of devoted scholars, but educational standards had slumped, as the universities fell back on the most arid Thomism and showed themselves hostile to any sign of change.

The exact reasons for the intellectual failure of later seventeenth-century Castile are extremely hard to establish. The inadequacies of contemporary education are obvious enough, but it is far from clear to what these inadequacies should be attributed. The Jesuit Mariana thought that much of the blame lay with his own Order, which had acquired a monopoly of the lower reaches of the educational system.

In his Discourse on the affairs of the Company of Jesus, written in 1605, he pointed out that his Order had taken over the teaching of 'humane letters' in the most important towns in Spain. 'There is no doubt,' he continued, 'that less Latin is known in Spain than fifty years ago. I believe – indeed, I am certain – that one of the major causes of this misfortune is to be found in the fact that the Company has been entrusted with these studies. ... Formerly, the secular teachers of grammar' were expert in various branches of learning, 'since they devoted their whole lives to the work. But among our members, there are hardly any who have any knowledge of these things; and laymen, seeing the posts occupied, are no longer willing to enter the profession.'[3]

Mariana was so passionate a critic of his own Order that his judgements are generally too partisan to be taken purely on trust. Certain aspects of Jesuit education were extremely good. The emphasis placed on theatrical productions in Jesuit schools seems, for instance, to have acted as a powerful stimulus to Spanish drama, and, as the curriculum of the Colegio Imperial at Madrid makes clear, science and mathematics were by no means neglected in the higher institutes of learning. Mariana himself, while criticising the primary education, admits that the more advanced studies were better organized. This comment perhaps provides a clue to the character of Jesuit education in Spain, for by no means all the students can have proceeded to the more advanced course of study. Since the average pupil in Jesuit schools did not begin the study of science, mathematics, and philosophy before the age of sixteen, it is possible that a large number had to be content with the 'humanistic' course in classical languages and learning, in which – as Mariana suggests – the standard of teaching often left much to be desired.

The Jesuits, however, were not the only teachers in Spain. Nor were they even particularly numerous, considering the size of the Religious Orders in the seventeenth century. The total membership of the Jesuit Order in Spain, as distributed among the four traditional Spanish provinces, was:[4]

3. *Obras del Padre Juan de Mariana* (Biblioteca de Autores Españoles, vol. 31, Madrid, 1854), p. 601.
4. Figures taken from A. Astraín, *Historia de la Compañía de Jesús*, 7 vols. (Madrid, 1912–25), vol. III, p. 183, vol. IV, pp. 753–4, vol. VI, p. 30.

	1580	1615	c. 1700
Aragon	200	390	523
Castile	500	613	560
Toledo	480	570	544
Andalusia	260	600	489
	1,440	2,173	2,116

While the Jesuits in the seventeenth century succeeded in winning the support of the Spanish Crown, and obtained from the King in 1621 the right for their own colleges to confer degrees, they never achieved a monopoly of education. The universities continued to fight them with every weapon at their disposal, and did their best to prevent the foundation of the Colegio Imperial. But the universities had nothing better to offer of their own. Indeed, it was precisely in order to give young Spanish nobles a better grounding in such subjects as science and mathematics that Olivares and his Jesuit confessor, Hernando de Salazar, originally devised the new college in Madrid.

But the Colegio Imperial was a failure. Similarly, the famous academy at Madrid where scientific and mathematical questions had been discussed since 1583, faded out of existence at the very time when the Colegio Imperial was coming into being. Somehow, the intellectual curiosity and excitement which had distinguished six-teenth-century Castile had disappeared. The Church, too, had lost its former vitality. There were too few seminaries to train a growing priesthood, and many of the clergy were notorious for their ignor-ance. Philip IV made various attempts to limit the wealth and expansion of the Church and tried, with some support from Rome, to inaugurate a reform of the Religious Orders. In 1677 a reduction in the number of the clergy and a fresh attempt at reform of the Orders were again seriously contemplated, but once again nothing of note was achieved. Vested interests were too powerful, opposition to change too strong, and the Crown was too weak to do what needed to be done.

Inert and immovable, the top-heavy Church of baroque Spain had little to offer a passive population but an unending succession of sedatives, in the form of Te Deums, processions, solemn masses, and heavy ceremonial which ministered to its apparently insatiable passion for display. Religious festivals in some places occupied a third of the year. The rites of the Church had degenerated into mere formalism, its dogmas into superstitions, and the dead weight of the vast apparatus of ecclesiastical bureaucracy lay heavy on Castile.

It would be a mistake, however, to assume that the supine, priest-ridden Castile of Charles II was typical of all Spain. In some parts of the peninsula there are unmistakable signs of a new vitality, both intellectual and economic. Unfortunately, however, so little is known about Spanish social and economic history in the second half of the seventeenth century that all assertions about movements of the Spanish economy must remain extremely tentative; but already by the last quarter of the century the first hesitant indications of economic revival can be discerned. The fact that different regions of the peninsula had remained in their own economic compartments, curiously detached one from another, meant that the rhythm of economic decline varied from one region to the next. It would seem that the decline of Castile began earlier, and lasted longer, than that of other parts of Spain. In the Principality of Catalonia, for instance, the commercial crisis dated from the 1630s, and the demographic and monetary crisis from the 1640s; and whereas Castile experienced violent in-flationary and deflationary movements throughout the 1660s and 1670s, the Catalan coinage was stabilized after the deflation of 1654. Valencia, which was also free from the scourge of Castilian *vellón*, experienced a downward movement of prices and wages in the 1650s and 1660s. On the whole it would appear that the economic move-ments of the peripheral provinces of the peninsula conformed more closely to general European movements than did those of Castile; and that just as western Europe as a whole was climbing out of its mid-century depression in the 1670s, so also the Spanish periphery was following suit.

Although their project bore no immediate fruit, it was a hopeful sign that thirty-two Aragonese representatives met under the presi-dency of Don Juan José in 1674 to consider methods for reviving the kingdom's economy and freeing it from the control of foreigners. Still more hopeful was the changed outlook of the post-revolutionary generation of Catalans. Its experiences between 1640 and 1652 had apparently administered a profound shock to the Principality, and forced it for the first time to come face to face with the realities of its own weakness in the world of great powers. After a century of relegation to the margin of Spanish history, the Catalans at last began to look beyond their own borders, and to turn their eyes once more to America as a possible replacement for the Mediterranean markets they had lost. Although they did not in fact secure official entry into the American trade until the beginning of the new century, they settled down in the 1660s and 1670s to the restoration of their shattered economy. In particular they set about the rebuilding of their textile industry, which, unlike that of Aragon, was not fettered by a protectionist legislation that tended to favour the production of inferior quality cloths. It was in the second half of the seventeenth century that the Catalan population, refreshed and reinvigorated by a century of French immigration, acquired its reputation for hard work and business enterprise. As economic opportunities increased, public order became more secure. The age of the bandit was passing, to be replaced by the less picturesque age of the industrious artisan.

The slow recovery of Catalonia, in spite of constant warfare with the French, was the prelude to the most crucial economic transformation in the history of modern Spain. Economic predominance in the peninsula was shifting from the centre to the periphery, where the burden of taxation was lighter, and where economic prostration had been less complete; and foreign travellers would increasingly contrast the vitality and populousness of the peripheral regions with the emptiness and misery of Castile. The growing intervention of the peripheral provinces in the political life of the Monarchy, as suggested by Don Juan José's abortive *coup*, was a further indication of this gradual shift of predominance from the centre to the circumference. In the late fifteenth and sixteenth centuries Castile had made Spain. Now in the late seventeenth century there was for the first time a possibility that Spain might remake Castile.

After the terrible collapse of 1680, it began to appear that even for Castile itself, the worst was at last over. The history of Castile is too easily equated with the living death of its wretched King, as if the year 1700, which saw the death of Charles II, saw also the end of Castile's prolonged agony, and the start of a new life under a new régime. But there are possibilities that further investigation will reveal a slight Castilian recovery during the last fifteen years of the century, in spite of the disastrous war with France of 1689 to 1697. After 1686 the monetary position in Castile appears to have been stabilized, and in 1693 the minting of *vellón* ceased. Moreover, the country at last acquired a ruler of real capacity in the Count of Oropesa, who served as first minister from 1685 to 1691. Oropesa made serious attempts to reduce taxation and to cut down Government spending, and although he was finally overcome by the opposition of strongly entrenched interests, he had at least achieved something, and marked out a path for others, more fortunate, to follow. But perhaps even more hopeful than the transient ministry of Oropesa was the first sign of intellectual revival, beginning again at the periphery, in Andalusia, which still retained its links with the outside world. For in Seville, although the university was moribund, medical circles in particular began to display new signs of intellectual life; and in 1697 a society was created for the purpose of 'furthering experimental philosophy' – an object that was to be partly promoted by the purchase of foreign books. Even in the soporific mental climate of Charles II's Spain, the Age of Reason was belatedly beginning to dawn.

2. THE CHANGE OF DYNASTY

The fall of Oropesa in 1691 left Spain without an effective Government. Indeed, it was followed soon after by the curious administrative experiment of dividing the peninsula into three large governmental regions, one under the Duke of Montalto, the second under the Constable, and the third under the Admiral, of Castile. This was little more than a medieval-style partition of the country among rival lords; and since it was imposed on a State which already possessed the most rigid and elaborate bureaucratic superstructure, it merely led to a further round of clashes of jurisdiction between Spain's perennially competing Councils and tribunals. But by this stage domestic changes in the peninsula had virtually ceased to be of any importance. Spain was no longer even remotely the master of its own fate. Overshadowed by the terrible problem of the royal succession, its future now largely depended on decisions taken in Paris, London, Vienna, and the Hague.

By the 1690s, the problem of the Spanish succession had become acute. Charles II had remained childless by his first marriage, to

María Luisa of Orleans, who died in 1689. It soon became apparent that his second marriage – an 'Austrian' marriage, to Mariana de Neuburg, daughter of the Elector Palatine and sister of the Empress – was also likely to be childless. As the hopes of an heir faded the great powers began their complicated manoeuvres for the acquisition of the King of Spain's inheritance. The new marriage had provoked Louis XIV into a fresh declaration of war, which involved yet another invasion of Catalonia, and the capture of Barcelona by the French in 1697. But in the Treaty of Ryswick, which ended the war in September 1697, Louis could afford to be generous. His aim was to secure for the Bourbons an undivided Spanish succession, and there was more hope of attaining this by diplomacy than by war.

The last years of the dying King presented a pathetic spectacle of degradation at Madrid. Afflicted with convulsive fits, the wretched monarch was believed to have been bewitched, and the Court pullulated with confessors and exorcists and visionary nuns employing every artifice known to the Church to free him from the devil. Their rivalries and intrigues mingled with those of Spanish courtiers and of foreign diplomats, who were collecting like vultures to prey on the corpse of the Monarchy. While France and Austria hoped to secure the entire prize for themselves, England and the United Provinces were determined to prevent either of them from obtaining an inheritance which would bring the hegemony of Europe in its train. But the task would not be easy, and time was running out.

At the time of the peace of Ryswick there were three leading candidates for the Spanish throne, each of whom had a strong body of supporters at the Court. The candidate with the best claims was the young Prince Joseph Ferdinand of Bavaria, the grandson of Philip IV's daughter, Margarita Teresa. His claims were supported by the Count of Oropesa, and had been pressed by the Queen Mother Mariana, who died in 1696. They were also acceptable to the English and the Dutch, who had less to fear from a Bavarian than from a French or Austrian succession. The Austrian candidate was the Archduke Charles, the second son of the Emperor, who was supported by Charles's Queen, Mariana de Neuburg, and by the Admiral of Castile. Finally, there was the French claimant, Louis XIV's grandson, Philip of Anjou, who claims were clouded by the Infanta María Teresa's renunciation of her rights to the Spanish throne at the time of her marriage to Louis XIV.

In 1696 Charles, who was thought to be dying, was induced by the majority of his councillors, headed by Cardinal Portocarrero, to declare himself in favour of the Bavarian Prince. Louis' skilful ambassador, the Marquis of Harcourt, set himself to undo this as soon as he reached Madrid on the conclusion of the Treaty of Ryswick. Still manoeuvring among themselves without regard for the King's wishes, the great powers agreed secretly in October 1698 on the partition of the Spanish inheritance between the three candidates. Naturally enough the secret was badly kept. Charles, imbued with a deep sense of majesty which his person consistently belied, was deeply affronted by the attempt to dismember his domains, and signed a will in November 1698 naming the Bavarian as his universal heir. This arrangement, however, was thwarted by the sudden death of the young Prince in February 1699 – an event which brought the rival Austrian and French candidates face to face for the throne. While frantic diplomatic efforts were made to avert another European conflagration, Charles fought with a desperate resolution to keep his domains intact. The news that reached him at the end of May 1700 of another partition treaty seems finally to have persuaded him where his duty lay. Alienated by dislike of his Queen from all things German, and deeply solicitous for the future well-being of his subjects, he was now ready to accept the almost unanimous recommendation of his Council of State in favour of the Duke of Anjou. On 2 October 1700 he signed the anxiously awaited will, naming Anjou as the successor to all his dominions. The Queen, who had always terrified her husband, did everything in her power to induce him to revoke his decision, but this time the dying King held firm. With a dignity on his death-bed that had constantly eluded the poor misshapen creature in his lifetime, the last King of the House of Austria insisted that his will should prevail. He died on 1 November 1700, amidst the deep disquietude of a nation which found it almost impossible to realize that the dynasty which had led it to such triumphs and such disasters had suddenly ceased to exist.

The Duke of Anjou was duly proclaimed King of Spain as Philip V, and made his entry into Madrid in April 1701. A general European conflict might still have been avoided if Louis XIV had shown himself less high-handed at the moment of triumph. But his actions alienated the maritime powers, and in May 1702 England, the Emperor, and the United Provinces simultaneously declared war on France. For a time the war of the Spanish Succession, which was to last from 1702 to 1713, seemed to threaten the Bourbons with utter disaster. But in 1711 the Emperor Joseph died, to be succeeded on the Imperial throne by his brother, the Archduke Charles, who had been the allies' candidate for the throne of Spain. The union of Austria and Spain beneath a single ruler – so uncomfortably reminiscent of the days of Charles V – was something that appealed to the maritime powers even less than the prospect of a Bourbon in Madrid. Accordingly, the English and the Dutch now declared themselves ready to accept a Bourbon succession in Spain, so long as Philip V abandoned any pretensions to the French throne. Agreement was formalized in the Treaties of Utrecht of 1713, which also gave Great Britain Gibraltar and Minorca. A further peace settlement in the following year between France and the Empire gave the Spanish Netherlands and Spain's Italian possessions to the Austrians. With the treaties of 1713–14, therefore, the great Burgundian-Habsburg empire which Castile had borne on its shoulders for so long was dissolved, and two centuries of Habsburg imperialism were formally liquidated. The Spanish Empire had shrunk at last to a truly Spanish empire, consisting of the Crowns of Castile and Aragon, and of Castile's American colonies.

The extinction of the Habsburg dynasty and the dismemberment of the Habsburg empire were followed by the gradual dismantling of the Habsburg system of government. Philip V was accompanied to Madrid by a number of French advisers, of whom the most notable was Jean Orry. Orry remodelled the royal household along French lines, and settled down to the gargantuan task of financial reform. The process of reform continued throughout the war, and culminated in a general governmental reorganization, in the course of which the Councils began to assume the shape of ministries on the French model. At last, after decades of administrative stagnation, Spain was experiencing that revolution in government which had already changed the face of western Europe during the preceding fifty years.

The most important of all the changes introduced by the Bourbons, however, was to occur in the relationship between the Monarchy and the Crown of Aragon. In the modern-style centralized state which the Bourbons were attempting to establish, the continuation of provincial autonomies appeared increasingly anomalous. Yet it did seem for one moment as if the Crown of Aragon might survive the change of régime with its privileges intact. Obedient to the dictates of Louis XIV, Philip V went to Barcelona in 1701 to hold a session of the Catalan Cortes – the first to be summoned since Philip IV's abortive Cortes of 1632. From the Catalan standpoint, these were among the most successful Cortes ever held. The Principality's laws and privileges were duly confirmed, and Philip conceded important new privileges, including the right of limited trade with the New World. But the Catalans themselves were the first to appreciate that there was something incongruous about so generous a handling of provincial liberties by a dynasty notorious for its authoritarian traits. Nor could they forget the treatment they had received at the hands of France during their revolution of 1640–52, and the terrible damage inflicted on the Principality by French invasions during the later seventeenth century. It was therefore perhaps not surprising that as Philip V's popularity increased in Castile, it declined in Catalonia. Finally, in 1705, the Catalans sought and received military aid from England, and proclaimed the Austrian claimant, the Archduke Charles, as Charles III of Spain. Allied troops were also enthusiastically welcomed in Aragon and Valencia, and the War of the Spanish Succession was converted into a Spanish civil war, fought between the two parts of the peninsula nominally united by Ferdinand and Isabella. The allegiances, however, were at first sight paradoxical, for Castile, which had always hated the foreigner, was supporting the claims of a Frenchman, while the Crown of Aragon, which had always been so suspicious of Habsburg intentions, was championing the claims of a prince of the House of Austria.

On this occasion, Catalonia, although a far more mature and responsible nation than it had been in 1640, proved to have made a disastrous mistake. The Government of the Archduke Charles in Barcelona was sadly ineffective, and would probably have collapsed within a few months if it had not been shored up by Catalonia's allies. Aragon and Valencia fell to Philip V in 1707, and were summarily deprived of their laws and liberties as a punishment for supporting the losing side. It was hard to see how the Principality could escape a similar fate unless its allies held firm, and firmness was the last thing to be expected of an increasingly war-weary England. When the Tory Government signed the peace with France in 1713 it left the Catalans in the lurch, as the French had left them in the lurch during their revolution against Philip IV. Faced with the equally grim alternatives of hopeless resistance and surrender, the Catalans chose to resist, and for months the city of Barcelona held out with extraordinary heroism against the besieging army. But on 11 September 1714 the Bourbon forces mounted their final assault, and the city's resistance reached its inevitable end. From 12 September 1714 Philip V, unlike Philip IV, was not merely King of Castile and Count of Barcelona; he was also King of Spain.

The fall of Barcelona was followed by the wholesale destruction of Catalonia's traditional institutions, including the *Diputació* and the Barcelona city council. The Government's plans for reform were codified in the so-called Nueva Planta, published on 16 January 1716. This document in effect marks the transformation of Spain from a collection of semi-autonomous provinces into a centralized State. The viceroys of Catalonia were replaced by Captain-Generals, who would govern in conjunction with a royal *Audiencia* conducting its business in Castilian. The Principality was divided into a new series of administrative divisions similar to those of Castile, and run by *corregidores* on the Castilian model. Even the universities were abolished, to be replaced by a new, royalist, university established at Cervera. The intention of the Bourbons was to put an end to the Catalan nation, and to obliterate the traditional political divisions of Spain. Nothing expressed this intention better than the abolition of the Council of Aragon, already accomplished in 1707. In future, the affairs of the Crown of Aragon were to be administered by the Council of Castile, which became the principal administrative organ of the new Bourbon state.

Although the new administrative organization went a good deal less far in practice than it went on paper, the passing of Catalan autonomy in 1716 marks the real break between Habsburg and Bourbon Spain. If Olivares had been successful in his foreign wars, the change would no doubt have come seventy years earlier, and the history of Spain might have taken a very different course. As it was, the change came too late, and it came in the wrong way. Spain, under the Government of the Bourbons, was about to be centralized and Castilianized; but the transformation occurred at a time when Castile's economic hegemony was a thing of the past. Instead, a centralized Government was arbitrarily imposed on the wealthier peripheral regions, to be held there by force – the force of an economically retarded Castile. The result was a tragically artificial structure which constantly hampered Spain's political development, for during the next two centuries economic and political power were perpetually divorced. Centre and circumference thus remained mutually antagonistic, and the old regional conflicts stubbornly refused to die away. The dichotomy of Castile–Aragon could not be summarily removed by the stroke of a pen – not even the pen of a Bourbon.

3. THE FAILURE

The firm establishment of the new Bourbon dynasty on the Spanish throne ended one epoch in the history of the peninsula and opened another. In the future – or so at least it was believed – there would be no more Pyrenees. Nor, for that matter, would there be any more Ebro. Spain was henceforth to be part of Europe, just as Catalonia and Aragon were to be part of Spain. The seventeenth century, the age of Spain's renewed regional fragmentation and of its renewed isolation from Europe, had at last, and none too soon, come to an end.

It is natural to look back over this century and wonder where things had gone wrong. Both contemporary and later generations could not fail to be struck by the extraordinary and terrible contrast between the triumphant Spain of Philip II and the broken Spain inherited by Philip V. Was not this a repetition of the fate of Imperial Rome? And could it not be interpreted by the confident rationalists of the eighteenth century as an object lesson in the disastrous consequences of ignorance, superstition, and sloth? To an age which took the idea of progress as its gospel, the Spain which had expelled the Moriscos and allowed itself to fall into the clutches of ignorant monks and priests had condemned itself to disaster before the bar of history.

In retrospect, it would seem that, in analyses of the 'decline', too much has been made of what were assumed to be exclusively

'Spanish' characteristics. While there *were* profound differences
between Spain and other west European nations, springing in particular from the Afro-European character of Spain's geography and
civilization, there were also marked similarities, which it is a mistake
to underplay. At the end of the sixteenth century there was no
particular reason to believe that the future development of the
peninsula would diverge so markedly from that of other parts of
western Europe as it was later to do. Habsburg Spain had, after all,
set the pace for the rest of Europe in the elaboration of new techniques of administration to cope with the problems of governing a
world-wide empire. The Spain of Philip II would seem to have had
at least as good a chance as the France of Henry III of making the
transition to the modern, centralized State.

The failure to make this transition was essentially a seventeenth-
century failure, and, above all, a failure of the second half of the
century. The economic depression of the earlier and middle years of
the century, although exceptionally severe in certain parts of the
peninsula, was not unique to Spain. France and England, as well as
Spain, were plunged in an economic crisis in the 1620s and a political
crisis in the 1640s. The real divergence came only after the middle of
the century, when the moment of most acute political crisis had
everywhere been passed. It was in the years after 1650 that certain
European States seemed to strike out on a new course, building up
their power by a more rational exploitation of their economic
possibilities and their military and financial resources – and this at a
time when the new science and the new philosophy were beginning
to teach that man could, after all, shape his own destiny and control
his environment.

This moment of exceptionally rapid intellectual and administrative advance in many parts of Europe was, for Spain, the moment of
maximum political and intellectual stagnation. Castile in particular
failed to respond to the challenge posed by the crisis of the mid-
seventeenth century, and relapsed into the inertia of defeat, from
which it took the best part of a century to recover. The immediate
explanation of this failure is to be found in the disastrous events of the
age of Olivares, and notably in the country's defeat in war. The strain
of war had precipitated the Conde Duque into constitutional experiments which entailed a radical reorganization of the country's

administrative structure, and he lacked both the military and economic resources, and the prestige that would have been conferred by foreign victories, to carry these experiments through to success. The result of his failure was even worse than if the experiments had never been tried. The frictions between the peoples of the peninsula were exacerbated by his efforts; and the extent of the failure effectively discouraged any attempt to repeat the experiment during the half-century when other States were reorganizing their administrative systems, in order to compete more effectively in the international struggle for power.

Yet the fatal over-commitment of Spain to foreign wars at a time when Castile lacked the economic and demographic resources to fight them with success, cannot be simply attributed to the blunders of one man. It reflects, rather, the failure of a generation, and of an entire governing class. Seventeenth-century Castile had become the victim of its own history, desperately attempting to re-enact the imperial glories of an earlier age in the belief that this was the sole means of exorcising from the body politic the undoubted ills of the present. That it should have reacted in this way was not inevitable, but it was made the more probable by the very magnitude of the country's triumphs in the preceding era. It was hard to turn one's back on a past studded with so many successes, and it became all the harder when those successes were identified with everything that was most quintessentially Castilian. For had not the successes derived from the military valour of the Castilians and their unswerving devotion to the Church?

It was one of the tragedies of Castile's history that it found itself, by the end of the reign of Philip II, in a position where it seemed that readjustment to the new economic realities could be achieved only at the price of sacrificing its most cherished ideals. However stern the warnings of the *arbitristas*, it was difficult for a society nurtured on war to find a substitute for the glory of battle in the tedious intricacies of mercantile ledgers, or to elevate to a position of pre-eminence the hard manual labour it had been taught to despise. It was no less difficult for it to draw on the ideas and the experiences of foreigners, especially when the foreigners were so often heretics, for Castile's instinctive distrust of the outside world had been amply reinforced by the religious revolutions of sixteenth-century Europe.

By a tragic succession of circumstances, the purity of the faith had come to be identified during the reign of Philip II with a fundamental hostility to ideas and values gaining ground in certain parts of contemporary Europe. This identification had led to a partial isolation of Spain from the outer world, which had constricted the nation's development to certain well-defined channels, and lessened its capacity to adapt itself to new situations and circumstances through the development of new ideas.

Yet the very violence of Spain's response to the religious upheaval of the sixteenth century demands a sympathetic understanding it does not always receive, for Spain was confronted with a problem more complex than that facing any other State in Christendom. It alone was a multi-racial society, in which the inter-penetration of Christian, Jewish and Moorish beliefs created a constant problem of national and religious identity. To this problem there was no obvious solution. The closing of the frontiers and the insistence on the most rigorous orthodoxy represented a desperate attempt to deal with a problem of unparalleled complexity; and it is hardly surprising if religious uniformity appeared the sole guarantee of national survival for a society characterized by the most extreme racial, political and geographical diversity. The price paid for the adoption of this policy proved in the end to be very high, but it is understandable enough that to contemporaries the cost of *not* adopting it should have seemed even higher.

While the policies adopted by Philip II made the task of his successors incomparably more difficult, they did not make it impossible. Certain aspects of the career of Olivares suggest that there was still room for manoeuvre, and that Castile still retained some freedom of choice. This freedom was lost in the half-century after 1640, partly because of the tragic events of the Olivares era, and partly because of the unredeemed mediocrity of the Castilian ruling class at a moment when the highest gifts of statesmanship were required if the Monarchy were to escape disaster. There was here a failure of individuals, over and above the collective failure of a society so profoundly disillusioned by its unbroken series of reverses that it had lost even the capacity to protest.

The degeneracy of the dynasty played an obvious part in this failure, but there is also a striking contrast in the calibre of the

ministers, the viceroys and the officials who ran the Monarchy for
Charles V, and those who ran it for Charles II. The over life-size
figure of the Conde Duque de Olivares appears in retrospect the last
of that heroic line which had shed such lustre on the sixteenth-
century Monarchy: such men as the diplomat, poet and commander
Diego Hurtado de Mendoza (1503–75), or Francisco de Toledo
(1515–82), the great viceroy of Peru. The insistent references of
Olivares to the 'lack of leaders' suggests a sudden collapse of the
country's ruling class, as the last great generation of Spanish proconsuls – the generation of the Count of Gondomar (1567–1626) –
finally passed away. But a satisfactory explanation of this collapse
has yet to be given. Is it to be found in the excessive inter-breeding
of an exclusive aristocratic caste? Or in the failure of the country's
educational system as its mental horizons narrowed, for was not
Diego Hurtado de Mendoza as much a product of the 'open' Spain
of Ferdinand and Isabella as the Duke of Medinaceli was a product
of the 'closed' Spain of the seventeenth century? The men of the
seventeenth century belonged to a society which had lost the strength
that comes from dissent, and they lacked the breadth of vision and
the strength of character to break with a past that could no longer
serve as a reliable guide to the future. Heirs to a society which had
over-invested in empire, and surrounded by the increasingly shabby
remnants of a dwindling inheritance, they could not bring themselves
at the moment of crisis to surrender their memories and alter the
antique pattern of their lives. At a time when the face of Europe was
altering more rapidly than ever before, the country that had once
been its leading power proved to be lacking the essential ingredient
for survival – the willingness to change.

4. THE ACHIEVEMENT

The drastic failure of Habsburg Spain to make the vital transition
should not, however, be allowed to obscure the extent of its achievement in the days of its greatness. If the failures were very great, so
also were the successes. For nearly two centuries, Spain had sustained
a remarkable creative effort, which added immeasurably to the
common stock of European civilization. In the Europe of the mid-
seventeenth century the influence of Castilian culture and customs

was widespread and fruitful, upheld as it was by all the prestige of an empire whose hollowness was only just becoming apparent to the outside world.

It is all too easy to take for granted what was perhaps the most remarkable of all Spain's achievements – the ability to maintain its control over vast areas of widely scattered territories, at a time when governmental techniques had scarcely advanced beyond the stage of household administration, and when the slowness of communications would seem at first sight to have made long-distance government impossible. While in course of time the failings of the Spanish governmental system made it the laughing-stock of the world, no other sixteenth- or seventeenth-century State was faced with so vast a problem of administration, and few succeeded in preserving over so long a period such a high degree of public order in an age when revolts were endemic.

The soldiers, the lawyers, and the administrators who made this achievement possible possessed in full measure the defects generally associated with a conquering race, but the best of them brought to their duties a sense of dedication which sprang from an unquestioning acceptance of the superiority of their society and of the absolute rightness of their cause. Nor did it seem in the sixteenth century as if this confidence was misplaced. Few nations had experienced such spectacular triumphs as the Castile of the Catholic Kings and of Charles V, and Castilians could be pardoned for thinking that they had been singled out for special favours by a God who had chosen them to further His manifold purposes.

It is this supreme self-confidence which gives Castilian civilization of the sixteenth century its particular quality, just as it was the sudden failure of confidence that gave a new and more poignant character to Castilian civilization of the seventeenth. Tremendous challenges faced the sixteenth-century Castilian and he rose to them with a kind of effortless ease which seems in retrospect deeply impressive. He had to explore, colonize, and govern a new world. He had to devise new methods of cartography and navigation – work that was done by such men as Alonso de Santa Cruz, the inventor of spherical maps, and Felipe Guillén, who perfected the compass in 1525. He had to study the natural history of the newly discovered American continent – the achievement of Bernardino de Sahagún, and of botanists like Francisco Hernández and José de Acosta. He had to improve the primitive techniques of mining and metallurgy, and to pioneer, like Pedro de Esquivel, new methods of geodesy. And he had to solve novel problems of political and social organization, and to grapple with the moral questions connected with the establishment of government over uncivilized and pagan races.

This last work, accomplished by the theologians of sixteenth-century Spain, and in particular by the great school of Salamanca led by the Dominican Francisco de Vitoria, illustrates one of the most striking characteristics of the Castile of Charles V and Philip II: the constant and fruitful alliance between theory and practice, between the man of action and the man of learning, which provided intellectuals with a strong incentive to formulate their theories with clarity and precision, and to direct their attention to the pressing problems of the day. The inherent tendency of the Castilian mentality to concern itself with the concrete and practical was thus encouraged by the demand of Castilian society that the scholar and the theologian should contribute to what was regarded as a collective national effort. Yet, at the same time, the need to meet this social demand led to no sacrifice, at least among the better scholars, of their independence of judgement and intellectual integrity. There is something deeply moving about the characteristic forthrightness and independence of the Jesuit Juan de Mariana (1535–1624), still campaigning for constitutionalism in a Castile where constitutionalism was fast dying, and steadfastly refusing to accept anything on trust. 'Nos adoramus quod scimus', he wrote to the Archbishop of Granada in 1597, at a time when the discovery of some mysterious lead books in Granada had convinced many of his gullible contemporaries that they had found irrefutable evidence for the doctrine of the Immaculate Conception and for the visit of St James to Spain. There could have been no better motto for the scholars of the Spanish Renaissance.

Paradoxically, however, alongside this empirical approach, there seems to have existed in many sixteenth-century Castilians a highly developed awareness of another world, beyond that cognizable by the human senses. Saint Teresa of Avila, that most practical of mystics, seemed to be entirely at home in both worlds – worlds that were caught and held in a strange juxtaposition by El Greco when he painted in 1586 the 'Burial of the Count of Orgaz'. The sombre, withdrawn faces of the witnesses to the miracle are the faces of men who seem only half to belong to the terrestrial world, because they feel themselves simultaneously to be citizens of another.

The mystical movement of the later sixteenth century possessed a degree of intensity which inevitably made it a transient phenomenon: it was all too easy for the mystical to degenerate into the mannered, and for the unpremeditated combination of the natural and the supernatural to degenerate into something that was merely arch. But at moments of apparently excessive strain Castilian art and literature had a capacity for self-revival by drawing fresh inspiration from the springs of popular tradition. The Castile of Cervantes resembled the England of Shakespeare in this ability of its writers and artists to synthesize the traditions of the populace with the aspirations of the educated, in such a way as to produce works of art simultaneously acceptable to both.

To some extent this ability disappeared during the course of the seventeenth century. The *conceptismo* of Quevedo and the *culteranismo* of Góngora were perhaps symptoms of a growing divorce between the culture of Court and country, which itself seemed to symbolize a slackening of the previously close-knit texture of Castile's national life. The *arbitristas* with their practical solutions went unheeded by the Court; the universities closed in on themselves; the men of letters and the men of action were drifting apart. One of the most marked intellectual repercussions of this was to be found in the realm of science, more dependent than the arts on a collective effort and a continuing tradition. In the early seventeenth century the continuity had barely been established, and society and the State had lost interest; and Castilian science, as a result, was either extinguished or went underground, to be pursued in secrecy by a few dedicated spirits in a mental climate totally uncongenial to their efforts.

The arts, on the other hand, continued to prosper, enjoying as they did the patronage of the great. Wide as was the gulf between Court and country, it could still be bridged by an artist of the calibre of Velázquez, drawing his inspiration impartially from both. But that fusion of the classical and the popular which had inspired so many of the greatest achievements of the Golden Age, was overlaid in the works of Velázquez by an extra dimension of awareness, peculiarly characteristic of the disillusioned Castile of Philip IV. For Velázquez caught in his paintings the sense of failure, the sudden emptiness of the imperial splendour which had buoyed up Castile for more than a century.

There is no doubt a certain paradox in the fact that the achievement of the two most outstanding creative artists of Castile – Cervantes and Velázquez – was shot through with a deep sense of disillusionment and failure; but the paradox was itself a faithful reflection of the paradox of sixteenth- and seventeenth-century Castile. For here was a country which had climbed to the heights and sunk to the depths; which had achieved everything and lost everything; which had conquered the world only to be vanquished itself. The Spanish achievement of the sixteenth century was essentially the work of Castile, but so also was the Spanish disaster of the seventeenth; and it was Ortega y Gasset who expressed the paradox most clearly when he wrote what may serve as an epitaph on the Spain of the House of Austria: 'Castile has made Spain, and Castile has destroyed it.'

Notes on Further Reading

1. BIBLIOGRAPHICAL AIDS

The essential bibliographical guide to Spanish history is: Sánchez Alonso, B., *Fuentes de la historia española e hispanoamericana* (3rd ed., 3 vols., Madrid, 1952). Since 1953 new books and articles on the history of Spain and Spanish America have been listed, with critical comments, in a quarterly periodical, *Índice Histórico Español* (University of Barcelona).

2. GENERAL

There are several general histories of Spain in Spanish, of which the most useful are:

Altamira y Crevea, R., *Historia de España y de la civilización española* (3rd ed., 4 vols., Barcelona, 1913). Contains much information not easily available elsewhere.

Ballesteros y Beretta, A., *Historia de España y su influencia en la historia universal* (2nd ed., 12 vols., Barcelona, 1943–8).

Soldevila, F., *Historia de España* (8 vols., Barcelona, 1952–9). Valuable for up-to-date bibliographical information, and for its attempt to study Spanish history from the standpoint of the peripheral provinces rather than from that of Castile.

Vicens Vives, J., *Aproximación a la historia de España* (2nd ed., Barcelona, 1960). A brilliantly suggestive attempt at an interpretation of Spain's historical development, in very brief compass. An English translation by Joan Connelly Ullman, entitled *Approaches to the History of Spain* was published by the University of California Press in 1967.

Studies written in, or translated into, English include:

Haring, C. H., *The Spanish Empire in America* (New York, 1952).

Hume, M. A. S., *Spain. Its Greatness and Decay (1479–1788)* (3rd ed., Cambridge, 1913).

Merriman, R. B., *The Rise of the Spanish Empire in the Old World and the New* (4 vols., New York, 1918–34, reprinted 1962). This remains fundamental for any study of sixteenth-century Spain, although some of it has been outdated by recent research, and it is not strong on economic and social developments.

Ranke, L., *The Ottoman and the Spanish Empires in the Sixteenth and Seventeenth Centuries* (London, 1843). Still far more suggestive and stimulating than many more recent works.

Lynch, J., *Spain under the Habsburgs* (2 vols., Oxford, 1964 and 1969). An admirably comprehensive and up-to-date survey of sixteenth- and seventeenth-century Spanish history.

3. ECONOMIC AND SOCIAL

Two important attempts have been made in recent years to map out the economic and social history of Spain:

Vicens Vives, J., *Manual de Historia económica de España* (Barcelona, 1959). English translation, *An Economic History of Spain* (Princeton, 1969).

Vicens Vives, J. (ed.), *Historia social y económica de España y América* (5 vols., Barcelona, 1957–9).

Both these works have the faults of pioneering studies, but provide extremely valuable introductions to subjects which still remain largely unexplored.

Braudel, F., *La Méditerranée et le monde méditerranéen à l'époque de Philippe II* (Paris, 1949, new and substantially revised edition, 1966), although covering the entire Mediterranean region, devotes many pages to Spain. One of the major historical works written in this century, it has opened up fresh lines of thought and research, and has helped to place the social and economic development of Spain in a wider, international, setting.

Chaunu, H. and P., *Séville et l'Atlantique* (8 vols., Paris, from 1955). An immensely ambitious attempt, inspired by the work of Braudel, to study the twin economies of Spain and its American empire between 1500 and 1650. Many years will be required for the digestion of the vast amount of material contained in these volumes. Some of the authors' interpretations of the evidence seem unlikely to stand the test of time, but the work as a whole (although extremely difficult to use) contains a quantity of interesting facts and ideas which will make it an invaluable quarry for generations of historians.

Hamilton, E. J., *American Treasure and the Price Revolution in Spain,* 1501–1650 (Cambridge, Mass., 1934). The classic account of the impact of American silver on the Spanish economy. Amplified by the work of the Chaunus, and recently subjected to considerable criticism for some of its interpretations, it remains fundamental for its information on prices and wages, and on the quantities of silver shipped to Spain. Professor Hamilton's articles and essays have been collected and edited in a Spanish translation in *El Florecimiento del capitalismo y otros ensayos de historia económica* (Madrid, 1948).

4. SPECIALIZED STUDIES

A book of this nature inevitably relies heavily on the work of others. Since it has not been possible to equip it with footnotes, the best alternative would seem to be a brief survey of some of the more important books and articles used in writing the various chapters. The survey is not intended to be complete, nor to provide a comprehensive coverage of the subject under review. It merely lists some of the works which I have found most helpful, and which may serve as useful guides – in addition to those mentioned above – to readers wishing to investigate more thoroughly some particular aspect of the period.

Chapters 1, 2, and 3 (The Union of the Crowns: Reconquest and Conquest: The Ordering of Spain).

1. *The fifteenth-century background*

Professor J. Vicens Vives has been responsible for a radical reinterpretation of fifteenth-century Spanish history. His works on the period include: *Juan II de Aragón: monarquía y revolución en la España del siglo XV* (Barcelona, 1953); *Historia crítica de la vida y reinado de Fernando II de Aragón* (Zaragoza, 1962); and, in Catalan, *Els Trastàmares* (Barcelona, 1956).

Henry IV of Castile is subjected to a professional analysis by Dr Gregorio Marañón, *Ensayo biológico sobre Enrique IV y su tiempo* (2nd ed., Madrid, 1934). The case for *La Beltraneja* is put by Orestes Ferrara, *L'Avènement d'Isabelle la Catholique* (Paris, 1958). Pierre Vilar provides a brilliant analysis of the decline of Catalonia in *Estudios de Historia Moderna*, vol. VI (1956–9), and in vol. 1 of his *La Catalogne dans l'Espagne Moderne* (Paris, 1962).

2. *The reign of Ferdinand and Isabella*

W. H. Prescott's *History of the Reign of Ferdinand and Isabella* (first published 1838) still has many merits, of which not the least is its readability. Another nineteenth-century study of the reign which is still of value is H. Mariéjol, *L'Espagne sous Ferdinand et Isabelle* (Paris, 1892), of which an English translation by Benjamin Keen appeared in 1961 (*The Spain of Ferdinand and Isabella*, Rutgers University Press), with an admirable preface and bibliographical survey, by the translator, of recent work on the reign. The chapter by J. M. Batista i Roca, 'The

Hispanic Kingdoms and the Catholic Kings' in *The New Cambridge Modern History*, vol. I (Cambridge, 1957), is an excellent brief account.

The problem of the origins of the 'modern state' is examined by Professor Vicens Vives in 'Estructura administrativa estatal en los siglos XVI y XVII', published in vol. IV of the *Rapports* of the XI⁰ Congrès International des Sciences Historiques (Stockholm, 1960), and by José Antonio Maravall, 'The Origins of the Modern State', *Journal of World History*, vol. VI (1961). José Cepeda Adán, *En torno al concepto del estado en los Reyes Católicos* (Madrid, 1956), is a study of the political beliefs and theories to be found in the Spain of Ferdinand and Isabella.

While J. Vicens Vives, *Política del Rey Católico en Cataluña* (Barcelona, 1940), examines the restoration of government in Catalonia, there is no recent survey of the administrative reforms in Castile, and the study by J. Gounon-Loubens, *Essais sur l'administration de la Castille au XVI⁰ siècle* (Paris, 1860), remains the essential work on the machinery of Castilian government as established by Ferdinand and Isabella. The religious policy of the Catholic Kings is examined by P. Tarsicio de Azcona, *La elección y reforma del episcopado español en tiempo de los Reyes Católicos* (Madrid, 1960), and he has also written in his *Isabel la Católica* (Madrid, 1964) the best biography of Isabella to date. Economic questions are treated in J. Klein's standard work, *The Mesta: a study in Spanish economic history* (Cambridge, Mass., 1920); R. S. Smith, *The Spanish Guild Merchant* (Duke University Press, 1940); and E. Ibarra y Rodríguez, *El problema cerealista en España durante el reinado de los Reyes Católicos* (Madrid, 1944). The best recent work on the coinage is O. Gil Farrés, *Historia de la moneda española* (Madrid, 1959).

For artistic and intellectual life in this, and later, reigns, see G. Kubler and M. Soria, *Art and Architecture in Spain and Portugal and their American Dominions, 1500 to 1800* (Pelican History of Art, London, 1959); Bernard Bevan, *History of Spanish Architecture* (London, 1938); G. Reynier, *La vie universitaire dans l'ancienne Espagne* (Paris, 1902); G. Brenan, *The Literature of the Spanish People* (Cambridge, 1951).

3. Castilian expansion

Perhaps the best general study of the beginnings of Castile's overseas expansion is R. Konetzke, *Das Spanische Weltreich: Grundlagen und Entstehung*, translated into Spanish as *El Imperio Español. Orígenes y Fundamentos* (Madrid, 1946). F. Braudel, 'Les Espagnols et l'Afrique du Nord de 1492 à 1577', *Revue Africaine*, vol. 69 (1928), is a valuable article on Spain's North African policy.

J. H. Parry, *The Age of Reconnaissance* (London, 1963) and *The Spanish Seaborne Empire* (London, 1966) are admirable general surveys.

See also the same author's *The Spanish Theory of Empire in the Sixteenth Century* (Cambridge, 1940). For the Spanish background to the settlement and organization of the New World, J. M. Ots Capdequi, *El estado español en las Indias* (3rd ed., Mexico, 1957), and Silvio Zavala, *Ensayos sobre la colonización española en América* (Buenos Aires, 1944), are particularly helpful. R. Ricard, *La conquête spirituelle du Mexique* (Paris, 1933; Eng. trans. *The Spiritual Conquest of Mexico*, Berkeley, 1966), examines the work of the friars, and G. Kubler, *Mexican Architecture of the Sixteenth Century* (2 vols., Yale, 1948), is a superb survey of the intense architectural activity in the first decades after the conquest, which never overlooks the social, religious, and economic conditions that made the building possible. The important debate over the correct method of approach to the American Indians has been extensively studied by Lewis Hanke, notably in *The Spanish Struggle for Justice in the Conquest of America* (Philadelphia, 1949) and *Aristotle and the American Indians* (London, 1959). The great unfinished biography of Bartolomé de Las Casas by Manuel Giménez Fernández (vol. I, Seville, 1953, vol. II, 1960) is overwhelmingly rich in its details of administration and politics in Spain and America in the early sixteenth century.

Chapters 4 and 5 (The Imperial Destiny: The Government and the Economy in the Reign of Charles V).

Ferdinand's foreign policy and methods of diplomacy are examined in Garrett Mattingly, *Renaissance Diplomacy* (London, 1955). A. Walther, *Die Anfänge Karls V* (Leipzig, 1911), is a remarkable study of the Burgundian-Spanish connexion and of the complicated interlude between the death of Isabella and the establishment of her grandson on the Spanish throne. The revolt of the *Comuneros* needs far more systematic and detailed investigation than it has so far received, but H. L. Seaver, *The Great Revolt in Castile* (London, 1928), is a helpful summary of existing knowledge. Much more perceptive, however, is the interpretative essay by José Antonio Maravall, *Las Comunidades de Castilla* (Madrid, 1963) which sees the revolt as the first 'modern' revolution. The differing historiographical approaches to the revolt are analysed by J. Pérez in an article in the *Bulletin Hispanique* LXV (1963), pp. 238–83. On the *Germanía* of Valencia there is a suggestive article by L. Piles Ros, 'Aspectos sociales de la Germanía de Valencia', *Estudios de Historia Social de España* II (1952).

Incomparably the best recent survey of the empire of Charles V is to be found in the chapter by Professor H. Koenigsberger in *The New Cambridge Modern History*, vol. II. Royall Tyler, *The Emperor Charles V* (London, 1956), is useful for its chronology of Charles's life and travels, and for its summary, in chapter XII, of recent Spanish work on the Emperor's finances. Bohdan Chudoba, *Spain and the Empire, 1519–1643* (Chicago, 1952), is a strange, and uneven, study of relations between the Spanish and Austrian Habsburgs, but contains information from the Czech archives that is not to be found elsewhere. Some of the essays printed in *Charles-Quint et son temps* – the outcome of a symposium held in Paris in 1958 to commemorate the fourth centenary of the Emperor's death – are very valuable, as also is the essay by F. Chabod, 'Milan o los Paises Bajos?' in *Carlos V. Homenaje de la Universidad de Granada* (Granada, 1958).

The government of Spain under Charles V has been sadly neglected, although some useful information is scattered through the posthumously published work of F. Walser, *Die Spanischen Zentralbehörden und der Staatsrat Karls V* (Göttingen, 1959). The important figure of Los Cobos has at last found a biographer in Hayward Keniston, *Francisco de los Cobos. Secretary of the Emperor Charles V* (Pittsburgh, 1960), but this remains strictly a personal biography, and there is no general study of the workings of the governmental machine under Cobos. The standard and indispensable work on the Council of the Indies – the only one of the Spanish Councils to have received an adequate study – is E. Schäfer, *El Consejo Real y Supremo de las Indias* (2 vols., Seville, 1935).

The economic history of the reign of Charles V has fared much better than its administrative history. The pioneer in this field has been R. Carande, whose *Carlos V y sus banqueros* (vol. 1, Madrid, 1943, vol. II, 1949, vol. III, 1967) has become a standard authority. J. Larraz, *La época del mercantilismo en Castilla, 1500–1700* (2nd ed., Madrid, 1943), is a very enlightening account of economic policy and practice in Habsburg Spain. H. Lapeyre, *Une Famille de Marchands: les Ruiz* (Paris, 1955), is an important study of a great Castilian merchant dynasty, and is complemented by the same author's *Simon Ruiz et les Asientos de Philippe II* (Paris, 1953), which shows the workings of the *asiento* system. The commercial system linking Spain to its American colonies is described by Chaunu (noted above) and by C. H. Haring, *Trade and Navigation between Spain and the Indies in the time of the Hapsburgs* (Cambridge, Mass., 1918). A detailed monograph on the golden age of Seville is greatly needed, but there is some interesting information to be found in the short survey by A. Domínguez Ortiz, *Orto y Ocaso de Sevilla* (Seville, 1946).

Chapter 6 (Race and Religion).

The influence of Erasmus on Spain has been exhaustively studied by M. Bataillon, *Érasme et l'Espagne* (Paris, 1937; revised and enlarged edition in Spanish translation, *Erasmo y España*, 2 vols., Mexico, 1950). Further light is thrown on the persecution of the Erasmians in J. E. Longhurst, *Erasmus and the Spanish Inquisition: the Case of Juan de Valdés* (Albuquerque, 1950). H. C. Lea, *A History of the Inquisition in Spain* (4 vols., New York, 1906-7), remains the fundamental work on the Inquisition, although Henry Kamen, *The Spanish Inquisition* (London, 1965), provides a more modern study.

On the Moors of Granada, the best study in print is Julio Caro Baroja, *Los Moriscos del Reino de Granada* (Madrid, 1957). It is greatly to be hoped that K. Garrad, *The Causes of the Second Rebellion of the Alpujarras*, to which acknowledgement is made in the text, will soon be published. H. Lapeyre, *Géographie de l'Espagne Morisque* (Paris, 1959), is an extremely meticulous statistical survey of the Morisco population before, and at the time of, the expulsion. There are important articles on the Moriscos of Valencia by T. Halperin Donghi in *Cuadernos de Historia de España*, vols. XXIII and XXIV (1955), and in *Annales. Economics. Sociétés. Civilisations* (1956).

For the Jews and *conversos* see Cecil Roth, *A History of the Marranos* (1932, reprinted Meridian Books, New York, 1959), J. Caro Baroja, *Los Judíos en la España moderna y contemporórea* (3 vols., Madrid, 1962), and A. Domínguez Ortiz, 'Los Conversos de orígen judío después de la expulsión', *Estudios de Historia Social de España*, vol. III (1955). A. A. Sicroff, *Les Controverses des Statuts de 'Pureté de Sang' en Espagne du XVe au XVIIe Siècle* (Paris, 1960), is an exhaustive study of the great debate about *limpieza de sangre*. On the attitude to honour, which is connected with the problem of *limpieza*, there is a famous article by Américo Castro, 'Algunas observaciones acerca del concepto del honor en los siglos XVI y XVII', *Revista de Filología Española*, vol. III (1916). Jewish influence on Spanish history is a dominant theme in Américo Castro's remarkable *La Realidad Histórica de España* (revised ed., Mexico, 1965) and his earlier *The Structure of Spanish History*, trans. Edmund L. King (Princeton, 1954), and he has inspired important researches into the subject. See in particular *Collected Studies in honour of Américo Castro's Eightieth Year*, ed. M. P. Hornik (Oxford, 1965).

Philip II's relations with the Papacy are summarized in J. Lynch, 'Philip II and the Papacy', *Transactions of the Royal Historical Society* (5th series, vol. XI, 1961), and his treatment of Archbishop Carranza is scrutinized by G. Marañón, 'El proceso del Arzobispo Carranza',

Boletín de la Real Academia de la Historia, vol. CXXVII (1950). The literature devoted to the religious history of the reign of Philip II is extraordinarily disappointing and unsatisfactory. M. Boyd, *Cardinal Quiroga, Inquisitor General of Spain* (Dubuque, Iowa, 1954), is little more than an introduction to an important subject, and is not entirely reliable. Aubrey Bell, *Luis de León* (Oxford, 1925), and 'Liberty in Sixteenth-Century Spain', *Bulletin of Spanish Studies*, X (1933), give some idea of the difficulties facing scholars in the early years of the reign, but this is an exceptionally difficult and delicate subject, on which much more work is required. Apart from the Jesuits, whose history has been related at length by A. Astraín, *Historia de la Compañía de Jesús* (7 vols., Madrid, 1912–25), the Spanish Religious Orders have been peculiarly neglected, and there is no reliable general survey of the impact of the Counter-Reformation on Spain. At present, Bataillon's great work on Erasmianism remains by far the best book on sixteenth-century religious movements in Spain, and its very importance may well have distorted the picture of Spanish religion by directing so much attention to one particular school of religious thought. Gerald Brenan, 'St John of the Cross. His life and poetry', *Horizon*, vol. XV (1947), contains some stimulating ideas about the reform movement and its opponents, and E. Allison Peers, *Handbook to the Life and Times of St Teresa and St John of the Cross* (London, 1954), is also useful on this subject. Professor A. A. Parker's booklet, *Valor actual del humanismo español* (Madrid, 1952), has some interesting pages on the growing reaction against Renaissance values in the later sixteenth century. E. Allison Peers, *The Mystics of Spain* (London, 1951), is an anthology of translated extracts from the writings of the mystics, with a brief introduction.

Chapter 7 ('One Monarch, One Empire, and One Sword').

There is no satisfactory biography of Philip II – a point which H. Lapeyre brings out well in a critical round-up of recent lives of the King, 'Autour de Philippe II', *Bulletin Hispanique*, vol. LIX (1957). G. Marañón, *Antonio Pérez* (6th ed., 2 vols., Madrid, 1958; abridged English translation under same title, London, 1954), provides, however, a psychological study of the King, as well as an exciting piece of detective work which claims to unravel the mystery of the Pérez affair (a subject which really requires a Namier-style investigation into the family backgrounds and clientage systems of the opposing factions at Court). J. M. González de Echávarri y Vivanco, *La Justicia y Felipe II* (Valladolid, 1917), is a brief anthology of incidents illustrating the

King's preoccupation with the maintenance of high standards of justice. Philip II's theory and practice of kingship need much more investigation, as does the governmental system in his reign, although H. Koenigsberger, *The Government of Sicily under Philip II of Spain* (London, 1951), is an excellent study of the administration in one of his dominions. G. de Boom, *Don Carlos* (Brussels, 1955), is a reliable, and sometimes moving, short life of the King's unfortunate son.

The bibliography of the revolt of the Netherlands is enormous, but falls largely outside the scope of this work. The revolt still needs to be studied from the standpoint of Madrid, and a systematic survey of Spanish policy towards the Netherlands has never been attempted. Luis Morales Oliver, *Arias Montano y la política de Felipe II en Flandes* (Madrid, 1927), gives the views of the King's chaplain on the causes of the revolt and the best means of ending it. J. Reglà, *Felip II i Catalunya* (Barcelona, 1956), while concerned with Philip's government in Catalonia, emphasizes the multiplicity of the problems which confronted the King at the time when the revolt of the Netherlands broke out. Don John of Austria's ambitions and activities are discussed at length in P. O. de Törne, *Don Juan d'Autriche et les projets de conquête de l'Angleterre* (2 vols., Helsinki, 1915 and 1928), while L. Van der Essen, *Alexandre Farnèse* (5 vols., Brussels, 1933–7), is a superb biography of his successor in the government of the Netherlands.

The annexation of Portugal is another subject which deserves closer study but J. M. Rubio, *Felipe II de España, Rey de Portugal* (Madrid, 1939), is a useful brief account. M. Van Durme, *El Cardenal Granvela* (Spanish translation from the Flemish, Barcelona, 1957), contains information on the part played by Granvelle in the annexation and its aftermath. A. P. Usher, 'Spanish Ships and Shipping in the Sixteenth and Seventeenth Centuries', *Facts and Factors in Economic History. Articles by Former Students of E. F. Gay* (Cambridge, Mass., 1932), gives some idea of the relative strength of the combined Spanish and Portuguese merchant fleet, while the Invincible Armada has found an ideal historian in Garrett Mattingly, *The Defeat of the Spanish Armada* (London, 1959).

On the revolt of Aragon, the standard work remains the *Historia de las Alteraciones de Aragón*, by the Marqués de Pidal (3 vols., Madrid, 1862–3).

Chapters 8, 9, and 10 (Splendour and Misery: Revival and Disaster: Epitaph on an Empire).

The classic account of the decline of Spain is to be found in the article by Earl J. Hamilton, 'The decline of Spain', *Economic History*

Review, VIII (1938). Valuable suggestions towards a new and wider synthesis are to be found in P. Vilar, 'Le temps du Quichotte', *Europe*, XXXIV (1956), and literature produced on the subject since Hamilton's article is surveyed by the author of this book in 'The decline of Spain', *Past and Present*, no. 20 (1961). There is a magisterial survey of the demographic crisis in the New World in W. Borah, *New Spain's Century of Depression* (University of California, 1951), and F. Chevalier, *La Formation des grands domaines au Mexique* (Paris, 1952; Eng. trans. *Land and Society in Colonial Mexico*, Berkeley, 1963), is a fine study of the reasons why Mexico became a country of vast landed estates in the seventeenth century. Engel Sluiter, 'Dutch–Spanish rivalry in the Caribbean area, 1594–1609', *The Hispanic American Historical Review*, vol. XXIX (1949), is useful for the impact of the Dutch on the Spanish-American colonial system, while H. Kellenbenz, *Unternehmerkräfte in Hamburger, Portugal- und Spanienhandel, 1590–1625* (Hamburg, 1954), studies the activities of the Dutch in relation to Spain's home economy. There is, unfortunately, very little of value on Spain's economic troubles (other than specifically monetary problems) although C. Viñas Mey, *El problema de la tierra en la España del siglo XVI* (Madrid, 1941), at least broaches the almost untouched subject of Spanish land-ownership, and J. Reglá, 'La expulsión de los moriscos y sus consecuencias', *Hispania* XIII (1953), provides new information about the economic effects of the expulsion of the Moriscos of the Crown of Aragon. Noël Salomon, *La Campagne de Nouvelle Castille à la fin du XVIᵉ Siècle* (Paris, 1964) and B. Bennassar, *Valladolid au siècle d'or* (Paris, 1967) offer valuable fresh insights into the neglected topic of sixteenth-century Castilian social history. An important general survey of seventeenth-century society is being written by Antonio Domínguez Ortiz: *La Sociedad Española en el siglo XVII* (vol. I, Madrid, 1964).

The literature on the reign of Philip III is particularly scanty and inadequate. On the Duke of Lerma, for instance, little advance has been made since E. Rott, 'Philippe III et le duc de Lerme', *Revue d'Histoire Diplomatique*, vol. 1 (1887), and J. Juderías, 'Los favoritos de Felipe III. Don Pedro Franqueza . . .', *Revista de Archivos, Bibliotecas y Museos*, XIX and XX (1908–9). Contemporary ideas about the position of the Favourite and other stock themes of contemporary political thought are, however, usefully examined in J. A. Maravall, *La teoría española del estado en el siglo XVII* (Madrid, 1944; French edition, *La philosophie politique espagnole au XVIIᵉ siècle*, Paris, 1955) and in Francisco Tomas Valiente, *Los Validos en la Monarquía Española del siglo XVII* (Madrid, 1963).

On the reign of Philip IV, A. Cánovas del Castillo, *Estudios del reinado de Felipe IV* (2 vols., Madrid, 1888–9, 2nd ed., 1927), retains its usefulness, but Martin Hume, *The Court of Philip IV* (London, 1907, 2nd ed., n.d., 1928?), although lively and readable, is showing signs of wear. J. Deleito y Piñuela has written in *El declinar de la monarquía española* (2nd ed., Madrid, 1947), and a number of other volumes, a series of informative but light-weight studies of Spanish society and customs in this period, and P. W. Bomli, *La femme dans l'Espagne du siècle d'or* (The Hague, 1950), is a study of the position of women, based, however, entirely on literary sources. The figure of Olivares has found a remarkable biographer in G. Marañón, *El Conde-Duque de Olivares* (3rd ed., Madrid, 1952), but this is overwhelmingly concerned with his personal, rather than his political, career. The first competent account of Spanish finances in the reign of Philip IV is to be found in A. Domínguez Ortiz, *Política y hacienda de Felipe IV* (Madrid, 1960), and the same author has written two particularly valuable articles in 'La ruina de la aldea castellana', *Revista Internacional de Sociología*, no. 24 (1948), and 'La desigualdad contributiva en Castilla durante el siglo XVII', *Anuario de Historia del Derecho Español*, vol. XXXI (1951).

For the Catalan revolution of 1640, see J. H. Elliott, *The Revolt of the Catalans* (Cambridge, 1963), and J. Sanabre, *La acción de Francia en Cataluña* (Barcelona, 1956), which deals with Catalonia during the French occupation. The first volume of P. Vilar, *La Catalogne dans l'Espagne moderne*, cited earlier, is particularly valuable for the history of Catalonia throughout this period. There is no good study of the Portuguese revolution of 1640, but F. Mauro, *Le Portugal et l'Atlantique au XVIIᵉ siècle* (Paris, 1960), provides a comprehensive survey of Portugal's Atlantic economy.

The second half of Philip IV's reign, after the fall of Olivares, is largely unexplored territory. F. Silvela, *Cartas de la venerable Sor María de Ágreda y del Señor Rey Don Felipe IV* (2 vols., Madrid, 1885–6), is, however, a magnificent edition of the correspondence between the King and the nun, and contains a useful introduction; and R. Ezquerra Abadía, *La conspiración del Duque de Híjar*, 1648 (Madrid, 1934), throws light on the causes of aristocratic discontent.

The reign of Charles II is in even worse shape. The Duque de Maura, *Vida y reinado de Carlos II* (2 vols., 2nd ed., Madrid, 1954) is a complex analysis of Court history. John Nada, *Carlos the Bewitched* (London, 1962), is a gloomily readable biography. The administrative history of Spain in this period has been entirely neglected, and the subject of the intellectual decline still awaits its historian, although there are essays of very uneven quality on Spanish science in *Estudios sobre la ciencia española del siglo XVII* (Madrid, 1935).

Index

Dates are those of birth and death, except for those after the names of kings, which are regnal dates

Academies, 342, 369

Acosta, José de, botanist, 384

Acuña, Antonio de, Bishop of Zamora (d. 1526), 157–8

Acuña, Hernando de (d. 1580), poet, 249, 284

Administration,
in Castile, 90–92, 257–9, 275–6, 366–7; local government, 93–6
in Spanish Monarchy, 170–81, 375–6, 377–8, 383
see also Aragon, Crown of; Conciliar system; Indies; Secretaries; Viceroys

Adrian of Utrecht 'Pope Adrian VI' (1459–1523), 102, 145, 201, 213
regent of Castile (1520–22), 154–5, 157

Africa, North, 53–4, 168, 232

Agriculture, 117–20, 189, 195–6, 293–8

Agustín, Antonio, Vice-Chancellor of Aragon, 143

Álamos de Barrientos, Baltasar (1555–1643), political theorist, 329

Alba, 2nd Duke of, Fadrique Álvarez de Toledo (d. 1531), 140, 172

Alba, 3rd Duke of, Fernando Álvarez de Toledo y Pimentel (1507–82), 160, 168, 233, 267, 272, 275
Court faction of, 261–3, 281, 328

Albert, Archduke (1559–1621), 275, 290

Alburqurque, 7th Duke of, Francisco Fernández de la Cueva (d. 1637), Viceroy of Catalonia, 331

Alburquerque, Leonor de, 34

Alcabala, 92, 202–3, 231, 269, 285–6

Alcalá, Duke of, Fernando Afán de Ribera y Enríquez (1584–1637), 319, 331

Alcalá de Henares, university of, 105, 127, 128, 129, 215, 217

Alcalde, 93, 96

Alcalde de Zalamea, El, 295

Alcaraz, Pedro Ruiz de, 213–4

Alcázarquivir, battle of (1578), 266, 271

Alemán, Mateo (1547–1620), writer, 246

Alexander VI, Pope, 53, 69, 77, 79, 102, 103, 104

Alfonso V, the Magnanimous, of Aragon (1416–58), 35, 36, 39–40

Alfonso V, of Portugal (1438–81), 20, 23

Algiers, 53–4

Aljubarrota, battle of (1385), 43

Almagro, Diego de (1472–1538), *conquistador*, 64

Almazán, 2nd Marquis of, Francisco Hurtado de Mendoza (d. 1615), Viceroy of Catalonia, 331

Almenara, 1st Marquis of, Íñigo de Mendoza y de la Cerda (d. 1591), 279–81

Alonso de Aragón, natural son of John II of Aragon, 87

Alonso de Aragón (1478–1520), natural son of Ferdinand II, Archbishop of Zaragoza, 142

Alpujarras, first revolt of (1499–1500), 51–2, 53, 123 second revolt of (1568–70), 236–41, 242

Alumbrados, see Illuminism

Álvarez de Toledo, house of (Dukes of Alba), 23, 260

America, *see* Indies

Andalusia, 186–8, 235–40, 348 reconquest of, 26, 46–52

Antwerp, sack of (1576), 264

Aragon, Crown of, 27 dynastic union with Castile, 18–19, 24–5, 42–4 traditional foreign policy of, 19–20, 23, 131–5, 140–41 population of, 24–5, 37 greatness and decline of, 27–31, 34–5, 36–41, 42

and the New World, 78–9, 375, 376 administrative organization of, 79–80, 82–4, 90–91 recruiting in, 82, 330–31, 332 Inquisition in, 107–8 fear of Castilianization, 255–7 lack of unity in, 350–52 and Bourbons, 375–8

Aragon, kingdom of, 25–6, 27–30, 332, 351–2, 376 revolt of 1591–2, 277–84

Aragón, Cardinal Pascual de (1625–77), 362

Aranda, Count of, Aragonese noble, 282

Aranjuez, 254, 367

Arbitristas, 300, 303, 310, 315–16, 317, 328 influence of, 324, 327, 380, 385

Arbués, Pedro de, inquisitor, 107

Architecture, 127, 253–4, 319

Archive, state, 171

Arias Montano, Benito (1527–98), chaplain of Philip II, 227, 242, 245, 247, 251

Aristocracy, in Andulasia, 26, 57 in Castile, 111–16; ideals of, 32–3; income and expenditure, 34, 111–13, 179, 195, 312–15; privileges of, 115–16, 203–5, 336; creations of, 314; faction struggles, 142, 147–8, 221–2, 259–62, 279

relations with Crown, in 15th
century, 15–16, 34; under
Ferdinand and Isabella,
86–92, 111–14; (1504–20),
114, 138–9, 141–3; during
revolt of *Comuneros*, 154–9;
under Charles V, 114,
204; under Philip II, 212,
259–62; under Philip III,
302, 312, 314; under Philip
IV, 336, 342, 348–9; under
Charles II, 363, 364–5,
see also Grandees, *Hidalguía*
in Crown of Aragon, 28, 112–
13; in Catalonia, 40–41,
340, 353, in kingdom of
Aragon, 277–9, 282
in the Indies, 63, 75
in Portugal, 270–72, 346
provincial aristrocracies in
Spanish Monarchy, 352
Armada, Invincible, 270, 285,
287–9
Army, 46–8, 133–4, 142, 350
in Netherlands, 263–4, 325–6,
326, 341
see also Billeting; Recruiting
Art, 127, 318–19, 367, 384–6
Asiento, 206, 264, 333
Auctions, 318
Audiencias, 97, 174–5, 178–9, 377
Ávalos, Hernando de, Toledan
noble, 148
Avis, house of, 43, 270
Ayamonte, 6th Marquis of,
Francisco
Antonio de Guzmán y
Zúñiga (d. 1648), 348

Ayatona, 4th Marquis of,
Guillermo Ramón de
Moncada (d. 1670), 362, 364
Azores, 43, 58
Azpilcueta Navarro, Martín de
(1491–1586), professor at
Salamanca, 191–2

Balboa, Vasco Núñez de (1475?–
1519), 62
Balearic Islands, 26, 232, 241,
375
Baltasar Carlos, son of Philip IV
(1629–46), 357
Bandits, Catalan, 304, 331, 371
Bankers, 38, 182, 199–200, 201,
206–7, 333
Castilian, 197, 287
see also Bankruptcies, royal
Bankruptcies, royal, (1557), 199–
200, 210–11, 231; (1575),
263, 269; (1596), 287, 290;
(1607), 290–91; (1627),
333–4; (1647), 356; (1653),
356; (1680), 367
Banks, 38, 264, 328
Barajas, 1st Count of, Francisco
Zapata de Cisneros (d.
1592), President of Council
of Castile, 275
Barbarossa, Kheireddin, 54
Barcelona, 27
decline of, 38, 40–41, 108
and revolt against Philip IV,
337, 340, 345, 353–4
captured by French (1697),
373; by Bourbons (1714),
377

Bedmar, Marquis of, Alfonso de la Cueva (1572–1655), ambassador to Venice 1607–18, 325

Behetrías, 68

Béjar, 2nd Duke of, Álvaro de Zúñiga (d. 1531), 145, 172

Benavente, 6th Count of, Antonio Alfonso Pimentel, 204

Bible, 105, 129, 225, n.3, 226

Biga and *Busca*, Catalan factions, 40

Bilbao, 121

Billeting, 295, 243, 344

Bishops, 99–102, 103, 204
see also Church

Black Death, 33, 37

Blake, Admiral, 186

Boabdil, King of Granada (1482–92), 47–51

Bodin, Jean, 192

Bourbons, 375–8

Bourgeoisie, 26, 34, 197–8, 310–11
see also Towns

Braganza, Catherine, Duchess of, 267

Braganza, Duke of, John IV of Portugal (1640–56), 338, 346–7, 354

Bravo, Juan (d. 1521), *Comunero* leader, 158

Brazil, 63, 270, 337, 338, 341–2, 355

Breda, 341

Breisach, fall of (1638), 341

Brill, captured by Sea Beggars (1572), 242

Burgos, 94, 157
as commercial centre, 33, 120–21, 187, 197, 361

Burgundian ceremonial, 160

Cabra, Count of, 48

Cabrera de Córboba, Luis, (1550–1623), historia, 254

Cadiz, 182, 289, 334, 361

Calderón, Rodrigo (1570–1621) (Court favourite, 303, 315, 322, 326

Calderón de la Barca, Pedro (1600–81), dramatist, 295, 319, 367

Calvinism, 224, 225, 232, 233

Cámara de Castilla, Council of, 174

Canaries, The, 43, 45, 58–9, 69

Cano, Melchor (1509–60), Dominican theologian, 224, 229, 244, 247

Capitalism, 198, 310–11

Capitulaciones, 59

Caravels, 56–7

Cardona, 6th Duke of, Enrique de Aragón (d. 1640), Viceroy of Catalonia, 345

Caribbean Sea, Dutch incursions into, 291

Carlos, Don, son of Philip II (1545–68), 209, 235, 252–3

Carranza, Bartolomé de, Cardinal (1503–76), Archbishop of Toledo (1558–76), 228–9

Carrera de las Indias, 185–6, 187
see also Treasure fleet

Carrillo, Alfonso, Cardinal
(1410–82), Archbishop of
Toledo (1446–82), 15, 20,
100, 104
Carrillo, Fernando de (d. 1622),
President of Council of
Finance, 321
Casa de Contratación, 122, 175, 182
Casas, Bartolomé de las (1474–
1566), Dominican, 73, 75
Cascales, Fray Pedro de, 251
Caspe, Compromise of (1412),
18
Castile,
in Middle Ages, 31–5, 42–3;
united with Aragon, 15–26,
43–4
crusading ideal of, 32, 46, 60–
62, 233, 241–3, 248, 288;
eclipse of, 324–5
see also Administration,
Church, Cortes, Trade, etc.
Castilianization, 255–8, 277, 328–
9, 378
Castilians,
views on, 256, 277
antipathy towards Aragonese,
143
Castilla, Pedro de, dean of
Toledo Chapter 221
Castrillo, 2nd Count of, García
de Haro y Avellaneda, 348,
362
Catalonia, Principality of,
in Middle Ages, 26, 27–31,
35, 36–41
Ferdinand the Catholic and,
79–80, 84, 107–8

Charles V and, 146–7
Philip II and, 234–5
Olivares and, 331–3, 336–7,
338–41, 343; revolt of 1640–
52, 344–6, 350, 351, 353–4,
362
Bourbons and, 375–8
see also Bandits; Cortes;
Trade
Cateau-Cambrésis, peace of
(1559), 231
'Catholic Kings', title bestowed
on Ferdinand and Isabella
by Alexander VI, 77
Cazalla, Dr Agustín (1510–59),
chaplain of Charles V, 225,
229–30
Celestina, La (1499), 128
Censorship, 225–7, 234
Censos, 189, 306, 308, 311
see also Juros
Cerdaña, County of (Catalan:
Cerdanya), 41, 131, 355
Cervantes Saavedra, Miguel de
(1547–1616), 241, 299, 319–
20, 385–6
Chancillerías 97–8, 102, 251
see also Audiencias
Charles V, Holy Roman
Emperor (1519–58), King of
Spain (as Charles I, 1516–
56),
and North Africa, 54–5, 168–9
as King of Spain, 139–147,
159, 164–5, 210
as Emperor, 146–51, 160, 166–
9, 209–10
see also Finance

Charles II of Spain (1665–1700),
357–60, 361–2, 372–4
Charles VIII, of France (1483–
98), 131, 133
Charles, Archduke (1685–1740),
Emperor Charles VI (1711–
40), 373–4, 375, 376
Charles, Prince of Viana (1421–
61), son of John II of
Aragon, 41
Chaunu, Pierre, historian, 194
Chaves, Fray Diego de, 250–51
Chièvres, Sieur de, Guillaume de
Croy (1458–1521), Grand
Chamberlain of Charles V,
138, 144–5, 150
Chile, 63, 74
Chinchón, 3rd Count of, Diego
Fernández de Cabrera y
Bodadilla (d. 1608), Treasu-
rer-General of Council of
Aragon, 233, 275, 279
Chivalry, romances of, 64–5
Church, 32, 99–106, 229–30, 312,
369–70,
in America, 71–2, 101–2
in Andalusia, 26, 52–3, 101,
237–8
taxation of, 103, 200–201, 286,
336
Cisneros, Francisco Jiménez de
(1436–1517), Archbishop of
Toledo (1495–1517), 52,
53–4, 104–5, 127, 213
regency of, 139, 142–4
Claris, Pau (1586–1641), Catalan
leader, 341, 344, 346, 347,
353

Clergy, 99–100, 102, 204, 221–2,
247
reform of, 103–4, 243–4, 369
and revolt of *Comuneros*, 154,
215
numbers of, 244, 312, 317; in
America, 71
see also Bishops; Church;
Religious Orders
Cloth,
in Castile, 111, 122, 123, 187,
189–91, 195
in Catalonia, 27, 38, 39, 187,
371
market for, in New World,
185, 187, 190–91, 195, 292–3
Cobos, Francisco de los (1477?–
1547), Comendador mayor
de León,
career, 143, 162, 165–6, 179–80
208
and administration in Castile,
171, 173, 178–9, 208
Coinage, *see* Currency
Colegio Imperial, 342, 368–9
Colegios Mayores, 220–1, 316
see also Universities
Colonization, methods of,
55–6, 58–62, 66–74
Columbus, Christopher (1451–
1506), 45, 59–62
Comuneros, revolt of, 151–9,
215, 221, 260–61, 263
Conchillos, Lope (d. 1521),
secretary of Ferdinand the
Catholic, 143
Conciliar system, 83–4, 170–81,
254, 302, 335, 350

Bourbon reorganization of,
375–6
see also *Juntas; and under
individual councils*
Conquistadores, 62–7, 174
Consulados, 120–2, 185
Contractualism, 28–31, 41, 80,
81–2
Conversos,
hostility towards, 106–10, 143,
220–4, 225–6
intellectual tendencies of, 128,
161, 213
Copernicus, 242
Córdoba, Gonzalo Fernández de
(1453–1515), the Great
Captain, 46, 50, 133–4, 139,
141
Córboda, Gonzalo Fernández de
(1585–1635), governor of
Milan, 334
Corn, 118–20, 189, 295–6, 297, 298
Corregidores, 94–8, 152, 154, 251
Corruption, 179–81
Cortes,
of Castile, 34–5, 92–3, 151–2,
201–5, 363; complaints of,
116, 166, 214, 296, 322;
sessions: (Madrigal, 1476),
86, 92; (Toledo, 1480), 89–
90; (1510), 94; (Valladolid,
1518), 139; (Santiago and
Corunna 1520), 145–6;
(Toledo, 1538), 150–1; 204
–5; (1548),190–1; (1552),
190; (1561), 231; (1574–5),
269; (1588–90, 1592–8), 285–
6; (1623–9) 328

of Crown of Aragon, 28–9,
80, 82, 201–2, 255–6; of
Aragon, 28–9; (1518), 145–
6; (1585), 278; (1592), 282–
3; (1626), 331, 332; of
Catalonia, 28–9; (1480–1),
81, (1599), 303; (1626), 331–
2; (1632), 337; (1701),
376; of Valencia, 28; (1604),
303; (1626), 331, 332
of Navarre, 141
see also *Servicios*
Cortés, Hernán, Marqués del
Valle de Oaxaca (1485–
1547), 62–6, 163
Council of Aragon, 83, 134, 170,
281, 377
Council of Castile, 89–91, 170,
174, 322, 377
Council of Finance (*Hacienda*),
173, 179, 198–9, 325, 335,
339, 356–7
Council of the Indies, 170, 174–
6, 302
Council of Italy, 170, 255
Council of Portugal, 274, 325
Council of State, 172, 260, 302,
336, 366, 374
Council of War, 172, 295
Counter-Reformation, 216, 224–
31, 243–47
Court, 127, 160, 161, 312–15,
322
Crato, Prior of, Don Antonio
(1531–95), 267, 271–3
Crespí de Valldaura, Cristóbal
(1599–1672), Vice Chancellor of Aragon, 362

Croy, Guillaume de (1500–21), Archbishop of Toledo (1518–21), 145, 158
Cruz, Isabel de la, 213–14
Cruzada, 53, 103, 201, 286
Cueva, Beltrán de la (d. 1492), 23
Currency, 124–5, 194–5, 274, 332–3, 370
   vellón, 304, 315, 333–4, 349, 356, 357, 367, 370, 372
   see also Prices
Customs duties, 124, 185, 202, 231, 274

Denia, Marquis of, *see* Lerma, Duke of
Deza, Pedro de (1520–1600), president of the *chancillería* of Granada, 238–9
Díaz del Castillo, Bernal (d. 1582), *conquistador*, 65
Díaz de Montalvo, Alonso (1405 –99), jurist, 98
Diplomatic service, Spanish, 132–3
Diputació, Catalan, 29–30, 40, 41, 81–2, 234, 341, 354, 377
Domestic service, 315
Donativos, 298, 336
Doria, Nicolás (1539–94), Provincial of the Carmelites, 247
Downs, battle of the (1639), 341
Drake, Sir Francis, 289
Duplessis Besançon, Bernard, Richelieu's agent in Catalonia, 347

Dutch, *see* Netherlands; United Provinces

Eboli, Prince of, Ruy Gómez de Silva (1516–73), 232, 250, 252, 261–2
Eboli, Princess of, Ana de Mendoza de la Cerda (1540– 91), 261, 266–8
Eboli faction, 261–4, 268, 273–4, 181, 329
Economic policies of Spanish Crown,
   Catholic Kings, 111, 120, 122–3
   Charles V, 189–91, 198–9
   see also Arbitristas; Finance
Education, 128–9, 225–7, 234, 315–17, 342, 367–9
   of royal officials, 90, 116, 178–9, 315–16,
   of clergy, 104–6
   see also Universities
Egas, Enrique de (d. 1534), architect, 127
Eguía, Miguel de, printer to Alcalá university, 217
Eixemeniç, Francesc (1340?– 1409), Calalan jurist, 28
El Greco (1541–1614), 384–5
Elizabeth I of England, 265, 288
Emmanuel I of Portugal (1495– 1521), 131
Empire, of Charles V, 146–7, 166–8, 209–11
   Spain and Imperial tradition, 160–61, 162–3
Encabezamiento, see Alcabala

Encomienda, 70–71, 74, 75

England,
Ferdinand's alliance with, 131, 134
hostilities with, 233–4, 287–9, 298, 334, 357; invasion projects, 264–5, 270, 276, 287–8
and Spanish succession, 375, 376–7

Enríquez, house of, 23, 34, 90, 113

Erasmianism, 71, 161–2, 215–18, 226, 229, 244

Eraso, Francisco de (d. 1570), secretary of state, 178

Escobedo, Juan de (d. 1678), secretary of Don John of Austria, 265–6

Escorial, 253

Espina, Juan de (d. (1642), connoisseur and collector, 318

Espinosa, Cardinal Diego de (1502–72), minister and Inquisitor General, 226, 232, 239, 262

Esquivel, Pedro de, professor of mathematics at Alcalá, 384

Essex, Earl of, 289

Évora (Portugal), riots, of 1637, 338

Excusado, 201, 234, 286

Factions, 142, 147–8, 221, 259–62, 279

Fairs, 42, 120, 188, 269, 287

Famine, 37, 120, 298
see also Harvests; Hunger

Fárax Abenfárax, Morisco leader, 235

Farnese, Alexander, Duke of Parma (1545–92), 268, 270, 289

Favourites, 301–2, 323, 350

Federalism, 31, 83–4, 257–8, 262, 283, 363

Ferdinand III of Castile (1217–52), 26

Ferdinand I (of Antequera), King of Aragon (1412–16), 18

Ferdinand II of Aragon (1479–1516), V of Castile, (1474–1504), the Catholic,
first marriage, 15–23; second marriage, 138; death, 142, 143
as King of Aragon, 41, 79–84, 107–8; rights in Castile, 77–8, 84–5
diplomacy and foreign policy 48, 53–4, 130–35, 140–42
joint government with Isabella, 77–8, 84–6; reconquest of Granada, 45, 48–51; overseas conquests, 57–61, 74–6; creation of State, 77–80, 82–6; government in Castile, 86–99; and Church 99–106; and Jews, 106–10; economic and social policies, 110–11, 116, 119–20, 122–5; achievements, 125–9, 153, 159; patronage of arts, 128
as regent of Castile, 136–41

Ferdinand I, King of Bohemia and Hungary, Holy Roman

Ferdinand I.—*continued*
  Emperor (1558–64), brother
    of Charles V, 200, 209
  as Infante, 140, 142, 144–5
Ferdinand, Cardenal Infante
    (1609–41), 323, 341
Feria, 3rd Duke of, Gómez
    Suárez de Figueroa (d.
    1634), Governor of Milan,
    general, 326, 342
Fernández de Lugo, Alfonso,
    conquistador in the Canaries,
    58–9
Fernandez Navarrete, Pedro,
    arbitrista, 316
Finance, Crown,
  Ferdinand and Isabella, 92–3;
    Charles V, 195, 199–211;
    Philip II, 231–3, 269–70,
    285–7; Philip III, 302, 321–
    2; Philip IV, 327, 333–4,
    339, 356–7; Charles II, 367;
    Philip V, 375
  see also Bankruptcies,
    Taxation
Flander, 290, 330, 341, 351
  cost of army in, 326, 339
  see also Netherlands; United
    Provinces
Fleet, Spanish, 121, 232, 276,
    287–9, 326, 241
  see also Shipping; Treasure
    fleet
Fonseca, Alonso (1475–1534),
    Archbishop of Toledo
    (1524–34), 214
Fonseca, Juan Rodríguez de, *see*
    Rodríquez de Fonseca

Francavilla, 1st Duke of, Diego
    Hurtado de Mendoza (d.
    1578), president of the
    Council of Italy, father of
    Princess of Eboli, 255
France,
  traditional hostility to Aragon,
    19, 41, 130–32, 133, 134
  civil wars in, 232, 270, 276,
    289; Fronde, 353, 355–6
  peace treaties with Spain:
    (1559), 231; (1598), 290;
    (1659), 355–6; (1678), 365;
    (1697), 373; marriage
    alliances, 321, 356
  war of 1635–59, 335, 339–40,
    341, 343, 350, 355–6
  French aid to Catalan rebels,
    346, 347, 349, 353–4; to
    Portuguese, 338, 357; to
    Neapolitans, 352
  war of 1673–8, 365–6
  and Spanish succession, 372–6
  see also under individual kings
Franche-Comté, loss of (1678),
    365–6
Franqueza, Pedro, Count of
    Villalonga (1547?–1614),
    Court favourite, 303
Friars, *see* Religious Orders
Fuenterrabía, siege of (1638), 339
Fuentes, Count of, Pedro
    Enríquez de Acevedo (d.
    1610), general, 325
Furió Ceriol, Fadrique (1527–
    92), Valencian humanist
    and political theorist, 257,
    263, 264

Galileo, 297

Galíndez de Caravajal, Dr Lorenzo (1472–1532), royal official and historian 145

Gattinara, Mercurino (1465–1530), Grand Chancellor of Charles V, 146, 150, 165, 170, 173, 174

Generalitat of Catalonia, 29–30, 40, 41, 81–2, 234, 341, 354, 377

Genoa, 27, 38–9, 169 merchants and bankers of, 110, 145, 197, 199, 206

Germaine de Foix (1488–1538), second wife of Ferdinand the Catholic, 138

Germanías of Valencia, 156–7, 159

Germany, Protestant princes of, 209

Gibraltar, 375

Girón, Pedro, *Comunero* leader, 142, 157

Gold, 183, 191

Golden Fleece, Order of the, 160

Gómez, Ruy, *see* Eboli, Prince of

Gondomar, Count of, Diego Sarmiento de Acuña (1567–1626), 382

Góngora Argote, Luis de (1561–1627), poet, 385

González, José, secretary of Olivares, 335, 356

González Dávila, Gil (1578–1658), historian, 312

González de Cellorigo, Martín, *arbitrista*, 298, 300, 310–11, 317–18, 320

González de Mendoza, Pedro (1428–95), Archbishop of Seville (1473–82) and of Toledo (1482–95), 100, 104, 105

Gracián, Baltasar (1601–58), 367

Granada, 45–52, 235–41

Granada, Fray Luis de (1504–88), Dominican mystical writer, 245

Grandees, 114–15, 314 *see also* Aristocracy

Granvelle, Antoine Perrenot de, (1517–86), Cardinal minister of Charles V and Philip II, 232, 258, 267–8, 271–6, 277

Granville, Nicholas Perronot de (1486–1550), minister of Charles V, 166

Great Captain, the, *see* Córdoba, Gonzalo Fernández de

Guidiel, Fray Alonso (1526–73), scholar, 245

Guerrero, Pedro (d. 1576), Archbishop of Granada (1546–76), 238

Guicciardini, Francesco, 140

Guilds, 111, 122, 156, 189–90

Guillén, Felipe (1492?–1561), mathematician and naturalist, 383

Gumiel, Pedro de, architect, 127

Guzmán, Gonzalo de, *Comunero* leader, 157

Guzmán, house of, 34, 113, 348

Guzmán de Alfarache, 186, 246

Hamilton, Professor Earl J.,
192–6

Harcourt, Marquis of, French
ambassador, 374

Haro, Luis de (1598–1661),
principal minister of Philip
IV, 350, 353, 355, 362

Harvests, 118, 189, 298, 334
see also Corn

Hawkins, Sir John, 233, 289

Henry IV, of Castile, the
Impotent (1454–74), 15, 18,
20, 22, 46

Henry III of France (1574–89),
289

Henry IV of France (1589–1610),
290, 321

Henry, Cardinal King of
Portugal (1578–80), 266,
271

Heresy, 212–19, 222, 225–30,
233, 234, 288

Hermandad, Santa, 86–7, 142

Hermandad de las Marismas, 57

Hernández, Francisca, former
Alumbrado, 217

Hernández, Francisco (1517–87),
doctor and naturalist, 384

Herrera, Juan de (1530?–97),
architect, 253, 319

Heyn, Piet (1578–1629), Dutch
privateer, 186, 335

Hidalgos, 114–15, 203–5
participation in conquest of
America, 63–6
employment in administra-
tion, 89–91, 95–7, 178–9
and *Comuneros*, 154–9, *passim*

Hidalguía,
ideals of, 32, 222–3
privileges of, 99, 115–16, 203–5
aspiration after, 65–6, 115–17,
179–80, 310
see also Aristocracy

Híjar, Duke of, Rodrigo
Sarmiento de Silva (1600–
64), 352

Hispania, concept of, 19

Hispaniola, 62, 70, 73

Honour, 32, 66, 222–3

Hospitals, 127, 243

Huguenots, 233–4, 334

Humanism, 105, 127–8, 161–2,
215–17, 224, 225, 242, 245–7
in Aragon, 19
in New World, 71

Hunger, 311
see also Famine

Idiáquez, Alonso de (d. 1547),
royal secretary, 178

Idiáquez, Juan de (1540–1614),
son of the preceding,
minister of Philip II,
267, 275–6

Idleness, 190, 299, 311–12, 317,
318

Illuminism, 213–15, 217, 224, 244

Index, 225–6, 244

Indians, 67–74, 292

Indies,
discovery and settlement of,
45, 62–75
government of, 78–9, 170–71,
174–5, 362
limitations on right of trade

with, 79, 124, 181–3, 361,
376
economic relationship with
Castile, 78–9, 122, 181–96
passim, 198–9, 200, 292–3
see also Seville; Silver
Indulgences, 103, 201
see also Cruzada
Industry, 122–3, 187–91
failure of, 193, 195–6, 207,
293, 298, 366–7
see also Cloth; Silk; Wool
Infantado, 3rd Duke of, Diego
Hurtado de Mendoza
(1461–1531), 142, 154, 261
Infantado, 5th Duke of, Íñigo
López de Mendoza (1536–
1601), 313–4
Inflation, *see* Currency
Inquisition, 107–9, 212–17
passim, 218–19, 224–6,
228–30, 242
in Crown of Aragon, 107–8,
234, 280–81
in Granada, 237
Investment, 39, 207, 310, 318, 328
see also Censos; Juros ·
Ireland, 290
Iron, Vizcayan, 121, 122, 188
Isabella I, the Catholic, Queen of
Castile (1474–1504),
marriage, 15–23; death, 130
and crusade against Islam, 53,
60
and slavery, 69
and Military orders, 88
and Nebrija's grammar, 128
see also Ferdinand

Isabella, Empress (1503–39),
wife of Charles V, 165
Isabella Clara Eugenia, Infanta
(1566–1633), 253, 290
Islam, crusade against, 26, 32,
53–4, 57, 106, 140, 241
Italy,
Aragonese interests in, 35, 140,
168;
Italian wars, 133–4
cultural and religious influence
of, on Spain, 127, 128, 161,
212–13, 227
Council of, 170, 225
see also under individual
Italian States

Jesuits, 247, 273, 342, 367–9
Jews, 20, 106–10, 116, 220–2
effects of expulsion, 107, 109–
10, 119, 120, 123
Portuguese, 304
see also Conversos
John II, Aragon (1458–79), 15,
19–21, 22, 23, 40–41, 140
John of Austria, Don (1545–78),
natural son of Charles V,
55, 240–41, 264–6, 268
John Maurice of Nassau, Prince,
355
Joseph Ferdinand of Bavaria,
Prince (1692–9), 373, 374
Juan, Prince (1478–97), son of
Ferdinand and Isabella, 135
Juan José of Austria, Don (1629–
79), natural son of Philip IV,
353, 356, 357, 361–2, 363–6
370

Juana, the Mad, Queen of
Castile (1504–55), 78, 135,
136, 138, 144, 155
Juana *la Beltraneja* (1462–1530),
15–16, 22–3
Juana, Infanta (1535–73), sister of
Philip II, 225, 271
Juntas, 302–3, 350
de Alivios, 364
de Gobierno, 362
de Noche, 275, 302
de Reformación, 322, 327
Jurisdiction,
aristocratic, 68, 81, 84, 96–7,
117, 278
ecclesiastical, 99, 100
military, 295
municipal, 67–8, 94–7
royal, 84–5, 94–8, 100–101, 212,
304; in New World, 68–9,
74–5, 174–6
see also Justice
see also Encomienda
Juros, 93, 195, 206–7, 287, 311,
336, 356
proposals for redemption of,
286, 318, 328
and see Censos
Justice, royal excercise of, 86,
98–9, 249–51
see also Jurisdiction
Justicia, of Aragon, 29, 279–80,
282, 283

Kingship,
in Crown of Aragon, 28–31;
in Spanish Monarchy, 167,
176-7

see also Monarchy, Spanish
concepts of: Catholic Kings,
77–8, 80, 85–6, 97–9;
Charles V, 166–7; Philip II,
249–51, 253, 254–5
royal absenteeism, 31, 83,
164–5, 176, 254–5, 329

Labour, 190, 196, 297–8, 318,
in New World, 70–71, 73–4
Land,
distribution and ownership of,
26–7, 32, 34, 50, 113, 297;
in New World, 59–60,
67–8, 74–5
Crown, 49–50, 89, 237
forms of tenure, 68, 81, 117–18
189
see also Agriculture
Language, 128, 141, 234, 245
La Noue, François de (1531–
91),
Huguenot leader, 289
Lanuza, Juan de, Justicia of
Aragon (1564–91), 282
Laso de la Vega, Pedro, *Comu-
nero* leader, 154, 157
Latifundios, 26, 292
see also Land
La Torre, Count of, Fernando
Mascarenhas, Portuguese
naval commander, 341
Law, 96–8, 329
Leyes Nuevas (1542), 73
see also Letrados
Leganés, Marquis of, Diego
Felipe de Guzmán (d.
1655), general, 318, 349

León, Fray Luis de (1527–91), theologian and poet, 219, 242, 245, 247

Lepanto, battle of (1571), 241–2

Lerma, Duke of, Francisco de Sandoval y Rojas, Marquis of Denia (1553–1625), favourite of Philip III, 301–4, 321–2, 323, 324

Lerma, Pedro de (d. 1541), humanist scholar, and Chancellor of Alcalá University, 217

Letrados, 90, 178–9

Levant Company, 332

Limpieza de sangre, 107, 220–24, 309

Lisbon, 271, 276, 337–8

Literature, 64, 128, 226–7, 245–7, 319–20, 385–6

Llorenç, Juan (d. 1520), leader of *Germanías*, 156

Loaisa, García de (1480?–1546), confessor of Charles V, Bishop of Osma (1525–32), Archbishop of Seville (1539–46), 172, 208

Local government, in Castile, 94–7
see also Jurisdiction

Lope de Vega Carpio, Felix (1562–1635), 319

Louis XI of France (1461–83), 15, 19, 22, 41, 77, 130

Louis XIV of France (1643–1715), 373, 374, 376

Loyola, St Ignatius (1491–1556), 214

Luna, Álvaro de (1390?–1453), favourite of John II of Castile, 18

Lutheranism, 212–15, 217

Madrid, 171, 253–4, 287, 305, 315

Majorca, 56, 232, 241

Manila galleon, 293

Manrique, Alonso (d. 1538), Archbishop of Seville (1524–38), Inquisitor General, 214–15, 216–17

Mantuan war (1628–31), 334–5

Manuel, Juan, adviser to Philip the Fair, 136

Margaret of Parma (1522–86), natural daughter of Charles V, 233, 268

Margaret of Savoy, Princess (1589–1655), Governess of Portugal, 337, 347

Margarit i Pau, Joan (1421–84), Cardinal, Chancellor of Joan II of Aragon, 19

María de Ágreda, Sor (1602–65), confidante of Philip IV, 350

María Teresa, Infanta (1638–83), daughter of Philip IV, 356, 373

Mariana of Austria (1634–96), 2nd wife of Philip IV, and Queen Regent, 357, 361, 362, 363, 364–5, 373

Mariana, Father Juan de (1535–1624), Jesuit historian, 218, 219, 367–8, 384

Marineo Sículo, Lucio (1444?–
1533), Italian humanist and
historiographer of Ferdinand
the Catholic, 89, 111, 313

Martin I of Aragon (1396–
1410), 16, 30

Martire d'Anghera, Pietro
(1457?–1526), Italian
humanist and historian, 128,
145, 156–7

Mary Tudor (1516–58), 210, 228

Maurice of Saxony (1521–53),
209

Maximilian I, Emperor (1493–
1519), 135, 146

Mazarin, Cardinal, 351, 352, 353

Medina del Campo, 154, 187–8
197, 294
fairs, of, 42, 120, 188, 269, 287

Medina de Ríoseco, 2nd Duke
of, Admiral of Castile, Luis
Enríquez de Cabrera y
Mendoza (d. 1596), 260

Medina-Sidonia, 9th Duke of,
Gaspar Pérez de Guzmán el
Bueno y Sandoval (d. 1664)
348

Medina de las Torres, 1st Duke
of, Ramiro Núñez de
Guzmán (d. 1668), 362

Medinacli, 8th Duke of, Juan
Francisco Tomás, de la
Cerda (d. 1691), minister of
Charles II, 315, 366

Mediterranean, 168–9, 231–2,
239, 241–2

Mendicant Orders, *see* Religious
Orders

Mendoza, house of, 23, 34, 113,
137, 260

Mendoza, Antonio de, Viceroy
of New Spain (1535–50)
and of Peru (1551–2), 175

Mendoza, Diego Hurtado de
(1503–75), statesman and
author, 382

'Mercantilism', 198
see also Economic Policies

Mercedes, 180, 283, 322

Merchants,
Castilian, 116–17, 121–2, 179,
197–8, 204
Catalan, 27, 36, 39, 332
foreign, 182, 186–7, 197, 361
see also Genoa
of Seville, 57, 59, 183, 187, 343
see also Trade

Mercury, 183, 269

Mesta, 33, 57, 119, 188

Mexico,
conquest and government of,
62, 64–6, 162, 174–6;
encomiendas, 70–71, 74; 75
Church in, 71–2, 102
silver, 183
'century of depression', 291–3
see also Indies

Milan, duchy of, 168, 286, 326

Military Orders, 26, 32, 88–9,
119, 201, 224

Millones, 285–6, 304, 328, 356

Minorca, 375

Miranda, Count of, Juan de
Zúñiga y Avellaneda (d.
1608), President of Council
of Castile, 301

Molina, Luis (1535–1600),
    Jesuit theologian, 247
Monarchy, Spanish,
    structure of, 166–7, 176–7,
        254–8
    see also Conciliar system
    proposed solutions to prob-
        lem of,
    see Castilianization; Eboli
        faction; Federalism;
        Olivares
Moncada, Sancho de, *arbitrista*,
    300
Mondéjar, 2nd Marquis of, Luis
    Hurtado de Mendoza, 3rd
    Count of Tendilla (d. 1566),
    237, 239
Mondéjar, 3rd Marquis, Íñigo
    López de Mendoza, 4th
    Count of Tendilla (1512–80),
    Captain-General of
    Granada, 236–40
Montesinos, Fray Antonio de
    (d. 1526?), Dominican,
    72–3
Moors, 26–7, 32, 45–56, 217
    Moorish survivals and
        influences, 52–3, 127, 236,
        308–9
    see also Moriscos
Moriscos, 110, 156, 168, 278
    2nd revolt of Alpujarras
        (1568–70), 235–41
    expulsion of, 305–8
    see also Moors
Mortara, 2nd Marquis of,
    Francisco de Orozco,
    general, 353

Moura, Cristóbal de (1538–1613),
    minister of Philip II, 271, 275,
    301
Mulay Hassan, King of Granada
    (d. 1485), 48
Münster, peace of (1648), 351
Murillo, Bartolomé Esteban
    (1617–82), artist, 367
Mysticism, 213, 244–6, 384–5

Nadal, Dr Jorge, historian, 194
Nájera, 1st Duke of, Pedro
    Manrique de Lara (d.
    1515), 142
Naples, 36, 131, 133–4, 139, 352
Nassau, Count Henry of, 172,
    173
Navagero, Andreas (1483–1529),
    Venetian historian, 197
Navarre, Kingdom of, 24, 25,
    140–42, 158–9, 170
Navigation, internal, 296–7
Nebrija, Elio Antonio de (1444–
    1522), humanist and
    grammarian, 128
Neo-Platonism, 244, 245
Netherlands,
    trade with Spain, 33, 120–21,
        137, 187, 188, 195, 290–92
    Flemish influences on Spain,
        127, 154, 160–61, 212;
        Spanish influence on
        Netherlands, 227
    political connexion with
        Castile, 135–7, 142–3, 160–
        61; Castilian reactions to
        Charles V's Flemish suite,
        145–6, 153, 155

Netherlands—*continued*
  and Imperial finances, 200
  revolt of (1566), 232, 242,
    258, 261–6, 268–9, 289–90
  see also Flanders; United
    Provinces
Nevers, Duke of, claimant to
  duchy of Mantua, 334
New World, *see* Indies
Nijmwegen, Peace of (1678),
  365
Nithard, Father Juan Everardo
  (1607–81), confessor of
  Mariana of Austria, 362, 363,
  364
Nueva Planta (1716), 377

Ocaña, Francisco de, Illuminist
  friar, 213
Offices, 89–91, 95–7, 178–80,
    263, 329
  municipal, 93–6, 212, 327
  sale of, 94, 304, 336, 356
  see also Administration;
    Limpieza de Sangre
Officials, royal, 91, 177–81
  see also Administration:
    Corregidores, etc.
Olivares, Conde Duque de,
  Gasper de Guzmán (1587–
  1645), favourite of Philip
  IV, 302, 318, 319, 323–49,
  379
Oquendo, Antonio de (1577–
  1640), admiral, 341
Oropesa, Count of, Manuel
  Joaquín Álvarez de Toledo
  y Portugal (d. 1707),

minister of Charles II, 363,
  372, 373
Orry, Jean (1652–1719), minister
  of Philip V, 375
Ortega y Gasset, Jose (1883–
  1955), 386
Osuna, Duke of, Pedro Tellez
  Girón (1579–1624), 325, 326
Ottoman Empire, *see* Turks
Oudegherste, Peter van, 328
Ovando, Nicolás de (1460?–
  1518), Governor of His-
  paniola (1502–9), 70

Padilla, Juan de (1484)–1521),
  Comunero leader, 150, 154–5,
  158
Palacios Rubios, Juan López de,
  jurist, 84
Papacy,
  relations with Spanish Crown,
    100–103, 227–31, 247
  taxes levied by papal conces-
    sion, 103, 201, 286, 336
Parma, *see* Margaret of; *and*
  Farnese, Alexander
Patronage, *see* Art
Patronato, 101–2, 174
Paul IV, Pope, 227–8
Peasantry,
  in Aragon, 278–9, 282
  in Castile, 117–18, 154, 189–
    90, 294–5
  in Catalonia, 37–8, 40, 81,
    340, 344
Peñaranda, 3rd Count of, Gaspar
  de Bracamonte (d. 1676),
  362

Pérez, Antonio (1540–1611),
    secretary of Philip II, 30n.,
        259, 261, 262, 264–8, 280–82
        329
Pérez, Gonzalo (1500?–66),
    secretary of Philip II, 178,
    259
Pérez, Juan, Franciscan monk of
    monastery of La Rábida, 60
Peris, Vincenç (d. 1522), leader
    of Valencian *Germanía*, 156,
    159
Peru, 62–6, 74–5, 175–6, 183,
    199, 293
Peter III of Aragon (1276–85),
    30
Philip, Archduke, the Fair, King
    Philip I of Castile (1504–6),
    135, 136–9
Philip II (1556–98),
    as prince, 165, 208–9
    ideas and methods of king-
        ship, 170, 249–60, 273–6,
        281–4; and Court factions,
        260–61; and affair of
        Antonio Pérez, 265–7, 280–
        81
    and heresy, 222, 230–31, 234;
        and Jesuits, 247, 273
    and Turks, 231–2, 241; revolt
        of Granada, 238–40
    and Dutch, 232–3, 250–51,
        258, 262–4, 268–9, 290
    and England, 264–5, 270, 276,
        287–9, 290
    and France, 270, 289–90
    and Portuguese succession,
        251, 171–5

    imperialism of, 268–70, 285,
        291
    death of, 290, 301
Philip III (1598–1621), 290, 300–
        301, 312, 314, 323
Philip IV (1621–65), 323–4,
        331–2, 349–50, 354, 356, 357
Philip V (1700–46), former
    Duke of Anjou, 373, 374–7
Pícaro, 246, 299, 311
Pizarro, Francisco (1476–1541),
    conquistador, 63–5
Plague, 37, 156, 298, 353, 361
Plateresque, 127, 253
Ponce de la Fuente, Constantino
    (d. 1559), canon of Seville,
    225
Poor law, 190
Population, 24–5
    of Castile, 118, 188, 293–4,
        298; of Madrid, 315; of
        Seville, 186;
    of Catalonia, 37, 337
    of Indies, 185, 292
    Morisco, 278, 307
Porreño, Baltasar, (1565–1639),
    writer, 251
Portocarrero, Cardinal Luis
    Fernández de (1635–1709),
    Archbishop of Toledo
    (1678–1709), 374
Portugal,
    in Middle Ages, 20, 26, 27,
        42–3
    population, 25
    overseas expansion and empire,
        43, 56–7, 270–71, 321, 325,
        355

Portugal—*continued*
  trade, 182, 270–71, 355
  origins and character of union
    with Castile (1580), 266–7,
    270–77; government under
    Spanish Crown, 337–8
  revolt of 1640, 346–7, 354,
    356, 357
Posts, 123
Potosí mines, 183
Prices,
  'price revolution', 192–6, 312–
    13
  17th-century fluctuations,
    333–4, 348–9, 356–7, 367,
    372
  estimated cost of living, 286
  price-fixing, 118, 189, 334
  see also Corn, Currency
Priego, 1st Marquis of, Pedro de
    Córdoba (d. 1517), 139,
    141
Printing, 64, 215, 217, 225
Privados, 301, 324, 350
Protestantism,
  in Spain, 212, 225
  international, 227, 233, 277,
    287–9
  see also Calvinism; Heresy;
    Lutheranism
Puebla, Dr Rodrigo de, ambas-
    sador to England, 132
Pulgar, Hernando del (1430?–
    91), secretary and chronicler
    of the Catholic kings, 98,
    218
Pyrenees, Treaty of (1659), 355,
    357

Quantity theory, 191
Quevedo y Villegas, Francisco
    Gómez de (1580–1645),
    320, 385
Quintana, Pedro de, Aragonese
    secretary of Ferdinand the
    Catholic, 143
Quiroga, Gaspar de (1512–94),
    Cardinal, Inquisitor-
    General (1573), Archbishop
    of Toledo (1577–94),
    242, 243, 262, 265

Ramirez de Prado, Alonso,
    member of Council of
    Castile, 317–18
Reconquista, 26–7, 31–3, 45–76,
    passim, 187
Recruiting,
  in Castile, 119, 240, 294, 339
  in Crown of Aragon, 82,
    240, 330, 332
  see also Union of Arms
Religious Orders, 154, 190, 215,
    220, 247, 312
  reform of, 103–4, 243, 247,
    369–70
  and mysticism, 213, 244
  friars in America, 71–2
  see also Jesuits
Remença peasants, 37–8, 40,
    81
Renaissance, *see* Humanism
Requesens y Zúñiga, Luis de
    (1528–76), Governor-
    General of the Netherlands,
    263, 264

Ribadeneyra, Pedro de (1527–
    1611),
    Jesuit writer, 245, 288
Ribagorza, Count of, Juan de
    Aragón (1544–73), 279
Ribagorza, county of, 278–9
Ribera, Juan de (1532–1611),
    Archbishop of Valencia,
    306
Richelieu, Cardinal (1585–1642),
    334, 335, 338, 342, 346, 349
Roads, 123
Rocroi, battle of (1643), 350
Rodríguez de Fonseca, Juan
    (1451–1524), (Chaplain to
    Isabella and Bishop of
    Burgos, 174
Rojas, Fernando de (1465?–
    1541), author of *La Celestina*,
    128
Ronquillo, Rodrigo (d. 1545),
    alcalde of Zamora, 158
Rosellón, county of (Catalan:
    Rosselló; French: Roussil-
    lon), 41, 131, 340, 349,
    355, 365
Ruiz, Simón, (1525–97), banker,
    198
Ruiz de la Mota, Pedro (d.
    1522), Bishop of Badajoz
    and Palencia, 151
Ryswick, Treaty of (1697), 373

Sahagún, Fray Bernardino de
    (1500?– 90), Franciscan
    missionary and historian,
    72, 383
St John of God (1485–1550), 243

St Teresa of Ávila (1515–82), 116,
    243, 247, 324, 384
Salamanca, university of, 129,
    191, 242, 246, 251, 316, 384
Salinas, Francisco de (1514?–
    90), professor of music, at
    Salamanca, 242
Salses, seige of (1639–40), 340
Salt, 291
Sánchez el Brocense, Francisco
    (1523–1600), scholar, 242
Santa Coloma, Count of,
    Dalmau de Queralt (d.
    1640), Viceroy of Catalonia,
    340, 343, 345
Santa Cruz, Alonso de, cosmo-
    grapher, 383
Santa Cruz, 1st Marquis of,
    Álvaro de Bazán (1526–88),
    admiral, 287–8
Santángel, Luis de (d. 1498),
    secretary of Ferdinand the
    Catholic, 60
Sardinia, 27, 30, 31, 124
Sauvage, Jean (d. 1518), Grand
    Chancellor of Charles V,
    146
Scholasticism, 245, 246, 368,
    384
Schomberg, Marshal, 357
Science, 297, 342, 367–9, 372,
    385
Sebastian, of Portugal (1557–
    78), 266, 270
Secretaries, royal, 91, 178, 258–9
Senior, Abraham, treasurer of the
    Hermandad, 107, 109
Sentencia de Guadalupe (1486), 81

Sepúlveda, Juan Ginés de (1490–1573), theologian, 73
Servicios, 93, 145, 150–51, 202–3, 208, 285–90
see also Taxation
Seville,
in Middle Ages, 32, 39, 42, 57
in 16th and 17th centuries, 186–7, 296–7, 309, 361
and American trade, 79, 182–3, 185–8, 193–5, 231, 269, 291; decline of, 293, 307, 336, 343, 361
heretical communities, 212, 226n.
Sheep, 33–4, 119, 120, 188, 202
see also Wool
Shipbuilding, 56–7, 111, 121, 187, 199
Shipping, Spanish, 276
Atlantic, 185–6, 194–5, 343
see also Treasure fleet
Cantabrian, 33, 42, 121
see also Fleet
Sicily, 168, 169, 352, 362n., 365
as possession of Crown of Aragon, 27, 30, 31, 131, 134
Siliceo, Juan Martínez (1486–1557), Cardinal Archbishop of Toledo (1546–57), 221–2, 229
Silk industry, 122–3, 187, 199, 202, 237, 296
Silver, 183–6, 191–4, 291, 336, 367
imports of, 184, 233, 269–70, 286–7, 291, 333; decline of, 322, 343

Portuguese need of Spanish, 270–71, 273
see also Treasure fleet
Simancas, 158, 171
Slavery, 69–71, 73–4, 145
Solariegos, 68
Soto, Fray Domingo de (1494–1560), theologian, 190
'Spanish Road', 326, 341
Spices, 27, 38, 270
Spínola, Ambrosio (1571–1630), general, 326, 341
Subsidies, see Servicios

Talavera, Hermando de (1428–1507), Archbishop of Granada (1492–1507), 50–52, 103
Tamarit, Francesc de, Catalan Diputat, 344
'Tanto monta, monta tanto', device of Catholic kings, 85
Tasa del trigo, 118, 189, 294
Tavera, Juan (1472–1545), Cardinal Archbishop of Toledo (1534–45), 68, 208
Taxation,
in Castile, 34; under Ferdinand and Isabella, 92–3, 119; under Charles V, 145, 147, 150–51, 201–2, 208; under Philip II, 231–2, 237, 285–6; under Philip III, 303–4; under Philip IV, 327–9, 336–7; under Charles II, 356–7, 364
in Crown of Aragon, 29, 201–2, 283, 303–4, 332–3, 337

exemptions from, 99, 111, 115,
203–5, 286, 336
ecclesiastical, *see* Church
see also Alcabala; Servicios
Tendilla, 2nd Count of, Íñigo
López de Mendoza first
Captain-General of Granada
(1492), 50
Tendilla, 4th Count of, *see*
Mondéjar, 3rd Marquis
Theologians, Juntas of, 250–51,
297
Tithes, 99, 102–3, 118, 201
Toledo, 147, 154, 158, 221,
296
Toledo, Archbishop of, 99
see also Carillo, Alfonso;
González de Mendoza,
Pedro; Cisneros, Francisco
Jiménez de; Croy, Guil-
laume de; Fonseca, Alonso;
Tavera, Juan; Siliceo, Juan
Martínez; Carranza,
Bartolomé; Quiroga,
Gaspar de
Toledo, Francisco de (1515–82),
Viceroy of Peru (1569–81),
176, 382
Toledo, García de (1514–78),
naval commander, 232
Toledo, Juan Bautista de (d.
1567), architect, 253
Tordesillas, Treaty of (1494), 63
Toro, battle of (1476), 86, 100
Towns,
in Castile, 22, 26, 87, 88,
93–7, 117, 197, 294
see also Comuneros; Cortes

in Crown of Aragon, 28, 40,
81, 156, 331
in Indies, 60, 67–8, 174–5
*see also under individual
towns*
Trade,
Castilian, 33–4, 120–22, 136,
187, 188, 196–8
see also Netherlands; Wool
Catalan, 27, 39, 124, 332
Portuguese, 182, 270–71,
354–5
with New World, *see* Seville
see also Merchants
Trastámara, house of, 18, 19,
271
Treasure fleet, 185–6, 188, 206,
289, 343
loss of, 186, 335, 357
see also Silver
Trent, Council of (1545–63),
224, 225, 238, 243–4
Tromp, Admiral, 341
Tunis, 53–5, 169, 241
Turks,
Charles V and, 54–5, 163,
168–9, 199
Philip II and, 55, 231–2, 239–
40, 241–2
see also Islam; Moriscos

Uceda, Duke of, Cristóbal
Sandoval y Rojas (d. 1624),
son of Duke of Lerma,
322, 323, 324
Union of Arms, 330–33, 337,
340, 341

United Provinces,
  trade with Spain and colonies,
    290–92
  Twelve Years' Truce (1609–
    21), 290, 304, 321, 325
  war with Spain (1621–48),
    341, 342, 350–51
  see also Flanders; Nether-
    lands
Universities, 104, 128, 316, 368–
  9, 377
  foreign study at prohibited,
    227, 234
  see also Education
Urriés, Ugo de, Aragonese
  secretary of Ferdinand the
  Catholic, 143
Utrecht, peace settlement of
  (1713–14), 375

Valdés, Alonso de (1490?–1532),
  humanist, and secretary of
  Charles V, 217, 259
Valdés, Hernando de (1483–
  1568), Inquisitor-General
  (1547–66), 224, 226, 229,
  247
Valdés, Juan de (1500?–41),
  brother of Alonso de
  Valdés, humanist, 162, 217
Valencia,
  in Middle Ages, 26–7, 28, 29,
    36, 42
  under Habsburgs, 303, 330,
    331, 332, 370;
    Germanías, 156–7, 159;
    Moriscos, 305–8
  under Bourbons, 376

Valenzuela, Fernando de (1636–
  89), favourite of Mariana of
  Austria, 365
Valera, Diego de (1412–87?),
  chronicler, 86
Valladolid, 171, 212, 294, 305
  see also Cortes
Valtelline, 325
Vargas, Alonso de, army com-
  mander, 282
Vasconcellos, Miguel de
  (d. 1640), secretary in
  Government of Portugal, 346
Vázquez, Mateo (1542–91),
  secretary of Philip II, 250,
  266, 275
Vázquez de Arce, Rodrigo
  (1529–99), President of
  Council of Castile, 301
Vázquez de Molina, Juan,
  secretary of Charles V and
  Philip II, 178, 237
Velázquez, Diego Rodríguez de
  Silva y (1599–1660), 320,
  341, 367, 385–6
Vélez, 1st Marquis of los, Pedro
  Fajardo (1477?– 154?), 156–7
Vélez, 2nd Marquis of los, Luis
  Fajardo (1508–74), 237, 240
Vélez, 3rd Marquis of los, Pedro
  Fajardo y Córdoba (1530?–
  80), minister of Philip II,
  262, 263, 265, 267
Vélez, 5th Marquis of los, Pedro
  Fajardo Zúñiga y Requesens
  (d. 1647), 346, 347
Vellón, 304, 333–4, 349, 356,
  357, 367, 372

Vergara, Juan de (1493–1557), professor of Greek at Alcalá, 217

Viceroys, 31, 39, 83, 174–7, 352, 377

Villafranca, 5th Marquis of, Pedro de Toledo (d. 1627), governor of Milan (1615–18), 325

Villahermosa, Duke of, Martín de Gurrea y Aragón (1526–81), 279

Villahermosa, Duke of, Hernando de Gurrea y Aragón (d. 1592), 282

Villalonga, Count of, *see* Franqueza, Pedro

Villanueva, Jerónimo de (d. 1653), Protonotario of Council of Aragon, 335, 344, 350

Villars, Marquis of, French ambassador in Madrid, 366

Villaviciosa, battle of (1665), 357

Villena, 2nd Marquis of, Diego López Pacheco (d. 1529), patron of Illuminists, 213

Vitoria, Francisco de (1480?–1546), Dominican theologian, 384

Vives, Juan Luis (1492–1540), humanist, philosopher, 162, 190

Vizcaya, 121, 188, 303–4, 336

Wages, 196, 298

Wales, Prince of (Charles I), 327

Women, 309

Wool, 33–4, 39, 57, 119–21, 137, 188, 366
duties on, 119, 231

Ximenes, *see* Cisneros, Francisco Jiménez de

Yuste, monastery of, 164, 210

Zafra, Hernando de, secretary of Isabella, 50, 91, 165

Zagal, El, King of Granada (1485–7), 48–9

Zamora, Bishop of, *see* Acuña, Antonio de

Zaragoza, 280–82

Zayas, Gabriel de, secretary of Philip II, 259, 264

Zumárraga, Fray Juan de (1475–1548), 1st Bishop of Mexico, 71

Zúñiga, Baltasar de (d. 1622), first minister of Philip IV, 324

Zúñiga, Juan de (1490?–1546), tutor to Philip II, 208

Zurbarán, Francisco de (1598–1664), painter, 367

Zurita, Jerónimo (1512–80), chronicler of Aragon, 141

READ MORE IN PENGUIN

In every corner of the world, on every subject under the sun, Penguin represents quality and variety – the very best in publishing today.

For complete information about books available from Penguin – including Puffins, Penguin Classics and Arkana – and how to order them, write to us at the appropriate address below. Please note that for copyright reasons the selection of books varies from country to country.

In the United Kingdom: Please write to *Dept. EP, Penguin Books Ltd, Bath Road, Harmondsworth, West Drayton, Middlesex UB7 ODA*

In the United States: Please write to *Consumer Sales, Penguin USA, P.O. Box 999, Dept. 17109, Bergenfield, New Jersey 07621-0120.* VISA and MasterCard holders call 1-800-253-6476 to order Penguin titles

In Canada: Please write to *Penguin Books Canada Ltd, 10 Alcorn Avenue, Suite 300, Toronto, Ontario M4V 3B2*

In Australia: Please write to *Penguin Books Australia Ltd, P.O. Box 257, Ringwood, Victoria 3134*

In New Zealand: Please write to *Penguin Books (NZ) Ltd, Private Bag 102902, North Shore Mail Centre, Auckland 10*

In India: Please write to *Penguin Books India Pvt Ltd, 706 Eros Apartments, 56 Nehru Place, New Delhi 110 019*

In the Netherlands: Please write to *Penguin Books Netherlands bv, Postbus 3507, NL-1001 AH Amsterdam*

In Germany: Please write to *Penguin Books Deutschland GmbH, Metzlerstrasse 26, 60594 Frankfurt am Main*

In Spain: Please write to *Penguin Books S. A., Bravo Murillo 19, 1° B, 28015 Madrid*

In Italy: Please write to *Penguin Italia s.r.l., Via Felice Casati 20, I–20124 Milano*

In France: Please write to *Penguin France S. A., 17 rue Lejeune, F–31000 Toulouse*

In Japan: Please write to *Penguin Books Japan, Ishikiribashi Building, 2–5–4, Suido, Bunkyo-ku, Tokyo 112*

In South Africa: Please write to *Longman Penguin Southern Africa (Pty) Ltd, Private Bag X08, Bertsham 2013*

READ MORE IN PENGUIN

A CHOICE OF NON-FICTION

The Pillars of Hercules Paul Theroux

At the gateway to the Mediterranean lie the two Pillars of Hercules. Beginning his journey in Gibraltar, Paul Theroux travels the long way round – through the ravaged developments of the Costa del Sol, into Corsica and Sicily and beyond – to Morocco's southern pillar. 'A terrific book, full of fun as well as anxiety, of vivid characters and curious experiences' – *The Times*

Where the Girls Are Susan J. Douglas

In this brilliantly researched and hugely entertaining examination of women and popular culture, Susan J. Douglas demonstrates the ways in which music, TV, books, advertising, news and film have affected women of her generation. Essential reading for cultural critics, feminists and everyone else who has ever ironed their hair or worn a miniskirt.

Journals: 1954–1958 Allen Ginsberg

These pages open with Ginsberg at the age of twenty-eight, penniless, travelling alone and unknown in California. Yet, by July 1958 he was returning from Paris to New York as the poet who, with Jack Kerouac, led and inspired the Beats . . .

The New Spaniards John Hooper

Spain has become a land of extraordinary paradoxes in which traditional attitudes and contemporary preoccupations exist side by side. The country attracts millions of visitors – yet few see beyond the hotels and resorts of its coastline. John Hooper's fascinating study brings to life the many faces of Spain in the 1990s.

A Tuscan Childhood Kinta Beevor

Kinta Beevor was five when she fell in love with her parents' castle facing the Carrara mountains. 'The descriptions of the harvesting and preparation of food and wine by the locals could not be bettered . . . alive with vivid characters' – *Observer*

READ MORE IN PENGUIN

A CHOICE OF NON-FICTION

The Time Out Film Guide   Edited by Tom Milne

The definitive, up-to-the minute directory of over 9,500 films – world cinema from classics and silent epics to reissues and the latest releases – assessed by two decades of *Time Out* reviewers. 'In my opinion the best and most comprehensive' – Barry Norman

The Remarkable Expedition   Olivia Manning

The events of an extraordinary attempt in 1887 to rescue Emin Pasha, Governor of Equatoria, are recounted here by the author of *The Balkan Trilogy* and *The Levant Trilogy* and vividly reveal unprecedented heights of magnificent folly in the perennial human search for glorious conquest.

Berlin: Coming in From the Cold   Ken Smith

'He covers everything from the fate of the ferocious-looking dogs that formerly helped to guard East Germany's borders to the vast Orwellian apparatus that maintained security in the now-defunct German Democratic Republic ... a pithy style and an eye for the telling detail' – *Independent*

Cider with Rosie/As I Walked Out one Midsummer Morning
Laurie Lee

Now together in one volume, Laurie Lee's two classic autobiographical works, *Cider with Rosie* and *As I Walked Out One Midsummer Morning*. Together they illustrate Laurie Lee's superb descriptive powers as he conveys the poignancy of a boy's transformation into adulthood.

In the Land of Oz   Howard Jacobson

'A wildly funny account of his travels; abounding in sharp characterization, crunching dialogue and self-parody, it actually is a book which makes you laugh out loud on almost every page ... sharp, skilful and brilliantly funny' – *Literary Review*

READ MORE IN PENGUIN

A CHOICE OF NON-FICTION

The Time of My Life Denis Healey

'Denis Healey's memoirs have been rightly hailed for their intelligence, wit and charm ... *The Time of My Life* should be read, certainly for pleasure, but also for profit ... he bestrides the post-war world, a Colossus of a kind' – *Independent*. 'No finer autobiography has been written by a British politician this century' – *Economist*

Chasing the Monsoon Alexander Frater

'Frater's unclouded sight unfurls the magic behind the mystery tour beautifully ... his spirited, eccentric, vastly diverting book will endure the ceaseless patter of travel books on India' – *Daily Mail*. 'This is travel writing at its best. Funny, informed, coherent and deeply sympathetic towards its subject' – *Independent on Sunday*

Isabelle Annette Kobak

'A European turned Arab, a Christian turned Muslim, a woman dressed as a man; a libertine who stilled profound mystical cravings by drink, hashish and innumerable Arab lovers ... All the intricate threads of her rebellious life are to be found in Annette Kobak's scrupulously researched book' – Lesley Blanch in the *Daily Telegraph*

Flying Dinosaurs Michael Johnson

Hundreds of millions of years ago, when dinosaurs walked the earth, we know that there also existed great prehistoric beasts call pterosaurs that could fly or glide. Now you can make these extraordinary creatures fly again. *Flying Dinosaurs* contain almost everything you need to construct eight colourful and thrillingly lifelike flying model pterosaurs – from the pterodactylus to the dimorphodon.

The Italians Luigi Barzini

'Brilliant ... whether he is talking about the family or the Mafia, about success or the significance of gesticulation, Dr Barzini is always illuminating and amusing' – *The Times*. 'He hits his nails on the head with bitter-sweet vitality ... Dr Barzini marshals and orders his facts and personalities with the skill of an historian as well as a journalist' – *Observer*

READ MORE IN PENGUIN

HISTORY

Frauen Alison Owings

Nearly ten years in the making and based on interviews and original research, Alison Owings' remarkable book records the wartime experiences and thoughts of 'ordinary' German women from varying classes and backgrounds.

Byzantium: The Decline and Fall John Julius Norwich

The final volume in the magnificent history of Byzantium. 'As we pass among the spectacularly varied scenes of war, intrigue, theological debate, martial kerfuffle, sacrifice, revenge, blazing ambition and lordly pride, our guide calms our passions with an infinity of curious asides and grace-notes ... Norwich's great trilogy has dispersed none of this magic' – *Independent*

The Anglo-Saxons Edited by James Campbell

'For anyone who wishes to understand the broad sweep of English history, Anglo-Saxon society is an important and fascinating subject. And Campbell's is an important and fascinating book. It is also a finely produced and, at times, a very beautiful book' – *London Review of Books*

Conditions of Liberty Ernest Gellner

'A lucid and brilliant analysis ... he gives excellent reasons for preferring civil society to democracy as the institutional key to modernization ... For Gellner, civil society is a remarkable concept. It is both an inspiring slogan and the reality at the heart of the modern world' – *The Times*

The Habsburgs Andrew Wheatcroft

'Wheatcroft has ... a real feel for the heterogeneous geography of the Habsburg domains – I especially admired his feel for the Spanish Habsburgs. Time and again, he neatly links the monarchs with the specific monuments they constructed for themselves' – *Sunday Telegraph*

READ MORE IN PENGUIN

HISTORY

Citizens Simon Schama

The award-winning chronicle of the French Revolution. 'The most marvellous book I have read about the French Revolution in the last fifty years' – Richard Cobb in *The Times*

The Lure of the Sea Alain Corbin

Alain Corbin's wonderful book explores the dramatic change in Western attitude towards the sea and seaside pleasures that occured between 1750 and 1840. 'A compact and brilliant taxonomy of the shifting meanings of the sea and shore' – *New York Review of Books*

The Tyranny of History W. J. F. Jenner

A fifth of the world's population lives within the boundaries of China, a vast empire barely under the control of the repressive ruling Communist regime. Beneath the economic boom China is in a state of crisis that goes far deeper than the problems of its current leaders to a value system that is rooted in the autocratic traditions of China's past.

The English Bible and the Seventeenth-Century Revolution
Christopher Hill

'What caused the English civil war? What brought Charles I to the scaffold?' Answer to both questions: the Bible. To sustain this provocative thesis, Christopher Hill's new book maps English intellectual history from the Reformation to 1660, showing how scripture dominated every department of thought from sexual relations to political theory ... 'His erudition is staggering' – *Sunday Times*

Fisher's Face Jan Morris

'*Fisher's Face* is funny, touching and informed by wide reading as well as wide travelling' – *New Statesman & Society*. 'A richly beguiling picture of the Victorian Navy, its profound inner security, its glorious assumptions, its extravagant social life and its traditionally eccentric leaders' – *Independent on Sunday*

READ MORE IN PENGUIN

HISTORY

London: A Social History Roy Porter

'The best and bravest thing he has written. It is important because it makes the whole sweep of London's unique history comprehensible and accessible in a way that no previous writer has ever managed to accomplish. And it is angry because it begins and concludes with a slashing, unanswerable indictment of Thatcherite misrule' – *Independent on Sunday*

Somme Lyn Macdonald

'What the reader will longest remember are the words – heartbroken, blunt, angry – of the men who lived through the bloodbath . . . a worthy addition to the literature of the Great War' – *Daily Mail*

Aspects of Aristocracy David Cannadine

'A hugely enjoyable portrait of the upper classes . . . It is the perfect history book for the non-historian. Ample in scope but full of human detail, accessible and graceful in its scholarship, witty and opinionated in style' – *Financial Times*

The Penguin History of Greece A. R. Burn

Readable, erudite, enthusiastic and balanced, this one-volume history of Hellas sweeps the reader along from the days of Mycenae and the splendours of Athens to the conquests of Alexander and the final dark decades.

The Laurel and the Ivy Robert Kee

'Parnell continues to haunt the Irish historical imagination a century after his death . . . Robert Kee's patient and delicate probing enables him to reconstruct the workings of that elusive mind as persuasively, or at least as plausibly, as seems possible . . . This splendid biography, which is as readable as it is rigorous, greatly enhances our understanding of both Parnell, and of the Ireland of his time' – *The Times Literary Supplement*